Exploring
Europe by RV

Exploring Europe by RV

ELEVEN ITINERARIES THROUGH
TWENTY-THREE COUNTRIES

---

by

Dennis and Tina Jaffe

A Voyager Book

Old Saybrook, Connecticut

Copyright © 1994 by Dennis Jaffe

All rights reserved. No part of this book may be reproduced or transmitted in any form by any means, electronic or mechanical, including photocopying and recording, or by any information storage and retrieval system, except as may be expressly permitted by the 1976 Copyright Act or by the publisher. Requests for permission should be made in writing to The Globe Pequot Press, P.O. Box 833, Old Saybrook, CT 06475.

Library of Congress Cataloging-in-Publication Data

Jaffe, Dennis.
Exploring Europe by RV : eleven itineraries through twenty-three countries / Dennis and Tina Jaffe. — 1st ed.
p. cm.
"A voyager book."
Includes index.
ISBN 1-56440-491-9
1. Europe—Guidebooks. 2. Recreational vehicles—Europe. 3. Camp sites, facilities, etc.—Europe—Guidebooks. I. Jaffe, Tina.
II. Title.
D909.J318 1994
914.04'559—dc20 94-27161
CIP

Manufactured in the United States of America
First Edition/First Printing

Contents

Overview Map of Europe

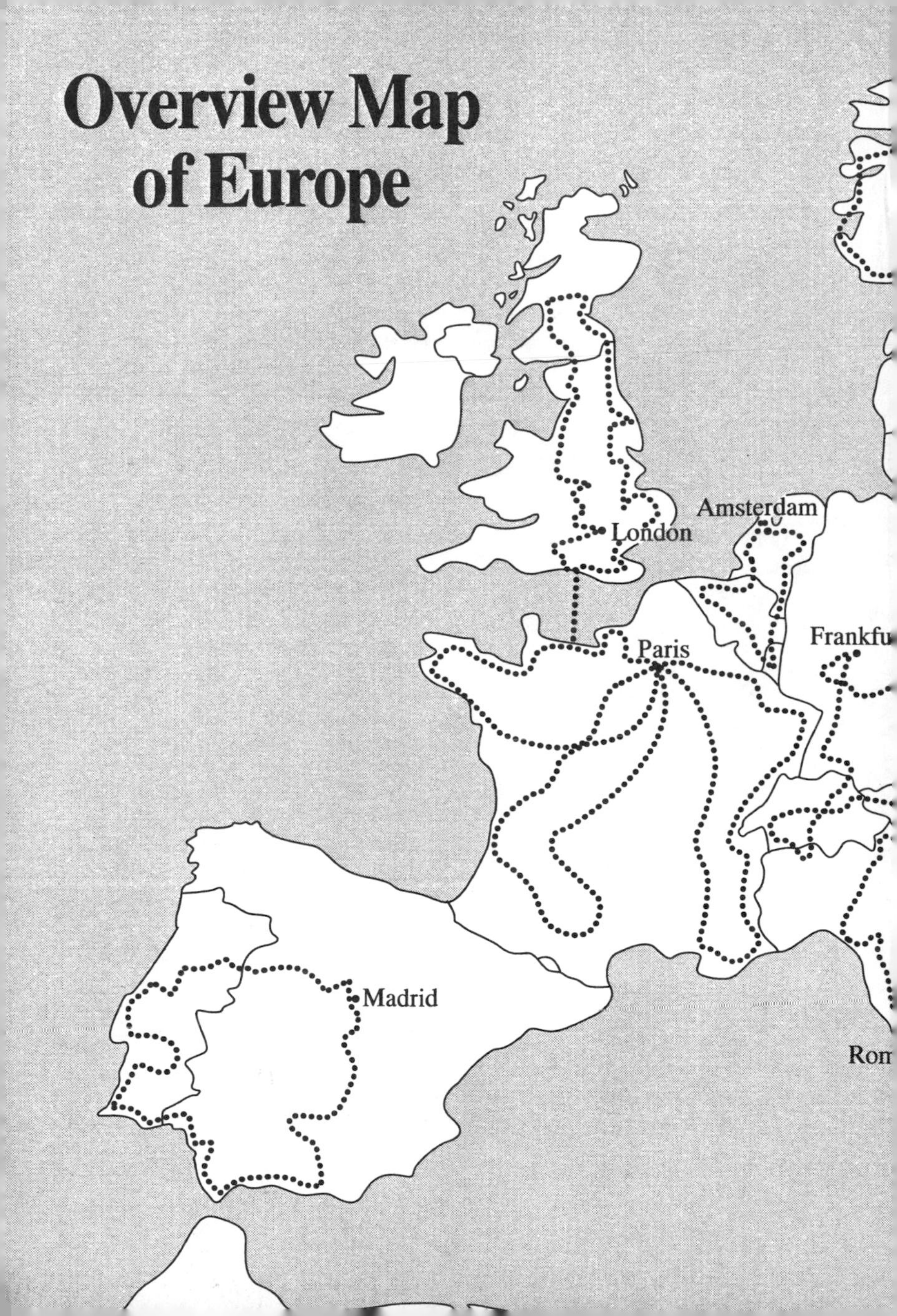

Copenhagen
erlin
Athens

Forward

A few months before I went to Europe for the first time, a lucky thing happened. Dennis Jaffe visited the California offices of TL Enterprises, publisher of *Trailer Life* and *Motorhome* magazines. He wanted to review the state of the American RV market in preparation for this book. He gave me more than he received, drawing from his wealth of knowledge as a longtime resident of Europe to answer a multitude of questions about RVing overseas.

A few weeks later I received a letter from Dennis with a suggested itinerary and camping map. Thanks to him, my RV trip in Switzerland was all I had hoped it would be. I wish I had had that kind of information about the other countries I visited. Of course, I had read whatever I could find on the subject of overseas RVing, but nothing was as specific and comprehensive as I wanted. The book you hold in your hands is sorely needed.

Traveling in a strange land, whether or not you speak the language, is bound to be a challenge. Cultural differences and customs affect such everyday matters as the hours when restaurants offer dinner. It may surprise you just how different Europe is. But, as the French say, "Viva la difference!" It is those differences that make the whole experience of foreign travel so exciting.

On the other hand, it doesn't hurt to be prepared. Armed with the reliable information in this book, you will find the treasures of the continent easier to reach and its roads easier to negotiate if you also know where you're going to spend the night and where you're heading tomorrow. Dennis and his wife, Tina, know exactly what an RVer needs to know in order to travel happily throughout Europe, and they've presented it here in an easy-to-read format with helpful maps. With the Jaffe's book as your guide, you have some wonderful adventures awaiting you!

Sherry McBride
Managing Editor
Trailer Life

Preface

There was a great temptation to begin this book with a warning label reading: "Danger! The information contained within may cause serious disruption to your lifestyle!"

At least that's what happened to us. In 1969 we were leading what can best be described as a normal, middle-class suburban existence. The only camping we had ever done was some backpacking in the Sierra Nevada Mountains of California, and we had never even seen the inside of an RV—that is, not until we took off with our then four- and six-year-old boys on a European camping trip. After picking up a new camper in Frankfurt, Germany, we spent the next six weeks on a fantastic adventure through Central and Southern Europe.

Things have never been quite the same since, for it was during that trip that the seeds were sown that so completely changed the direction of our lives. The following summer "European camping fever" struck once again, and we returned to Europe in search of a cure. After a month of touring Scandinavia, again in a camper, we went home to California, incurably afflicted.

A few years later the opportunity arose to sell our interest in a group dental practice. This prompted much soul searching and many long discussions regarding future plans, the meaning of life, and other such heady topics. We finally decided that we would take an extended European camping trip. So we sold the practice, along with our house and cars, and off we went. That was in May 1975, and we've been in Europe ever since.

In writing this book we have drawn upon our experiences of living in Europe and traveling to all parts of the continent in a variety of RVs: campers, luxury motorhomes, and towing travel trailers. Over the years there have been lots of wonderful experiences and adventures—and some that were not quite so wonderful. Along the way we have encountered many different people, some in the most unlikely places and under the most outrageous circumstances. Several lasting friendships have resulted from these "on the road" encounters. Rather than fill these pages with detailed accounts of our lives and experiences in Europe, however, we would prefer to share with you the kind of first-hand information that will help you to get the most enjoyment possible out of exploring Europe by RV.

Dennis and Tina Jaffe
Praia do Zavial, Portugal

How to Use This Book

In Part I, we introduce you to the "hows" and "whys" of European RV travel, including suggestions on selecting a vehicle, information about European campgrounds and tips on driving.

In Part II, which makes up the bulk of this book, we describe eleven in-depth itineraries that cover the best of Europe, from England to Turkey and from Norway to Portugal. Each itinerary is prefaced by a description of the countries through which it passes. Particular emphasis is placed on topics of special interest to the RV traveler, such as camping and driving in each country.

The itineraries cover areas that we have personally explored and are designed to provide the framework for a two-to-four-week vacation. By linking two or more routes together, a much longer trip is possible. Obviously, each traveler has his or her own concept of what is interesting and what constitutes a reasonable pace of travel. For that reason we have avoided using a rigid, day-by-day approach.

The minimum recommended touring times, given at the beginning of each itinerary, are really just rough approximations for your planning purposes. For some travelers, a day in Madrid or Munich is sufficient, while for others a full week is hardly enough. You may choose to use these itineraries as the entire basis for a journey, or they may be used to provide a framework upon which to build your own personalized European RV experience. Some travelers like to have everything laid out for them and want the convenience, organization, and predictability that a detailed itinerary provides, while others prefer a looser, more spontaneous arrangement. The choices are entirely yours. The itineraries are designed so that they can be used either way.

Travel is a highly personal experience, and there is no right or wrong way of going about it. John Steinbeck expresses this feeling so well in *Travels with Charley in Search of America,* when he says, "Once a journey is designed, equipped and put in process, a new factor enters and takes over. A trip, a safari, an exploration, is an entity, different from all other journeys. It has personality, temperament, individuality, uniqueness. A journey is a person in itself; no two are alike. — We find after years of struggle that we do not take a trip; a trip takes us."

Information regarding maps, phone numbers, addresses, RV-rental procedures, driving regulations, international driving signs, ferry services, and all other information subject to change was believed to be accurate at press time. Neither the authors nor the publisher can be held responsible for changes that occur subsequent to the publication of this guide.

PART I

BEFORE YOU GO

Under way in the Alps

Introduction

WHY AN RV?

If you are one of the millions of people who own a camper, motorhome, or travel trailer, you already know that this is the only way to travel! What you may not realize is just how easy it is to expand your travel horizons to include the very best that Europe has to offer.

If you have never traveled in a recreational vehicle, or RV, let us consider just a few of the advantages of this mode of travel. When we took our first trip to Europe in 1969, we chose a camper because it seemed like a great way to travel with small children. We wanted the independence of having our own transportation but didn't want to hassle with checking in and out of hotels and having to eat all of our meals in restaurants. At that time there were no such travel books available, and we had no idea of what such a trip would entail.

Then we saw an ad in a travel magazine for a VW camper to be picked up in Germany, used for a European vacation, and then shipped back to the United States. This seemed like a great idea, and the price was right—just under $3,000, shipping included! And so began our love affair with Europe and the RV lifestyle.

Now, some 25 years later, there have been some changes besides the added pounds and gray hairs. For one thing, a VW camper costs about $30,000; and those two little kids that we dragged along on that first trip are now grown men, a doctor and a physicist who, having been bitten by the travel bug at such an early age, are busy undertaking exciting travels of their own. We like to think that all of their traveling around Europe had a very positive effect on the boys' development.

Although the Europe of the 1990s is quite different from the place that we first visited in 1969, many aspects of European RV travel have, surprisingly, remained much the same. For example, the independence from reservations and fixed schedules that characterizes RV travel in North America is also very much a part of the European RV travel experience. There is no need for constant packing and unpacking. You can sleep in the same comfortable bed every night; only the scenery changes. When you are in the mood, you can eat out in restaurants, or you can eat "at home" whenever and wherever you like. This is particularly advantageous in Europe, where most restaurants have fixed hours for serving meals. We usually like to have our dinner early. In many parts of Europe, however, especially in the Mediterranean countries, most restaurants do not serve dinner until 7:00 P.M. or, in Spain, until 8:00 P.M. or later.

With an RV such problems are easily solved. You can eat where and when you choose to. What you eat is limited only by what you have in your refrigerator and how creative you can be within the confines of a small kitchen. This is a nice option to have, particularly when traveling with children.

It's also nice not always to have to eat the local fare. On one occasion, early in the morning, after an uncomfortable all-night ferry ride from Piraeus to the Greek island of Crete, we decided to treat ourselves to a hearty breakfast at a local restaurant. We tried several places in the port city of Iraklion, and the only warm food we could manage to find was spaghetti. Not exactly enthralled with the idea of a Greek spaghetti breakfast, we repaired to our camper for a delicious breakfast of pancakes, eggs, and ham.

Another plus of European RV travel is the opportunity that it gives you to have fun shopping for food in colorful and often exotic local markets. Even in the most remote places, language deficiencies notwithstanding, we always seem to manage to come home with something quite enjoyable. When all else fails, including pointing, we have on occasion, much to the amusement of the assembled locals, resorted to making piglike sounds for pork and mooing for beef. This type of "charades" shopping is no longer necessary in most parts of Europe, as modern, self-service supermarkets with clearly discernible products on display are now quite common. Just for the fun of it, however, we often go out of our way to shop at the quaint village and roadside markets that one finds all over Europe.

Another of the joys of traveling through Europe in an RV is the opportunity that it affords to meet and exchange viewpoints with people of various nationalities and backgrounds. Local markets, sightseeing attractions, and, in particular, campgrounds provide fertile ground for such encounters. Campgrounds in Europe, just as in the United States, are great places to meet people and to swap yarns and travel tips. As camping is such a popular pastime throughout Europe, chances are that at any time your neighbors might be German, Dutch, English, or perhaps Spanish or Italian. You will find that they will be as curious about you as you are about them. Over a bottle of the local wine, language difficulties seem to melt away. Lasting friendships are often the souvenirs brought back from such meetings.

Impromptu picnics are yet another benefit that the RV traveler enjoys. Many times in the course of our travels, we have pulled off the road to enjoy a wonderful meal of locally purchased delicacies against an inspiring backdrop; a Swiss alpine meadow and a beautiful, deserted Portuguese beach are just two of many such places that come to mind. On one occasion we parked our motorhome at the harbor in Oslo and bought fresh shrimp right off the fishing boat. The picnic that followed, with a view of the colorful harbor in the background, was memorable. The choices and possibilities for such alfresco dining are endless.

WHY EUROPE?

As wonderful as RV travel in North America is, it's just that much better in Europe. When it comes to the sheer concentration of breathtaking scenery, cultural and historic attractions, romantic hideaways, and outstanding culinary delights, there is simply no other place on Earth where so much is packed into as small an area. The variety and quality of experiences to be enjoyed are boundless. The magnificent chateaux of France, the towering Alps, the great cities and museums—the Louvre in Paris and Madrid's Prado—quaint Portuguese fishing villages, romantic castles on the Rhine, and fiestas and folkfests such as Seville's Spring Fair and Munich's Oktoberfest are just a few of the myriad attractions awaiting you, all within an area that is only one-third the size of the United States.

As an example of what a typical European RV trip might encompass, let's take a brief look at one of our itineraries. Our Alpine Heights and Old World Delights route covers a distance of some 2,000 miles and takes us through six countries and a variety of experiences that include castles on the Rhine, Switzerland's famed Matterhorn, and, in the French Alps, Chamonix and the towering Mount Blanc. The historic cities of Munich, Heidelberg, and Zurich as well as such romantic me-

Back in the camper after grocery shopping in Spain

dieval towns and villages as Rothenburg on the Tauber and Oberammergau, host to the world-famous Passion Play, are also visited. Mozart's magical Salzburg, the Black Forest, and the tiny Principality of Liechtenstein make up yet another part of this itinerary. All of this and a great deal more, depending on your pace of travel, can be enjoyed in anywhere from three weeks to three months.

THE ECONOMICS OF EUROPEAN RV TRAVEL

There are many ways of touring Europe with an RV. The parameters are determined only by your budget and imagination. To give a rough approximation of what RV travel in Europe costs, here are some average prices as of spring 1994, based on an exchange rate of 1.70 German deutsche marks, 1.50 British pounds sterling, and 135 Spanish pesetas to the U.S. dollar.

Two persons traveling in a motorhome and utilizing electrical hookups will pay between $15 and $30 per night for a campground. German campgrounds provide the best value for the money; those in Spain, which are among the most expensive in Europe, cost about 25 percent more. If you are traveling with a trailer rather than in a camper or motorhome, most campgrounds charge an additional $3.00 to $4.00 per night. Food and restaurant costs vary widely but are roughly comparable to prices in the United States and Canada.

Motorhome rental rates also vary widely, with the type of vehicle, the season, and the point of origin as determining factors. The best deals for rental motorhomes are found in Germany during the spring and fall. In the high-season months of July and August, a fully equipped 5.5- to 6-m (18- to 20-ft.) mini-motorhome will cost around $150 to $175 per day. In the spring and fall, prices are approximately 25 percent lower. The average cost of renting a VW camper in the spring or fall is about $100 per day, while a luxury 7-m (24-ft.) class A motorhome rents for approximately $200 per day.

These prices compare favorably with the cost of renting a car and paying for a hotel room and meals. If you do most of your cooking in the camper and use restaurants and campgrounds only occasionally, you can save substantial amounts of money. When traveling with kids in an RV, in addition to the convenience offered, the savings over other modes of travel are significant.

Getting Around

EUROPEAN RVS

A wide variety of European-manufactured RVs, offering great differences in quality, features, amenities, and, of course, price, are available. There are some notable differences between American and European RVs. For one thing, European vehicles tend to be smaller and lighter. As the price of fuel in Europe is three to four times that of the United States, fuel economy takes on a much more important role in RV design. Consequently, great emphasis is placed on weight reduction and obtaining the maximum performance from a power plant.

The European motorhomes most commonly available for rental are the 5.5- to 6-m (18- to 20-ft.) type with a bunk over the cab and a convertible table/double-bed combination. These units are powered by a four-cylinder, 2- to 2.5-diesel engine with a five-speed manual transmission. With a turbocharger, these rigs develop between 75 and 100 hp and are surprisingly peppy.

Fuel economy is not the only reason for the emphasis on smaller vehicles. Many of Europe's loveliest towns and villages and many of the most interesting places to visit would be very difficult, and in many cases impossible, to negotiate in a 12-m (39-ft.) Winnebago. Also, the access and layout at most campgrounds favor the use of a smaller, more maneuverable vehicle. Paved or graveled drive-through motorhome or trailer pads are a rarity. In many instances, to pull into a site that would be better suited for bicycle and a tent (a small tent at that), it is necessary to run a slalom course between rows of trees, hedges, and other obstacles, often with the entire campground population critically looking on.

The tendency toward smaller and lighter vehicles applies also to trailers. Because of the high fuel costs and expensive registration fees for cars with large-displacement engines, few Europeans have a vehicle suitable to towing a heavy American-style trailer or fifth wheel. Most European trailers are rated at less than 2,000 kg (4,400 lb) fully loaded.

To retain the mobility and maneuverability to explore comfortably the charming and often "off the main road" places that make touring

Europe such a delight, we recommend limiting the maximum size of a motorhome to about 7–7.5 m (23–25 ft.) in length, with a width of not more than 2.3 m (7.5 ft.). The ideal-size motorhome for two people, in terms of economy and comfort, is 5.5–6 m (18–20 ft.). With such a motorhome you will be able to drive and park just about everywhere that you can with a conventional auto. The maximum length for a trailer should not exceed about 6.5 m (21 ft.). This size will allow you to enjoy all of the comforts of home, including a separate bathroom with toilet, hot-water shower, kitchen, central heating, and comfortable sleeping space for up to four adults.

SHIPPING YOUR OWN RV

The high cost and inconvenience of shipping an RV make this an impractical option for any trip of less than a few months. For longer trips there is a lot to be said for traveling in the comfort of your own, familiar rig, and by amortizing the shipping costs over a longer period of time, you can save money over the cost of renting for such a long period.

In addition to the already mentioned size factor, however, there are several things to keep in mind when driving an American RV in Europe. Although some U.S. RV manufacturers, such as Winnebago, Holiday Rambler, and Airstream, are represented in Europe, the network of dealers and the availability of spare parts are extremely limited.

In addition, the European electrical standard is 220–240 V/50 cycle. To hook up an American rig at a campground, you will need to use a transformer to convert the electricity from the 110-V North American standard. But as there is little need, outside of the American military community in Europe, for 110-V current, such transformers are not generally sold at camping-supply stores in Europe. With luck, however, you can find someone to purchase one for you at an American military installation. There is a firm near Frankfurt that sells transformers: Trueblood RV, Justinianstrasse 22, 60322 Frankfurt, Germany; phone (69) 34 53 54. Your best bet is to have a transformer installed in your vehicle before coming to Europe—merely wiring the vehicle for 220 V without a transformer will not allow you to use your 110-V refrigerator or other 110-V appliances.

Most European RVs are equipped with cassette-type toilets. These have a small holding tank that can easily be removed from outside the vehicle and carried to a special receptacle. They may also be emptied into a regular toilet. Few European campgrounds have facilities for emptying the large, built-in holding tanks found on most American motorhomes and trailers. Dumping facilities at municipal sewerage plants can often be used for this purpose. There is also an expanding European network of motorhome service posts or kiosks where tanks can be emptied. These facilities are designated by a sign, usually blue and white, that features a motorhome pictogram.

The most inexpensive and efficient way to ship an RV from the United States or Canada to Europe is via an RO–RO (roll on–roll off) automobile transport vessel. Although you can make all the arrangements yourself, you will save much grief and aggravation by dealing with a customs broker. As this is a big-ticket item and rates may vary considerably, it will pay to get several quotes. You will find listings in the yellow pages in all major port cities in the United States and Canada.

PURCHASING AN RV IN EUROPE

Unless you purchase a vehicle with North American specifications, such as the VW camper van, you can count on having a lot of difficulty in importing it into the United States or Canada. As RVs in Europe are generally more expensive than in the United States, in most cases it is not worth the effort and expense. At this writing the VW overseas purchase and delivery plan is no longer available. When making your travel arrangements, check with VW of America, Auburn Hills, MI 48326 (phone 313–340–5000, fax 313–340–5045) to see if this plan has been reinstituted.

Another possibility if you are considering a long stay abroad is to buy a new or used RV with European specifications and sell it before you return home. To get an idea of what is available on the European market, you can write to some of the camping publications for back issues of their magazines (see the list on p. 22). The best RV selection and the lowest prices are found in Germany. Most vehicles in Great Britain have right-hand drive, which is not a very practical setup for driving on the continent.

One of the biggest disadvantages of purchasing an RV just for use in Europe is that you never know how long it will take to sell the vehicle at the end of your trip. Unless you have unlimited time, you might find yourself literally giving it away the day before you fly back home or having to leave the vehicle with a dealer to be sold on consignment. One way to avoid this problem is to arrange a long-term lease or a guaranteed buy-back from the dealer that you purchase the vehicle from. Most of the larger firms that advertise in the German and French camping magazines will answer correspondence in English.

RV EXCHANGE

If you are already an RV owner, you might consider an exchange with a European RVer. We know several people who have done this, and it's worked out quite well. For details contact the Vacation Exchange Club, P.O. Box 650, Key West, FL 33041; phone (800) 638–3841. You may also choose to place an ad in one of the European camping magazines listed on p. 22.

RENTING AN RV

For the majority of people who are planning a trip of several weeks to a month or two, the most practical solution to finding a suitable vehicle is to rent a motorhome at or near one of the major European gateways. Motorhome rental in Europe is quite popular, and there is a good selection of vehicles available to fit every taste and budget. These vehicles range from VW campers to luxurious American-style motorhomes.

The rental firms listed on pp. 12–16 will answer correspondence in English. Most of these firms are conveniently located in or near the starting places for the itineraries described in this book. The list also includes several U.S.-based agencies that will make arrangements for you to pick up an RV in Europe.

Rental prices vary widely, with substantial discounts available in the off season. The high and low seasons are not the same in all countries; and in some countries, such as Germany, there are differences within the country that are related to the school vacation schedule. It pays to contact several different companies to compare vehicles and prices. Be sure to get a clear explanation of just what is included in the rental price. Extra charges are often made for such items as bedding, kitchen utensils, cleaning, additional mileage, insurance options, and emergency road-service protection. As an ever-increasing number of Europeans discover the advantages of RV travel, there are many rental firms that sell out well in advance, especially during the peak summer months. To avoid disappointment, start gathering information well in advance. Six months prior to your departure is not at all too soon.

A valid driver's license, in some cases an international driver's permit, and your passport are all that are required to rent an RV. Insurance and the necessary documents will be provided by the rental company.

RV Rental Firms

U.S.-Based European RV Rental Firms

Avis
World Headquarters
900 Old Country Road
Garden City, NY 11530
Phone (800) 331–1084
Fax (516) 222–4796
Motorhomes for rent in France, the Netherlands, and Switzerland

Foremost Euro-Car
5658 Sepulveda Boulevard #201
Van Nuys, CA 91411
Phone (800) 272–3299
Fax (818) 786–1249

Global Motorhome Travel
1142 Manhattan Avenue,
Suite 300
Manhattan Beach, CA 90266
Phone (800) GMT–EURO
Fax (310) 318–9795

Hertz Auto Rental
5601 NW Expressway
Box 25722
Oklahoma City, OK 73132
Phone (800) 654–3001
Fax (405) 728–6684

Austria

Autohaus Hanzl
Drasche Strasse 36
A–1230 Vienna–Inzersdorf
Phone (222) 31 98 093

Happycar
(Gerhard Lettner)
Breitenfurt Strasse 201/1
A–1230 Vienna
Phone (222) 80 43 840

Belgium

Colruyt
Steenweg naar Edingen 247
B–1500 Halle (Brussels)
Phone (2) 36 01 371

Vrebos
Donkerstraat 19
B–3040 Neerijse (Brussels)
Phone (16) 47 73 83

Denmark

Camperudlejning
Olsevej 1, Sandby
DK–4171 Glumso
Phone/fax 53 64 34 52
(Near Copenhagen)

RAFCO A/S
Englandsvej 380
DK–2770 Kastrup
Phone (45) 31 51 15 00
Fax (45) 31 51 10 89
(Near Copenhagen Airport)

Finland

Touring Cars
Paivaränta
SF–70420 Kuopio
Phone (71) 34 18 00
Fax (71) 34 13 44

France

Avis Car-Away
15/17 rue Fournier
F–92110 Clichy
Phone (1) 47 30 14 04
Fax (1) 47 30 14 64
(Near Paris)

Hertz/Trois Soleils
BP 15
F–67117 Ittenheim
Phone 88 69 17 17
Fax 88 69 11 28
(Near Paris)

EuropCar/Inter Rent
201 quai de Stalingrad
F–92130 Issy-les-Moulineaux
Phone 40 93 55 99
(Near Paris)

Germany

Europcar Autovermietung
Tangstedter Landstrasse 81
D–22415 Hamburg 62
Phone (40) 52 01 28 11
Fax (40) 52 01 09 14
(Berlin, Frankfurt, Hamburg)

Karstadt Reisemobil Miet Service
Hafen Strasse 70
D–45356 Essen 11
Phone (201) 36 70 51
Fax (201) 36 70 50
(Essen, Munich, Hamburg)

Schafhautle Reisemobile
Feuergasse 4
D–74321 Bietigheim–Bissingen
Phone (7142) 66 866
Fax (7142) 43 953
(Stuttgart)

Jumpertz Reisemobile
Rudolf Diesel Strasse 8
D–52428 Julich
Phone (2461) 52 021
Fax (2461) 42 34
(Near Cologne)

Moses Reisemobile
Kurt Schumacher Strasse 1
D–61267 Neu-Anspach
Phone (6081) 8046
Fax (6081) 7855
(Frankfurt)

Great Britain
DD Motorhomes Ltd.
Eastbourne Road
GB–Halland
East Sussex, BN8 6PS
England
Phone (825) 84 07 23
Fax (825) 84 04 54
(Near London)

Motorhome Rentals Ltd
Lowood Garage
12 Kings Avenue, Clapham
GB–London, SW4 8BQ
England
Phone (71) 72 06 492
Fax (71) 72 06 721

Turner's Motor Caravan Centre
11A Barry Road
East Dulwich
GB–London, SE22 OHZ
England
Phone (81) 69 31 132
Fax (81) 69 31 134

St. Andrews Motorhome Hire
Ardennes House
Cupar Road
GB–Pitlessie Cupar KY7 7SU
Scotland

Greece
Camper Caravans
4 Nikis Street
GR–10110 Athens
Phone (1) 32 30 55 25

I. Galatoulas Co.
330 Athinin Ave.
Haidari
Phone (1) 58 12 103

Global Transport Touristik Service
Dieselstrasse 27
D–61184 Karben
Germany
Phone (6039) 43 011
(Book in Germany, pick up in Greece)

Italy
Freedom Holiday
Via Cristoforo Colombo, 2339
I–00124 Roma Casalpalocco
Phone (6) 60 94 212
Fax (6) 50 90 338

Rome Camper
Via Pontina, km 13,400
I–00128 Roma
Phone (6) 64 81 504

The Netherlands
Lokhorst Autoverhuur
Langestraat 48
NL–1211 HA Hilversum
Phone (35) 21 73 33
Fax (35) 23 54 02
(Near Amsterdam)

Tigchelaar Recreatie
Boeimeesingel 6
NL–4819 AA Breda
Phone (76) 28 14 81
Fax (76) 21 33 11

KAV Auto Verhuur
Klokkenbergweg 17
NL–1101 AK Amsterdam
Phone (20) 69 69 730
Fax (20) 69 64 211

Norway
Gumpens Auto
Setesdalsvn. 90
N–4617 Kristiansand S.
Phone (42) 29 590
Fax (42) 29 594

Auto Camping A/S
N–5230 Espeland/Bergen
Phone (5) 24 05 38
Fax (5) 24 38 20

Portugal
Delta Car
Av. Sao Joao de Deus, 17-B
P–1000 Lisbon
Phone (1) 84 81 428
Fax (1) 80 03 36

A. Dias & Santos
Tv. de St Antonio a Graca, 8B/C
P–1100 Lisbon
Phone (1) 87 31 91
Fax (1) 87 31 92

Spain
Camper Europa
Velazquez, 146
Despacho, 305
E–28002 Madrid
Phone (1) 56 28 270
Fax (1) 56 31 806

Caravan Travel
Ctra. de Alcobendas a Barajas,
km. 5,800
E–28100 Alcobendas (Madrid)
Phone (1) 65 40 249
Fax (1) 65 43 583

Switzerland
Petersen's Motor Homes
Wibachstrasse 4
CH–8153 Rumlang
Phone (1) 81 73 233
Fax (1) 81 72 454
(Near Zurich)

Kossler Wohnauto Vermietung
Monchaltorferstrasse 16
CH–8132 Egg/ZH
Phone (1) 98 40 748
Fax (1) 98 41 989
(Near Zurich)

Moby Campers
Moslistrasse 12
CH–4532 Feldbrunnen
Phone (65) 22 96 10
Fax (65) 23 82 12
(Near Zurich)

Turkey
Europcar Autovermietung
Tangstedter Landstrasse 81
D–22415 Hamburg 62
Germany
Phone (40) 52 01 28 11
Fax (40) 52 01 09 14
(Book in Germany, pick up in Turkey)

Global Transport Touristik Service
Dieselstrasse 27
D–61184 Karben
Germany
Phone (6039) 43 011
(Book in Germany, pick up in Turkey)

VEHICLE INSURANCE

If you rent a vehicle in Europe, the insurance will be part of the rental package. In some cases you may be offered an optional low- or no-deductible coverage. If you purchase a vehicle in Europe, you will have to have liability insurance; this is required by all European countries along with proof of insurance in the form of a "Green Card." Non-European residents visiting Europe can obtain tourist insurance that is underwritten by American International Underwriters (AIU) and sold through the American Automobile Association (AAA). For further information contact AAA National Headquarters, Foreign Motoring Insurance, 1000 AAA Drive, Heathrow, FL 32746–5063; phone (800) 222–4599, fax (407) 444–8567.

EUROPEAN VS. AMERICAN CAMPGROUNDS

One of the major differences that RVers from North America notice when touring Europe is the number of major cities that have easily accessible campgrounds. Munich, London, Paris, Stockholm, Copenhagen, Lisbon, Zurich, and Vienna are just a few of the capitals and large cities with such facilities. In Paris, for example, there is a municipal camp-

Campground signs are easy to follow

ground along the Seine River, right in the heart of the Bois de Boulogne.

It's safe to say that just about every place that you may want to visit, whether at the beach, in the mountains, or in a city, has at least one campground reasonably close by. In France and in several other countries, a number of campgrounds are located on the grounds of elegant chateaux and ancient castles.

There is a great variation in types of campgrounds, and there is no really "typical" European campground. Just about all sites provide hot showers, flush toilets, and electricity. In the course of your travels, you are likely to encounter everything from highly personalized family operations that are little more than a large backyard with a few electrical outlets and a small bathhouse to enormous camping villages that hold thousands of people and have all of the facilities and amenities—as well as many of the problems—found in a small city. In some countries, such as France and Switzerland, many of the campgrounds are operated by local municipalities—in others, for example, Spain and Italy, most sites are privately owned. As a rule the municipal campgrounds tend to have fewer frills and offer the best values. Although it is difficult to generalize, the standards of cleanliness and maintenance are highest in Northern Europe and tend to decline as one heads south. Standards at campgrounds in the former Soviet bloc countries of Eastern Europe are considerably below those of the Western European countries.

As the popularity of camping continues to grow throughout Europe, there is an increasing trend toward expanding and improving facilities. In most countries some sort of rating system monitored by the tourist authorities is used. The more stars or check marks that a campground is awarded, the more facilities that are provided and, generally speaking, the higher the standards of maintenance and cleanliness.

Toilets and Showers

At many campgrounds and public facilities in Southern and Eastern Europe, you will encounter the notorious "Turkish toilet," or "squatter." In place of a proper sit-down toilet, a porcelain tray with a hole in the middle and raised platforms for your feet on either side of the hole is set into the floor. The first time that we saw one of these things, we thought it was some kind of strange shower—since there was no place to sit, we couldn't believe that it was a toilet. Looming above this device is a water tank and a chain-activated flushing mechanism that, when operated, releases a mini–tidal wave. If you are not sufficiently nimble, this can leave you soaked up to the ankles. These toilets are one of the best arguments we've encountered for having a camper with a built-in toilet.

Hot showers are included in the price at some sites, while at others coin- or token-operated showers are provided. Be sure to inquire as to how long a token will operate the shower. Tina learned this lesson the hard way on a cold night at a campground on Spain's Costa del Sol. She had just gotten all soaped up when the water suddenly stopped flowing.

Hookups

As mentioned earlier, the European electrical standard is 220 V/50 cycles. Some campgrounds have individual meters and make a hookup charge and also charge per kilowatt-hour, while others make an all-inclusive charge. Most European RVs are wired with 10-A circuits. This allows the use of approximately 2,200 W. Not all campgrounds, however, provide 10 A of electricity. At some places in southern Spain and

France, we have received only 3 or 4 A. To roughly calculate the allowable wattage, simply multiply the voltage by the amperage. For example, 220 V x 10 A = 2,200 W.

Heat-producing appliances such as hair dryers, toasters, and heaters draw a lot of power, usually from 1,000 to 2,000 W. To avoid overloads, check on the amount of power available before plugging in. (This can also save you a lot of inconvenience. The circuit breakers at many campgrounds are in locked boxes; if they are tripped, it is necessary to find someone with the key to turn the power back on. If this happens at night, you will be without power until morning at many campgrounds.)

In 1984 a European-wide standard known as CEE 17 was introduced for campground plugs and sockets. The idea was to establish a uniform safety standard and to eliminate the need for having several types of adapters. Yet many campgrounds still have not switched over. The Swiss have one type of plug, the French a totally different kind. Most campgrounds will provide the necessary adapters. If you are driving a rig with U.S. or Canadian specifications, however, you will need to use a step-down transformer to change the current from 220 to 110 V. As there is little demand for 110-V current in Europe, these transformers are difficult to obtain. We have encountered several travelers who were not fully enjoying their vehicles because they had neglected this item. As it is often necessary to park some distance from power points, most Europeans travel with a 25-m (83-ft.) cable roll. If you are purchasing one of these, be sure that it is suitable for outdoor use.

All campgrounds provide drinking-water taps, usually with a hose connected to allow filling an RV tank. Don't, however, expect to find a water hookup for each vehicle. To ensure being able to fill your tank, it is a good idea to carry a length of hose with you, as in most cases you will have to park some distance from a water point. A half-inch fitting will fit the majority of European taps. Although tap water is safe to drink throughout Europe, we usually prefer drinking bottled water because of the more pleasant taste.

As we mentioned earlier, most European RVs are equipped with cassette-type chemical toilets. The lower half of the unit is detachable and can be readily emptied in the specially designated receptacles provided at most campsites. If these "Chem WC" units are not present, the cassette can also be emptied in a regular toilet. Dump stations for emptying fixed sewerage tanks are not commonly found in Northern Europe, and they are practically nonexistent in the Southern and Eastern European countries.

In Northern and Central Europe, the majority of campgrounds have coin- or token-operated washers and dryers. European machines have longer cycles and operate differently from American appliances, so be sure to read the posted instructions or ask for assistance. In Southern and Eastern Europe, few campgrounds have laundry machines. Some campgrounds will take your laundry and for a modest charge return it clean and neatly folded.

Most sites have a campstore and a restaurant or snack bar. Many also provide fresh rolls in the morning. Ask at the reception area when you check in.

Campground Charges

Rather than levying a comprehensive charge for a site, most European campgrounds itemize their fees, making a charge for each individual, vehicle, tent, and trailer as well as for the use of electricity. Many campgrounds even charge extra if you have a dog. Costs vary widely, depending on the facilities provided and on the location of the campground. In prime resort areas during high season, charges are often out of proportion to the services provided. Substantially lower rates are available in the off season. A price list is always posted at campground reception areas. The use of credit cards at campgrounds is in its infancy but is growing rapidly. The most commonly accepted cards are MasterCard and Visa.

Registering at a campground is a simple matter. You will be asked to present either an International Camping Carnet or your passport. The Carnet is an internationally recognized identification card that includes proof of liability insurance for camping-related claims. (For details see p. 35.) Unless you are staying for just one night, payment is expected when you leave.

Free Camping

By "free camping," or *camping sauvage,* as it is called in France, we mean overnighting outside of a regular campground. Whether or not to free camp is very much an individual matter. We know some people to whom staying in a campground is anathema, while others would never even consider free camping.

There are arguments for and against each position; our personal preference is to combine both. There are many occasions when the facilities, favorable location, and security offered by an official campground outweigh the freedom, adventure, convenience, and economy that free camping offers. At other times it's wonderful to be able to be independent and to enjoy a particularly scenic spot with all of the comforts of your home-on-wheels available.

When deciding whether or not to free camp, there are two primary considerations: Is it legal, and is it safe? In a number of countries, free camping is expressly prohibited. Greece is one such country; there are even multilingual signs to this effect posted at the border. But that's the official version. Practically speaking, it is possible to free camp in most parts of Greece, and, for that matter, in the rest of Europe, providing that you use a little discretion. Obviously, this includes not parking where NO CAMPING signs are posted or setting up just outside of an official campground or resort, where you are likely to incur the wrath of the local business community, who tend to look upon free campers as a threat to their livelihoods. When in doubt it is best to ask for permission. We once enjoyed a lovely week on an idyllic beach on Crete, under the watchful eyes of the local police, until one day someone complained and our friendly policeman knocked on our camper door and, in broken English, ordered us to pack up and leave in "seven minutes." On other occasions we have parked our rig and spent several days, without incident, in the center of such diverse cities as Zurich and Seville while enjoying the local sights.

Things did not work out quite so well on another occasion. While parked with our motorhome at a lonely beach in Spanish Basque country, we were awakened at 3:00 A.M. by the sound of a car pulling up. As several men approached our rig, we fired up our motor and were out of there in a lot less than seven minutes, breaking our previously established Greek record for getting our show on the road.

As more and more communities pass ordinances prohibiting free camping, a number of other localities are adopting RV-friendly policies and establishing parking sites, many with water taps and dump stations, to encourage RVers to visit their areas. This movement is especially apparent in Germany and France. These "official free-camping sites" are designated with a motorhome pictogram. It is also possible in most regions to obtain permission from local farmers to park on their property for a modest sum. In France and England as well as in several other countries, there are many reasonably priced rural sites that provide just the basics for camping: water, toilet, and sometimes electrical facilities. The number of camping units at these sites is usually limited to five or six.

Facilities for the Physically Disabled

When it comes to providing wheelchair-accessible facilities at campgrounds and tourist attractions, the Northern and Central European countries are far ahead of their Southern and Eastern European neighbors. To obtain information on renting or purchasing European motorhomes suitable for wheelchair users, contact Trueblood RV, Justinianstrasse 22, 60322 Frankfurt, Germany; phone (69) 34 53 54.

For information on wheelchair-accessible facilities, contact the national tourist offices for the countries that you intend to visit. Information is also available from Moss Rehabilitation Hospital Travel Information Service, 1200 West Tabor Road, Philadelphia, PA 19141–3009 (phone 216–456–9600) and The Society for the Advancement of Travel for the Handicapped, 26 Court Street, Penthouse, Brooklyn, NY 11242 (phone 718–858–5483).

EUROPEAN CAMPING MAGAZINES

Camp Magazin
Gansemarkt 24
Postfach 30 54 24
D–20317 Hamburg
Germany
Phone (40) 34 700
Fax (40) 34 58 90

Pro Mobil
Anzeigenabteilung
D–70162 Stuttgart 10
Germany
Phone (711) 18 21 639
Fax (711) 18 21 349

Camping Car
24, avenue de Mousquetaires
F–94420 Le Plessis-Trevise
France
Phone (1) 45 93 72 72
Fax (1) 45 93 25 93

Motor Caravan Magazine
Link House
Dingwall Avenue
GB–Croydon CR9 2TA
England
Phone (81) 68 62 599

DRIVING IN EUROPE

For many people the idea of driving a motorhome or towing a trailer overseas carries with it an aura of danger and adventure. Visions of thousands of tiny foreign cars buzzing around Parisian traffic circles at near-supersonic speeds and of jet-propelled Mercedes and Porsches blowing away all comers on the German autobahns are, at the least, intimidating. While there is some basis for such thoughts, driving in Europe need not be any more harrowing than driving at home. (For those of you living in Los Angeles or New York, that may offer little consolation.)

Actually, driving in Europe these days is a very civilized business. In recent years, along with an increasing level of affluence, a whole new generation of drivers has come on the road. Licensing requirements have been stiffened; in most countries a considerable number of hours of driver training with a certified instructor is part of the licensing process. Great improvements in highway design and maintenance have also gone a long way toward making driving safer and more pleasurable. Modern superhighways now extend to all corners of the continent, and even the once fearsome Alps have been tamed. The gently ascending Brenner Autobahn, which connects Austria and Italy, and the Gotthard Tunnel under the Swiss Alps are two of the most important transalpine links. The new Channel Tunnel, which transports motor vehicles on rail cars, provides for the very first time the opportunity to drive directly between France and England.

While these new high-speed motorways and tunnels have their advantages, don't plan on seeing the real charm of Europe while whizzing through the countryside or under a mountain at 110 kph (66 mph). Selective use of superhighways and tunnels to cross difficult mountain stretches or to bypass congested or uninteresting areas makes good sense. Otherwise, get off of these and get into the real Europe.

Our experience, after more than a quarter million miles in Europe behind the wheel of cars, cars towing trailers, and various campers and motorhomes, is that the vast majority of European drivers are courteous and considerate. There are some very definite exceptions, and those are the ones to watch out for. The best overall strategy is to drive defensively and always to expect the unexpected. When uncertain about who has the right of way, don't push your luck—yield!

The farther south one goes, the more animated driving becomes. In

Italy and France horn honking, arm waving, and various gestures are meant more as friendly warnings than as expressions of personal hostility; California-style freeway shootings are unknown in Europe, at least so far.

Drinking and driving are taken seriously, and permissible blood-alcohol levels are low—in some countries, 0 percent. Being a foreigner or feigning ignorance of the law will get you very little sympathy. Should you get into trouble, you will find that your consular authorities can do little more for you than arrange for an English-speaking attorney and, if it comes to that, visit you in jail. Don't spoil a good trip. If you drink, don't drive.

European traffic regulations are logical and differ only slightly from those in North America. Driving is, with the exceptions of Great Britain and Ireland, on the right, with passing on the left. As a rule, priority is given to traffic coming from the right. Traffic entering a roundabout or traffic circle has the right of way over those already in the circle in most countries. When in doubt, take a defensive stance and yield.

A standardized system of international road signs is used throughout Europe, with only minor local variations. The signs are self-explanatory and follow a logical pattern. Triangular signs indicate danger, round signs denote restrictions such as speed limits and no passing, and rectangular signs provide information such as the location of campgrounds (see the appendix, pp. 362-69, for illustrations). Major national and international routes are well marked (refer to the chapters on driving in individual countries for details). The major international routes are designated with the letter "E."

Places are often known by different names in different languages. For example, Switzerland is *Die Schweiz* in German, *La Suisse* in French, and *La Svizzera* in Italian. Many cities also have several names. In our itineraries we have indicated, where appropriate, the different spellings of these names.

Just as each U.S. state and each Canadian province has its own license plate, so does each European country. Individual countries are identified by an international symbol. For example, "F" is for France, "D" for Germany. (See the appendix for a complete list.) If you know the codes, it is possible in many countries to identify the city or county that a vehicle is registered in.

Even though European highways are well marked, an automobile compass is a handy gadget to have along. We have, more than once, caught ourselves leaving a city or campground and speeding off in the wrong direction. The addition of this inexpensive item has saved us many hours of driving and much aggravation. Stick one in your bag before you leave.

PARKING

Although parking regulations vary from place to place, there is one constant: Parking a motorhome in most major European cities is a very difficult, or impossible, proposition. The saving grace is the almost universal existence of efficient public transportation. This allows you to leave your vehicle at a campground or in the suburbs of a large city and take a train or bus into town.

Many large cities have park-and-ride schemes. A single parking meter is often used to control a large area; put your money in the meter and place the ticket that you receive on the windshield. Some locales limit the length of stay by requiring the use of a blue cardboard clock disk. This is set upon arrival and placed inside the windshield. These disks may be obtained from automobile clubs and most service stations.

Trip Planning

The key to a successful trip, whether a weekend outing or a globe-circling expedition, lies in the planning and preparation. For many people a good part of the enjoyment of travel derives from poring over maps, searching through travel brochures, and reading about the places to be visited. This all serves to heighten the enjoyment of the main event. The more knowledge that you bring with you, the more rewarding your trip will be. As Samuel Johnson said, "He, who would bring home the wealth of the Indies, must carry the wealth of the Indies with him. So it is in traveling, a man must carry knowledge with him if he would bring home knowledge."

Obviously, the length of time that you have to travel and the thickness of your wallet will be deciding factors in the type of trip you take. Due to the relatively high cost of getting to Europe, the flying time involved, and the jet-lag factor, it does not make much sense to plan an RV tour that is shorter than two weeks. Ideally, you should have three weeks or longer. Figure that the better part of two days will be spent traveling to and from Europe and that checking out and returning a rental motorhome will consume another day. That leaves, at best, ten or eleven days out of those fourteen days for actual travel in your motorhome. If two weeks are all that you can manage, try to keep your itinerary limited to one or two regions that you can comfortably explore in the allotted time. Our Benelux route (Tiptoeing through the Tulips) and our French itineraries (France a la Carte) can each be covered comfortably in a two-week period.

Even though Europe is small as compared to the United States and Canada, it is packed full of so many interesting places to visit that fourteen days are not sufficient time to "do it all." We have been RVing in Europe for the past twenty-five years and still haven't "done it all." A few years ago we met a young American family at Munich's Thalkirchen campground who were traveling in a van and doing their own version of *If It's Tuesday, This Must Be Belgium.* Bleary-eyed and haggard, they looked a lot more like people who *needed* a vacation than people who were *on* vacation. No wonder! They told us that they had three weeks and that during that time they were determined to "do Europe." It looked more like Europe had done them instead.

For a vacation that gives you lasting fond memories rather than nightmares, think in terms of travel quality rather than quantity. With a planning map of Europe, where distances look deceivingly short, spread out on the kitchen table, it is very tempting to draw some lines between the dots, perhaps from Frankfurt to Istanbul or from London to Helsinki. But such a trip will have you hopping all over Europe without seeing much more than monotonous stretches of superhighways and gas stations. That's not really the Europe that you came to see. Resist the temptation to do it all at one time. Remember that what appear as straight lines on a map often turn out to be winding, climbing roads on which you may average only 30 or 35 kph (18 or 21 mph).

Be sure also to allow time for traffic jams and other unexpected occurrences. Fortunately, with the development of the European Community, long delays at border crossings are now a thing of the past. Sufficient time to shop for food, fuel, and the basic necessities should also be included in your planning. In addition, allow time for impromptu shopping stops at village markets along your route.

When planning your sightseeing, remember that however ambitious your intentions, there are just so many museums and cathedrals that the human organism can absorb in a given period of time. Plan a trip that will get you off the autobahns and motorways and onto the many quiet country roads that make RV travel in Europe such a delight. Some of your most memorable experiences will be those that happen spontaneously, in places that have no stars and are not even listed in the guidebooks. Take the time to stop and smell the flowers. Some of the greatest joys of traveling on your own come from just stumbling upon that quaint English village church or an idyllic lake at the end of some unmarked road in the Finnish wilderness.

A wrong turn on such a road one summer led us to a Gypsy encampment. There were tents, horses, wagons, and kids all over the place. Except for the fact that the poverty was very real, this looked like a Hollywood movie set. The Gypsies were curious about our motorhome, and for us it was a fascinating and memorable experience—we hadn't even known that there were Gypsies in Finland.

In your planning be sure to allot time for the unexpected. Use the itineraries in this book as a framework upon which to build your own memorable experiences. Above all, don't be afraid to venture out on your own. Give yourself the time to explore some of those back roads. You won't pick a winner every time, but you will hit the jackpot often enough to make it worthwhile.

MAPS

For a broad overview and for general planning purposes, the *Planning Map of Europe,* available from the AAA, is highly recommended. When touring, we have had the best experience with the Michelin series of road maps. They are the most accurate, are easy to read, and are printed on good-quality paper. Detailed map references are given at the beginning of each of our itineraries.

Michelin maps are readily available throughout France and at most larger European bookstores. In the United States and Canada, they may be found at most bookstores with extensive travel sections.

For information on obtaining these maps, contact the following Michelin distributors. In the United States: Michelin Travel Publications, Michelin Tire Corporation, One Parkway South, Greenville, SC 29602; phone (803) 458–6470, fax (803) 458–6630. In Canada: Ste. Canadienne des Pneus Michelin, 175 Boulevard Bouchard, Dorval, Quebec H9S 5T1, Canada; phone (514) 636–5920, fax (514) 636–6828. In Great Britain: Michelin Tyre PLC, Davy House–Lyon Road, Harrow, Middlesex HA1 2DQ, England; phone (81) 861–2121, fax (81) 863–0680.

CAMPGROUND DIRECTORIES

There are a number of good campground guides available in Europe; however, most of these are not written in English. The best of the English-language guides is published in England by The Caravan Club. This two-volume set includes descriptions of selected campsites throughout Europe along with reasonably detailed directions for locating campgrounds. U.K. sites are listed in a separate volume. To order or to obtain additional information, contact The Caravan Club, East Grinstead House, East Grinstead, West Sussex RHI9 IUA, England; phone (0342) 32 69 44, fax (0342) 41 02 58. A less detailed guide, also in

English, is available from The Automobile Association, Farnum House, Basing View, Basingstoke, Hampshire RG21 2EA, England; phone (256) 20 123, fax (256) 49 33 89.

If you can understand some basic German, you will find the two-volume campground guide published by the German automobile club, ADAC, to be very useful. For further information contact ADAC, Am Westpark 8, 81373 Munchen 70, Germany; phone (89) 76 760, fax (89) 76 76–2500.

WHEN TO GO

SUMMER

If you must travel during July and August, then Northern and Eastern Europe—and in particular the Scandinavian countries—are your best bet for avoiding the overcrowded campgrounds, the long lines at museums and palaces, and the horrendous traffic that plague the Central European mountains and the beach resorts of Southern Europe. Scandinavian summers, while often unpredictable, still provide the best weather for touring. Spring and autumn in the northern countries are usually cold and rainy, and many campgrounds are closed.

In the summer the interior regions of Spain and southern France are far less congested than along the coast. Although these are wonderful places to tour, if you venture into these regions in July, August, and early September, be prepared for unmercifully hot weather. Portugal north of Lisbon is a delightful area of sandy beaches, mountains, and fortified hilltop villages, and it is relatively uncrowded and has a mild summertime climate. Although many Western Europeans are now taking advantage of the lifting of travel restrictions and the bargain prices in Eastern Europe, most of that region is still not overly crowded in the summer. The Atlantic coast of France and the dramatic Normandy and Brittany coasts are also well suited for summertime touring, although you will find these areas to be more crowded than Scandinavia.

SPRING

April in Paris may sound cozy and romantic in a song title, but in reality, April in Paris—and, for that matter, in much of Northern and Central Europe—often means cold and rainy weather. That is not to say that the sun never shines in March and April, but if you plan to travel in early spring, you should be prepared for cold temperatures, rain, and even snow in many areas. A number of Alpine passes are closed due to snow until late May and often until mid-June. To allow for bad weather, spring travel plans should include at least a few city and museum visits.

In most large cities, campgrounds are open in March; in the beach and mountain regions, many do not open until mid-April or early May. Springtime is the loveliest time to travel in Southern Europe. Tourist attractions are just awakening from their winter hibernation and uncrowded campgrounds are freshly scrubbed and newly painted, awaiting the first guests of the season. Flowers are blooming everywhere and the sun is usually shining. The Easter season in Spain is a time of many colorful pageants and festivals, including Seville's famed April Fair. April through early June is our favorite time for traveling in the south of Europe.

Autumn

Autumn in much of Europe is also an ideal time for touring. The summertime throngs of tourists have departed, museums and castles can be enjoyed at leisure, and the weather is usually mild and pleasant. September and October are our favorite months for traveling in the Alps. The changing colors of the leaves are a spectacular sight, and the weather is ideal for hiking. Autumn is also the time for many of Central Europe's rollicking beer and wine festivals.

Winter

Winter travel in Southern Europe can be very pleasant if you stick to the most southerly portions of Spain, Portugal, the Greek island of Crete, and the Turkish Riviera. Most campgrounds along the coast stay open all year.

By contrast, winter in the inland and mountainous regions of Southern Europe can be nasty and cold. Most campgrounds are closed and roads are often covered with snow and ice.

Even Spain and Greece often experience severe winter weather in their interior regions. On our first trip to Greece, we were free camping at a highway rest stop just north of Thessaloniki in late November and were astonished to wake up in the morning to find our motorhome enveloped in a blanket of snow!

Unless you are planning on a ski vacation, winter camping in Central and Northern Europe is not advised. Outside of the winter resorts, few campgrounds are open, and driving and weather conditions are not conducive to touring.

SHARING AN RV

A great way to cut the cost of an RV vacation is to share the cost of renting an RV with friends or family. The expense of renting a large motorhome that can comfortably accommodate four persons is much less per couple than the cost of renting a smaller single unit. By pooling fuel costs, campground fees, and highway tolls, substantial additional savings can be realized.

Keep in mind, however, that traveling together in an RV brings people very close together: these tight confines, especially during a spell of rainy weather, can place a heavy strain on even the best of relationships. It takes very special friends to be able to share a camper and finish the trip still friends. If you are seriously considering this option, try it out for a week or so before coming to Europe.

TRAVELING WITH CHILDREN

Without a doubt, an RV is the optimal way of traveling with children of all ages. In addition to the obvious economic benefits of combining accommodations and transportation for the whole family in one unit and the savings involved in not having to eat all of your meals in restaurants, there are many other advantages to family motorhome vacations.

For one thing, you always have a comfortable bed handy. When it's nap time for you or the children, there is no need to curl up in an uncomfortable car or train seat. You can stop and stretch out and sleep for as long as you like. If someone craves a snack or a cup of coffee, there is no need to search for a restaurant that is open. Simply pull over to the side of the road and your menu will be limited only by the contents of your kitchen and the talents and imagination of the chef. Need to change a diaper, or need a toilet in a hurry? No problem! Everything that you need is literally right at your fingertips.

It's not just the physical and economic considerations that make European RV travel so appealing for family vacations, though—it is also the opportunity that this mode of travel provides for meeting kids from other countries. When it comes to language problems and hesitation to cross cultural and ethnic barriers, children are far less inhibited than their parents.

On a trip along the Dalmatian coast of Yugoslavia some years ago, before the recent war madness, we pulled our camper off of the road for a picnic lunch. We shared a small, grassy clearing with a Yugoslav family who had also stopped for lunch. Before we knew it our sons were off having a great time busily playing and chatting away with the local kids. These kids spoke not a word of English and ours certainly spoke no Serbo-Croatian, but there they were, playing as if they had been friends for years. We soon found ourselves drawn into sharing lunch with the parents. After a few shots of Slivovitz, the fiery Yugoslavian plum brandy, we were all having a great time and had no problem communicating in spite of the lack of a common language. When they were younger, our boys accompanied us on many of our RV trips, learning much about other ways of life and making many friends along the way.

ESCORTED MOTORHOME TOURS

An interesting option, particularly for that first European RV experience, is to take an organized, all-inclusive motorhome tour. These unique tours offer a comprehensive package that includes a fully equipped motorhome, reserved campgrounds, an extensive program of guided sightseeing tours and excursions, entertainment, some meals, and the flight to and from Europe. Each tour is accompanied by a full-time, multilingual couple who serve as "wagonmasters" and hosts. Sightseeing excursions are conducted in modern motor coaches with local professional guides. The European motorhomes supplied are state of the art and are equipped with hot and cold running water, shower, toilet, refrigerator, stove, bedding, and crockery. In addition to on-the-spot information from the wagonmasters, participants receive a detailed day-by-day, kilometer-by-kilometer trip log that highlights points of interest along the route and makes it virtually impossible to get lost. Within the parameters of the planned tour, there is a great deal of individual freedom. Driving in a convoy is not required, and plenty of time is given for impromptu picnics and just to stop and smell the flowers.

This mode of travel provides that often sought but seldom found blending of the independence of vagabonding with the security and camaraderie that go with group travel. Although previous RV experience is helpful, it is not required. The vehicles, designed for European conditions, are compact and easy to handle. If you can drive a pickup truck or station wagon, you'll have no trouble with one of these rigs. It is also possible to take one of these tours and, after its conclusion, continue traveling on your own with the same motorhome.

Several tours are scheduled yearly and include various regions of Europe. These trips are very popular and are usually booked up well in advance. For additional information contact Overseas Motorhome Tours, 222K South Irena Street, Redondo Beach, CA 90277; phone (800) 322–2127.

Useful Information

DOCUMENTS

Passport

An up-to-date passport is required of all U.S., Canadian, and British citizens for entry into any European country. If you do not have an International Camping Carnet, a passport is required when registering at most campgrounds. It is also required when changing money or cashing traveler's checks. Be sure that your passport is valid for your return trip home—an expired passport may be renewed by consular authorities abroad, but this is often inconvenient and time consuming.

Visas

Visas are not currently required for entry into the Western European countries. The situation in the former Communist countries is in a state of flux. To avoid any unpleasant surprises, check with the national tourist office or embassy of the country you intend to visit.

International Driving Permit

This document is a multilanguage translation of the relevant information on your home driver's license. It is valid only when used together with an up-to-date license from your place of residence. Although it is not required in Western Europe, it is advisable to obtain this document—should you have an accident or problems involving the police, it is a handy document to have. In view of the changing situation in Eastern Europe, it is advisable to check with the national tourist offices or embassies of the countries that you plan on visiting for current requirements.

For details on obtaining an International Driving Permit, contact your automobile club or the American Automobile Association, 1000

AAA Drive, Heathrow, FL 32746–5063; phone (407) 444–7000, fax (407) 444–7380.

INTERNATIONAL CAMPING CARNET

No one should camp in Europe without an International Camping Carnet. This handy card greatly simplifies registering at a campground, eliminating the necessity of leaving your passport at the campground reception desk. Some campgrounds require the Carnet for admission, and it is required at all campgrounds in Denmark. Holders of the card receive a discount at many sites. During the course of your trip, this discount will usually more than pay for the cost of the card. Included in the price of the Carnet is liability insurance that covers the Carnet holder and his or her family for property damage and personal injury caused as a result of any camping activity occurring at a campground. It is valid for one year and is sold only to members of issuing organizations.

In the United States and Canada, the International Camping Carnet may be obtained from the Family Campers and RVers Association, 4808 Transit Road, Building 2, Depew, NY 14043–4906 (phone and fax 716–668–6242); and in the United Kingdom, from The Caravan Club, East Grinstead House, East Grinstead, West Sussex, RHI9 IUA, England (phone 342–32 69 44, fax 342–41 02 58).

INTERNATIONAL GREEN INSURANCE CARD

Your U.S. or Canadian automobile insurance is not valid in Europe. To drive a motor vehicle in a European country it is necessary to have an International Green Insurance Card, commonly known as a Green Card, valid for that country. If you rent or lease overseas, this will be provided along with the other vehicle documents. Be sure that the card is valid in all of the countries in which you intend to travel.

Short-term liability insurance may be purchased at most border crossings, but this is a time-consuming and expensive procedure. If you are driving your own vehicle in Europe, you can obtain coverage from American International Underwriters through the AAA. Contact AAA Foreign Motoring Insurance, 1000 AAA Drive, Heathrow, FL 32746–5063; phone (800) 222–4599, fax (407) 444–8567.

HEALTH CONSIDERATIONS

INOCULATIONS

There are currently no inoculation requirements for travel to Europe. Check with the U.S. Public Health Service prior to departure for current status. An updated tetanus vaccination is beneficial in case of accidental injury.

INSURANCE

Check with your medical insurance carrier to see if your coverage is valid in Europe. Medicare does not cover overseas medical expenses. Find out exactly what information is required to present a claim for medical expenses incurred overseas.

Most European medical facilities will not honor U.S. health insurance plans; in most cases you will have to pay for treatment and submit a receipt to your insurance company for reimbursement. The Canadian health insurance plans provide for some overseas coverage. In many cases it is necessary to arrange supplementary insurance.

PRESCRIPTIONS

Take along an adequate supply of any medications that you require. Obtain a copy of the prescription from your doctor. Be sure that the generic name is indicated, as the same drug is often marketed under different brand names in different countries. Having a prescription for medication that you are carrying can also save you problems with customs authorities.

PREVENTION

Although there are no serious health risks associated with travel in Europe, it is a good idea to have your doctor prescribe medicine for diarrhea. Tap water, unless otherwise posted, is safe to drink throughout Europe. If you have any doubt, use bottled water. Fruits and vegetables should be thoroughly washed prior to consumption.

If you wear glasses or contact lenses, take along an extra pair as well as a copy of your prescription. Denture wearers can save much time and potential embarrassment by bringing along a spare.

The International Association for Medical Assistance to Travelers (IMAT) can provide you with a list of English-speaking doctors who meet U.S. and British standards of training. In the United States contact the IMAT, 417 Center Street, Lewiston, NY 14092 (phone 716–754–4883); in Canada write the IMAT at 40 Regal Road, Guelph, Ontario N1K 1B5, Canada.

KEEPING IN TOUCH

To some people a vacation means total escape—the less that they have to do with what is going on in the world the better. Many travelers, however, particularly on longer journeys, find it comforting to touch base occasionally with what's happening out there. Same-day editions of *USA Today,* the *International Herald Tribune,* and the *Wall Street Journal* are available in most major European cities and resorts. The most important British papers are also widely available, as are the European editions of *Time* and *Newsweek* magazines.

English-language radio programs can be picked up on the U.S. Armed Forces Radio Network in areas where U.S. forces are still present. With a shortwave receiver you will be able to listen to the English-language broadcasts of The Voice of America, the BBC, Radio Canada International, and other international stations.

TELEPHONES

It is now a simple matter to telephone the United States or Canada from anywhere in Europe. The simplest—and usually cheapest—way to do this is with a phone card such as AT&T, MCI, or Sprint. With these cards you can dial a direct number, place your call with an English-speaking operator, and be billed at home for the call. (Direct-dial numbers are listed in the *International Herald Tribune* and *USA Today.*) Whenever possible, avoid making long-distance calls from hotels, as rates are often three to four times the rate charged at public phones.

Post offices often have comfortable facilities for telephoning. Fax machines also are available for public use at most post offices.

Each country has a designated code number that must be used when making international calls. For example, the number for the United States and Canada is (1); for the United Kingdom, it is (44). When making an international call, if the area code begins with a zero (0), this must be dropped when calling from outside that country.

Prepaid phone cards and credit cards can be used in most countries, in phones equipped with a slot for this purpose. This eliminates the need for having to carry a lot of coins.

Mail

American Express offices abroad will hold mail at no charge for American Express Card or traveler's check holders. You may also have mail sent to any campground or to any city c/o General Delivery (Poste Restante). Persons traveling together should have mail addressed to both parties so that either party can pick up the mail.

MONEY

Credit Cards

The use of credit cards is rapidly catching on all over Europe, although their use is not as extensive as in North America. It is now possible to pay by card for gasoline and diesel in most countries. Visa and MasterCard may also be used on the French and Spanish toll roads and for the major trans-Alpine tunnels. A limited number of campgrounds accept credit cards. Payment at most better restaurants and shops may also be made by card.

Traveler's Checks and Cash

For both safety and convenience, any large sums of money should be carried in the form of traveler's checks. When exchanging money, try to do so at banks or official exchange offices. Shops and campgrounds often give less favorable rates.

If you have a bank card with an international "pin" number, you may obtain cash in the local currency at automatic teller machines

(ATMs) located in major cities and popular tourist areas. Do not plan on being able to cash personal checks abroad. Money can be exchanged after regular business hours at major train stations and airports.

SAFETY AND SECURITY

The concept of just what constitutes reasonable safety precautions to take when traveling varies greatly from person to person. Some travelers are so preoccupied with the threat (or presumed threat) of being ripped off, mugged, or even kidnapped and sold into slavery that they never really let go and enjoy their vacations. To others, safety and security when traveling are not even a topic for consideration.

As with most issues, the answer lies somewhere in the middle. Statistics continue to show that Europe, major cities included, is a considerably safer place to live and to vacation in than is the United States. This is not to say, of course, that Europe is free of crime. Wherever you travel, reasonable precautions should be taken; and in certain high-risk areas, such as Seville and the south of Spain, Amsterdam, Berlin, and the major Eastern European cities, additional care should be exercised.

Here are a few suggestions for reducing your risk of being robbed:

- Always lock your vehicle and engage the steering-wheel lock. If you have an alarm system, be sure to activate it.
- Never leave valuables, such as money, passports, and cameras, in the vehicle.
- Leave the glove compartment open to show that there is nothing of value in it.
- Where possible, park in supervised or guarded areas. The extra money spent for parking fees or given to local kids for "protection" is cheap insurance.
- When camping outside of campgrounds in high-risk areas, stay away from deserted places. Hotel parking lots, service stations, and even police stations are preferred spots.
- Keep copies of your passport information and photo pages as well as a list of credit-card numbers and where to report losses.
- If your passport is lost or stolen, report the loss immediately to the local police. Take the police report to your nearest consulate; in most instances you will be issued a temporary passport within a day.

- When walking on the street, keep your purse on the side away from traffic to discourage moped-mounted purse snatchers.
- Avoid conspicuous jewelry, flashing large amounts of money, and other obvious displays of affluence.
- Wear a money belt or other concealed holder.

ADDITIONAL SOURCES OF INFORMATION

National tourist offices will supply you with much useful information to help with planning your trip. (See the list in the appendix, pp. 357-61.) When traveling through an area, you will find that local tourist offices also have a wealth of useful material. They can assist in locating a campground or a good restaurant, furnish local maps, and provide any number of other helpful services.

PART II

WHERE TO GO

A typical campground office

Introduction to Itineraries

The following eleven itineraries present RVing in Europe at its best and include a wide variety of cultural and historic attractions, major cities, out-of-the-way hamlets and villages, and some of Europe's most scenic drives. The starting cities have been chosen for their ease of access and ready availability of rental motorhomes. All of the itineraries trace a circular route, allowing you the flexibility of being able to start and finish at any point along the way.

By combining various itineraries or parts of itineraries, you can also design your own custom tour. Convenient places for joining together different routes are indicated in the text and on the maps.

ROADS

In our choice of highways, we have avoided the autobahns and other high-speed motorways wherever feasible, in favor of the back roads and country lanes that are a so much more interesting part of the European motoring experience.

PLACES TO VISIT AND THINGS TO SEE

Descriptions of various towns and places of interest are not intended to be all-encompassing but are meant to provide you with enough information to decide whether or not to stop and explore further. Material from local tourist offices and from guidebooks, such as the Michelin Green Guides, Cadogan Guides, or Fodor's Travel Guide series, can fill in whatever details you might need.

CAMPGROUNDS

For each town or city that is described in the text and denoted on the accompanying map with a circled number, for example, ⑦, we have selected one or more campgrounds. These campgrounds are designated by a letter indicating the country and a number that corresponds to the listing in the text and in the index. The distance between campgrounds is rarely more than 175 km (105 mi.), or a few hours' comfortable driving time.

Where there are several campgrounds, we have picked the best ones available, based on a number of factors. These include the convenience and attractiveness of the location, type of facilities available, cleanliness, and level of friendliness and service.

To give you some general guidelines in choosing a site, we have rated each with from one to four stars (★). These ratings are at best subjective and, of course, can change for better or worse from year to year. It is also important to note that in some cases, depending on the weather or sometimes just on the mood of the manager, a given campground may open or close a few days to several weeks earlier or later than the dates listed.

If in the course of your travels you come across an interesting campground that you would like to share with us or if our description of a campground is no longer accurate, please write to us care of The Globe Pequot Press, P.O. Box 833, Old Saybrook, CT 06475.

Campground Ratings and Descriptions

The ratings are as follows:

★ Satisfactory
★★ Good
★★★ Very good
★★★★ Superior

The amenities present, such as a snack bar or restaurant, swimming pool, and so on, are indicated by the icons displayed below.

Campstore on site or grocery store nearby
Restaurant or snack bar on site or nearby
Swimming (pool, lake, beach) on site or nearby
Tennis

- Coin-operated laundry machines
- Wheelchair accessible (at least one toilet)
- Propane or butane gas
- Playground

MAPS

For each itinerary a map is provided that shows the main route, places of interest, and campgrounds. Circled numbers on the map correspond to places of interest described in the text, and campground locations are shown with the symbol ▲. To find details about a particular campground, look up its location in the index.

BRITISH BYWAYS

Great Britain

CAPITAL: London

POPULATION: 57,800,000

CURRENCY: pound sterling (£), divided into 100 pence

LANGUAGES: English, Welsh, Scots, and Gaelic

RELIGIONS: Church of England and Roman Catholic

POLICE: 999

FIRE: 999

AMBULANCE: 999

ROAD SERVICE: 999

BANKS: weekdays 9:30 A.M.–3:30 P.M.; some major banks open Saturday morning; major airports have 24-hour service

STORES: weekdays and Saturday: 9:00 A.M.–5:30 P.M.; some stores earlier on Wednesday or Thursday; London department stores open until 7:30 or 8:00 P.M.

HOLIDAYS: January 1; January 4, bank holiday; Good Friday and Easter Monday (movable); first and last Mondays in May, bank holidays; August 2, Scotland only; August 30, bank holiday; December 25 and 26; December 27, bank holiday

EMBASSIES: *United States,* 24/31 Grosvenor Square, W1A 1AE London; phone (071) 499–9000, fax (071) 409–1637. *Canada,* 38 Grosvenor Street, London W1X 0AA; phone (071) 258–6600, fax (071) 258–6533

Let's begin with a few definitions so that we are all on the same wavelength. The term *Great Britain* refers to England, Scotland, and Wales. With the inclusion of the province of Northern Ireland, this becomes the *United Kingdom.* The *British Isles* include Great Britain and Ireland (an entirely separate nation of some 3.5 million inhabitants). The republic of Ireland occupies most of the island of Ireland, which it shares with Northern Ireland. The whole of the British Isles, including Ireland, is just slightly larger than the U.S. state of Arizona and has a population of some 60 million. So much for geography!

One of the nicer things about traveling in Great Britain is the opportunity it presents of visiting a European country without having to hassle with the difficulties of getting by in a foreign language. This is the only place in Europe where you can navigate in miles and order your beer by the pint.

Even in these closing years of the twenty-first century and in the face of an increasing number of social and economic problems, which include a challenge to the preservation of the monarchy, the strong British sense of history and tradition has helped to preserve and protect many of the country's treasured sites and institutions. One can still watch the pomp and circumstance of the changing of the guard at Buckingham Palace, enjoy the performance of a Shakespearean play at Stratford-upon-Avon, or just have a pint and join in a game of darts at a local pub.

DRIVING

Once you have gotten over the confusing and sometimes terrifying experience of driving on the left-hand side of the road and passing on the right, driving in Great Britain is—with the exception of London, Birmingham, and the other major cities—quite pleasant. Motorists are disciplined, generally courteous, and amazingly tolerant of drivers with foreign license plates. This is probably due to the fact that Britons experience a similar disorientation when driving on the continent. Be particularly alert at roundabouts (traffic circles) and when you are tired: In an emergency situation your immediate reaction will be to get the vehicle back on the "right" side of the road.

An advantage of driving in Great Britain is that the distances are short. For example, it is only some 240 mi. (400 km) from the center of London to the Scottish border in the north. The network of high-speed roads ("motorways") is not as extensive in England as in countries like Germany or France; in Wales and Scotland it is practically nonexistent. Only 4 percent of Britain's 232,500 mi. (375,000 km) of roads are motorways, yet these carry more than 30 percent of the traffic. The obvious conclusion is to avoid the motorways in favor of the smaller roads.

Getting around, especially during the summer vacation period and on holiday weekends, can be slow going. The British tendency to construct traffic circles (roundabouts) with great frequency along the major highways leads to some horrendous traffic backups. In many instances there are no bypasses, so major roads go right through the center of large towns and cities.

The extensive network of country roads that meander from village to village provide a wonderful way to enjoy the delightful countryside. In some areas, however, vision is obscured by tall hedgerows. To avoid nasty surprises slow down at bends in the road.

The motorways are designated by the letter "M" and are not subject to tolls. Primary roads are marked with an "A." The major trunk roads have the least number of digits. Thus "A1" indicates a major four-lane highway, while "A658" and "A4104" indicate secondary country roads. The roads designated with the letter "B" are predominantly narrow, often quite scenic country lanes.

With the exception of the fact that driving is on the left-hand side of the road, traffic regulations are similar to those in other European countries. When entering a roundabout, unless otherwise marked, traffic on your right has the right of way. Remember that you are going around toward the left!

The wearing of seatbelts is obligatory. This also applies to rear seatbelts when fitted. As in other countries, there are strong penalties for driving under the influence of alcohol. Gasoline in Britain is called *petrol* and is sold by the imperial gallon (1.2 U.S. gallons).

The speed limit for motorhomes on the motorways is 70 mph (112 kph) and on surface roads 60 mph (96 kph). Be careful when driving through towns—unless otherwise posted, the speed limit is 30 mph (51 kph). Trailers longer than 23 ft. (7 m) and wider than 7½ ft. (2.3 m) are not permitted. All accidents involving injuries must be reported to the police.

CAMPING

Great Britain, a country that lays claim to being the birthplace of camping, is well equipped to care for its many camping visitors. In addition to the more than 1,100 official campsites that are located throughout the country, there are thousands of informal sites at farms and country inns.

For example, The Caravan Club lists some 3,600 Certified Locations with varying levels of amenities. Only five RVs are permitted on these sites at the same time. Access is restricted to Caravan Club members or to members of affiliated clubs, such as the AAA and the Family Campers and RVers Association (4808 Transit Road, Building 2, Depew, NY 14043–4906; phone/fax 716–668–6242). Members are required to show an International Camping Carnet as well as their membership card in the affiliated organization.

In some parts of England, campgrounds are located on the grounds of horseracing tracks. The Forestry Commission also has campgrounds in a number of scenic locations. Details may be obtained from the Forestry Commission, 231 Corstorphine Road, Edinburgh EH12 7AT, Scotland; phone 031–334–0303.

A directory of selected sites in Britain is available at any British Tourist Authority (BTA) office. These sites are rated as to type and quality of facilities, with from one to five check marks. With the exception of campgrounds operated by the major camping clubs, the International Camping Carnet is rarely required. Major BTA offices offer a campers' advisory service to assist in locating campgrounds and, in the peak season, to help in making reservations.

Between mid-June and mid-September sites in the more popular areas, such as London, north Wales, and Cumbria, are often full. To avoid disappointment in obtaining a pitch (site), try to schedule your arrival for early in the day, or make advance reservations. British campgrounds are generally well laid out, with attention given to providing sufficient space and privacy.

Although an increasing number of campgrounds provide cafes, restaurants, and camp stores, this type of facility is not nearly as common in Britain as on the continent. Most sites have converted to the European Community standard CEE-type electrical plug and socket. Where these are not in use, adapters are usually available. Current supplied is 220 V/50 cycle.

German-type propane bottles can be filled at a limited number of Calor Gas depots. Carry a Euro-Set of gas adapters with you. These are available at most camping supply shops in Germany. When booking a ferry passage to or from Great Britain, check with the ferry company to see if you are permitted to transport gas bottles (the regulations vary from company to company). It is prohibited to use a gas cook stove in motorway service-station areas.

Free camping is prohibited but widely tolerated if you are discreet about it. When camping on private property be sure to obtain the owner's permission.

For additional information about camping in Great Britain, contact The Caravan Club, East Grinstead House, East Grinstead, West Sussex RH19 1UA, England (phone 342–32 69 44, fax 342–41 02 58) or The Camping and Caravanning Club, Greenfields House, Westwood Way, Coventry CV4 8JH, England (phone 203–69 49 95, fax 203–69 48 86).

Itinerary: London · The Cotswolds · The Lake District Southern Scotland · East Anglia · Southern England

START: London

COUNTRY: Great Britain

DISTANCE: 1,320 mi. (2,112 km)

MAPS: Michelin #986 *Great Britain–Ireland;* #402 *Midlands, The North Lake District & Borders;* #403 *Wales, West Country, Midlands;* #404 *South East, Midlands, East Anglia*

MINIMUM RECOMMENDED TOURING TIME: 21 days

INTRODUCTION

Once you get over the strange feeling of driving on the "wrong side of the road," touring in Great Britain, with its diversity of attractions, is a delight. People are friendly, and even though some of the regional accents take a bit of getting used to, it is comforting to travel in a country where conversation with the locals does not require a stack of phrase books. Britain also makes an excellent starting point for a European tour. With the new cross-Channel tunnel link to France and good ferry connections to various European ports, touring on the continent from England is a simple matter.

In laying out this itinerary, we have covered a broad range of interests and tastes and have included large cities as well as quaint villages. After the frenzied pace of London, we venture into the quiet of the English countryside, a region that has retained the thatched-roof-cottage charm that captivates visitors from all parts of the world. Our route passes through a number of picturesque, characteristically English villages, such as Saffron Walden in East Anglia and the castle-dominated hamlet of Arundel in South Hampshire.

These and many other spots along the way are ideal places to park and get out of your vehicle, to stretch your legs and enjoy the local sights, and perhaps to take in a meal at a traditional pub. (In spite of all the bashing of British food, the fare at many village pubs is actually quite good and is also reasonably priced.) As an alternative to eating out, you always have the option of picnicking or parking your vehicle alongside a scenic meadow or by a quiet stream and "eating at home." The Lake District and Yorkshire Dales are particularly well suited for such impromptu dining.

Visits to such diverse attractions as the Roman emperor Hadrian's Wall in the north of England, Shakespeare's birthplace in Stratford-upon-Avon, the universities at Oxford and Cambridge, and the Beatles Museum at the Liverpool docks span centuries of English history and culture.

Britain is a land of imposing cathedrals, and along the way we will see London's historic Westminster Abbey, the York Minster, and the cathedrals at Winchester and Salisbury. Our route also traces portions of the North Sea and Channel coasts, with excursions inland through the northern moors and the lush gardens of Kent.

We recommend several additional areas for touring. An excursion into Wales, in particular the magical beauty of Snowdonia and the rugged Welsh coastline, will be well rewarded. From Wales there is regular ferry service to Ireland, where rambling, uncrowded country lanes and hilltop castles present a tempting destination for a week or two of RV travel.

The Scottish Highlands are another such tempting touring destination. Located just a few hours north from either Glasgow or Edinburgh, this is one of Europe's last and most beautiful unspoiled regions. The rugged cliff-lined coast of Cornwall in the southwest corner of England is yet another area of great natural beauty.

When to Go

Britain is often the butt of nasty jokes that deride its notoriously bad weather. Having experienced this inclement weather firsthand on several occasions, we can offer little solace in that department. Of course, the lush green meadows and forests that we encounter throughout our travels in Britain are dependent upon lots and lots of rain.

When the sun does shine and the flowers are in bloom, there are few places on Earth that can match the English countryside for charm and beauty. Your best chances for capturing those elusive rays of British sunshine are in July and August. As a general rule the rains are more fre-

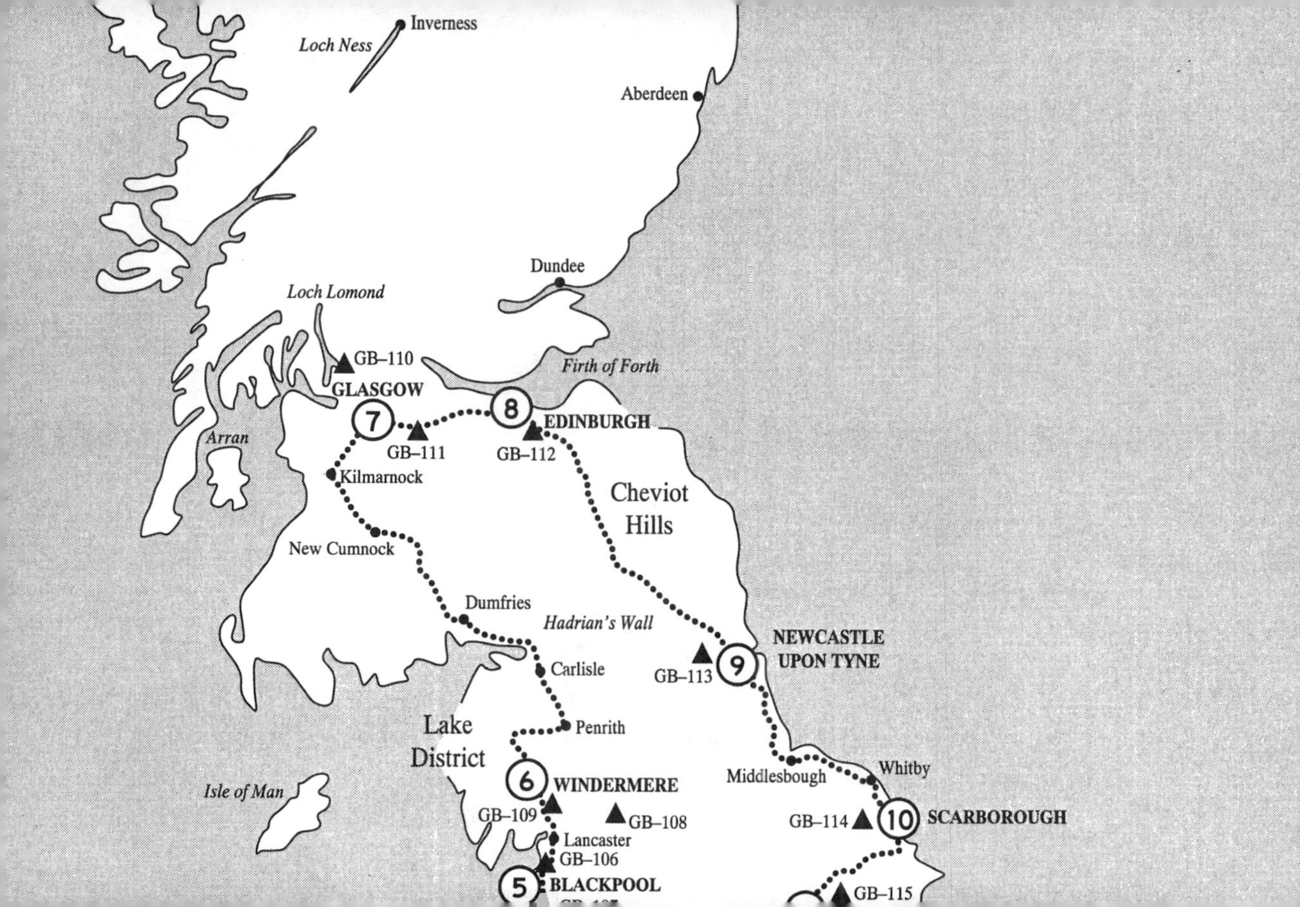

Inverness
Loch Ness
Aberdeen
Dundee
Loch Lomond
GB–110
Firth of Forth
GLASGOW
7
8
EDINBURGH
Arran
GB–111
GB–112
Kilmarnock
Cheviot Hills
New Cumnock
Dumfries
Hadrian's Wall
NEWCASTLE UPON TYNE
GB–113
9
Carlisle
Lake District
Penrith
Middlesbough
Whitby
6
WINDERMERE
Isle of Man
GB–109
GB–108
GB–114
10
SCARBOROUGH
Lancaster
GB–106
5
BLACKPOOL
GB–115

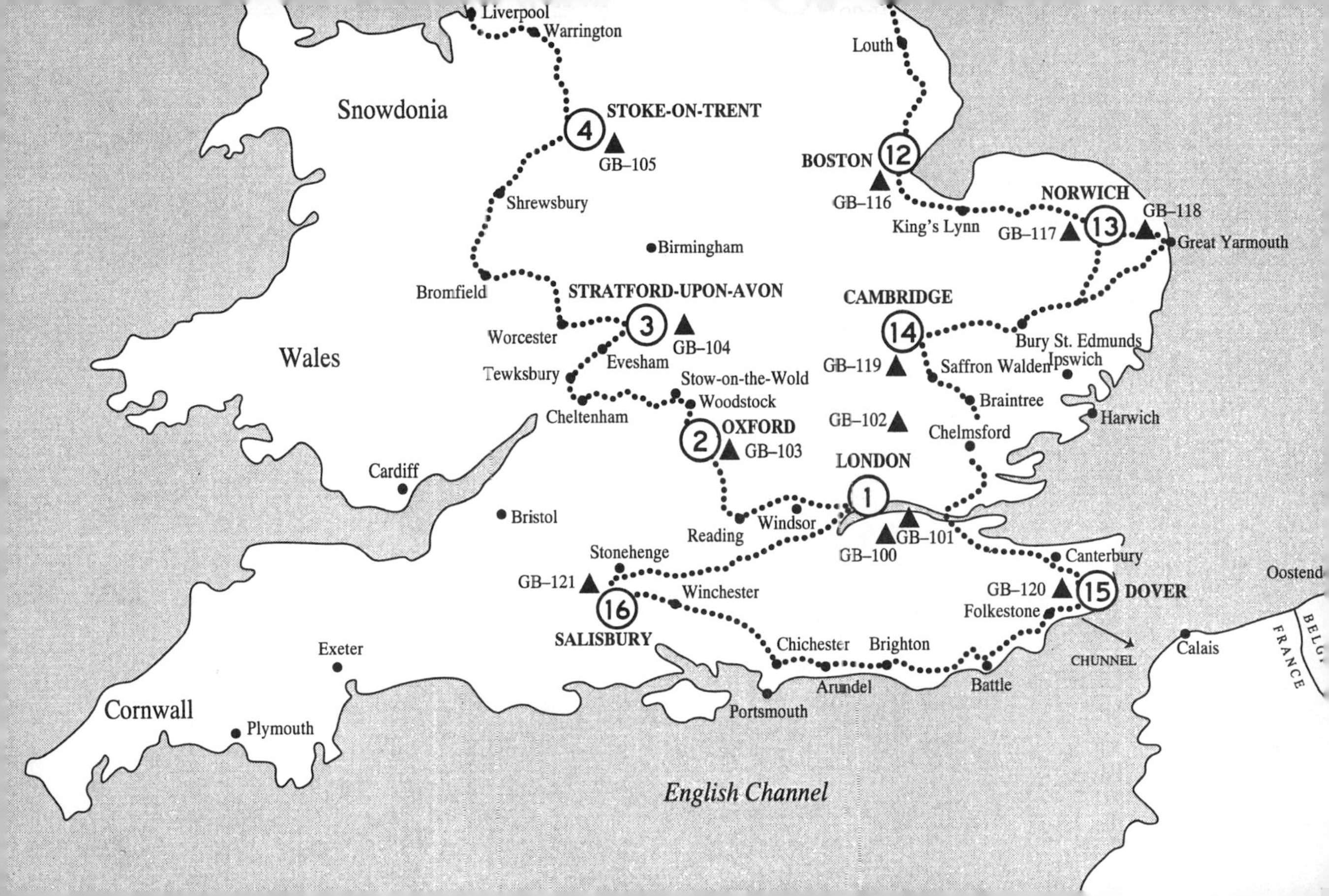
Liverpool
Warrington
Louth
Snowdonia
4
STOKE-ON-TRENT
GB–105
12
BOSTON
GB–116
NORWICH
13
GB–117
GB–118
King's Lynn
Great Yarmouth
Shrewsbury
Birmingham
Bromfield
3
STRATFORD-UPON-AVON
GB–104
CAMBRIDGE
14
GB–119
Worcester
Wales
Evesham
Tewksbury
Stow-on-the-Wold
Woodstock
Cheltenham
Bury St. Edmunds
Saffron Walden
Ipswich
Braintree
Harwich
2
OXFORD
GB–103
GB–102
Chelmsford
LONDON
1
Cardiff
Bristol
Reading
Windsor
GB–101
GB–100
Stonehenge
Canterbury
GB–121
16
SALISBURY
Winchester
15
DOVER
GB–120
Folkestone
Oostend
BELG
FRANCE
Calais
CHUNNEL
Exeter
Chichester
Brighton
Arundel
Battle
Portsmouth
Cornwall
Plymouth
English Channel

quent the farther north and west you get from the center of England.

Unlike summer in many other parts of Europe, British summers are rarely uncomfortably hot. The average daily minimum and maximum temperatures for London in July are 54°F and 72°F (12°C and 22°C). If you do opt to do this itinerary in the summer, be prepared to share the roads, attractions, and campgrounds with lots of other similarly minded folks. Many campgrounds are filled to overflowing, and waiting in long lines to take a shower or to visit a castle or museum can take much of the fun out any vacation. Our recommendation is to wait until the summer crowds thin out a bit and to do your traveling in September or during the pre-season months of May and June. In any case be prepared for rain and chilly weather at any time and pack accordingly.

Highlights

London
Oxford
The Cotswolds
Stratford-upon-Avon
The Lake District
Edinburgh
York Minster
Cambridge
Stonehenge

Expanding Horizons

There are numerous possibilities along this route to connect by ferry with various itineraries on the continent. The Channel Tunnel also provides a rapid link between Dover and Calais, giving you the opportunity for joining with our France and Benelux itineraries.

- **To France a la Carte Itinerary I:** From Dover take the ferry to Calais and head south to link up at Rouen (see p. 158). This is the shortest English Channel crossing. There are also ferry connections from Brighton to Dieppe and between Portsmouth and the French ports of Le Havre, Caen (Cabourg), and Cherbourg (see p. 159).
- **To Tiptoeing through the Tulips Itinerary:** Take the Dover–Zeebrugge ferry (see p. 141).
- **To Viking Trails Itinerary:** Take the ferry from Newcastle to Bergen and Stavanger, Norway, or to Goteborg, Sweden (see pp. 109, 113).

ON THE ROAD

Numbered sites correspond with circled numbers on the itinerary map.

1. LONDON

With its rich history and wonderful attractions, London is an important part of any visit to England. This is a city to explore on foot and via public transportation (several money-saving schemes are available from London Transport). Driving an RV through the city's narrow, crowded streets and lanes—even without the "wrong way" traffic—would be madness. There are several good campgrounds within easy striking distance of London that are located close to bus and train transport to provide convenient access to the city.

Greater London covers an area of some 620 sq. mi. (1,600 km^2) and is home to a heterogeneous mixture of nearly 7 million people. But, fortunately for the visitor, most of the interesting sights and attractions are located within the approximately one-square-mile area known simply as "the City." A modern metropolis struggling to come to grips with massive traffic congestion, urban renewal, purple-haired punkers, and a flood of immigrants from all corners of the former British Empire, London is still, in many ways, the quaint old city of Buckingham Palace, Big Ben, the Tower of London, brightly costumed Beefeater guards, and all of the other trappings that inspired Samuel Johnson in 1777 to say, "When a man is tired of London, he is tired of life."

To get a broad overview of the city, take London Transport's two-hour sightseeing tour. Then go back and concentrate on a few of the attractions that you are most interested in. Be sure to leave some time for just strolling about. London is one of the world's great walking cities.

Obtaining information about London is no problem. In fact, there is so much available that it is difficult to sort it all out. The British Travel Centre, 12 Lower Regent Street, has all of the information that you could possibly need. Bookstores and newsstands are full of guidebooks, maps, and magazines with entertainment listings.

For recorded information on London happenings, call (071) 730–3488. For information about colorful pubs in London and in the rest of Britain, contact The Pub Information Centre, 93 Buckingham Palace Road; phone (071) 222–3232.

Here are just a few of our favorite London attractions.

Westminster Abbey has been the traditional place for coronations, weddings, and the final resting place for English monarchs ever since William the Conqueror was crowned there in 1066.

Buckingham Palace, the London home of the queen, is the scene of one of England's most colorful spectacles, the Changing of the Guard. This takes place in the forecourt of the palace daily at 11:30 A.M. April through July and on alternate days the rest of the year. When the queen is in residence, the royal standard flies over the east wing. Behind the palace are some forty acres of lovely formal gardens.

The Tower of London has been under the vigilant eyes of the colorfully outfitted Beefeater Guards since 1550. With its exhibits of the Crown Jewels and menacing implements of torture, it is one of London's most popular attractions.

The House of Parliament, overlooking the **Thames River,** is topped by **Big Ben,** the world's most famous clock. Practically within shouting distance of the Parliament is another famous address, **10 Downing Street,** the official residence of the prime minister.

St. Paul's Cathedral, London's largest and most impressive church, is a masterpiece of Renaissance architecture. Designed by Christopher Wren, it contains the tombs of two of England's greatest military heroes: Admiral Nelson and Lord Wellington, conqueror of Napoleon at Waterloo.

Concentrated within a small area are some of the world's most outstanding museums, filled with treasures gathered during the days when the sun never set on the British Empire. The **British Museum,** across from London University in the fashionable Bloomsbury District, includes the **Elgin Marbles** (from the Parthenon in Athens), the **Rosetta Stone** and the original **Magna Carta** as part of its permanent exhibit. The **Tate Gallery** and the **Victoria and Albert Museum** house impressive collections of fine and applied art. The **National Gallery,** on bustling **Trafalgar Square,** displays one of the world's finest collections of old masters. **Madame Tussaud's,** the grand-mere of all wax museums, has been a London institution since 1802.

Hampton Court Palace, 10 mi. (16 km) southwest of the center of London, is a Renaissance masterpiece that was the favorite country residence of Henry VIII. Over a period of time, five of his wives lived there with him. It is said that the ghosts of Jane Seymour and Catherine Howard inhabit the premises. The palace was devastated in a tragic 1992 fire.

London Campgrounds

GB–100 ★★★ Crystal Palace Camping. Open year-round. Six mi. (10 km) south of London Bridge. Access is easiest from the southern London ring road A205. Turn off at Crystal Palace/Crystal Park exit and follow signs to site. Located at the north end of the park next to the large TV tower and Crystal Palace Sports Centre. Entrance to site is between two mini-roundabouts. A medium-size well-shaded site in a pleasant park setting. Most pads are graveled and terraced. Very busy at all times. Reservations are advised. Crystal Palace Camping, London SE19 1UF; phone (081) 77 87 155. Convenient public transportation at entrance. –500 yd.

GB–101 ★★★ Co-operative Woods Camping (Abbey Wood). Open year-round. Approximately 10 mi. (16 km) east of London center. Take M25 motorway toward London and take exit #2 onto A2 in direction of London; then follow signs to campground. Approaches are well posted. A large oasis of green grass and shade trees in the heart of a built-up urban area. Reservations advised in July, August, Easter. Abbey Wood Camping, Abbey Wood, London SE2 OLS; phone (081) 310 2233. Thirty-five minutes by train to London from Abbey Wood Station, 500 yd. Mini-golf, cinema.

GB–102 ★★ Lee Valley Campsite (Chingford). Open April 1–October 30. In Leyton, 10 mi. (16 km) north of London center. From A25 motorway take exit #26 and follow A121 toward Walton Abbey; then take A112 north to Chingford. Approaches are well marked. A large, slightly sloping meadow with some hard sites. Train to London from Chingford Station, 1,000 yd.

London→ Oxford, 57 mi. (95 km)

From any of the London campgrounds, head west in the direction of **Heathrow Airport.** From there follow signs farther west to the Victorian town of **Windsor** on the Thames River. **Windsor Castle,** a royal residence for nine centuries, is set in a magnificent 4,800-acre park. From Windsor head west on B3024 to **Reading,** a prosperous university and manufacturing town on the Thames. A329 continues through a series of small villages along the Thames and joins with A34. This will take you into **Abington,** a jewel of a town on the banks of the Thames. From Abington follow signs into Oxford.

2. Oxford

Site of Britain's oldest university, Oxford is the quintessential college town, even though it now must share the limelight with such twentieth-century intrusions as an automobile manufacturing plant. The university complex is composed of some thirty-five more or less autonomous colleges. Among the most interesting colleges to visit are **Christ Church,** with the largest quad, and **Magdalen College** (pronounced "maudlin"), with its deer park and riverside walking path.

Oxford Campground

GB–103 ★★★ Oxford Camping International. Open year-round. On the south side of town, on the Abington Road about a mile from the town center. From A34 (the Oxford ring road), turn off onto A423, cross the railroad tracks and follow signs to campground. A medium-size, level grassy site, with individual plots separated by low picket fences. Bus to town, 200 yd. –500 yd.

Oxford → Stratford-upon-Avon, 84 mi. (140 km)

A portion of the route runs through the **Cotswolds,** a delightful, hilly, wool-producing region of honey-colored stone cottages and grazing sheep. Leave Oxford on A34, following this to the village of **Woodstock.** Just south of the village, set in an enormous park is **Blenheim Palace,** England's largest private home and the birthplace of Winston Churchill. Continue through Woodstock and after 1.8 mi. (3 km) turn off onto B4437. This narrow country lane winds its way through a series of tiny villages: **Charlbury, Ascot under Wychwood,** and **Shipton.** At **Stow-on-the-Wold,** the marketing center for this sheep-raising region since medieval times, take A429, which follows an old Roman road, into **Burton-on-the-Water.** Continue on A436 to **Cheltenham,** an elegant spa with a number of fine Regency buildings. From Cheltenham follow signs to **Tewkesbury,** a sleepy medieval town at the junction of the Avon and Severn rivers. Take A438 and A435 to **Evesham** and then follow signs to Stratford-upon-Avon.

3. Stratford-upon-Avon

In spite of the commercialization of its famous native son and the busloads of tourists who make the pilgrimage to visit anything and anywhere associated with the celebrated Bard of Avon, Stratford has much to recommend a visit. It is especially attractive in the early morning and evening hours, before the arrival and after the departure of the tourist hordes. There are five principal sites associated with Shakespeare that may be visited: **The Birthplace, The New Place, Hall's Croft, Anne Hathaway's Cottage,** and **Mary Arden's House.**

Stratford Campground

GB–104 ★★★ Dodwell Park. Open year-round. Two mi. (3.2 km) southwest of Stratford on B439. A small, partly sloped grassy site with some hard-surface pads. Adequate parking available in Stratford.

Stratford → Stoke-on-Trent, 108 mi. (180 km)

Head west from Stratford to **Worchester,** a quiet town on the Severn River with a fine **900-year-old cathedral.** From Worcester take B4204, B4197, and B4202, by way of the villages of **Martle** and **Great Witley,** into **Cleobury Mortimer.** Then take A4117 west to **Bromfield** and continue into **Shrewsbury** via A49. Shrewsbury, with its many half-timbered houses, is one of the best-preserved medieval and Tudor towns in all of England. A53 leads across the Shropshire countryside into Stoke-on-Trent.

4. Stoke-on-Trent

Famous since Roman times for its pottery and china production, Stoke-on-Trent is the home of the **Wedgwood China Works.** The **City Museum** contains one of the world's finest ceramic collections.

Stoke-on-Trent Campground

GB–105 ★★ Trentham Gardens Camping. Open year-round. On A34 at Trentham, 1.8 mi. (3 km) south of Stoke. An expansive, partly sloping, grassy site with hard pads. Nearby bus to town.

Stoke-on-Trent → Blackpool, 108 mi. (180 km)

From Stoke follow A50 to **Warrington.** Continue on A561 through **Liverpool.** A teeming industrial city and one of Britain's major seaports, Liverpool is perhaps best known as the home of the Beatles. The group's story and meteoric rise to fame are chronicled in a series of exhibits at **Britannia Pavilion** at **Albert Dock.** Follow A561 through Liverpool along the waterfront and continue on A565 to **Southport.** Then follow signs to **Preston,** the scene of one of Cromwell's major victories during the English Civil War. From Preston take A584 along the coast into Blackpool.

5. Blackpool

Once a quaint fishing village, Blackpool mushroomed to become Britain's largest and most garish holiday resort. The skyline is dominated by a 520-ft. (158-m) imitation of the Eiffel Tower. A raucous amalgam of piers, amusement parks, hotels, and fast-food emporiums, Blackpool is a British Coney Island and Miami Beach all in one place.

Blackpool Campgrounds

GB–106 ★★★ Sunset Holiday Hamlet (Hambleton). Open March 1–October 31. Located 9 mi. (15 km) northeast of Blackpool, at the mouth of the River Wyre. Take A588 from Poulton-le-Fylde to Knott End. A level, medium-size site with hard-surface pads. No public transportation. Difficult parking in Blackpool.

GB–107 ★★★ Blackpool South Caravan Club Site. Open March 5–December 31. Three mi. (5 km) southeast of Blackpool. From Blackpool take A583 and follow signs to site. A medium-size, level site, shielded by fences from the busy road. Convenient bus to Blackpool. –3 mi.

Blackpool → Windermere, 51 mi. (85 km)

Take A586 east out of Blackpool to A588 following signs to **Lancaster,** site of an impressive castle. Continue north on A6 to **Windermere.**

6. Windermere and the Lake District

Cumbria, with its rugged mountains, shimmering lakes, and fertile valleys, provides some of Britain's most spectacular scenery and has been a source of inspiration for such noted poets as William Wordsworth and

Samuel Coleridge. Within the **Lake District National Park** is a series of long, finger-shaped mountain lakes arranged like spokes around the hub of a wheel. The best way to explore this lovely region is on foot. Distances between the lakes are short, and well-marked hiking trails abound. Windermere and the neighboring resort of **Bowness,** situated along **Lake Windermere,** Britain's largest lake, make a convenient base for exploring the region.

Lake District Campgrounds

GB–108 ★★★★ Wild Rose Caravan & Camping Park (Appleby-in-Westmoreland). Open year-round. In the Eden Valley midway between the Lake District and Yorkshire Dales. Located 22 mi. (35 km) northeast of Windermere. From center of Appleby take B6260 south and turn off to campground at Soulby-Ormside. A beautifully landscaped, 40-acre grassy site with a number of gravel pads. An award-winning site, this is one of Britain's best campgrounds.

GB–109 ★★★★ Limefitt Park (Troutbeck by Windermere). Open March 12–October 31. Located 2.4 mi. (4 km) north of Windermere on A592 in the direction of Ullswater. A large, sloping, grassy meadow in a beautiful valley on what was once a sheep farm. The eighteenth-century barns now house modern sanitary facilities. This is an ideal base from which to tour the Lake District. Bus to Windermere.

Windermere → Glasgow, 149 mi. (250 km)

From Windermere take A592 through the Lake District National Park and over the 1,476-foot-high **Kirkstone Pass** to **Penrith.** Then follow A6 north to **Carlisle.** At nearby Solway Firth you can view intact parts of **Hadrian's Wall.** This massive, 76-mile-long stone wall was built by the Roman emperor in A.D. 120 as a defense against marauding tribes from the north. Continue from Carlisle into Scotland, following signs to **Dumfries.** Straddling the Nith River, Dumfries is best known as the home of the poet Robert Burns. From Dumfries, A76 follows the course of the Nith across the sparsely settled region of grassy hills and dales of the Southern Uplands. From **New Cumnock** the road continues into **Kilmarnock,** home of Johnny Walker, the world's largest whiskey-bottling concern. **Dundonald Castle,** 4 mi. (6.4 km) southeast, is worth a visit. A77 runs the remaining 18 mi. (30 km) into Glasgow.

7. Glasgow

Glasgow, Scotland's largest city and its chief industrial center, is one of the best overall examples of a Victorian city remaining anywhere in the world. Although its origins are ancient, most of medieval Glasgow was sacrificed during the mid-nineteenth-century flurry of building activity that characterized the Industrial Revolution. Of particular interest is the lively Glasgow **Barras.** Held every weekend, this is reputed to be the largest open-air flea market in the world.

Glasgow Campground

GB–110 ★★★ Tullichewan Caravan Park (Balloch, Loch Lomond). Open year-round. Located 19 mi. (30 km) northwest of Glasgow at the southern end of Loch Lomond. From Dumbarton take A82 north for 4.2 mi. (7 km). Turn right onto A811 toward Balloch and follow signs to campground, which is located at the foot of the hill. A large, grassy site surrounded by rolling hills.

GB–111 ★★★★ Strathclyde Caravanning & Camping Park (Motherwell). Open April 1–October 31. Located 11 mi. (18 km) southeast of Glasgow. From motorway M47 take exit 5 and follow signs to Strathclyde Park. A large, grassy area with paved sites. This is part of an extensive vacation complex with water sports and other recreational activities.

Glasgow → Edinburgh, 40 mi. (65 km)

Take A89 or the M8 east from Glasgow to Edinburgh.

8. Edinburgh

Scotland's capital is pleasantly situated on the Firth of Fourth, a fjord-like inlet in the North Sea, and is surrounded by green rolling hills, forests, and water. Edinburgh is the center of the country's cultural and academic life. **Edinburgh Castle,** constructed by the English in 1513 and perched high atop **Castle Rock,** is the city's most dominant feature. From the castle battlements, on a clear day you can see all the way

Scottish castle

across the Firth of Fourth. **Queen Margret's Chapel,** constructed in 1076 and located within the castle walls, is the city's oldest building.

The seventeenth-century **Lady Stair's House** contains a collection of memorabilia honoring Scotland's three most notable literary figures: Sir Walter Scott, Robert Burns, and Robert Louis Stevenson. Of Edinburgh's many museums and galleries, the two most notable are **The National Gallery of Scotland,** with a fine collection of old masters, and **The Scottish National Gallery of Modern Art.** For an interesting insight into everyday life in Georgian Scotland, visit the faithfully restored **Georgian House,** on St. Andrew's Square in the New Town. The road that runs down from Edinburgh Castle to **Holyrood Palace,** a royal residence since the sixteenth century, is known as the **Royal Mile** and passes through the oldest and most interesting part of the city. Edinburgh is a city that is made for pub crawling. Numerous pubs provide a welcome sanctuary during the capital's many rainy days.

Edinburgh Campground

GB–112 ★★★★ Mortonhall Caravan Park (Lothian). Open April 1–October 31. Located 6 mi. (10 km) east of the city center. From bypass road A720 turn off at Lothianburn exit and follow campground signs. A large, partly hilly, grassy site in a beautiful park setting on an old estate. Public transportation, 700 yd.

Edinburgh → Newcastle upon Tyne, 112 mi. (180 km)

Take A68 southeast from Edinburgh across the granite slopes of the **Cheviot Hills,** which form a natural boundary between Scotland and England. The road runs through the **Northumberland National Park.** The best-preserved 12 mi. (20 km) of Hadrian's Wall traverse the park, a vast solitary region that encompasses rocky sand-topped moors, once-mighty castles, and attractive market towns and villages. The northern reaches of the park include a wild forested area that surrounds **Kielder Water,** England's largest man-made lake. From the junction of A68 with A696, take A696 to **Otterburn,** a town renowned for its mill and fine woolens. Continue on A696 into Newcastle upon Tyne.

9. Newcastle upon Tyne

Situated on the north bank of the Tyne River some 12 mi. (20 km) from the sea, Newcastle is one of England's major industrial, recreational, and cultural centers. Although its origins are ancient, present-day Newcastle displays much of the concrete and chrome of a modern industrial city. Interspersed among the modern buildings are a number of fine Victorian structures. Newcastle takes its name from the "new castle" built in 1080 by the son of William the Conqueror.

Note: To connect with our Viking Trails Scandinavian itinerary, take the ferry from Newcastle to Goteborg or to Stavanger and Bergen. The Bergen–Stavanger crossing takes from twenty-four to twenty-six hours. There are two to three crossings weekly, depending on the season. For details contact The Color Line, P.O. Box 1422 Vika, 0115 Oslo, Norway; phone (47) 294–4470, fax (47) 283–0776.

The Newcastle–Goteborg crossing takes about twenty-four hours. There are three crossings weekly. For additional information contact Scandinavian Seaways, Scandinavia House, Parkeston Quay, Harwich, Essex CO12 4QG, England; phone (0255) 241 234, fax (0255) 241 471.

Newcastle Campground

GB–113 ★★ Gosforth Park Racecourse Campsite. Open May 15–September 15. At the north edge of the city on the racetrack grounds. From Newcastle center take A1 north in the direction of Morpeth. In Gosforth turn off to the racetrack. Approaches are well marked. A large, fenced meadow between the racecourse and a forest. Bus to town.

Newcastle upon Tyne → Scarborough, 72 mi. (120 km)

Leaving Newcastle, follow the coast down to **Middlesbough.** Continue south on A174 and trace the coastal edge of the **North York Moors National Park** to the picturesque seaside village of **Whitby,** which lies at the mouth of the Esk River. The hilltop **Whitby Abbey,** founded in 657, is one of the earliest vestiges of Christianity in Britain. This is a delightful stretch of coastline where grassy bluffs slope down to meet a series of broad sandy beaches. **Robin Hood's Bay,** just south of Whitby, is one of the most captivating spots along the entire coast.

10. Scarborough

Continue along the coast to Scarborough, a spa since 1662 and one of Britain's first seaside resorts.

Scarborough Campground

GB–114 ★★★ Jacob's Mount Caravan & Camping Site. Open March 1–October 31. Located 1.8 mi. (3 km) west of Scarborough on A170, in the direction of Thirsk. A medium-size grassy site with a full range of facilities. Convenient public transport to Scarborough.

Scarborough → York, 42 mi. (70 km)

Take A164 south and continue on this to York.

11. York

An ancient fortress town with some of the best-preserved medieval buildings in Europe, York makes a good base from which to visit the delightful Yorkshire countryside. To best appreciate the beauty of this medieval gem, first get an aerial perspective by taking the 2½-mi. (4-

km) walk atop the massive thirteenth-century walls. Then stroll through the old town center. The main focus of interest and the point of convergence of many of the town's narrow alleys and lanes is the **York Minster,** northern Europe's largest Gothic cathedral. The enormous stained-glass windows are the finest in England. For a glimpse of life in the region some 1,000 years ago, visit the reconstructed village at **Jorvik Viking Centre.**

York Campground

GB–115 ★★ Rowntree Caravan Park. Open year-round. Directly in the city, on the Ouse River. Approaching York from the A64 in the direction of Leeds, turn off at the YORK sign onto A1036 and follow signs to campground. A medium-size site with paved pads. Conveniently located within easy walking distance of the town center.

York → Boston, 102 mi. (170 km)

Take A1079 southeast from York to **Beverly.** From there head south across the Humber River and follow signs to **Louth** via A18. Continue from Louth along A16 into Boston.

12. Boston

Boston, a prosperous thirteenth-century Hanseatic wine and wool trading center, was the place from which the pilgrims who founded Boston, Massachusetts, originated. From the top of the massive keep of nearby **Tattershall Castle,** 11 mi. (18 km) northwest, you can enjoy a panoramic view of the surrounding fenlands.

Boston Campground

GB–116 ★★★ Tattershall Park Country Club (Tattershall). Open March 1–October 31. Located 11 mi. (18 km) northwest of Boston. Follow signs to Tattershall and then to campground. A large, well-equipped site in the middle of a 300-acre vacation park, with every conceivable recreational activity, including lakes and watersports.

Boston → Norwich (Great Yarmouth), 72 mi. (120 km)

Leave Boston on A17 and follow this into **King's Lynn.** Straddling both sides of the Ouse River, King's Lynn, a member of the ancient Hanseatic League, at one time served as an important trading partner with Germany and the Scandinavian countries. Boston is also the center of a centuries-old glassblowing industry. The **Wedgwood Crystal Factory** is open for visits. Continue east across the fenlands to Norwich via B1145 and A1067.

13. Norwich/Great Yarmouth

Norwich, an important trading and cultural center built around a fine old Norman castle, is the gateway to a vast, sparsely inhabited wetlands region of peat bogs, rundown windmills, and an elaborate network of interconnecting waterways that is known as the Norfolk Broads. The medieval old-town center of Norwich contains a number of fine old dwellings, including a twelfth-century cathedral. Situated 16 mi. (25 km) to the east is Great Yarmouth. With its fifteen miles of sandy beaches and a host of recreational facilities, Great Yarmouth is one of Britain's largest and most popular seaside resorts.

Norwich/Great Yarmouth Campgrounds

GB–117 ★★ Norfolk Showground Campground (Norwich). Open April 1–October 10. Located 2.4 mi. (4 km) west of Norwich. Turn off A47 at the Longwater intersection and follow signs to Bawburgh and Norfolk Showground. A large, pleasant, tree-ringed site in a country setting at the corner of the Norfolk fairgrounds. Bus to town. –2 mi.

GB–118 ★★★ Vauxhall Caravan Park (Great Yarmouth). Open May 1–September 30. Just west of town on A47 in the direction of Norwich, 500 yd. from train station. A large, level, sprawling meadow with some paved pads. Bus to beaches.

Norwich/Great Yarmouth → Cambridge, 72 mi. (120 km)

From Great Yarmouth head southwest on A143 to **Bury St. Edmunds,** an ancient market town with a strong Georgian and Victorian imprint. Continue to Cambridge on A45.

14. Cambridge

The stately college buildings overlooking the gently flowing Cam River and the surrounding lush green lawns and gardens give Cambridge the distinctive character that has made it the role model for university towns throughout the Western world. With the most important colleges all located within a short distance of one another, this is an ideal town to explore on foot or by bicycle. No visit to Cambridge is complete without a ride along the Cam in a flat-bottomed punt, preferably with a picnic lunch and some chilled white wine. The most interesting colleges to visit are **Trinity, King's,** and **Queen's colleges.** The **Fitzwillian Museum,** one of England's oldest public museums, houses a fine collection of Egyptian and Chinese antiquities along with a diverse selection of paintings.

Cambridge Campground

GB–119 ★★★ Highland Farm Camping Park (Comberton). Open April 1–October 31. Located 4.2 mi. (7 km) southwest of Cambridge center. Take exit 12 from A11 motorway and follow A603 toward Sandy for ½ mile. Then turn off on B1046 to Comberton and follow signs to campground. A level, grassy area with paved sites divided by bushes and hedges. Bus to Cambridge, 400 yd. –1 mi.

Cambridge → Dover, 114 mi. (190 km)

Take A1301 south from Cambridge to **Saffron Walden,** a charming market town with some of the finest medieval buildings in East Anglia. The fifteenth-century **Sun Inn** was used as Cromwell's headquarters during the English Civil War. Leave Saffron Walden and head southeast on B1053 across the gentle East Anglian countryside to **Braintree.** Continue into **Chelmsford.** Situated on the outskirts of London, this has been an important market town since Roman times.

From Chelmsford take A12 to the M25 Motorway. Take the motorway south for a short stretch through the tunnel under the Thames. At the intersection with A2, follow signs across the garden-filled county of Kent to **Canterbury.**

Rich in historical associations and a popular tourist destination since the fourteenth century, Canterbury is best known as the setting for Chaucer's **Canterbury Tales.** It was also in Canterbury, in 1170, that

Thomas Becket was murdered by knights of King Henry II. The town's most impressive building is the cathedral. Founded by St. Augustine at the close of the sixth century, this imposing structure has been enlarged and rebuilt numerous times over the centuries. From Canterbury take A2 into Dover.

Note: To connect with our Tiptoeing through the Tulips itinerary, after visiting Cambridge, follow signs toward Ipswich and then continue to the ferry port at Harwich. There are daily sailings to the Hoek van Holland and Rotterdam. The crossing takes seven to eight hours. For details contact Sealink Ferries, Charter House, Park Street, Ashford TN24 8EX, England; phone (0233) 647 047.

15. Dover

An important Channel-crossing port since Roman days, when it was called Dubris, Dover is England's principal gateway to the European continent. On a clear day you can just about make out the French town of Boulogne, 26 mi. (43 km) across the English Channel. A few miles west of the town are the famed white chalk cliffs of Dover. The English terminus of the Channel Tunnel is located between Dover and Folkstone.

Note: To connect with our Tiptoeing through the Tulips itinerary, take the ferry from the port of Dover to Zeebrugge, Belgium. The crossing takes about four hours. For more information contact P&O European Ferries, Channel House, Channel View Road, Dover CT17 9TJ, England; phone (0304) 203 388.

Dover Campground

GB–120 ★★★ Hawthorn Farm Caravan & Camping Site (Martin Mill). Open March 1–October 31. Three mi. (4.8 km) northeast of Dover. Take A258 from Dover toward Deal and turn off at Martin Mill. A large, somewhat hilly, grassy site in a parklike setting. Many shrubs and hedges. Occasional noise from nearby train line. ▣ ▨–0.9 mi. ◙ ☐

Dover → Salisbury, 174 mi. (290 km)

From Dover follow the coast road through **Folkestone** (ferry connections to France) and continue past the picturesque old port town of

Rye to **Hastings,** a popular seaside resort. Four miles inland from Hastings is the small market town of **Battle.** It was here, in 1066, that the Battle of Hastings took place. This Norman conquest marked the last time that Britain was successfully invaded. The coast road continues to **Brighton,** one of Britain's most fashionable beach resorts.

From Brighton continue west and inland to the village of **Arundel.** With its magnificent castle and well-preserved half-timbered dwellings, Arundel is one of the most delightful spots in southern England. At the old Roman town of **Chichester,** continue inland, taking A286 north to Mid-Lavant. Continue on B2141 across the East Hampshire countryside, a placid region of thatched and half-timbered cottages, to **Winchester,** once the capital of England. The **Winchester Cathedral** is one of Britain's finest. In the **Great Hall of Winchester Castle,** you will find the legendary Round Table of King Arthur.

Note: To connect with our France a la Carte Itinerary I, continue from Brighton along the coast to Portsmouth. From there you can take the ferry to Cabourg on the Normandy coast. The crossing time is six to seven hours, and there are several daily departures. For details contact Brittany Ferries, the Brittany Centre, Wharf Road, Portsmouth PO2 8RU, England; phone (075) 827701.

16. Salisbury/Stonehenge

An impressive cathedral town surrounded by rolling hills and four rivers, Salisbury lies 21 mi. (35 km) to the west across the Wiltshire Meadows from Winchester. **Amesbury,** 6 mi. (10 km) to the north at the edge of the Salisbury Plain, is the jumping-off point for visiting the mysterious prehistoric stone monuments at Stonehenge.

Note: To connect with our Iberian Interlude itinerary, take A30 southwest from Salisbury to Exeter. From there follow B3212 through the Dartmoor National Park to Plymouth. There are two to three crossings weekly from Plymouth to Santander, Spain. From Santander drive south through Burgos to join our itinerary at Madrid. For details about ferries contact Brittany Ferries, The Brittany Centre, Wharf Road, Portsmouth PO2 8RU, England; phone (075) 827701.

Salisbury Campground

GB–121 ★★ Coombe Nurseries Touring Caravan Park (Nether-

hampton). Open year-round. Take A3094 west to village of Netherhampton and follow campground signs. Near the race track. A small meadow divided by hedges. –1 mi.

Salisbury → London, 75 mi. (125 km)

From Salisbury take A30 back to London.

VIKING TRAILS

Denmark

CAPITAL: Copenhagen

POPULATION: 5,200,000

CURRENCY: krone (kr. or DKr), divided into 100 ore

LANGUAGES: Danish; English is widely spoken

RELIGION: Lutheran

POLICE: 112

FIRE: 112

AMBULANCE: 112

ROAD SERVICE: Copenhagen area, twenty-four hours 313–12144 or check directory under FALCK

BANKS: weekdays except Thursday 9:30 A.M.–4:00 P.M.; Thursday 9:30 A.M.–6:00 P.M.; exchange offices are often open until 10:00 P.M.; the provinces differ at times

STORES: weekdays 9:00 A.M.–5:30 P.M. and Fridays until 7:00 or 8:00 P.M.; Saturday 9:00 A.M. to 1:00 or 2:00 P.M.

HOLIDAYS: January 1; Good Friday and Easter Monday (movable); Common Prayer Day (movable); Ascension Day (movable); June 5, Constitution Day (shops close at noon); December 25 and 26

EMBASSIES: *United States,* Dag Hammarskjolds Allee 24, 2100 Copenhagen; phone (031) 423–144, fax (035) 430–223. *United Kingdom,* 36–38–40 Kastelsvej, 2100 Copenhagen; phone (031) 264–600. *Canada,* Kr. Bernikowsgade 1, 1105 Copenhagen; phone (033) 122–299, fax (033) 140–585

To some people, tiny Denmark is the fairy-tale kingdom of Hans Christian Andersen and the little mermaid, whose likeness overlooks Copenhagen's harbor. To others, it's the prototype for a modern, progressive country whose liberal welfare policies put it at the forefront of the European social movement. The Danes are a friendly and industrious people whose pervasive sense of humor sets them apart from their somewhat more dour northern neighbors in Sweden and Norway. With a population smaller than that of Greater Los Angeles, Denmark, a member of NATO and the European Community, is an active participant in the mainstream of modern European life.

This is a spotlessly clean country where everything seems to function efficiently, and yet it is a place where a genuine warmth and enjoyment of life have not been sacrificed on the altar of modern industrialization. Old traditions have been maintained, and the gently rolling countryside is dotted with carefully restored half-timbered thatched-roofed cottages as well as many elegant manor houses and castles.

Packed into this tiny kingdom, a constitutional monarchy since 1849, are a multitude of sights and attractions that include, to name just a few, Copenhagen, the country's rollicking capital; the broad sandy beaches and dunes of the Jutland Peninsula; historic castles, such as Kronborg Castle, the inspiration for Shakespeare's *Hamlet;* and scores of picture-postcard villages with thatch-roofed cottages.

DRIVING

The extensive network of highways and secondary roads are well maintained, and there are no toll roads. Danish motorists are a very civilized breed, and with the exception of the greater Copenhagen area, traffic is rarely a problem.

Major international routes are marked with green and white signs bearing the prefix "E." Primary roads are designated by one- or two-digit numbers on a yellow sign. Secondary roads are denoted with three-digit numbers on a white sign.

It is mandatory to drive with low-beam headlights on during the day. The wearing of seatbelts is also required. Children between ages four and six must wear an "approved" restraining device.

Penalties for driving under the influence of alcohol are severe for tourists as well as the locals. In cases of traffic violations, police are empowered to collect fines on the spot. If you want to contest the fine, it is necessary to post a bond.

The speed limit for motorhomes on the autobahns is 110 kph (66 mph). Unless otherwise posted, the speed limit in towns and built-up areas is 50 kph (30 mph). Outside of built-up areas, it is 80 kph (48 mph).

The ferry connections between the numerous islands are frequent and efficient; there are also many convenient ferry connections with other countries. One obvious advantage to motoring in a nation as small as Denmark is the fact that you are never more than a few hours' drive away from any part of the country.

CAMPING

With more than 500 campgrounds distributed throughout the country, there is a campsite near practically every town. A free map showing the location of all official campgrounds may be obtained from the Danish Tourist Board. With respect to sanitary facilities and cleanliness, Danish campgrounds rate among Europe's best. The sites are inspected and are rated by the tourist authorities with from one to three stars, based on the amenities provided. Most campgrounds in this kids-friendly country have playgrounds; many also have swimming pools.

Camping is a popular pastime among the Danes, and many of the people whom you will meet at Danish campgrounds will be locals. The majority of campgrounds are open from May 1 until early September, and approximately 100 sites are open all year.

Wheelchair users will find Denmark to be a particularly accessible country. Public transportation, buildings, and vacation facilities, including campgrounds, have been designed with wheelchair accessibility in mind. Most two- and three-star sites have dump stations for gray and black water.

An International Camping Carnet is required for all visitors to a Danish campground. Those who do not have a Carnet can purchase a Danish Camping Pass, valid throughout the country at any campground. Free camping is generally prohibited; however, you may camp on private land with the owner's permission. The regulation against free camping in beach and dune areas is strictly enforced, with offenders subject to being fined on the spot.

For additional information about camping in Denmark, contact Campingradet, Hesselogade 16, DK 2100 Copenhagen O, Denmark.

Finland

CAPITAL: Helsinki

POPULATION: 5,000,000

CURRENCY: marrka (FMk), divided into 100 pennia

LANGUAGES: Finnish and Swedish; English widely spoken

RELIGION: Evangelical Lutheran

POLICE: 0

FIRE: 0

AMBULANCE: 0

ROAD SERVICE: Autaliitto—Finnish Autoclub, twenty-four hours (90) 694–0496

BANKS: weekdays 8:30 A.M.–4:00 P.M.

STORES: weekdays 9:00 A.M.–3:00 P.M.; Saturday 8:30 A.M.–1:00 P.M. or 9:00 A.M.–2:00 P.M.

HOLIDAYS: January 1; January 6, Epiphany; Good Friday and Easter Monday (movable); April 30 and May 1, Mayday eve and day; Ascension (movable); Pentacost (movable); June 21 and 22, Midsummer eve and day; All Saints' Day (movable); December 6, Independence; December 24–26

EMBASSIES: *United States,* Itainen Puistotie 14A, 00140 Helsinki; phone (90) 171931, fax (90) 174681. *United Kingdom,* 16–20 Uudenmaankafu, 00120 Helsinki 12; phone (90) 647922. *Canada,* Pohgjois Esplanadi 2513, 00101 Helsinki; phone (90) 171141, fax (90) 601060

Often referred to as the land of light and lakes, Finland, an independent republic since 1917, is distinguished from its Scandinavian neighbors Sweden and Norway by its lack of mountains. But, while flat, the landscape is far from uninteresting. The nearly 200,000 lakes, shimmering birch and pine forests, and thousands of offshore islands offer visitors a placid natural beauty. As much as 65 percent of Finland is covered with forest, which makes it the most densely forested land in Europe.

This is a place to unwind, to take a sauna—a national pastime, to commune with nature, and to enjoy the occasional fortress or museum. Next to Iceland, Finland is Europe's most northerly country and as such is commonly perceived as a frigid expanse of ice and snow. Thanks to the proximity of the Gulf Stream and the Baltic Sea, however, Finland enjoys a pleasant summer climate, with a mean temperature in the southern lakes area that is the same as that of the northern coast of Spain. Winters are relatively mild.

DRIVING

The main roads in the southern half of the country are paved and well maintained. In the more sparsely populated north, there are numerous gravel roads, many of which may be in poor condition during the spring thaw. As a rule of thumb, highways designated with one or two digits are generally kept in good condition, while the three-digit roads are not as well maintained. Highway numbers are being changed to conform to a Scandinavian-wide system. For details check with the local auto club or tourist office.

When driving, particularly in the north, watch out for animals on the road. Elk and reindeer can be a hazard. Of the overall road network, some 45 percent of the roads are paved. There are no toll roads. The use of seatbelts by the driver and all passengers, front and back, is mandatory. Severe penalties, including imprisonment, are imposed for driving under the influence of alcohol. The police are authorized to collect fines on the spot for traffic violations. All vehicles must use headlights at dusk, in the dark, or in fog or rain. Outside of built-up areas, low beams must be turned on at all times of the day. To free camp outside of official campgrounds, the landowner's permission is generally necessary.

The speed limit for motorhomes on the major highways is 120 kph (72 mph); in towns and built-up areas, unless otherwise posted, it is 50 kph (30 mph). Outside of built-up areas, it is 80 kph (48 mph).

CAMPING

There is a network of more than 350 campgrounds throughout the country, with the highest concentration in the coastal, lake, and main tourist regions. The season is short, with most sites open from June 1 to September 1. Seventy campgrounds stay open all year.

The majority of campgrounds are run by local municipalities and vary greatly as to size, facilities, and amenities. Sites are graded with from one to three stars. The one-star sites are often small and without electrical hookups or showers. Restaurants and campstores are not as common as in the rest of Europe.

The International Camping Carnet or Finnish Camping Pass is required at most sites. The Finnish pass can be purchased at campgrounds throughout the country.

Many campgrounds are located at a beach or alongside a lake, and a great many campgrounds have individual wooden huts with saunas. In contrast to most of Europe, open campfires in designated places are permitted. Free camping, while not officially allowed, is tolerated in most regions. If in doubt, obtain permission locally.

Electrical hookups are relatively expensive but provide plenty of amperage. The two-prong German Shuko system is widely used. It is difficult to fill foreign gas cylinders.

For additional information about camping in Finland, contact The Finnish Travel Association, Camping Department, Mikonkatu 25, P.O. Box 776, 00101 Helsinki, Finland; phone (90) 170 868, fax (90) 654 358.

Norway

CAPITAL: Oslo

POPULATION: 4,300,000

CURRENCY: krone (Nkr or NOK), divided into 100 ore

LANGUAGES: Norwegian; English is widely spoken

RELIGION: Lutheran

POLICE: 002

FIRE: 002

AMBULANCE: 002

ROAD SERVICE: NAF Emergency Centre Oslo, twenty-four hours (02) 341–600

BANKS: weekdays 8:15 A.M.–3:30 P.M.; Thursday until 5:00 P.M.; all post offices exchange money

STORES: weekdays most shops are open 9:00 A.M.–5:00 P.M. (Thursday until 7:00 P.M.); Saturday 9:00 A.M.–1:00 or 2:00 P.M.

HOLIDAYS: January 1; Easter Friday and Monday (movable); May 1, Labor Day; Assumption Day (movable); May 17, Constitution Day; Pentacost (movable); December 25 and 26

EMBASSIES: *United States,* Drammensveien 18, 0244 Oslo 2; phone (02) 448–550, fax (02) 430–777. *Canada,* Oscar's Gate 20, 0244 Oslo; phone (02) 466–955/9, fax (02) 693–467. *United Kingdom,* Thomas Heftyesgate 8, Oslo 2; phone (02) 552–400

Few places in the world, if any, can match the spectacular scenery of Norway's fjords. The intimate interaction of sea and mountains along the more than 1,600 km (960 mi) of jagged coastline is awe-inspiring. The interior, while not as spectacular, is wonderfully green, heavily forested, and filled with rushing rivers and waterfalls. In a country blessed with such natural beauty and one of the lowest population densities in the world, it is little wonder that a visit to Norway is primarily an outdoor experience.

The two major cities, Oslo and Bergen, have a combined population of just 660,000, while the rest of the country's four million inhabitants live primarily in small towns and villages.

Norway is a country with a close relationship to the water. A large portion of its food supply comes from the sea, the countless fjords, and the rivers. The sea, in the form of oil from the vast North Sea deposits, also provides the country with substantial revenues. These oil revenues and cheap electricity from hydroelectric power contribute significantly to maintaining Norway's high standard of living, one of the highest in the world.

As is the case in neighboring Sweden, only a small percentage of the land (3 percent) is suitable for farming. Fruits and vegetables are not plentiful, and food prices in general are considerably higher than in the rest of Europe.

DRIVING

Because of the light traffic and abundance of magnificent scenery, driving in Norway is a pleasant experience, even though negotiating some of the narrow mountain roads with an RV can be a bit intimidating. Primary roads, particularly in the south, are good and well maintained. In the north and in the fjord regions, roads are mostly narrow and winding. Secondary roads are often gravel and in places in need of maintenance, especially just after the spring thaw. Short stretches of the motorway upon entering Bergen and Oslo are subject to tolls. The Norwegian Tourist Board (see p. 360) issues a map that shows roads that are unsuitable for trailers. Trailers wider than 2.3 m (7.5 ft.) are not permitted in the country without special permission obtained from Vegdirektoratet, Postboks 8109 Oslo 1, Norway; phone (02) 63 95 00.

Driving in Norway, particularly along the west-coast fjords, involves frequent ferry crossings. In July and the first half of August, it may be necessary to wait as long as several hours for a ferry. Reservations are recommended. In most cases these can be made at travel agencies throughout the country.

A free booklet with timetables for most of the domestic and international routes is available from the Norwegian Tourist Board. The narrow roads and many ferry crossings should be factored in when estimating how far you plan to drive on a given day. We have found that 200–250 km (120–150 mi.) a day is a comfortable distance to cover in an RV, especially in western Norway.

The road numbering system is currently undergoing change, as is the case in neighboring Sweden. As this may take several years to complete, your best bet is to follow place names rather than route numbers.

The wearing of seatbelts is mandatory: however, there is no restriction on children occupying a front seat as long as the seatbelt fits. Penalties for drinking and driving are severe, and you can be imprisoned for drinking the equivalent of less than one can of beer.

Speed limits are strictly enforced, and foreign motorists are required to pay on-the-spot fines in Norwegian kroner. The speed limit for motorhomes on the motorways is 90 kph (54 mph); in towns and built-up areas, unless otherwise posted, it is 50 kph (30 mph). Outside of built-up areas, it is 80 kph (48 mph). During the day you are required to drive with low beams on at all times.

CAMPING

Camping in Norway is a popular pastime among Norwegians as well as foreign tourists. There are some 1,400 organized campgrounds, the majority of which are concentrated in the southern portion of the country, particularly along the coast. Between Trondheim and North Cape, there are only a few dozen.

The sites are classified by the Tourist Board with from one to five stars, according to facilities and amenities provided. The major tourist centers have well-equipped sites; while in the more remote areas, campgrounds tend to be small and simple, with basic facilities and few amenities.

At many campgrounds the electricity supplied is limited to 2 A of power, barely enough for a light and a small refrigerator. The German two-prong Schuko electrical plugs are the most widely used, although a few sites have switched over to the CEE 17 standard. As it may often be necessary to park some distance from an electrical outlet, a minimum of 25 m (75 ft.) of extension cord is recommended.

Built-in RV propane tanks can be filled at PRO-GAS plants in Bergen, Kristiansand, Oslo, Stavanger, and Trondheim. Gas cylinders can be filled at AGA Gas outlets throughout the country.

The International Camping Carnet is required at many campgrounds. Where signs do not specifically prohibit it, free camping is widely tolerated. It is prohibited to park an RV closer than 150 m (495 ft.) to a residence without permission. Open fires are not allowed.

For additional information about camping in Norway, contact the Norwegian Automobile Club, Storgt. 2, N–0155 Oslo 1, Norway (phone 02–42 94 00) or Norsk Campingbilforening, P.O. Box 19, N–1401 Ski, Norway.

Sweden

CAPITAL: Stockholm

POPULATION: 8,700,000

CURRENCY: krona (SKr), divided into 100 ore

LANGUAGES: Swedish; English is widely spoken

RELIGION: Lutheran

POLICE: 90000

FIRE: 90000

AMBULANCE: 90000

ROAD SERVICE: (020) 910–040 throughout country

BANKS: weekdays: 9:30 A.M.–3:00 P.M. (Stockholm); 10:00 A.M.–2:00 P.M. in country; one bank always open in town 4:30–6:00 P.M.

STORES: weekdays 9:00 A.M.–5:00 or 6:00 P.M.; Saturday 9:00 A.M.–1:00 P.M.; either Monday or Friday larger shops open until 8:00 P.M.

HOLIDAYS: January 1; January 6, Epiphany; Good Friday and Easter Monday (movable); May 1, Labor Day; Ascension Day (movable); Pentacost (movable); June 22, Midsummer; All Saints' Day (movable); December 25 and 26

EMBASSIES: *United States,* Strandvagen 101, 115–89 Stockholm; phone (08) 783–5300, fax (08) 661–1964. *United Kingdom,* Skarpogatan 6–8, 11527 Stockholm; phone (08) 667–0140. *Canada,* Tegelbacken 4, 7th floor, 10323 Stockholm; phone (08) 237–920, fax (08) 242–491

Europe's fourth-largest country, Sweden occupies the eastern half of the Scandinavian Peninsula and, with a population of 8½ million, is one of the world's least densely settled nations. With the exception of the capital, Stockholm, and the west coast industrial cities of Goteborg and Malmo, which account for nearly one-third of the population, Sweden is essentially a rural country, with most of the population concentrated in the south.

Although the landscape is not as spectacular as that of neighboring

Norway, as you explore the countryside you will find a pleasant variety of scenery: clear glacial lakes, dense forests, and—in the northwest, along the border with Norway—mountains and rushing rivers. The northern provinces contain some of the last unspoiled wilderness in Europe, ideal for hiking, fishing, and camping. Throughout the country you will experience a feeling of spaciousness and communion with nature not often found in the more crowded countries to the south.

Sweden's rocky terrain, poor soil, and short growing season make agriculture difficult. With only 7 percent of its land arable, much of the country's fruit and vegetables must be imported. As a consequence, grocery and restaurant prices are among the highest in Europe.

Sweden's social welfare system, established following the depression of the 1930s, provides a wide range of cradle-to-grave benefits. The standard of living is one of the world's highest. Stores are well stocked with a wide variety of quality goods of Swedish design and manufacture, including many quality glass and ceramic products.

This is an easy country in which to travel. Facilities for tourists are well organized and spotlessly clean, and some 80 percent of the population speak English. Although very modern, in many aspects the Swedes also pay great attention to their traditions and heritage. As Sweden has been neutral since the nineteenth century, the country's many fine castles and other historical buildings suffered none of the destruction that two world wars imposed upon most of the rest of Europe.

DRIVING

Sweden's road network is extensive and well maintained, although many of the roads in the central and far northern regions are gravel. The approximately 1,100 km (660 mi.) of motorways are toll-free. The motorways are designated by green signs, and the major international routes by green and white signs bearing the prefix "E." The road-numbering system is currently undergoing change. As this may take several years to complete, your best bet is to follow place names rather than route numbers.

With the exception of Stockholm, traffic is rarely heavy and parking in most towns and at tourist attractions, even for an RV, is not a problem. Diesel-powered motorhomes exceeding 6,000 kg (2,727 lb) are classified as trucks and as such are subject to a road tax of 20 kronor per 100 km (60 mi.) traveled.

The wearing of seatbelts is mandatory, and children age seven and under may not occupy a front seat unless an approved restraining device is worn. Penalties for drinking and driving are severe, and you can be prosecuted for drinking the equivalent of less than one can of beer. Calling the police to the site of an accident is not necessary—however, if you leave the scene of an accident without exchanging relevant information with the other parties involved, you may be subject to imprisonment.

Radar controls are widespread and speeding laws are strictly enforced, but there are no on-the-spot fines. The speed limit for motorhomes on the motorways is 110 kph (66 mph); in towns and built-up areas, unless otherwise posted, it is 60 kph (36 mph). Outside of built-up areas, it is 90 kph (54 mph).

During the day you are required to drive with low beams on at all times. When driving in the more remote northern regions, watch out for elk on the road. Collision with these massive animals is one of the most frequent causes of accidents.

CAMPING

Camping is an extremely popular pastime. Between early July and mid-August at the more than 750 officially registered Swedish campgrounds, the majority of guests are Swedes. Campgrounds are inspected by the Tourist Board and are classified according to facilities with from one to three stars. The more amenities, the more stars. This does not mean, however, that you should avoid the one- and two-star sites. Many of these simple campgrounds are spotlessly clean and are located in beautiful scenic locations. Swimming pools and saunas are common.

Either a Swedish Camping Card or an International Camping Carnet is required at most sites. The Swedish Camping Card may be purchased at campgrounds in Sweden or ordered in advance from Swedish Camping Site Owner's Association (SCR), Box 255, S–45117 Uddevalla, Sweden. So-called Camping Checks are discount coupons that can be purchased in combination with ferry tickets.

As a money saver, many campgrounds offer a "quick stop" service.

Fees are reduced by one-third for those who check in after 9:00 P.M. and leave before 9:00 A.M. Most campgrounds are open from June 1 to September 1, and some 200 sites remain open all year.

Swedish law requires all RVs to have a closed drainage system. For those rigs that are not so equipped, approved tanks may be rented at the campground. The CEE 17 electrical connections are not commonly in use. The majority of campgrounds use the two-prong German Schuko system.

Butane gas, commonly used in Southern Europe, is not used in Sweden. Foreign propane tanks can be filled at Primus Svenska or AGA Gas AB stations throughout the country. Propane in Sweden is called *gasol.*

Allmansratten (everyman's right), a principle anchored in ancient Swedish law, gives everyone the right to camp on any unfenced land but dictates that you stay at least 100 m (330 ft.) from dwellings and that the owner's permission be obtained. Everyman's right does not apply to RVs. Vehicles are only permitted on authorized public roads and tracks. There are severe penalties for littering, including imprisonment.

For additional information about camping in Sweden, contact SCR at the address noted above.

Itinerary: Copenhagen • Southern Sweden • Stockholm • Southern Finland • Helsinki • The Finnish Lake District • The Swedish Lake District • The Norwegian Fjords • Southern Norway • Oslo • Jutland • The Island of Fyn

---

START: Copenhagen

COUNTRIES: Denmark, Finland, Norway, Sweden

DISTANCE: 5,880 km (3,528 mi.)

MAPS: Michelin #985 *Scandinavia—Finland* (shows location of many campgrounds)

MINIMUM RECOMMENDED TOURING TIME: 24–28 days

INTRODUCTION

RV travel in the Scandinavian countries, where distances between towns are great, elicits a strong affinity for nature and a freer, more open feeling than is experienced when traveling in much of Central and Southern Europe. In the course of this itinerary, you will encounter many uniquely Scandinavian art and architectural treasures. Norway's fascinating wooden stave churches and Finland's soaring architectural creations reflect the rugged, open character of the region. Churches and cathedrals, in this predominantly Lutheran domain, are somber and devoid of the baroque and rococo ornamentation that characterizes religious architecture in the mainly Catholic Central and Southern European regions.

Scandinavia is a region of great natural beauty, much of it closely associated with the water. This is revealed as we board oceangoing ferries, trace the rugged coastlines, and explore the sprawling lake regions. We travel from the ancient city of Trondheim in the north to Kristiansand at the southern tip of the country; and from the cabs of our own motorhomes and from the decks of the ferry boats that ply the

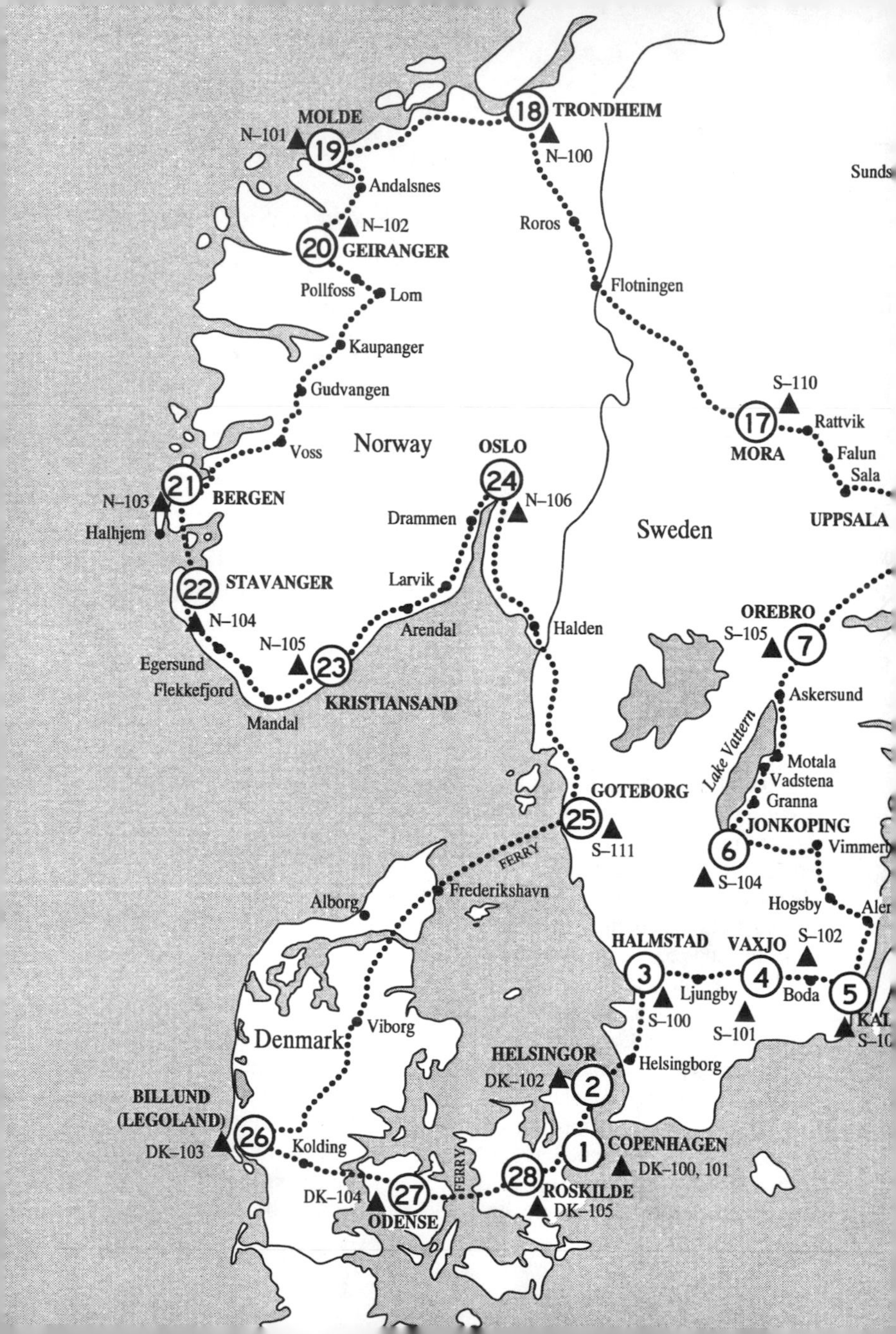
MOLDE
N–101
19
18
TRONDHEIM
N–100
Andalsnes
N–102
20
GEIRANGER
Roros
Pollfoss
Lom
Flotningen
Kaupanger
Gudvangen
S–110
17
Rattvik
MORA
Falun
Sala
UPPSALA
Voss
Norway
OSLO
24
N–106
21
BERGEN
N–103
Halhjem
Drammen
Sweden
22
STAVANGER
Larvik
N–104
Arendal
Halden
OREBRO
S–105
7
N–105
23
Egersund
Flekkefjord
KRISTIANSAND
Mandal
Askersund
Lake Vattern
Motala
Vadstena
Granna
GOTEBORG
25
S–111
JONKOPING
6
S–104
FERRY
Frederikshavn
Alborg
Hogsby
HALMSTAD
3
VAXJO
4
S–102
Ljungby
Boda
5
S–100
S–101
Viborg
Denmark
HELSINGOR
DK–102
2
Helsingborg
BILLUND
(LEGOLAND)
26
DK–103
Kolding
1
COPENHAGEN
DK–100, 101
FERRY
28
ROSKILDE
DK–104
27
DK–105
ODENSE
Sunds

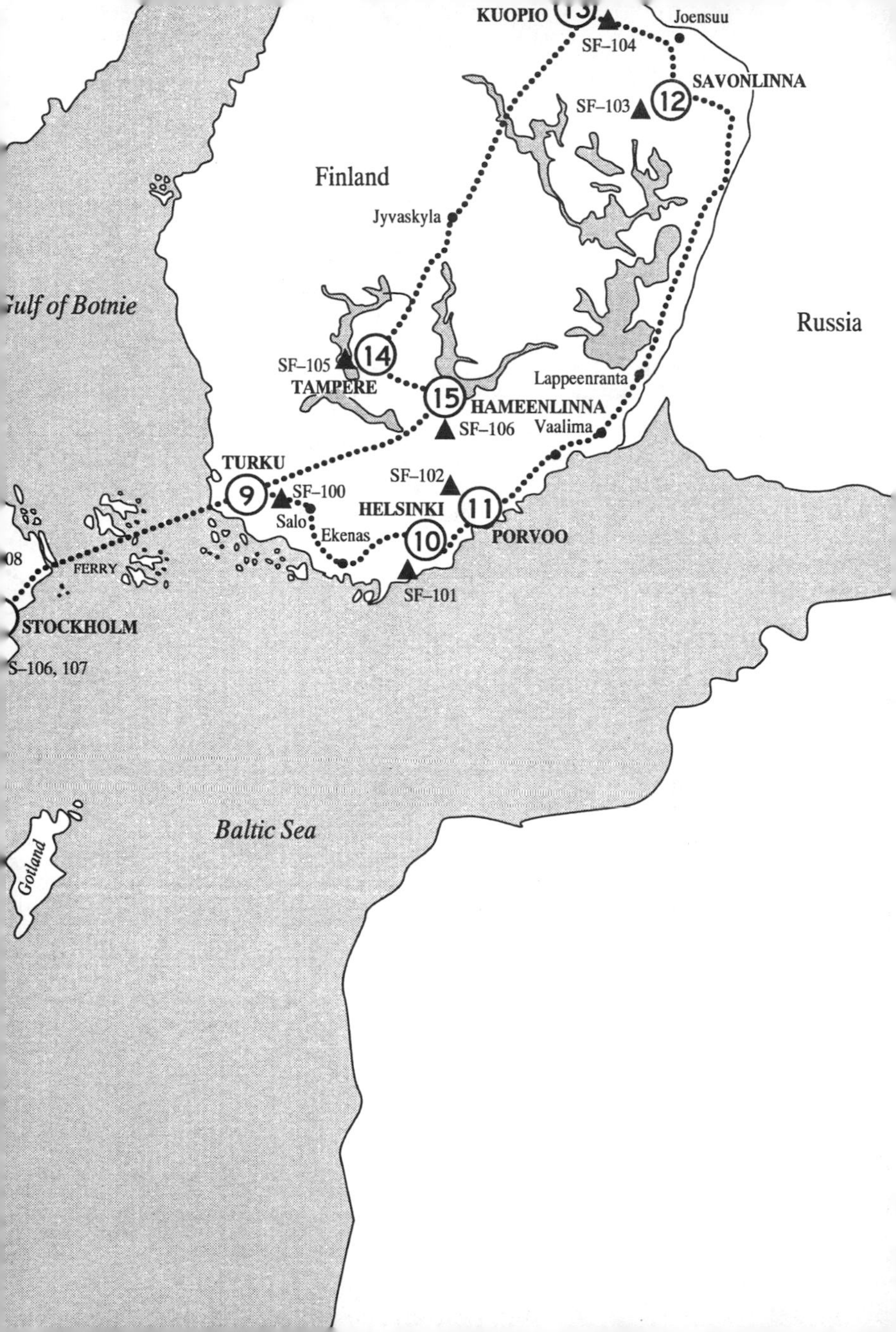
KUOPIO
13
SF–104
Joensuu
SAVONLINNA
12
SF–103
Finland
Jyvaskyla
Gulf of Botnie
Russia
SF–105
14
TAMPERE
15
HAMEENLINNA
SF–106
Lappeenranta
Vaalima
TURKU
9
SF–100
Salo
Ekenas
SF–102
HELSINKI
11
PORVOO
10
SF–101
08
FERRY
STOCKHOLM
S–106, 107
Baltic Sea
Gotland

fjords, we experience the awesome beauty of the precipitously steep, rock-walled fjords that extend into Norway's jagged west coast like so many long fingers.

Of the four Scandinavian capitals, each unique in its own right and each an important seaport, Copenhagen, with Tivoli Gardens, the Little Mermaid, and some of the most tempting shopping anywhere, is by far the liveliest. Helsinki, not much more than a stone's throw from St. Petersburg, exhibits a pleasing blend of modern Finnish and traditional Russian influences in its architecture. Stockholm, an efficient, modern city with a well-preserved old town and an impressive new museum built to house a sunken seventeenth-century ship, retains visibly strong links with its past. The Norwegian capital, Oslo, is home to one of the world's great sculpture gardens and boasts several fine museums that pay tribute to Norway's explorers, from the early Vikings to the twentieth-century adventurer Thor Heyerdahl.

When to Go

Scandinavia is one of the few places in Europe where a camping vacation during the summer months is advisable. Even in July and August, when the locals are on vacation, campgrounds and tourist facilities are pleasantly free of crowds. Although some of the more popular destinations, such as Copenhagen, Stockholm, and Oslo do attract many summertime visitors, it is nothing when compared to Florence or Rome in high season.

Summer weather is usually mild; however, you should be prepared for rain at any time. Days, even in the south, are long, with twilight occurring around midnight and the first glimmer of light appearing in the sky from 2:00 to 3:00 A.M. In May, early June, or September, you will pretty much have things to yourself. The difficulty of traveling in Scandinavia in the off season is that many campgrounds and tourist facilities are closed. This is particularly true before June 15 and after September 15.

Highlights

Tivoli Gardens, Copenhagen
Drottingholm Palace, Stockholm
Skansen, Stockholm
Gripsholm Castle, Mariefred
Norwegian fjords
Vigeland Sculpture Gardens, Oslo

A quiet campground in Denmark

EXPANDING HORIZONS

- **To Tiptoeing through the Tulips Itinerary:** From Stavanger take the ferry to Amsterdam (see p. 132). From Stavanger or Bergen take the ferry to Newcastle (see p. 64). From Goteborg take the ferry to Amsterdam (see p. 132).
- **To British Byways Itinerary:** From Goteborg take the ferry to Harwich (see p. 69).

ON THE ROAD

Numbered sites correspond with circled numbers on the itinerary map. Note: There have been recent changes in the numbering of the Swedish and Norwegian highways. To verify the current situation, obtain an updated map when you arrive in Sweden and Norway.

1. Copenhagen (Kobenhavn)

The Danish capital ranks as one of the great cities of Europe, offering its visitors a rich assortment of delights and diversions. **Tivoli Gardens,** a unique amusement park; the **Royal Palace;** bustling shopping streets; fine museums; and a swinging nightlife are all concentrated in a central area easily covered on foot. Public transportation is excellent and parking extremely difficult. It is best to leave your rig parked at one of the area's several campgrounds.

Without a doubt the main attraction in Copenhagen is Tivoli, a fabulous package of fun and fantasy that no visitor should pass up. Tivoli has something for everyone; exciting rides, a gambling casino, restaurants, discos, circus acts, and music from classical to rock. All of this takes place in a magical setting of thousands of twinkling colored lights and fresh blossoms. The park is open May 1 to mid-September.

Be sure to allot time, and plenty of money, to explore the **Stroget,** Copenhagen's principal shopping district. Packed with people, street performers, and exclusive shops, this is a shopper's paradise.

The statue of Hans Christian Andersen's **Little Mermaid,** on the Langeline Promenade, which overlooks the harbor, is a well-known Danish landmark.

Copenhagen Campgrounds

DK–100 ★ Bellahoj Camping. Open June 1–August 31. Directly in the city next to the Bellahoj Exhibition Hall. Located 4 km (2.4 mi.) west of city center. Situated just off the 02 ring road. Approaches are well marked. A large grassy area with no shade. Very crowded in July and early August. Convenient bus to Copenhagen center.

DK–101 ★★★ Absalon Camping. Open year-round. Located 9 km (5.4 mi.) west of Copenhagen center. Take A1 west. After signs reading RODOVRE and then BRONDBYOSTER, turn off at the campground sign. A large, grassy meadow in a rural setting with some shade trees. Parcels are separated by hedges. Commuter train to city center, 500 yd.

Copenhagen → Helsingor, 40 km (24 mi.)

Take Hwy. 152 north from Copenhagen along the harbor and follow signs to Helsingor. At **Humlebaek** (35 km/21 mi.), in an idyllic park setting that overlooks the sea, is the **Louisiana Art Museum,** which has a collection that is one of the world's great assemblages of modern art.

2. HELSINGOR

This old trading port is best known as the site of **Kronborg Castle,** the setting of Shakespeare's *Hamlet.* From the castle there is a wonderful view across the Oresund to the Swedish coast. Helsingor has a number of fine old houses and is also home to the **Danish Museum of Technology.**

Helsingor Campground

DK–102 ★ Gronnehave Camping. Open year-round. Located at the beach in the northeast edge of town in the direction of Hornbaek. A small, partly grassy, partly shady site that overlooks the Swedish coast. A ten-minute walk to Kronborg Castle.

Helsingor → Halmstad, 75 km (47 mi.)

Take the ferry from Helsingor across the Oresund to the Swedish port of **Helsingborg.** The pleasant boat trip takes about twenty-five minutes and offers a seaside view of Kronborg Castle. The ferries run at approximately thirty-minute intervals. To avoid a long wait at the dock in July and August, reservations are recommended. Contact Scandlines, phone (in Denmark) (45) 49 26 26 83. From Helsingborg head north on E6/E20 to Halmstad.

3. HALMSTAD

Halmstad, an attractive town on Laholm Bay, is one of Sweden's most popular summer resorts. Most of the activities take place at nearby **Tylosand,** 9 km (5.4 mi.) to the west. The long sandy beach, lined with grass-covered dunes, is one of the country's finest. On the road to Tylosand, you will see the **Miniland Leisure Park,** which features scale models of Sweden's most popular attractions. In Halmstad, on the banks of the Nissan River, there is a remarkable 14-yd.-high sculpture of a woman's head by Picasso.

Halmstad Campground

S–100 ★★★ Hagons Camping. Open May 1–September 1. Located

6 km (3.6 mi.) southeast of town. From Halmstad follow signs toward Ostra Stranden. Approaches are well marked. A twenty-acre grassy site with parcels separated by bushes. About 250 yd. to the beach. Bus to town, 100 yd.

Halmstad → Vaxjo, 129 km (77 mi.)

From Halmstad take Hwy. 25 east, following signs to **Ljungby** and then to Vaxjo.

4. VAXJO

With its strategic location at the northern end of Lake Vaxjo, Vaxjo has been an important trading center since its founding in Viking times. The town itself has little of interest, with the exception of its **twelfth-century cathedral.** The **Utvandranas Hus (Emigrant's House)** is filled with exhibits and documents that trace the migration of some one-quarter million local inhabitants who left this region for a new life in America during the second half of the nineteenth century.

Vaxjo is best known as the center of Sweden's **crystal glass industry.** Orrefors, Boda, and Kosta are among the local companies whose artistic creations have given the Swedes a worldwide reputation in fine glass manufacture. It is possible to tour the works and to purchase products directly. For details contact the tourist offices in Vaxjo and Orrefors.

Vaxjo and Glass-Region Campgrounds

S–101 ★★★ Evedals Camping (Vaxjo). Open year-round. On Lake Helgasjon, near the boat harbor. Take Hwy. 23 north toward Oskarshamm. After 2.5 km (1.5 mi.) turn off and follow campground signs to site. A large, grassy area with many trees in a pleasant lakeside park near Kronberg Castle. A good base for visiting the area's glass factories.

S–102 ★★ Kosta Bad & Camping (Kosta). Open May 1–September 15. On Hwy. 28, approximately 500 yd. southwest of the Kosta glassworks. Turn off from Hwy. 123 at the south edge of town by the Gulf station. A medium-size, grassy site in the center of a large vacation complex.

Vaxjo → Kalmar, 110 km (66 mi.)

From Vaxjo take Hwy. 25 southeast to **Eriksmala.** To visit the glassworks at **Kosta,** head north and take Hwy. 28 the 13 km (7.8 mi.) to Kosta. Ten km (6 mi.) east of Eriksmala on Hwy. 25, you will come to the **Boda Glassworks.** Continue on Hwy. 25 to **Nybro** and from there to Kalmar. To visit the **Orrefors Glass Factory,** take Hwy. 31 northwest from Nybro for the 13 km (8 mi.) to **Orrefors.**

5. Kalmar

Kalmar, one of the oldest towns in Sweden, occupies a favored location on the Kalmar Sound, the body of water that separates the island of Oland from the mainland. During the Viking era it was an important trading center and later became a member of the Hanseatic Trading League. The town's most impressive sight is its massive seaside castle. Built in the eleventh century, the castle was extensively reconstructed some 500 years later by King Vasa. In addition to containing richly furnished apartments and a cleverly constructed below-sea-level dungeon, the castle houses the **Kalmar Provincial Museum.** Just north of Kalmar the nearly 6-km (3.6-mi.) **Oland Bridge,** Europe's longest, links the island of Oland with the mainland.

Kalmar Campground

S–103 ★★ Stensos Camping. Open year-round. Take E22 south from the town center and follow signs for SJUKHUS (hospital). A twenty-eight-acre forested area adjacent to a vacation complex. Open-air entertainment in summer. Bus to Kalmar, 200 yd. Parking is available at Kalmar Castle.

Kalmar → Jonkoping, 265 km (164 mi.)

Follow the coast road E66/34 north from Kalmar to **Alem.** Here the road splits. Take Hwy. 34 inland to **Hogsby** and from there north to **Berga.** Continue north on Hwy. 34 to intersect with Hwy. 33 at **Vimmerby.** Head east on Hwy. 33, following signs to Jonkoping.

6. Jonkoping

Beautifully situated on the southern end of **Lake Vattern,** Sweden's second-largest lake, Jonkoping is a pleasant town that is best known as the home of the **Swedish Match Company.** It was here, in the mid-nineteenth century, that the safety match was developed. The unusual Match Museum, located on the site of the original factory, chronicles the development and production of matches.

Jonkoping Campground

S–104 ★★★ Rosenlunds Campingplats. Open year-round. Situated in Jonkoping at Lake Vattern. From Jonkoping center take E4 to Rosenlund. Then follow signs to the campground. A large, partly sloping meadow with some birch trees but not much shade. Difficult access to the lake. Bus to town, 500 yd. –700 yd. –1,000 yd.

Jonkoping → Orebro, 185 km (111 mi.)

Follow the lake north on E4 to **Granna,** a popular resort and one of the few towns in the region whose old wooden houses have not been destroyed by fire. Continue along E4 to **Odeshog** and then on Hwy. 50 to **Vadstena,** a small town known for its fine-quality lace. Vadstena is also the site of an unusual blue-limestone church. Stay on Hwy. 50 through **Motala** and **Askersund.** Some 25 km (15 mi.) north of Askersund, take E3 into Orebro.

7. Orebro

Orebro is an important commercial center serving the mining and farming regions of central Sweden. **Orebro Castle,** located on an island in the Svartan River, is an impressive four-towered structure that on numerous occasions served as the meeting place of the Riksdag (Swedish Parliament).

Orebro Campground

S–105 ★★★ Krono Camping Gustavsik. Open May 19–August 22. Located 1 km (0.6 mi.) south of Orebro. Turn off of E3 to Gustavisk and follow camping signs. A large, grassy site with some shade. Adjacent to a sports and vacation complex that has a large indoor and outdoor swimming pool.

Orebro → Stockholm, 195 km (117 mi.)

From Orebro follow E3 east into Stockholm.

8. STOCKHOLM

Situated at the confluence of Lake Malaren and the Baltic Sea, Stockholm is a delightful assemblage of traditional and modern architecture. The region's clear blue waters provide the unifying element to a city that is spread out over fourteen islands and surrounded by some 23,000 additional islands that constitute the famed **Skargarden** (Stockholm Archipelago). For a duck's-eye view of one of Europe's most beautiful cities, take an orientation cruise on one of the many sightseeing boats that ply the local waters.

Sweden's accomplishments in the ecological realm are demonstrated in a very practical way when one observes the bathers in the clear waters of the downtown harbor area and by the multitude of parks and green belts scattered throughout the city. The narrow lanes and medieval buildings of Stockholm's **Gamla Stan** (Old Town) constitute a living museum that captures the essence of seventeenth-century Sweden.

While in the Gamla Stan, visit the immense Italian baroque **Royal Palace** and observe the colorful changing-of-the-guard ceremony. The **Royal Armory** and **State Apartments** are open to the public. Stockholm, an art lover's paradise, offers its visitors a choice of some fifty museums and galleries. The **Millesgarden,** located in a quiet residential neighborhood on the island of Lindigo, contains a wonderful open-air display of the works of Carl Milles, Sweden's most famous sculptor.

At **Skansen,** a beautiful seventy-five-acre island park, you will find a sprawling **Open Air Museum,** where farmhouses, churches, stone houses, and other buildings, painstakingly moved from all over the country and furnished in their original styles, are on display. Many traditional handicrafts, including glass blowing, are demonstrated.

On August 10, 1628, the *Vasa,* a Swedish man-of-war, sank in Stockholm's harbor on its maiden voyage. This incredibly well-preserved ship was raised in 1961 and can now be seen in a specially built museum, the **Vasamuseet,** on the island of **Djurgarden.**

The **Royal Palace of Drottingholm,** the "Versailles of the North," is beautifully situated on a small island in Lake Malaren. Although you can drive your RV to visit the palace and there is plenty of parking, taking the passenger ferry from Stockholm makes for a wonderful day's outing.

Another delightful excursion is the three-hour boat trip along the southern shore of Lake Malaren to **Gripsholm Castle.** This towering sixteenth-century fortress is one of Sweden's most romantic castles. Gripsholm is also home to the **Swedish National Portrait Gallery.** The collection of some 3,400 portraits is one of the world's largest.

Stockholm Campgrounds

S–106 ★★★ Bredangs Camping. Open year-round. In the suburb of Bredang. Located 10 km (6 mi.) south of Stockholm center. Take Bredang exit from E4 Stockholm–Nykoping and follow campground signs. A large, grassy site with no shade. In a quiet setting by Lake Malaren; 400 yd. to lakeside beach. A five-minute walk to subway station and an eighteen-minute ride to Stockholm central station. Parking in Stockholm is very difficult. Remodeling planned for 1994.

S–107 ★★ Flottsbro Camping (Huddinge). Open year-round. Located 16 km (10 mi.) southwest of Stockholm center. Take E4 south from Stockholm. Turn off at Huddinge and take Hwy. 259 to Flottsbro. A small, newly opened site in a pleasant forested area. Adjacent to a large vacation complex. Train connection to Stockholm, 900 yd.

S–108 ★★★ Strandbadets Camping Mariefred (Mariefred). Open May 1–September 30. Located 2 km (1.2 mi.) east of Mariefred on Lake Malaren. From Stockholm take E4 to Sodertalje Interchange, then E3 to Mariefred. Approaches are well marked. A large meadow in a forested area. The site is divided into sections by trees. Direct access to the lake with views of Gripsholm Castle.

Stockholm → Turku, Finland, 270 km (162 mi.) by sea

The twelve-hour ferry cruise affords a wonderful opportunity for seeing the Swedish archipelago. The ferries are modern, well-equipped vessels and offer all the amenities of a luxury cruise ship. The boat leaves Stockholm at 8:00 A.M., arriving at Turku at 8:00 P.M. For more information contact EuroCruises, 303 West 13th Street, New York, NY 10014–1207 (phone 202–691–2099, fax 212–366–4747) or Viking Line, Mastokatu 1, SF-00160 Helsinki (phone 9–0–12351, fax 9–0–123 5292).

9. Turku

In an idyllic setting at the mouth of the Aura River, Turku is a major seaport for passenger and commercial traffic between Finland and Sweden. The city, Finland's oldest, developed around an ancient trading post and was the country's capital until 1812. The origins of **Turku Castle** date back to the thirteenth century, when it guarded the harbor. Badly damaged during World War II, the castle, now restored, houses a splendid banquet hall. The castle is also home to the **Turku Historical Museum. Turku Cathedral,** built in the thirteen to the fifteenth centuries, is the most significant medieval church in Finland. For an early-morning appetite booster, explore the colorful food and flower markets in the square next to the Orthodox church.

Turku Campground

SF–100 ★★ Ruissalo Camping. Open June 1–August 31. On the Ruissalo Peninsula 10 km (6 mi.) southwest of Turku center. Follow campground signs from the Satama dock area. A twenty-five-acre, partly hilly site in an attractive wooded location. Waterslide and bathing area. Sauna. Bus to Turku center at entrance. Limited parking available in Turku.

Turku → Helsinki (Helsingfors), 140 km (84 mi.)

Take E18/1 east from Turku by way of **Salo** into **Helsinki.** For a slightly longer—50 km (31 mi.)—but far more scenic route, at Salo turn off onto Hwy. 52 through the heavily forested countryside to **Ekenas,** an attractive small town with many interesting old wooden buildings. Take Hwy. 53 to **Lohja.** The fourteenth-century village church, built of unadorned stone, contains some fine sixteenth-century wall paintings. Nine km (5.4 mi.) north of Lohja, turn onto the motorway E18/1, which runs into Helsinki.

10. Helsinki (Helsingfors)

A relatively young city, by European standards, Helsinki was founded in 1550 and has been Finland's capital since 1812. After a tragic fire in 1808 that nearly destroyed the entire city, Helsinki was rebuilt under the direction of the German architect Carl Ludwig Engel. Most of the buildings in the city center date back to this project. The classical old wooden structures stand in sharp contrast to the works of such famous modern Finnish architects as Eero Saarinen and Alvar Aalto.

Although its population has expanded to approximately half a million, Helsinki is a pleasant, open city with trees and parks everywhere. Some 30 percent of the city's area is devoted to greenbelts and parks. The suburb of **Tapiola**—called the Garden City of Finland—is a model of imaginative architecture and urban planning. For an informative glimpse into the world of modern Finnish architecture, visit the **Soumenrakennustaiteen Museo (Museum of Finnish Architecture).**

The heart of this bustling city is the **Kauppatori Market Square.** Located at the edge of the South Harbor in front of the Esplanade, the marketplace is a beehive of colorful activity as venders hawk their fresh fish, vegetables, and flowers every morning except Sundays. Just behind the market square is the imposing **Senate Square,** where a statue of Czar Alexander II is flanked by three stately buildings, the **University,** the **Government Palace,** and the most impressive of Helsinki's landmarks, the **Cathedral of St. Nicholas.** Raised above the square, the cathedral dominates the sea approach to the city.

For an interesting insight into Finnish life in earlier times, visit the **Open-Air Museum** on **Seurasaari Island.** Authentically furnished farm and manor houses were transported here from all parts of the country and painstakingly reassembled. **Suomenlinna Sveaborg** is a massive eighteenth-century fortress that occupies a rocky island guarding the approaches to Helsinki harbor. There are several interesting museums on the island. Excursion boats leave regularly from the market square for the fifteen-minute ride.

The **Temppeliaukio Church** is one of the most unusual modern churches in Europe. The church, carved out of solid rock, is crowned by a 70-ft. copper dome.

Helsinki Campground

SF–101 ★★ Rastila Camping. Open May 1–September 30. Located 16 km (10 mi.) east of Helsinki center in the suburb of Rastila. Take Hwy. 7 over the Vuosaaria Bridge and follow campground signs. A thirty-acre, level, partly shaded site in a residential area. Convenient public transportation to Helsinki center, 100 yd. Parking in Helsinki is difficult. Sauna.

Helsinki → Porvoo, 45 km (28 mi.)

From Helsinki follow the coast road E18/7 to Porvoo.

11. Porvoo

An important trading center since the Middle Ages, Porvoo received its town charter from the Swedish king Magnus Eriksson in 1346. The old town and the small Gothic cathedral in which Czar Alexander issued the proclamation guaranteeing Finland's independence are the main attractions. Attracted by its narrow lanes, pastel-colored old wooden houses, and proximity to Helsinki, many of Finland's art and literary set have made Porvoo their home.

Porvoo Campground

SF–102 ★★★ Kokonniemi Camping. Open June 4–August 15. From E18/7 take exit Harabacka/Porvoo and follow signs for 6 km (3.6 mi.) to the campground. A large, attractive site in a wooded area with many shrubs and flowers. Gravel pads for larger RVs. No public transportation to Porvoo. Parking in town is not a problem. Thirty-minute walk into Porvoo.

Porvoo → Savonlinna, 300 km (180 mi.)

Continue along the east coast on E18/7 to **Kotka,** Finland's principal export harbor and the site of a major naval battle between Russia and Great Britain during the Crimean War. Several of the nineteenth-century frigates used in the battle are on display. From Kotka continue to **Vaalima,** which lies on the border with Russia. It is possible to drive from here to St. Petersburg. Check with the Russian Consulate in Helsinki for visa requirements.

From Vaalima take Hwy. 387 the 60 km (36 mi.) to **Lappeenranta,** a lively, modern resort that is the southern gateway to the **Saimaa lake region.** The town contains an interesting **fortress (Linnoitus),** Finland's oldest **Orthodox church,** and a **Cavalry Museum.** Take Hwy. 6, which at times runs along the Russian border through **Imatra,** a town known for its powerful waterfalls, and continue across the lakes into Savonlinna.

12. Savonlinna

Situated in the heart of the lovely Saimaa lake district, Savonlinna provides an excellent base for touring this extensive complex of lakes and forests. **Olavinlinna Castle,** romantically positioned on a tiny island, is Finland's finest medieval castle. The three-towered fifteenth-century fortress has been extensively restored, and the interior is used as a conference center. In July the castle's courtyard is the venue for the colorful **International Savonlinna Opera Festival,** one of Europe's major operatic events. Excursion boats ply the extensive lake system, offering a variety of pleasant cruises. **Kerimaki,** 25 km (16 mi.) northeast of Savonlinna on Hwy. 71, is the site of the world's largest wooden church. Constructed in 1847, it seats 5,000 persons.

Savonlinna Campground

SF–103 ★★★ Vuohimaki Camping. Open June 4–August 22. Located 6 km (3.6 mi.) west of town center. Take Hwy. 14 from Savonlinna in the direction of Mikkeli. Turn off after 3 km (1.8 mi.) and follow campground signs. A large, scenic, partly terraced meadow with few trees. Sandy beach and swimming in the lake. Bus to Savonlinna, 200 yd. Parking available for visiting castle.

Savonlinna → Kuopio, 210 km (130 mi.)

This route takes us through some of Finland's most scenic lake country. From Savonlinna head north on Hwy. 471 to **Enonkoski.** Take the ferry across a narrow isthmus in the lake and continue to **Pollakka.** After 7 km (4.2 mi.) turn right onto Hwy. 476 and take this to **Ylamylly** on Hwy. 17, the main Joensuu–Kuopio road. From here it's 115 km (69 mi.) of delightful driving to Kuopio.

13. Kuopio

A modern city beautifully placed on a peninsula in the lake, Kuopio is the seat of the Finnish Orthodox Church. The **Orthodox Church Museum** houses a rare collection of icons and artifacts. Additional treasures are to be found at the **Convent of Lintula** and the **Monastery of Valamo.** Both are located near **Heinavesi,** some 50 km (30 mi.) southeast of Kuopio, and can be reached by excursion boat from Kuopio or by road on Hwy. 476, along our route from Savonlinna to Kuopio. Instead of turning right on Hwy. 476 after Pollakka, turn left to Heinavesi.

Kuopio Campground

SF–104 ★★★★ Rauhalahti Camping. Open May 28–August 22. Take Hwy. 5 south from Kuopio. Approaches are well marked. A fifty-acre, grassy site in a beautiful lakeside location. Surrounded by a forest. Paved pads for RVs. Several children's playgrounds. Open-air entertainment, sauna. Convenient bus to town.

Kuopio → Tampere, 310 km (186 mi.)

From Kuopio take Hwy. E63/9 south to **Jyvaskyla,** a modern university town with several buildings designed by Alvar Aalto. Continue through the lake country to Tampere.

14. Tampere

Tampere is Finland's second-largest city and its leading industrial center. A city of parks, clean air, fountains, pools and statues, it's hard to believe that there is so much industry here.

Of special interest is the **Sarah Hilden Art Museum,** a striking contemporary building with a fine collection of modern Finnish and international works. The **Haihara Doll Museum** in nearby **Kaukajarvi,** has a unique collection of more than 1,000 dolls from seventy countries. In a magnificent natural setting at the edge of the lake is the unusual **Pyÿnikki Open-Air Theater,** where an amphitheater revolves around a fixed stage to change scenes.

Tampere Campground

SF–105 ★★★ Harmala Camping. Open May 7–August 22. Located 2 km (1.2 mi.) south of Tampere center at Lake Pyhajarvi in the suburb of Harmala. Approaches are well marked. A large, grassy site with plenty of shade. Sandy beach, water slide, sauna.

Tampere → Hameenlinna, 78 km (47 mi.)

Take E 12/3 southeast to Hameenlinna.

15. Hameenlinna

The birthplace of noted Finnish composer Jean Sibelius, Hameenlinna is also the site of a restored **medieval castle. Hattula Church,** 6 km (3.6 mi.) to the north, is the best known of Finland's medieval churches. The interior walls are covered with a number of fine sixteenth-century frescos.

Hameenlinna Campground

SF–106 ★★★ Aulanko Camping. Open May 17–September 15. At the north end of town, 4 km (2.4 mi.) from the town center. Approaches are well marked. A large, grassy site with plenty of trees. Adjacent to a golf course. Swimming in the lake. Access from pier and sandy beach. A beautiful scenic location.

Hameenlinna → Turku, 140 km (84 mi.)

Follow Hwy. 10 into Turku. You can take the ferry from Turku to Stockholm (see p. 98).

Stockholm → Uppsala, 60 km (36 mi.)

Head north from Stockholm on E4 to Uppsala.

16. Uppsala

Modern Uppsala is an attractive and lively university town dominated by its enormous **cathedral.** Consecrated in 1435, the cathedral has been the seat of the archbishop of Sweden for some six centuries. Among the notables buried in the cathedral is the eighteenth-century Swedish naturalist Carl Linnaeus. The **Cathedral Museum** houses one of the best collections of religious garments in Europe. The imposing **castle** that sits in a strategic position on a rise at the southeast corner of the city was built in the sixteenth century by King Gustav Vasa. **Uppsala University,** Scandinavia's oldest, was founded in 1477.

Uppsala Campground

S–109 ★★ Granebergs Camping. Open May 1–August 31. Located 8 km (4.8 mi.) south of Uppsala center. Follow signs from E4. A small municipal site at the lake. Small, sandy beach with swimming in the lake. Bus to Uppsala at entrance. Parking in Uppsala is difficult.

Uppsala → Mora, 265 km (159 mi.)

From Uppsala take Hwy. 72 northwest to **Sala.** Then pick up Hwy. 70 and follow it to **Borlange.** This route takes us across the Swedish heartland province of **Dalarna,** a major tourist region and one of the country's most attractive areas. The road cuts through dense forests interrupted by an occasional pristine lake and sweeps across the fertile valleys watered by the Osterdalalv and Vasterdalalv rivers. Dalarna is noted for the brightly colored little wooden horses that are a traditional local craft. At the industrial town of Borlange take Hwy. 60 to **Falun,** the largest city in Dalarna and, since Viking times, a major copper-producing center. Guided tours of the mines are available. Leave Falun on Hwy. 80 and continue to **Rattvik,** a popular resort on the shores of **Lake Sijan.** The large, clear blue lake is ringed by gently rising wooded hills. Continue along the lake on Hwy. 70 to Mora.

17. Mora

A pleasant, small market town at the northwest corner of the lake, Mora was the home of Andreas Zorn, Sweden's most famous painter. Many of his works are on display at the **Zorn Museum.** A lakeside **open-air museum** depicts the living conditions in the region during the Middle Ages. In **Nusnas,** on the lake just a few kilometers east of Mora, you can watch the traditional Dalarna wooden horses being carved.

Mora Campground

S–110 Mora Camping. Open year-round. In town, 400 yd. northwest from the church. Approaches are well posted. A twenty-five-acre site in a partly wooded, partly grassy meadow. Beautifully situated on a peninsula in the Osterdalalv River. Swimming in the lake and indoor pool. Easy walk to town center.

Mora → Trondheim (Norway), 465 km (279 mi.)

From Mora take Hwy. 70 northwest across the rugged Dalarna high

A rustic campsite in Norway

country to the Norwegian border crossing at **Flotningen.** Continue on Hwy. 26 to the old copper-mining town of **Roros.** Then follow Hwy. 30 across a rugged, mountainous stretch of countryside to **Storen.** From there continue on E6 into Trondheim.

18. TRONDHEIM

Dramatically positioned on a peninsula that juts into Norway's broadest fjord, Trondheim is the country's third-largest city. Once the capital of a Viking kingdom, Trondheim was founded by King Olav Tryggvason in A.D. 997. The city's most impressive structure and Scandinavia's largest medieval building is the **Nidaros Cathedral,** built at the end of the eleventh century as a shrine to St. Olav. The cathedral serves as the coronation place for the country's monarchs.

The rococo-style **Stiftsgaarden,** located in the center of the old town, is the largest wooden building in Scandinavia. Among the several interesting museums in the area are the **Ringve Museum,** which features a collection of musical instruments from all over the world, and the **Trondelag Folk Museum,** located in nearby **Sverresborg.**

Trondheim Campground

N–100 Heimdal ★★ Sandmoen Camping. Open year-round. In Heimdal, 10 km (6 mi.) south of Trondheim. Turn off of E6 at campground sign. A large, slightly sloping site with some shade trees, 1 km (0.6 mi.) from main road. Bus to Trondheim, 400 yd. Adequate parking in Trondheim.

Trondheim → Molde, 225 km (135 mi.)

Take E6 south from Trondheim to **Heimdal,** then follow Hwy. 65 east along the fjord to **Orkanger.** Where the road splits into Hwy. 65/71, continue on Hwy. 71 to **Halsa** and the remaining few kilometers into Molde.

19. MOLDE

A pleasant country town on the Moldefjord, Molde is a quiet summer resort. Although the town was founded in the fifteenth century, it was mostly destroyed during World War II and has been rebuilt in the modern style.

Molde Campground

N–101 ★★ Kviltorp Camping. Open year-round. Located 3 km (1.8 mi.) east of town center. Turn off of Hwy. 62 at the airport. A small, pleasant, sloping site on the Moldefjord. Bus to town, 100 yd. Ample parking in Molde.

Molde → Geiranger, 155 km (93 mi.)

Take Hwy. 64 from Molde to **Andalsnes,** a lively resort and important supply port for the offshore oil fields. From Andalsnes take Hwy. 63 to **Valldal,** along an incredibly beautiful stretch of road. From Valldal it's just a few kilometers to the ferry landing at **Linge.** The crossing to **Eidsdal** takes ten minutes and there is continuous service. From Eidsdal continue on the **Eagles Road,** a winding, climbing series of hairpin turns that affords breathtaking views of the fjords before descending into Geiranger.

20. GEIRANGER

Geiranger is a small resort, magnificently set at the head of the **Geiranger Fjord.**

Geiranger Campground

N–102 ★★★ Grande Fjord Camping. Open May 1–September 30. On Hwy. 58, about 2 km (1.2 mi.) north of town in the direction of Alesund. Adjacent to a motel. A small, partly flat, partly terraced site. Steep approach to entrance. Swimming in the fjord. Good base for hiking and exploring the fjords. –1.2 mi.

Geiranger → Bergen, 400 km (250 mi.)

From Geiranger follow signs to **Pollfoss** and then to **Lom** on Hwy. 15. From Lom take Hwy. 55, **Sognefjell Road,** through the **Jotunheim Mountains.** The road climbs to 1,440 m (4,752 ft.) before descending into **Sogndal,** a small town at the foot of the spectacular **Sognefjord,** Norway's largest fjord.

Continue to the ferry port of **Kaupanger.** This small fjord settlement has a fine thirteenth-century **stave church** and an **open air museum.** From Kaupanger take the ferry to **Revsnes** and then to **Gudvangen.** Along this short stretch of fjord lies some of the most magnificent scenery in the entire country.

There are several ferries daily. For details and reservations contact a travel agent before leaving Trondheim or Kaupanger Ferjeekspedisjon, 5880 Kaupanger, Norway; phone (47) 57 67 81 16.

From the ferry dock at **Gudvangen** take E16, which climbs quickly and steeply to offer a breathtaking panoramic view of the fjord. Continue to **Voss,** a popular year-round resort with a fine **medieval church** and **folk museum.** E16 runs through a series of tunnels for the remaining 80 km (50 mi.) into Bergen.

21. BERGEN

Norway's second-largest city and principal west-coast seaport, Bergen is one of Scandinavia's most attractive and interesting cities. The oldest and most appealing section of town lies at the edge of the busy harbor. Here you will find a lively fish market (Torget) that offers an incredible variety of freshly caught fish. Reminders of Bergen's heyday as a prosperous member of the Hanseatic Trading League are to be found in the old warehouses that line the harbor and in the **Hanseatic Museum. St. Mary's Church,** the oldest building in Bergen, was built in the mid-twelfth century.

Troldhaugen (Troll's Hill), the summer home of Norway's most noted composer, Edvard Grieg, occupies an idyllic setting on Nordas Lake. One of Norway's finest wooden churches, the richly decorated twelfth-century **Fantoft Stave Church** is located in the nearby village of **Paradis.**

Note: To connect with our British Byways itinerary, take the ferry from Bergen or Stavanger to Newcastle (see p. 64). The crossing takes twenty-four to twenty-six hours. There are two to three crossings per week, depending on the season. For details contact The Color Line, P.O. Box 1422 Vika, 0115 Oslo, Norway; phone (47) 294–4470, fax (47) 283–0776.

Bergen Campground

N–103 ★★ Lone Camping (Haukeland). Open year-round. In Haukeland, 20 km (12 mi.) east of Bergen on E16 in the direction of Voss. Adjacent to a Fina service station. A medium-size site, pleasantly situated on Lake Haukeland. Bus to Bergen, 100 yd. Bergen parking is difficult.

Bergen → Stavanger, 150 km (90 mi.)

Although it is possible to take the ferry directly from Bergen to Stavanger, the route that we have selected combines a bit of island hopping by ferry with some scenic driving stretches. This is a more interesting and less expensive route.

From Bergen head south on Hwy. 1 to the ferry port at **Halhjem.** The ferry to **Sandvikvag** is in continuous service daily from 6:00 to 12:45 A.M. The crossing takes fifty minutes.

From Sandvikvag follow signs to **Skjersholmane** at the southern tip of the island and take the twenty-minute ferry ride to **Velevag.** Cross the island to **Bokn** and from there continue by ferry to Stavanger (fifty minutes).

22. Stavanger

Once a prosperous fishing and trading center, Stavanger, more than any other Norwegian city, has felt the effects of the discovery of vast oil deposits in the North Sea. The population has soared from 10,000 to almost 100,000 over the past fifteen years, and the once quaint fishing harbor is now jammed with oil tankers and drilling rigs.

Stavanger Campground

N–104 ★★ Camping Mosvangen. Open June 1–August 31. Located 4 km (2.4 mi.) southwest of Stavanger. Take E18 toward Oslo. After the tunnel take Ullandhaug exit and follow signs to campground. A medium-size, hilly site. On Lake Mosvangen (no swimming).

Stavanger → Kristiansand, 270 km (162 mi.)

From Stavanger follow the coast road, Hwy. 44, across the flat and stony **Jaren region,** one of the few districts in this mountainous country to support agriculture. The highway passes through the fishing ports of **Egersund** and **Flekkefjord,** with its delightful Dutch houses. At Flekkefjord the road joins with Hwy. 18 and after a climbing winding stretch, you will come to the town of **Mandal.** The beaches in this region are some of the finest in Scandinavia.

23. Kristiansand

The largest town in southern Norway, Kristiansand is an important transportation center. An impressive **seventeenth-century fortress** guards the approaches to the harbor, and there is an **open-air museum** at the northeast edge of town.

Note: There is daily ferry service to Hirtshals, Denmark. The crossing takes four and one-half hours. For details contact The Color Line (see p. 109).

Kristiansand Campground

N–105 ★★ Camping Dvergnestangen. Open year-round. Located 6 km (3.6 mi.) east of town center. Turn south off of E18 6 km (3.6 mi.) northeast of Kristiansand onto Hwy. 401, then follow campground signs. A large, grassy, sloping site with plenty of shade trees and some rocks. Swimming in the fjord. Convenient stop before taking ferry. Adequate parking in Kristiansand.

Kristiansand → Oslo, 285 km (177 mi.)

Continue east on E18 from Kristiansand. The road hugs the coast passing through **Arendal,** a once thriving whaling port, and **Larvik,** birthplace of the noted explorer Thor Heyerdahl. E18 continues along the **Oslo Fjord,** through timber country and the logging port of **Drammen** into Oslo.

24. Oslo

Founded in the eleventh century, Oslo soon developed into one of Norway's most important religious centers—this in spite of the fact that the seat of the crown and of the church were first established in Trondheim and later in Bergen. In the fourteenth century Haakon V shifted the capital from Bergen to Oslo. From 1624 to 1924 the city was called Christiania.

One of the best places to begin a tour of Oslo is at the **Town Hall.** The modern, twin-towered brick structure, completed in 1950, looks out over the harbor at the head of the Oslo Fjord. The interior contains a stunning assortment of contemporary masterpieces by Norwegian artists and artisans.

The **Akerhus Fortress,** built in the thirteenth century on a steep cliff overlooking the fjord, is one of Oslo's oldest historical monuments. During the German occupation in World War II, the fortress was used as a military headquarters. The **Norges Hjemmefront Museum** (War Resistance Museum) on the fortress grounds pays tribute to those Norwegians who resisted the takeover of their country.

Three museums on the **Bygdoy Peninsula** document Norway's close association with the sea. The **Viking Ship Museum** contains three Viking ships that date back some 1,200 years. Housed in a separate museum just a few steps away are Thor Heyerdahl's original rafts, *Ra* and *Kon Tiki.* Another building encloses the polar exploration ship *Fram* used by the Norwegians Roald Admundsen and Fridtjof Nansen.

The dramatic works of sculptor Gustav Vigeland are magnificently displayed in the beautiful, seventy-five-acre **Frogner Park.** For a panoramic view of the city, climb to the top of the **Holmenkollen Ski**

Jump. The **Ski Museum** at the foot of the jump traces the development of skiing back more than 2,000 years.

Oslo Campground

N–106 ★★ Camping Bogstad. Open year-round. At the north edge of the city, 9 km (5.4 mi.) from Oslo center. On the south edge of Lake Bogstad, near the ski jump. Approaching from the south on E18, follow signs towards Drammen. Turn off of motorway at campground sign. Approaches are well marked. A thirty-six-acre, grassy site with some terracing and large shade trees. Located in a pleasant forested area practically in the city. Bus to Oslo, 500 yd. Limited parking in Oslo at most tourist attractions.

Oslo → Goteborg (Gothenburg), 320 km (198 mi.)

Leave Oslo on E6 and follow this south along the Oslo Fjord to **Halden** at the border with Sweden. The road continues along the coast into Goteborg.

25. Goteborg (Gothenburg)

Sweden's second-largest city and largest seaport, Goteborg is often referred to as the "Gateway to Northern Europe." The harbor, home to nearly half of the country's merchant fleet, is also one of the busiest fishing ports in Scandinavia.

The **Liseberg Amusement Park,** only a few minutes from the center of town, features exciting rides, restaurants and attractive gardens. This is the largest park of its kind in Northern Europe and one of the cleanest and best run anywhere.

The massive bronze figure of Poseidon that dominates the **Gotaplatsen,** the cultural heart of the city, is by the Swedish-American sculptor Carl Milles. Goteborg has several good museums, including the **Maritime Museum,** with exhibits that show the development of shipping and fishing from the Viking period to the present.

Note: To connect with our Tiptoeing through the Tulips itinerary, take the ferry from Goteborg to Amsterdam (see p. 132 for details). There are two crossings weekly. The trip takes twenty-four hours. For details contact Scandinavian Seaways, Scandinavia House, Parkeston Quay, Harwich, Essex CO12 4QG, England; phone (0255) 241 234, fax

(0255) 241 471.

To connect with our British Byways itinerary, take the ferry from Goteborg to Harwich (see p. 69). There are three crossings weekly; the crossing time is twenty-three and one-half hours. For details contact Scandinavian Seaways, listed above.

Goteborg Campground

S–111 ★★★ Krono Camping. Open year-round. Located 7 km (4.2 mi.) south of city center. Take E6 south to Molndal and follow campground signs. A large, level site near the sports field. Conveniently situated for visiting Goteborg. Bus to city, 100 yd.

Goteborg → Billund (Legoland), 250 km (150 mi.)

Take the ferry across the **Kattegat** to the Danish port of **Frederikshavn.** There are six crossings daily. The crossing takes 3¼ hours. For details contact Stena Line BV, Postbus 2, NL–3150 AA Hoek van Holland, The Netherlands; phone (31) (01747) 4140, fax (31) (01747) 87045. From the ferry dock in Frederikshavn take Hwy. E45 to Alborg, North Jutland's largest town and site of an interesting **Viking burial ground.** Continue south on E45 until the turnoff to Hwy. 13. Take Hwy. 13 to **Viborg** and continue south to **Vejle.** Then head west on Hwy. 28 to Billund.

26. Billund (Legoland)

The headquarters of the Lego Company is the site of one of the world's most unusual amusement parks. An entire miniature town, along with replicas of some of the world's best-known buildings, has been constructed out of millions of tiny plastic Lego building blocks.

Billund Campground

DK–103 ★★★ Camping Billund. Open May 1–October 18. Located 2 km (1.2 mi.) northeast of Billund. Turn off from Hwy. 28 and follow campground signs. A large, level site with little shade. The campground is divided into sections by hedges. About 500 yd. to Legoland. –300 yd.

Billund → Odense, 90 km (54 mi.)

Take Hwy. 176 southeast from Billund to **Kolding.** Take E20 from Kolding and cross the bridge onto the island of **Funen.** From the bridge take Hwy. 161 across the flat farmlands to Odense.

27. Odense

Denmark's third-largest city recently celebrated its 1,000th birthday. Odense is best known as the birthplace of Hans Christian Andersen. The famous storyteller used the city and its surroundings as the setting for many of his tales. The main attraction is **Andersen's birth house,** a charming half-timbered dwelling in the center of the old town that contains many articles that belonged to the author. **Den Fynske Landsby,** at the south edge of town, is one of Denmark's largest open-air museums. Here a typical Funen village has been built to portray rural life during the eighteenth and nineteenth centuries.

Odense Campground

DK–104 ★★★ Camping Odense. Open March 27–September 26. From E20 take exit 50 and follow signs on Hwy. 162 toward Odense Centrum. The turnoff to the site is just past a Texaco station. Approaches are well marked. The large, grassy site is divided into sections by hedges. Bus to center of Odense, 800 yd. Parking in Odense is difficult.

Odense → Roskilde, 120 km (74 mi.)

Take Hwy. 160 east to the ferry port at **Kundshoved.** There is continuous service over the fifty-minute route. After driving off of the ferry at **Halskov,** follow E20 east to **Ringsted.** Take exit 35 and then continue on Hwy. 14 into Roskilde.

Note: A bridge is under construction to replace the ferry.

28. Roskilde

Its origins steeped in legend, Roskilde was Denmark's capital until the early sixteenth century. In a scenic location at the head of the Roskilde Fjord, the city has a number of interesting attractions, including the imposing 800-year-old **Roskilde Cathedral,** the traditional burial place of

Danish kings and queens. The **Viking Ship Museum** houses the remains of five Viking ships recovered from the Roskilde Fjord.

The **Lejre Research Center,** in nearby **Lejre,** is an unusual living museum. Primitive dwellings have been constructed and are inhabited by people who live in them under Iron Age conditions.

Roskilde Campground

DK–105 ★★★ Roskilde Camping. Open April 4–September 27. Turn off of Hwy. 6 just north of town, toward Veddelev, and follow campground signs. A large, grassy, partly hilly meadow with some shade trees. In a beautiful wooded setting overlooking the fjord. Bus to town, 200 yd. Parking in Roskilde is difficult but possible. ▪ ▪–500 yd. ▪ ▪ ▪

Roskilde → Copenhagen, 65 km (39 mi.)

Follow Hwy. 156 directly into Copenhagen.

TIPTOEING THROUGH THE TULIPS

Belgium

CAPITAL: Brussels

POPULATION: 9,985,000

CURRENCY: Belgian franc (BF), divided into 100 centimes

LANGUAGES: Flemish, French, and German; English is widely spoken

RELIGIONS: Roman Catholic and Protestant

POLICE: 101

FIRE: check local directories

AMBULANCE: 100 or (02) 649 11 22

ROAD SERVICE: Touring Club (02) 512 78 90; Royal Automobile Club (02) 287 09 11

BANKS: weekdays 9:00 A.M.–4:00 P.M.; some banks close for lunch; in Brussels at Gare Nord & Midi (train station) open 6:00 A.M.–10:00 P.M.

STORES: Monday–Saturday 9:00 A.M.–6:00 P.M.; Friday until 9:00 P.M.; bakeries and some small food shops open on Sunday

HOLIDAYS: January 1; Easter Monday (movable); May 1, Labor Day; Ascension Day (movable), Pentacost (movable); July 21, Independence Day; Assumption Day (movable); All Saints' Day (movable); November 11, Armistice; December 25 and 26

EMBASSIES: *United States,* Boulevard du Regent 27, B–1000 Brussels; phone (02) 513 38 30. *Canada,* 2 Avenue de Tervuren, B–1000 Brussels; phone (02) 735 60 40. *United Kingdom,* Britannia House, rue Joseph II 28, B–1040 Brussels; phone (02) 217 90 00

With 10 million inhabitants packed into an area roughly the size of Maryland, Belgium is Europe's most densely populated nation and one of the world's most heavily industrialized countries. At first glance this hardly seems like the kind of place conducive to RV travel. Statistics, however, can be misleading. Belgium, with its historic medieval cities and its pleasant countryside, has much to offer camping visitors.

A constitutional monarchy since 1831, the country is split roughly in half along ethnic lines. These ethnic divisions enhance the country's appeal as a tourist destination. The French-speaking Walloons live primarily in the southern part of the kingdom; while the Flemings, who speak a Dutch dialect called *Flemish,* primarily occupy the northern portion of the country. Although officially classified as bilingual, Brussels, the capital, is primarily a French-speaking enclave in Flemish territory.

Thickening this polyglot brew are the people in the eastern part of the country, near Eupen and Arlon, whose native tongue is German. In Brussels and most of the major tourist destinations, English is widely spoken, particularly among young people.

The variety that Belgium offers its visitors is not restricted to language. The north of the country is a flat, heavily cultivated region of fens, canals, and rivers that are a natural extension of the Netherlands, Belgium's northern neighbor. As in the Netherlands, much of the land along the North Sea coast has been reclaimed from the sea. The seacoast, although a mere 60 km (36 mi.) long, contains some lovely sandy beaches and dunes and includes Ostend, the country's most important seaport and coastal resort. The southeastern part of Belgium is a rugged, wooded region where the hills rise to some 600 m (1,980 ft.).

Throughout its history Belgium has known many conquerors and has been the site of some of Europe's most significant battles. It was on the plains of Waterloo, just south of Brussels, that Napoleon met his final defeat in 1815. More recently, during World War II, it was in the Ardennes Forest that the decisive Battle of the Bulge took place. Following the massive destruction suffered during World War II, the historic cities were faithfully restored. Brugge, Ghent, and the diamond center of Antwerp should be included in any visit to Belgium.

DRIVING

Belgium is served by a network of excellent high-speed motorways that extend from Brussels at the hub to all corners of the country. There are no toll roads. The extensive system of highways and secondary roads is well maintained, and driving throughout the country, with the exception of the heavy truck traffic in and around the major cities, is quite pleasant. Road signs for the motorways are white on green; the route numbers are prefixed with "A" or "E." Principal surface streets have the prefix "N." The most difficult challenge that you will face driving through Belgium is keeping track of where you are. Road signs are written in the language of the region. Therefore, you will need to know that *Anvers,* for example, is French for "Antwerp," which in Flemish is *Antwerpen.* The first time we drove in Belgium looking for a restaurant that a Flemish friend had recommended in Doornik, near the French border, we drove through the town three times before it finally dawned on us that what the Flemish knew as *Doornik* was actually signposted as TOURNAI. Throughout this book we will use the Flemish, French, and English spellings. Fortunately, Belgium is a small country, so you can't go too far astray without running into another country.

Note that at intersections, traffic approaching from the right has the right of way. This is particularly important to know since STOP and YIELD signs are not widely used. Cars within a traffic circle have priority over traffic entering the circle. Streetcars always have the right-of-way. Seatbelts are compulsory in both front and back seats, and children under age twelve are not allowed in the front seats. The speed limit for motorhomes on the motorways is 120 kph (72 mph); outside built-up areas it is 90 kph (54 mph). In towns the speed limit, unless otherwise posted, is 50 kph (30 mph). Throughout the country the police are empowered to collect fines from foreign motorists on the spot.

Cycling is a very popular Belgian pastime. Wherever you drive, be on the lookout for the ubiquitous cyclists.

CAMPING

With more than 500 officially registered sites, you are never very far from a campground in Belgium. These sites are classified by the government with one to four stars. Sites rated with one and two stars do not have hot showers.

Many Belgian campgrounds are really more residential trailer parks than campgrounds, and they provide little space and few facilities for travelers. A recent law mandates that registered campgrounds reserve at least 15 percent of their sites for travelers. During the summer months, especially along the coast, it is difficult to find a spot at many of these parks.

Although there are no campgrounds within Brussels itself, there are several sites in the outlying suburbs with convenient public transportation into the city.

An International Camping Carnet is not required, although a number of campgrounds offer discounts to Carnet holders. Rates at every registered campground must be posted at the entrance to the facility. In many resort areas an additional tourist tax is charged.

It is often possible to camp on farms and other private property, but the owner's permission must always be obtained in advance. With the exception of overnight stops at motorway and highway rest stops, free camping is not allowed. To free camp on municipal property, try to obtain the permission of the local authorities. If this is not possible, be as inconspicuous as possible and chances are that no one will bother you.

A free map showing the locations of some 400 campgrounds is available from the Belgian National Tourist Offices (see p. 357). Additional information about camping in Belgium may be obtained from Royal Camping and Caravaning Club of Belgium, rue Madeleine, 31, 1000 Brussels; phone (02) 51 32 87.

Luxembourg

CAPITAL: Luxembourg

POPULATION: 400,000

CURRENCY: Luxembourg franc (LuxF); Belgium currency can be used in Luxembourg

LANGUAGES: Luxembourgisch, French, and German; English widely spoken

RELIGION: predominantly Roman Catholic

POLICE: 012

FIRE: 012

AMBULANCE: 012

ROAD SERVICE: Auto Club of Luxembourg 450–045

BANKS: weekdays 8:30 A.M.–noon and 1:30–4:30 P.M.

STORES: Monday 2:00–6:30 P.M.; Tuesday–Friday 8:30 A.M.–noon and 2:00–6:30 P.M.; usually close by 3:00 P.M. on Saturday

HOLIDAYS: January 1; Easter Monday (movable); May 1, Labor Day; Ascension Day (movable); Pentacost (movable); June 23, National Day; Assumption Day (movable); All Sants' Day (movable); December 25 and 26

EMBASSIES: *United States,* 22 Boulevard Emmanuel–Servais, 2235 Luxembourg; phone (352) 460–123, fax 461–401. *Canada,* 24–26 Avenue de la Liberte, 1014 Luxembourg; phone (352) 402–420, fax 402–455. *United Kingdom,* 14 Boulevard Roosevelt, 2450 Luxembourg Ville; phone (352) 29864/66

The Grand Duchy of Luxembourg is a tiny nation of just under 2,600 km² (1,000 sq. mi.) with a polyglot population of 400,000 inhabitants. While French is the official language, German is almost universally spoken, as is the local dialect, a tongue-twisting hybrid of French and German known as Luxembourgisch. Luxembourg contains some lovely unspoiled scenic areas that include parts of the Ardennes forest and the upper Moselle valley.

DRIVING

Driving conditions are essentially the same as in neighboring Belgium.

CAMPING

Luxembourg has some 120 campgrounds scattered throughout the country. Most of these are small, pleasant sites with few amenities. Free camping is not allowed; however, it is often possible to obtain permission to camp on private land. Additional information about camping in Luxembourg may be obtained from the National Tourist Offices (see p. 360).

The Netherlands

CAPITAL: Amsterdam; seat of government: The Hague

POPULATION: 15,300,000

CURRENCY: Dutch guilder (or florin), divided into 100 cents

LANGUAGES: Dutch; English is widely spoken

RELIGIONS: Roman Catholic, Protestant, and unaffiliated

POLICE: no single number; check directory

FIRE: check local directories

AMBULANCE: check local directories

ROAD SERVICE: ANWB; phone (070) 31 47 714

BANKS: weekdays 9:00 A.M.–4:00 P.M.; money can also be changed at GWK offices Monday–Saturday 8:00 A.M.–8:00 P.M., Sunday 10:00 A.M.–4:00 P.M.; in major cities open twenty-four hours

STORES: weekdays 9:00 A.M.–6:00 P.M. (some close for lunch); many shops closed Monday until 1:00 P.M.; Thursday and Friday evening shopping until 9:00 P.M.

HOLIDAYS: January 1; Good Friday and Easter Monday (movable); April 30, Queen's Day (shops open unless Sunday); May 5, Liberation; Ascension (movable); Pentacost (movable); December 25 and 26

EMBASSIES: *United States,* Lange Voorhout 102, 2514 EJ The Hague; phone (070) 310–9209, fax (070) 361–4688. *Canada,* Sophialaan 7, 2514 The Hague; phone (070) 361–4111, fax (070) 356–2823. *United Kingdom,* Lange Voorhout 10 2514 ED The Hague; phone (070) 36 45 800

Although the terms *Holland* and *the Netherlands* are often used interchangeably, there is, as a Dutch friend reminded us recently, a slight difference. The name *Holland* refers to the western provinces of North and South Holland, which constitute the country's economic and cultural heartland; while *the Netherlands* ("low lands") is the technically correct term for the entire country. For all but the most hard-core purists, the two terms can be used interchangeably.

With one of the highest population densities in the world, land is at a premium. As you tour the countryside, you will not see any unusued land, with the exception of the national parks in the eastern provinces. More than 20 percent of Holland's land area has been reclaimed from the sea in a series of remarkable engineering projects. These reclaimed areas, known as *polders,* provide a great deal of fertile acreage to help support the country's flourishing vegetable, flower, and dairy industries.

Despite the fact that the Netherlands is very much a modern country—the Dutch watch American sitcoms on their Japanese TVs and munch on Big Macs while playing the latest computer games—much of traditional Holland has been preserved. Many classic Dutch windmills, whose functions have been taken over by modern pumps, have been restored and retained as historical monuments; and colorful cheese markets are still held in ancient town squares, much as they were hundreds of years ago.

This tiny country has a rich cultural history and is home to more than 600 museums, including some of the world's most renowned. Holland's castle legacy is as rich as any country in Europe, with hundreds of fine castles and manor houses dotting the landscape.

Although this is not usually thought of as a beach country, Holland's North Sea coast has more than 250 km (150 mi.) of sandy beaches and dunes that offer a pleasant respite from the rigors of city sightseeing.

The Dutch, who in many aspects of their lives are quite conservative, are also a friendly and broadminded people, exhibiting a tolerance and respect for different ideas and values that are rarely found in other parts of Europe.

DRIVING

Holland has an extensive network of well-maintained roads that allow visitors to reach any part of the country within a few hours. There are no toll roads. Bicycling is a way of life in the Netherlands, and an extensive network of cycle paths is integrated into the overall traffic control system. As Dutch cyclists often tend to take their place on the road for granted, caution is advised when cyclists are about.

Traffic regulations are similar to those in other European countries.

Wearing seatbelts is compulsory; children ages four to eleven can only occupy the front seat if wearing a seatbelt that does not cross the chest. The permissible blood-alcohol level is 0.5. In the cities, streetcars have the right-of-way, and yellow curbs mean no parking.

The speed limit for motorhomes on the autobahn is 120 kph (72 mph); the speed limit in towns and built-up areas, unless otherwise posted, is 50 kph (30 mph). Outside of built-up areas it is 80 kph (48 mph) and on some main highways 100 kph (60 mph). In some districts the police are authorized to collect fines on the spot for traffic violations.

International highways are designated with the green "E" symbol. The red "A" denotes national highways. Other roads are designated with the letter "N." The strange, squat roadside markers seen in many areas are called "toadstools" and are used to designate cycle paths and country lanes. Scenic routes are indicated with hexagonal road markers.

CAMPING

With more than 1,000 designated sites and another 1,200 so-called mini-campings in a country of some 15 million inhabitants, the Netherlands has one of Europe's highest concentrations of campgrounds.

With few exceptions, Dutch campsites are well organized and maintain a high standard of cleanliness. Inspections are performed regularly, and the tourist authorities rate campgrounds with a system of stars and flags. The number of stars, from one to five, indicates the standard of sanitary facilities and overall maintenance; the number of flags denotes the extent and quality of general and recreational facilities.

Hot showers and electrical hookups are universal, although obtaining "really hot water" is difficult on occasion. Many sites have converted from the German two-prong Schuko plugs to the three-prong blue EEC 17 plugs and outlets.

Dump stations for motorhomes, even for gray water, are still a rarity. Trash disposal is regulated throughout the country, and campgrounds provide separate containers for various categories of refuse.

Mini-campgrounds are usually located on farms, and the number of RVs or tents is limited to ten per farm. Facilities are modest, but these inexpensive sites, where guests can experience life on a Dutch farm, are ideal for the self-contained-motorhome traveler. For additional information contact the local VVV (tourist offices) or, in Holland, call Mr. Wim van den Berg of the Stichting Vrije Recreatie at (01837) 2741.

An International Camping Carnet is not required to stay at a Dutch campground. Holland is one of the more progressive countries when it comes to providing wheelchair-accessible facilities; many campgrounds are accessible to wheelchair users.

Camping outside of official sites is prohibited and subject to a fine. In recent years the Dutch police have become stricter in enforcing this regulation. For additional information about motoring and camping in Holland, contact ANWB, Wassenaarsweg 220, 2596 EC The Hague, the Netherlands; phone (070) 314 71 47.

Itinerary: Amsterdam · The Dutch Countryside · Brussels and Northern Belgium · Luxembourg

START: Amsterdam

COUNTRIES: Belgium, Luxembourg, the Netherlands

DISTANCE: 1,100 km (660 mi.)

MAPS: Michelin #407 *Benelux;* #212 *Brugge–Rotterdam– Antwerpen;* #213 *Bruxelles–Oostend–Liege;* #214 *Mons–Dinant–Luxembourg;* #215 *Luxembourg*

MINIMUM RECOMMENDED TOURING TIME: 10 days

INTRODUCTION

This is an itinerary that explores three tiny countries—Belgium, the Netherlands, and Luxembourg—whose combined area is less than that of the state of Maine. In the course of a few hours, you can drive from one end of a country to another. Within this small multicultural area, however, there is much of interest to see and experience. The so-called Benelux countries are modern and progressive states that have preserved many of their old traditions and customs.

This itinerary starts in Amsterdam, with its winding canals and world-class museums. In the old seaport of Edam, you can watch the famous Edam cheese being made; and in many parts of the Netherlands, you will still see traditional Dutch windmills and drawbridges. In Belgium you can tour the historic battlefield at Waterloo and explore such well-preserved medieval cities as Brugge and Ghent; and in the Jewish quarter of Antwerp, you can watch diamonds being cut and polished. The hills and valleys of Belgium's Walloon region or the Grand Duchy of Luxembourg offer a pleasant contrast to the flat landscape of the eastern provinces of Holland and Belgium. The food of the region is varied and reflects the different cultural influences.

North Sea
Netherlands
Germany
Den Helder
NL–102
NL–103
2
ALKMAAR
Purmerend
3
EDAM
NL–104
AMSTERDAM
1
Haarlem
NL–100
NL–101
Lisse
Breukelen
Leiden
DEN HAAG
16
NL–109
Gouda
Delft
15
NL–108
ROTTERDAM
Soest
Amersfoort
4
UTRECHT
NL–105
Zwolle
5
APELDOORN
NL–106
De Hooge
National Park
de Hooge Veluwe
ARNHEM
6
NL–107
Nijmegen
Entschede

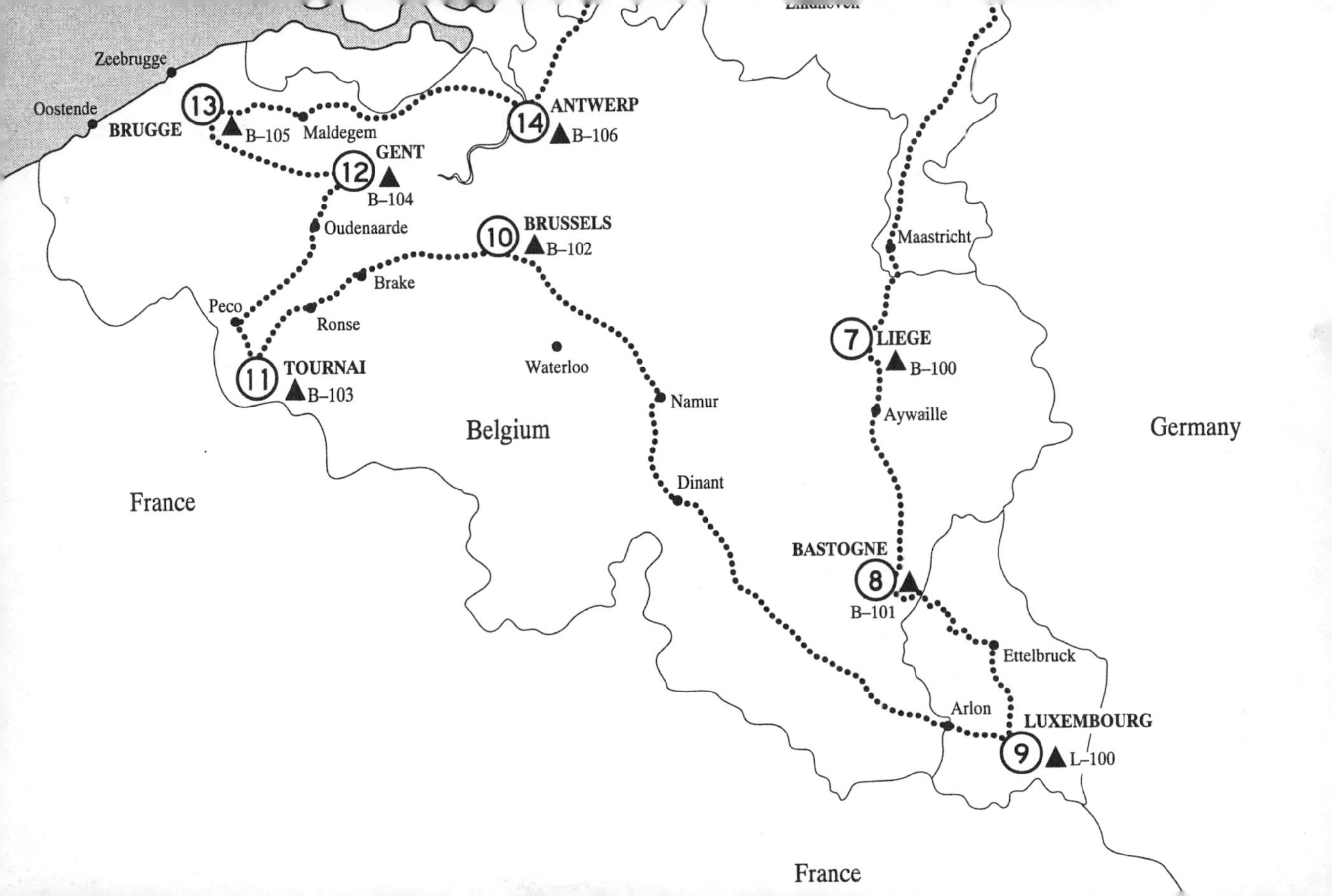

Zeebrugge
Oostende
13
BRUGGE
B–105
Maldegem
14
ANTWERP
B–106
12
GENT
B–104
Oudenaarde
10
BRUSSELS
B–102
Brake
Peco
Ronse
11
TOURNAI
B–103
Waterloo
Namur
Belgium
France
Dinant
Maastricht
7
LIEGE
B–100
Aywaille
Germany
BASTOGNE
8
B–101
Ettelbruck
Arlon
LUXEMBOURG
9
L–100
France

When to Go

Early April to mid-May is when the Dutch tulip fields are in bloom. Although this colorful spectacle draws many tourists and the countryside is full of tour buses, campgrounds are not crowded.

Summers throughout the region are generally mild, particularly near the coast, where the often brisk sea breezes keep the temperatures from rising above the mid-20s Centigrade (high 70s Fahrenheit). Rain can come at any time. Showers, however, occur most frequently in the inland areas during the summer and in the coastal regions in the autumn.

Campgrounds, especially along the coast, tend to be crowded with locals in July and August. September is a quiet time for touring, but the weather is often windy and rainy.

Highlights

The Grand'Place, Brussels
Van Gogh Museum, Amsterdam
Het Loo Gardens, Apeldoorn
Old Town, Brugge

Expanding Horizons

- **To Viking Trails Itinerary:** Take the ferry from Amsterdam to Goteborg (see p. 112).
- **To British Byways Itinerary:** Take the ferry from Zeebrugge to Dover (see p. 69) or from Hoek van Holland to Harwich (see p. 69).

ON THE ROAD

Numbered sites correspond with circled numbers on the itinerary map.

1. Amsterdam

Amsterdam is one of those great European cities where no matter what it is that you are looking for there is a good chance that you will find it. Founded in 1275 as Amestelledamme, the city is rich in tradition and boasts of having the largest historical inner city in Europe. Nearly 7,000 buildings, most of them constructed in the seventeenth and eighteenth centuries, are under protection as historical landmarks.

This is a city that lives with its past but is not encumbered by it. Ams-

Canal in Amsterdam (Courtesy Netherlands Board of Tourism)

terdam is a progressive European capital where it is not unusual to find a shop displaying the latest in computers and electronic gadgets housed in a meticulously restored seventeenth-century townhouse. In the notorious red-light district, one of the city's prime tourist attractions, an assortment of young and some not-so-young ladies also display their wares in shop windows. It's all a part of Amsterdam, a city of many moods and faces—at times cultured and refined, at other times brash and vulgar.

Some of the world's great museums are located in Amsterdam. Most famous of the more than forty museums is the **Rijksmuseum,** where the outstanding collection of Dutch masters includes the works of Rembrandt, Vermeer, and Frans Hals. Just down the street is the **Vincent Van Gogh Museum,** housing the largest collection of Van Goghs anywhere in the world. The third in this trio of great museums, all located within a few steps of the **Museumplein (Museum Square),** is the **Stedelijk Museum,** a leading modern art museum.

The **Anne Frank House,** where the Frank family hid from the Nazis for two years and where Anne Frank wrote her famous diary, is now a museum. No one who visits here remains unmoved by this heroic and tragic story.

In the heart of Amsterdam's large Jewish quarter is the faithfully restored **Rembrandt House,** in which the artist lived from 1639 to 1658. Amsterdam has been a major diamond-cutting center since the sixteenth century. For a fascinating look into the world of diamonds, visit one of the several diamond-cutting workshops that are open to the public. The **Albert Cuyp Market,** near the Museumplein, is one of Holland's largest and most colorful open-air markets.

The heart of Amsterdam is located in an area ringed by a series of concentric and intersecting canals. The more than 100 km (60 mi.) of canals are spanned by some 1,000 bridges. Unlike Rome and Paris, Amsterdam is not a city of spectacular monuments. It is a place that takes some time to get to know; one of the best ways to do this is to take a sightseeing cruise through the canals and harbor. Then stroll on your own through the city's fascinating quarters and along the canals, which are lined with colorful houseboats and fine old houses.

One thing that you do not want to do is to drive or try to park an RV in Amsterdam. Parking is extremely difficult, and those who do manage to find a parking spot are subject to one of Europe's highest break-in rates. Leave your vehicle in the campground and use Amsterdam's excellent public transportation system.

Note: To connect with our Viking Trails itinerary, take the ferry from Amsterdam to Goteborg. There are two crossings weekly. The trip takes twenty-four hours. For details contact Scandinavian Seaways, Scandinavia House, Parkeston Quay, Harwich, Essex CO12 4QG, England; phone (0255) 241 234, fax (0255) 241 471.

Amsterdam Campgrounds

NL–100 ★★★ Gaasper Camping. Open year-round. On Lake Gaasper 10 km (6 mi.) southeast of Amsterdam Central Station. From Autobahn A9 take Gaasperplas/Weesp S113 exit and follow signs to campground. Approaches are well marked. A large, partly shaded, grassy site in a park setting on a small lake. Individual gray-water drains for RVs. A five-minute walk to Amsterdam subway. This is a convenient and pleasant site from which to explore Amsterdam and vicinity.

NL–101 ★★★ Camping Het Amsterdamse Bos. Open April 1–October 31. Located 10 km (6 mi.) southwest of Amsterdam Central Station. From Autobahn A4 (Badhoevedorp–Ouderkerk) take Amstelveen exit and follow signs south to campground. Located in the Amsterdamse Park just east of Schiphol Airport. A large, grassy site with many shade trees. Individual sites divided by hedges. Convenient tram to Amsterdam, numbers 171, 172.

Amsterdam → Alkmaar, 35 km (21 mi.)

From Amsterdam center head north either on the Autobahn A9 or Hwy. N203, which runs parallel to it, and follow the signs to Alkmaar.

2. ALKMAAR

Founded in the tenth century, Alkmaar is a delightful old town best known for its colorful **Cheese Market.** The market is held Friday mornings from late April through mid-September.

Alkmaar Campgrounds

NL–102 ★★ Camping Alkmaar. Open April 1–October 1. At the west edge of town, on the road to Bergen. A medium-size meadow divided by bushes and hedges. Convenient bus to town. –900 yd.

NL–103 ★★★★ Camping Molengroet. Open year-round. Located 3 km (1.8 mi.) north of Alkmaar off of N245, in the direction of Schagen. Approaches are well marked. A twenty-five-acre, grassy area with many shrubs and trees, located in the heart of a large waterpark. Free bus to Alkmaar. Extensive entertainment program. Sauna, windsurfing, horseback riding nearby. A convenient base for visiting Edam and the countryside north of Amsterdam.

Alkmaar → Edam, 28 km (17 mi.)

Take N244 south and then east from Alkmaar across the **polders** (reclaimed lands) to **Purmerend** and then to Edam.

3. Edam

A pleasant little market town with an attractive seventeenth-century town square, Edam is known worldwide for its fine cheese. The cheese-making process can be seen at several of the local factories.

Volendam and the island of **Marken** are popular tourist centers a few miles south of Edam. This is one of the best areas in the country to observe people who still wear colorful folk costumes and who live in picturesque houses. These towns can also easily be visited as part of a day trip from Amsterdam.

Edam Campground

NL–104 ★★ Camping Strandbad. Open April 1–October 1. At the sea, 6 km (3.6 mi.) east of the town center along the dike road. A large, grassy site on a peninsula with little shade. Small, rocky beach. Parking is available in Edam.

Edam → Utrecht, 50 km (30 mi.)

Return to Amsterdam by following the coast road that runs along the dike. Drive south from Edam by way of **Monnickendam** and then **Uitdam.** From Amsterdam head south following signs to Utrecht by way of **Abcoude, Loenen,** and **Breukelen.**

4. Utrecht

The Netherlands' fourth-largest city, Utrecht was founded by the Romans in A.D. 47. Although the city has fallen prey to extensive urban renewal, the **medieval center,** ringed by an ancient moat, still contains a number of interesting old buildings. The pace of life here is noticeably calmer than in the town's more modern sections. The **Cathedral of St. Materiel,** in the center of the old town, is one of The Netherlands' finest examples of ecclesiastical architecture. Five km (3 mi.) northwest of the city, in the village of **Haarzuilens,** in a lovely setting surrounded by water, is the formidable **De Haar Castle.**

Utrecht Campground

NL–105 ★★ Camping de Berekuil. Open April 1–October 30. Located 3 km (1.8 mi.) northeast of Utrecht. From A28 (Utrecht–Amersfoort) take Zeist exit, cross the autobahn, and follow campground signs. A medium-size, grassy site next to a brook. Plots are divided by hedges.

Utrecht → Apeldoorn, 56 km (36 mi.)

Head northeast from Utrecht to **Soest.** The **Royal Palace** is located in a beautiful park at the north edge of Soest. Continue on N221 to **Amersfoort,** a lively town that was an early member of the Hanseatic Trading League. From Amersfoort take N344 the remaining 40 km (24 mi.) into Apeldoorn.

5. Apeldoorn

A fashionable, park-lined residential town, Apeldoorn serves as a good jumping-off point for visiting the 13,343-acre **National Park de Hooge Veluwe.** The park, a vast, unpopulated expanse of forest and sandy dunes, is an unusual sight in this densely populated country. The **Het Loo Palace** is a restored eighteenth-century royal residence with extraordinary gardens.

Apeldoorn Campground

NL–106 ★★★ Aegon Vakantiepark Rabbit Hill. Open March 26–November 1. Located 12 km (7.2 mi.) west of Apeldoorn. Located at the junction of N302 and N344. A large, shady site in a forested area. Individual water hookups. Part of a large vacation complex. Bus to town, 500 yd. This is a convenient site from which to visit the national park and the Kroller Muller Museum.

Apeldoorn → Arnhem, 30 km (18 mi.)

From Apeldoorn follow signs to Arnhem. The route leads through the National Park de Hooge Veluwe and passes through the villages of **Hoenderloo** and **Otterlo.**

6. Arnhem

Arnhem is a large, modern city that was rebuilt after having suffered nearly complete destruction during World War II. It was here that the disastrous battle depicted in the film *A Bridge Too Far* was fought. Significant mementos of that campaign can be seen at the **Airborne Museum** and the **Airborne Cemetery.**

The faithfully reconstructed country houses, windmills, and farms at the **Openlucht (Open-Air Museum)** just north of Arnhem present a living picture of traditional rural Dutch life. The **Kroller Muller Museum,** 10 km (6 mi.) north of the city in a magnificent wooded setting in the heart of the national park, is one of Europe's finest art museums.

Arnhem Campground

NL–107 ★★★ Kampeercentrum Der Hooge Veluwe. Open April 1–November 1. Located 6 km (3.6 mi.) northwest of Arnhem center. From Arnhem follow signs to suburb of Schaarsbergen and then to campground. A thirty-five-acre vacation complex in a park setting. Bus to Arnhem, 200 yd. Campground is well situated for visiting national park and Kroller Muller Museum.

Arnhem → Liege (Luik), Belgium, 160 km (96 mi.)

From Arnhem head south to **Nijmegen,** an important industrial center. From there continue south on N271 following the **Maas River** to **Maastricht,** an industrial and tourist center at the southernmost tip of the Netherlands. Follow the river into Liege.

7. Liege (Luik)

With a population of nearly half a million, Liege is Belgium's third-largest city, the capital of the Province of Walloon, and a major industrial center. The old town center retains many vestiges of Liege's 1,300-year history. The **Meuse River** meanders through the city and, in the downtown area, is crossed by numerous bridges.

Of Liege's many churches (more than one hundred steeples dot the skyline) the Romanesque **Church of St. Barthelemy** is one of the most attractive. Its intricate, twelfth-century copper baptismal fonts depicting five biblical scenes in relief are among Belgium's finest art treasures.

Although the mines have been shut down, Liege was the first European town to mine coal on a large scale. You can see a replica of a nineteenth-century coal mine in the **Musee de la Vie Walloone (Museum of Walloon Life).**

Liege Campground

B–100 ★ Camping du Syndicat d'Initiative (Tilff). Open April 1–October 15. In the suburb of Tilff, 10 km (6 mi.) south of Liege center. From Liege take autobahn E9 south towards Bastogne and take Tilff exit. In Tilff follow campground signs from the church. A small partly shaded site with limited facilities. –500 yd.

Liege → Bastogne (Bastenaken), 85 km (51 mi.)

Heading south from Liege on N33, go through **Tilff** and **Comblain au-Pont.** Then continue east on N33 to intersect with N15 at **Aywaille.** Follow N15 south to Bastogne.

8. Bastogne (Bastenaken)

Located near the border with Luxembourg, Bastogne was the site of the historic World War II Battle of the Bulge. There are several interesting war museums and monuments in the town.

Bastogne Campground

B–101 ★★ Camping de Renval. Open year-round. At the northeast edge of town, on the road to Marche. Approaches are well marked. A large, partly shaded site. Parking available in Bastogne. –900 yd.

Bastogne → Luxembourg, 60 km (36 mi.)

Take N34 east from Bastogne toward **Esch** and **Ettelbruck.** After you cross into Luxembourg, the road number changes to N15. At Ettelbruck, at the gateway to the hilly **Ardennes** region, head south on N7 into Luxembourg City.

9. Luxembourg

Luxembourg, the capital of the Grand Duchy, is a delightful 1,000-year-old medieval city and one of Europe's major banking centers. During the Middle Ages Luxembourg was one of the world's strongest fortified cities. Although many of these fortifications were dismantled in the last century, much of interest remains, including the **Casemates,** a 22-km (13-mi.) labyrinth of underground passages and fortifications.

Luxembourg Campground

L–100 ★★★ Camping Kockelscheuer. Open Easter–October 31. Located 4 km (2.4 mi.) south of Luxembourg on the road to Bettembourg. A medium-size, grassy site that is divided into sections by bushes. Part of a large sports complex with bowling, squash, tennis, and sauna. Bus to Luxembourg, 500 yd. Parking in the city is difficult.

Luxembourg → Brussels (Bruxelles), 190 km (114 mi.)

From Luxembourg take N4 west to **Arlon** and continue on N48 to **Dinant,** a popular tourist center on the Meuse River. The town is noted for its impressive fortress and hammered copperware. Continue on N17 along the Meuse into **Namur,** a charming fortified town at the junction of the Meuse and Sambre rivers. From Namur take N4 into Brussels.

10. Brussels (Bruxelles)

The cosmopolitan Belgian capital has a population of just over 1 million and is home to several major international organizations, including NATO and the European Community. The city's main attraction is the incredibly ornate **Grand'Place.** The colossal square, located in the center of the Old Town, is lined with a pleasant assortment of Gothic and baroque buildings.

The **Manneken Pis,** the irreverent seventeenth-century statue of a small boy urinating that has become the symbol of the city, is located just a few blocks from the Grand'Place. **Waterloo,** about 20 km (12 mi.) south of the capital, is the site of Napolean's famous 1815 defeat by the British general Wellington.

Brussels Campground

B–102 ★★ Camping Paul Rosmant R3CB. Open April 1–September 30. In the suburb of Wezembeek, 10 km (6 mi.) east of

Brussels center. From Brussels autobahn ring take Wezembeek/Oppem exit and follow campground signs that read R3CB. A small, grassy site adjacent to a park. Convenient commuter train into Brussels, 500 yd. Parking in Brussels is very difficult. –1.2 mi.

Brussels → Tournai (Doornik), 75 km (45 mi.)

From Brussels take N8 west to **Brake** and from there continue on N48 to **Ronse,** a pleasant textile manufacturing town. N48 continues from Ronse into Tournai.

11. Tournai (Doornik)

Tournai, founded by the Romans, is one of Belgium's oldest and most important historic cities. The twelfth-century **Cathedral of Notre Dame** is one of the finest examples of Romanesque architecture in Western Europe. In nearby **Antoing,** 6 km (3.6 mi.) southeast, there is a splendid sixth-century castle.

Tournai Campground

B–103 ★★★ Camping de l'Orient. Open year-round. Located 2 km (1.2 mi.) east of town. From intersection of N7 and E42, continue on N7 toward Tournai and follow campground signs. A medium-size site with some shade trees. Adjacent to a small lake. Bus to town. –500 yd.

Tournai → Gent (Ghent), 65 km (39 mi.)

Follow N50 toward **Kortrijk.** After 20 km (12 mi.) turn off at **Pecq** and take N453. Follow the **Schelde River** into **Oudenaarde (Audenarde),** a quiet medieval town with a number of fine old buildings. Then continue on N60 the remaining 20 km (12 mi.) into Gent.

12. Gent (Ghent)

A thriving industrial city of some 250,000, Gent is the capital of East Flanders. Rich in tradition, the city's old town contains more historic buildings than any other Belgian city. **'S Gravensteen,** the formidable castle of the Counts of Flanders, with its nearly 6½-ft.-thick walls, was built in the twelfth century.

De Haar Castle in Haarzuilens, near Utrecht (Courtesy Netherlands Board of Tourism)

Gent Campground

B–104 ★★★ Camping Blaarmeersen. Open March 1–October 15. Located 3 km (1.8 mi.) west of Gent center. Follow N466 from Gent in the direction of Tielt. At west edge of Gent, turn off at camping sign to campground. A large, grassy site with few shade trees. Some individual sites divided by hedges. Adjacent to the Blaarmeersen recreation center and lake. One-hour walk into Gent, or bus, 300 yd. Parking in Gent is very difficult.

Gent → Brugge (Bruges), 40 km (24 mi.)

From Gent take N9 into Brugge.

13. Brugge (Brugges)

Virtually a living open-air museum, Brugge has maintained a medieval mood and presence matched by few cities north of the Alps. If you have time to visit just one Belgian city, it should be Brugge. During the Middle Ages this was an important seaport, connected to the sea at Zeebrugge at the mouth of the Zwin River. The boat excursions along the old canals are a delightful way to get acquainted with Brugge.

Note: To connect with our British Byways itinerary, take the ferry from the port of Zeebrugge to Dover. The crossing takes about four hours. For more information contact P&O European Ferries, Channel House, Channel View Road, Dover CT17 9TJ, England; phone (0304) 203 388.

Brugge Campground

B–105 ★★ Camping Lac Loppem. Open year-round. In the suburb of Loppem, 5 km (3 mi.) south of Brugge center. A large, partly shaded site on a lake. Bus to Brugge, 500 yd. Parking is difficult in Brugge.

Brugge → Antwerp (Antwerpen/Anvers), 80 km (48 mi.)

Leave Brugge on N9 heading east. At the Maldegem interchange pick up N49 and follow this into Antwerp.

14. Antwerp (Antwerpen/Anvers)

Lying on the Schelde River close to the Dutch border, Antwerp is Belgium's second-largest city and one of the most cosmopolitan in Europe. The city has a centuries-old tradition as a major banking and trade center as well as one of the world's most important diamond-cutting centers.

Antwerp was the home of the painter **Peter Paul Rubens.** The house in which he lived and painted for nearly thirty years is now a museum.

Antwerp Campground

B–106 ★★ Camping Vogelzang. Open April 1–September 30. At the south end of town, next to the Crest Hotel. Approaches are well marked. Take exit 5 from the autobahn ring. A large, grassy site with little shade. Convenient for visiting Antwerp. Bus to center, 300 yd. Parking in Antwerp is difficult.

Antwerp → Rotterdam, the Netherlands, 45 km (27 mi.)

Take N1 north from Antwerp to **Breda.** At the Dutch border the road changes to N263. **Bouvigne Chateau,** a seventeenth-century moated castle with extensive gardens, is located in Ginneken on the south edge of the city. From Breda take A16 into Rotterdam.

15. ROTTERDAM

It was from Rotterdam's harbor, **Delfshaven,** that the Pilgrims set sail for America in 1620. Although this historic section of the city survived massive bombing raids during World War II and has been carefully preserved, the rest of Rotterdam was devastated. The Netherlands' second-largest city has been rebuilt in a bold, modern style and, with the exception of the **Delfshaven quarter,** offers little of historical interest. Tours of the busy harbor and of the **Delta Project,** the world's largest flood-control project, are available.

Note: To connect with our British Byways itinerary, take the ferry from Hoek van Holland to Harwich. There are daily sailings. The crossing takes seven to eight hours. For details contact Sealink Ferries, Charter House, Park Street, Ashford TN24 8EX, England; phone (0233) 647 047.

Rotterdam Campground

NL–108 ★★ Stadscamping Rotterdam. Open April 1–October 1. Located 3 km (1.8 mi.) north of Rotterdam center. Approaches are well marked. A medium-size, nicely shaded, grassy site. Parcels divided by hedges. Bus to downtown at entrance. Parking in Rotterdam is difficult. –800 yd.

Rotterdam → Den Haag ('S Gravenhage), 20 km (12 mi.)

From Rotterdam follow the road along the canal into **Delft.** Well-known for its characteristic blue and white tiles, Delft is a delightful town of tree-lined canals and Gothic and Renaissance houses. It is only a few kilometers from Delft to the center of Den Haag.

16. DEN HAAG ('S GRAVENHAGE)

The official seat of the Dutch government, Den Haag is a stately old dowager of a city. Its abundance of pleasant parks and wooded areas have earned it the distinction of being known as the Netherlands' greenest city. Although it has a fine royal palace and numerous museums, the attraction that seems to draw the greatest number of visitors is **Madurodam,** a delightful replica, in miniature, of a typical Dutch town. **Scheveningen,** once a simple fishing village, is now the country's most famous beach resort and the center of The Hague's night life.

Den Haag Campground

NL–109 ★★★★ Camping Delftse Hout (Delft). Open April 1–October 31. At the east end of Delft. Approaches are well marked. A large meadow with bushes and trees. Part of a lake and park complex. Bus to Delft/Den Haag.

Den Haag → Amsterdam, 60 km (36 mi.)

From Den Haag follow signs to **Leiden,** one of Holland's oldest and most picturesque towns. Continue north across the tulip fields to **Haarlem,** the center of the Dutch bulb industry. Midway between Den Haag and Haarlem, in **Lisse,** are the **Keukenhof Gardens,** where each spring the national flower exhibition is held. From Haarlem follow signs the 15 km (9 mi.) back to Amsterdam.

FRANCE A LA CARTE

France

CAPITAL: Paris

POPULATION: 56,900,000

CURRENCY: French franc (FF), divided into 100 centimes

LANGUAGE: French

RELIGION: Roman Catholic

POLICE: 17

FIRE: 18

AMBULANCE: 17

ROAD SERVICE: 17

BANKS: weekdays 9:00 A.M.–noon and 2:00–4:00 P.M. in cities, some banks open on Saturday but then close on Monday

STORES: Tuesday–Saturday 7:00 A.M.–7:00 P.M.; some bakeries and stores open on Sunday, closed on Monday; many shops close from noon to 2:00 P.M.

HOLIDAYS: January 1; Easter Monday; May 1, Labor Day; May 8, VE Day; Ascension Day (movable); Pentacost (movable); July 14, National Day; August 15, Assumption; November 1, All Saints' Day; November 11, Armistice Day; December 25

EMBASSIES: *United States,* 2 Avenue Gabriel, 75383 Paris, Codex 08; phone (01) 4296–1202, fax (01) 4266–9783. *Canada,* 35 Avenue Montaigne, 75008 Paris; phone (01) 4443–3200, fax (01) 4443–3497. *United Kingdom,* 35 Rue du Faubourg, St. Honore, 75383 Paris, Codex 08; phone (01) 4266–9142

A way of life, a state of mind, a bastion of culture and intellect, a faded dowager living with memories of a glorious past, or a progressive leader in the emergence of a new, self-confident and independent Europe? Take your choice! One, all, or none of the above—France has been for years and continues to be one of Europe's great enigmas.

Covering the largest area of the European countries and with a population of nearly 57 million, France is most definitely a force to be reckoned with in modern Europe. For travelers contemplating their first European trip, France presents a real dilemma. The question that always arises is: How much and for how long?

Probably no other country in the world offers such an interesting amalgamation of the past, present, and future. Whether you travel for a few weeks or for several months, you will encounter reminders of the country's incredibly rich history that include, to name just a few: prehistoric megaliths in Brittany; 30,000-year-old cave paintings in the Dordogne; the well-preserved Roman amphitheaters in Arles, Nimes, and Orange; the sumptuous Palace of Versailles; the imposing châteaux and mansions of the Loire Valley; and the World War II monuments and invasion beaches.

Don't get the idea, however, that France is a nation wallowing in its past. Quite to the contrary; this is a country that is very much involved in "what's happening." After all, the term *avant garde* is French; and such projects as the supersonic Concorde, the high-speed TGV (*train grande vitesse*), and the Channel Tunnel link with Great Britain are at the forefront of modern European technology.

For RV explorers France has attractions to suit all tastes and the largest number of campgrounds in Europe. This is also a country of great natural beauty, which includes the broad sandy beaches and dunes of the Atlantic coast, the rugged cliffs and delightful coves of Brittany and Normandy, and the magnificent Alps and Pyrenees. Quaint villages, cities with manicured tree-lined boulevards, sidewalk cafés wherever you go, opulent palaces, elegant châteaux, towering cathedrals, and intriguing ancient walled cities such as Carcassonne and Aigues Morte are all part of what makes a visit to France a unique and fascinating experience. Be sure to include Paris in your plans.

Volumes have been written trying to explain the characteristics of the French. They have been described as haughty, arrogant, romantic, charming, and just about every other adjective in the dictionary. Over the years we have spent a lot of time traveling in different parts of the country—camping, cycling, and skiing—and have had nothing but positive experiences. We have also had the opportunity to observe many American tourists in their encounters with the French. If there is one bit of advice that we can offer, it is to learn at least a few key words and phrases of the language. Nothing seems to go further in establishing friendly contact than addressing the French in their own language.

DRIVING

Driving an RV in France is a pleasure. The countryside, except for some grimy industrial areas in the north, is a scenic delight. The network of roads is extensive, and even the secondary roads are well maintained. Some of the most enjoyable touring that we have experienced in Europe has been on these secondary roads, marked in yellow on the Michelin maps. These roads are usually less congested, as most of the heavy truck and tourist traffic stick to the main highways. Roadside rest areas, ideal for picnic stops, are frequent and often placed in scenic locations—although few, with the exception of those on the toll roads, have toilet facilities.

If you are in a hurry, you can always hop on a modern high-speed turnpike (autoroute) just about anywhere in the country. France is second only to Germany in the number of high-speed motorways. Be prepared, however, to pay for the privilege of whizzing across the country. With the exception of a few major urban centers and the Brittany Peninsula, French motorways are toll roads, and the charges are steep for RVs. (Visa and MasterCard are accepted for payment.)

The previous *laissez faire* attitude toward the combination of alcohol and driving has been replaced by one of strict enforcement, with the imposition of breath tests and heavy on-the-spot-fines. In some districts police are authorized to collect fines directly for traffic violations. Seatbelts are compulsory, and children under age ten may not ride in the front seat.

The speed limit for motorhomes on the autoroutes is 130 kph (78 mph). The speed limit in towns and built-up areas, unless otherwise posted, is 50 kph (30 mph). Outside of built-up areas it is 90 kph (54 mph), and on four-lane highways it is 110 kph (66 mph).

CAMPING

France deservedly bears the title of "Europe's Most RV-Friendly Nation." With more than 11,000 campgrounds scattered throughout the country, there is just about no place that you might want to visit that does not have a campground nearby. Sites are rated with from one to four stars, based on the types of amenities present.

Many municipalities maintain their own campgrounds. These are generally less luxuriously outfitted than the private sites and are quite reasonably priced. Many are located in scenic areas and parks owned by the municipality. Of the more than 11,000 campgrounds, some 2,300 are small, informal sites located in rural areas and on farms. These sites usually have fewer amenities than the larger campgrounds and are limited, depending on location and classification, to from six to twenty-five vehicles or tents at a time. These sites provide a wonderful opportunity to view life on a French farm. Look for the signs CAMPING A LA FERME and CAMPING RURAL.

At the luxury end of the scale are the forty-six campgrounds belonging to the chain Castels & Camping Caravaning. These upscale sites are located on the grounds of elegant châteaux and manor houses. For a color brochure describing these luxury campgrounds, contact Castels & Camping Caravaning, Secretariat, B.P. 301, 56008 Vannes Cedex, France; phone (33) 97 42 55 83, fax (33) 97 47 50 72.

All French campgrounds are listed in a guide published annually by the French Camping Federation. The guide is available at most bookshops in France.

Camping sauvage, as free camping in known in France, is tolerated in most parts of the country. The rest areas on many of the French autoroutes are particularly well suited for an overnight stay. It is prohibited to free camp in many of the state forests and in the national parks. In many municipalities along the Mediterranean, free camping is not allowed. To enforce this ban, beach-area parking lots are outfitted with height barriers. But in contrast to this motorhome-unfriendly attitude, an increasing number of localities are providing specially designated parking areas for RVs. These are equipped with service islands for emptying tanks and filling up with fresh water. Look for signs with a motorhome pictogram.

The EEC 17 standard electrical hookups are still not used at most campgrounds. An adapter is required to use plugs from other countries. These are available at many campgrounds and can also be purchased at most electrical shops. It is very difficult to get propane bottles from other countries filled in France.

If your previous European camping experience has been limited to Northern Europe, France will probably provide the setting for your first encounter with the so-called continental toilet. Many French campgrounds, particularly the one- and two-star sites, are equipped with these hole-in-the-floor "squatter" toilets.

The International Camping Carnet is required at campgrounds in national parks and at some private sites. Additional information about camping in France may be obtained from the Federation Francaise de Camping et de Caravaning, 78, rue de Rivoli, 75004 Paris, France; phone (1) 42 72 84 08, fax (1) 42 72 70 21.

Itinerary I: Paris • Normandy • Brittany • The Loire Valley

START: Paris

COUNTRY: France

DISTANCE: 1,500 km (900 mi.)

MAPS: Michelin #989 *France;* #230 *Brittany;* #231 *Normandy;* #232 *Pays de Loire*

MINIMUM RECOMMENDED TOURING TIME: 10 to 14 days

INTRODUCTION

What better place than Paris in which to start a European tour? There are several motorhome rental firms in the greater Paris area (for details see p. 13). If you are flying directly into Paris, before picking up your vehicle, you might find it most convenient to check into a hotel and use that as a base from which to see the city's sights. Paris is a place in which to avoid driving whenever possible. Traffic and parking are on a par with downtown Manhattan. Gridlock is common; and parking, particularly for an RV, is next to impossible.

If you already have a vehicle or do not want to stay in a hotel, there are several campgrounds in Paris and its suburbs. The closest site is located in the Bois de Boulogne along the Seine River and is conveniently situated with respect to public transportation to the major Paris sights (for details see p. 156).

From Paris we head across the fertile farmlands of Normandy to Rouen, the "museum city." We then follow the Seine to the Normandy coast and visit the scene of the World War II Allied landings. In the medieval town of Bayeux, we can view the famed 900-year-old tapestry before moving on to the dramatically situated Abbey of Mont St. Michel.

Upon entering Brittany we trace the course of the jagged Emerald Coast and along the way visit sandy beaches and attractive fishing villages. The rich farmlands, lush forests, and magnificent chateaux of the Loire Valley present a strong contrast to the often windswept and rugged expanses of Brittany. From the Loire it is just a short ride back to Paris, with a stop to view the palace at Fontainebleau.

When to Go

Visiting Paris in early spring can be a damp, often gloomy experience. Late spring, early summer, and September are much more likely to provide the pleasant weather that presents Paris at its best. If you choose August you and all the other tourists in town will be humming, "Where have all the Parisians gone?" The answer is, "They have gone on vacation," to the other places described in our French itineraries. A Paris devoid of Parisians may sound wonderful to some people, but with most of the interesting restaurants and nightspots closed and the streets virtually deserted, Paris loses much of its appeal.

The popular Loire Valley is a place to avoid during the second half of July and all of August. If you are traveling during these busy months, try to arrange your schedule so that you visit Normandy and Brittany, where summer crowds are somewhat more manageable. This region, however, should be avoided in early spring and late autumn, as the weather is often cold and rainy and most campgrounds are closed. The best months for traveling this itinerary are June and September.

Highlights

Paris
Palace of Versailles
Normandy Invasion Beaches
Mont St. Michel
Brittany Sea Coast
Loire Valley Chateaux

Expanding Horizons

- **To France Itinerary II:** To see more of France, from Tours in the Loire Valley you can easily link up with our tour of Bordeaux, the Wine Country, and the Dordogne (for details see p. 175).
- **To France Itinerary III:** To connect with our Alsace, Provence, and Riviera routes, after completing the present itinerary, at Fontainebleau, instead of returning to Paris, follow signs to Reims (for details see p. 190).

Cherbourg
Guernsey
Jersey
St
Perros-Guirec
Emerald Coast
Lannion
DINARD
ST. MALO
9
8
Morlaix
Brest
St. Brieuc
F–111
F–110
MONT
ST. MICH
Dinan
Brittany
QUIMPER
10
F–112
Rennes
F–113
Pont
Aven
Auray
F–114
Quiberon
NANTES
F–115
F–116
11
La Baule
Loire River

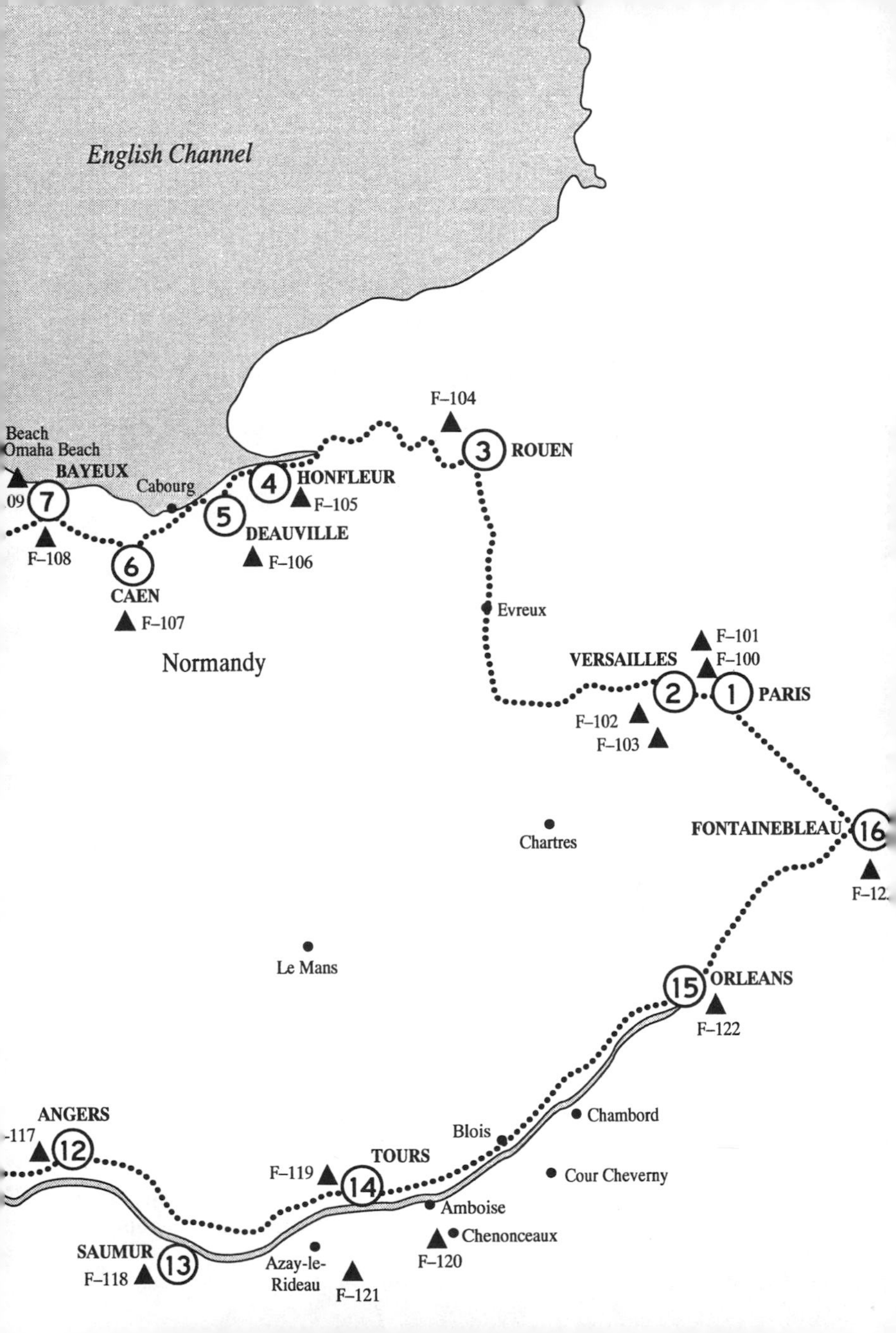

English Channel
Beach
Omaha Beach
BAYEUX
09
7
F–108
Cabourg
6
CAEN
F–107
5
DEAUVILLE
F–106
4
HONFLEUR
F–105
F–104
3
ROUEN
Normandy
Evreux
F–101
F–100
VERSAILLES
2
1
PARIS
F–102
F–103
Chartres
FONTAINEBLEAU
16
F–12
Le Mans
15
ORLEANS
F–122
Chambord
Blois
Cour Cheverny
ANGERS
-117
12
TOURS
F–119
14
Amboise
Chenonceaux
F–120
SAUMUR
13
F–118
Azay-le-
Rideau
F–121

- **The Grand Tour de France:** To combine all three French itineraries, after completing the present itinerary, continue with Itinerary II. At Beziers follow signs to Arles and Itinerary III (for details see p. 181).
- **To Tiptoeing through the Tulips Itinerary:** Head north from Paris on the Autoroute du Nord A1 to join up with our Benelux route at Tournai (for details see p. 139).
- **To British Byways Itinerary:** From Cabourg on the Normandy coast, take the ferry to Portsmouth, on the southern coast of England. The crossing time is six to seven hours (for details see p. 70).

ON THE ROAD

Numbered sites correspond with circled numbers on the itinerary map.

1. PARIS

Within the confines of a book such as this, it would be presumptuous to try to describe all or even most of the things to see and do in Paris. We will, however, list just a few of our favorites.

There is a wealth of information about Paris available. If you are not careful, you can be deluged with brochures and pamphlets and spend all of your time in Paris reading about the places that you came to see! Of the numerous Paris guidebooks, we have found the *Green Michelin Guide to Paris* to be the most useful. This is available in English at many Paris bookstores. *Plan de Paris par Arrondissement,* a street guide with separate maps of each district that includes the Metro stations, can be purchased at most bookshops and kiosks. The monthly English-language magazine *Passion* and the weekly *Pariscope* and *7 a Paris* offer detailed entertainment listings. The main Paris tourist office is at 127 Avenue des Champs-Elysees (open daily 9:00 A.M.–8:00 P.M.); phone 47 23 61 72.

With a population of more than 2 million, Paris is France's largest city. Although there has been tremendous expansion in recent years, most of this growth has radiated out from the central core toward the vast suburban areas that ring the city. Fortunately the old city nucleus, which contains Paris's most famous attractions, has been spared. From a tourist's perspective, this is an easy city to visit. The major sights and attractions are within easy walking distance of one another.

The history of Paris extends back to pre-Roman times. Although much development took place during the reign of Louis XIV and later under Napoleon, the broad boulevards, charming squares, and parks of the present-day city are the result of an extensive urban-development project undertaken in the mid-nineteenth century under the direction of Baron Georges Haussmann.

Paris is divided into twenty individual districts *(arrondissements),* each with its own town hall, or *marie.* As you negotiate your way through the city, keep the Seine River as your reference point. The Seine divides Paris into the *Rive Gauche* (Left Bank) and the *Rive Droit* (Right Bank). This division is more than just geographic. The Left Bank is known for its bohemian atmosphere; while the Right Bank, with its expansive boulevards and impressive buildings, takes on a more formal character. Try to allot sufficient time to capture the mood and spirit of the city, but forget about seeing *everything*—it's impossible!

The Left Bank

The Eiffel Tower is France's best-known landmark. This 1,000-ft.-tall steel tower was constructed for the World Exposition of 1889.

The **Hotel des Invalides,** just a few minutes' walk from the Eiffel Tower, is an impressive neo-classical structure built during the reign of Louis XIV. The lower level contains the **Tomb of Napoleon.**

The **Mosquee de Paris (Paris Mosque)** is one of the most impressive examples of Muslim Architecture in the western world. The **Pantheon,** an eighteenth-century temple built in the classical style, contains the tombs of Rousseau, Voltaire, and Hugo.

The **Luxembourg Palace and Gardens** were originally built for Marie de Medici in the early seventeenth century. The palace and extensive formal gardens offer a pleasant respite from the bustle of the surrounding Latin Quarter. **Montparnasse,** just to the south of the gardens, is the old artists' quarter, once the haunt of such Paris notables as Picasso, Hemingway, and Sartre.

The Right Bank

The Louvre, one of the world's great museums, occupies an enormous Renaissance palace on the Right Bank of the Seine. During the construction of the Palace at Versailles this was home to the royal court. The collection numbers some quarter of a million artworks and includes Da Vinci's *Mona Lisa.* The recently added glass pyramids are part of an ongoing modernization program.

The **Arc de Triomphe** and **Place de L'Etoile** were designed by Napoleon to honor his victorious armies. The massive 165-ft.-high arch is set in the Place de L'Etoile, an enormous plaza that has twelve avenues radiating from its center.

Place de la Concorde, one of the world's great squares, is a study in balance and proportion that faces the Seine amidst some of the city's most impressive landmarks. The 3,000-year-old **Obelisk** in the center of the square was a gift from the Viceroy of Egypt in 1829.

The **Marais** is a delightful quarter, a few minutes' walk from the Louvre. More than one hundred carefully restored, elegant old mansions are located there. Many now house interesting museums whose courtyards provide a delightful venue for concerts and theater performances. The **Musee d'Orsay,** a former train station, contains an outstanding collection of late-nineteenth- and early-twentieth-century art.

Beaubourg, otherwise known as **Le Centre National d'Art et de Culture Georges Pompidou,** is a fun place with an outstanding modern art collection housed in an innovative modern building. The museum is in the center of the old Les Halles market district. The neighboring streets are filled with musicians, clowns, acrobats, and a variety of other street performers.

Sacre-Coeur and **Montmartre,** the Mountain of Martyrs, the highest of the Parisian hills, is capped by the white-domed **Basilica of Sacre-Coeur.** From the gallery of the basilica there is a wonderful view of the city.

The **Cathedral of Notre-Dame,** magnificently situated on the Ile de le Cite, one of several islands in the Seine, is a Paris landmark and one of the most magnificent examples of Gothic architecture in the world.

Paris Campgrounds

F–100 ★★ Camping Caravanning du Bois de Boulogne. Open year-round. Access from the Peripherique, the motorway that rings Paris. Exit at Porte Maillot, Bois de Boulogne, and follow signs through the park to the campground. Of the several Paris area campgrounds, this is the closest to the center of the city, 6 km (3.6 mi.). Located in the Bois de Boulogne, Paris's largest park, the fifteen-acre, partly shaded site is pleasantly situated on the banks of the Seine between two bridges, the Pont de Suresnes and the Pont de Puteaux. Very crowded in summer; arrive early to ensure a space. An International Camping Carnet is required. From April to October there is a private shuttle bus from the campground to the Port Maillot station, 4 km (2.4 mi.). Public bus (#244) into Paris, 500 yd. Parking for an RV in Paris—*"c'est absolument impossible."*

F–101 ★★ Camping Caravanning International. Open year-round. In the Paris suburb of Maisons–Laffitte, 18 km (11 mi.) northwest of Paris center. (Maisons–Lafitte is the site of one of France's most attractive Baroque mansions.) From Autoroute A13 take Poissy exit. Then take D154 and N308 to Maisons-Laffitte. Follow signs to campground. A pleasant park on the banks of the Seine. Commuter train to Paris, 400 yd. Camping Carnet required.

Paris → Versailles, 24 km (14 mi.)

From the Bois de Bologne campground take N10 to Versailles. If you are in a hurry, you can take the A13 Autoroute.

2. Versailles

Europe's finest chateau and garden complex, Versailles was constructed in the late seventeenth century at the height of the reign of Louis XIV and has served as the inspiration for numerous palaces throughout Europe.

From Versailles it is only twenty-five minutes on the line C commuter train into Paris. For your visit to Paris, you can stay at a campground in Versailles and avoid the traffic and navigation problems involved in driving into the Paris campground.

Versailles Campgrounds

F–102 ★★ Camping Municipal de Porchefontaine. Open year-round. From the chateau take avenue de Paris and, after 2 km (1.2 mi.) turn right at the fourth traffic signal. Well posted with camping signs in town and at approaches from Paris. A medium-size, sloping, well-shaded site adjacent to a forest and a sports complex. Very crowded in summer. This is the most convenient campground for visiting the chateau. A forty-five-minute walk to chateau. Bus, 300 yd. Train to Paris, 1,000 yd.

F–103 ★★★ St. Quentin en Yvelines Camping du Parc Etang. Open year-round. Located 6 km (3.6 mi.) west of Versailles. From A12 turn off at St. Quentin en Yvelines and follow signs to Bois d'Arcy and campground. A twenty-five-acre, partly sloping, partly shaded site located within a large recreation complex that includes horseback riding, golf, fishing, and sailing. **Camping Carnet required.** Direct rail service to Paris and Versailles, station 1,000 yd.

Versailles → Rouen, 145 km (87 mi.)

From Versailles head west on N12 towards **Dreux.** Continue west to the intersection with N154 and take this into **Evreux,** an attractive, ancient walled city. There is an impressive twelfth-century cathedral in the town center. From Evreux follow N15 into Rouen.

3. Rouen

A busy port on the Seine River, Rouen is the capital of upper Normandy. Because of the quality and variety of the city's museums, it is known as the **Ville Musee (Museum City).** It was in Rouen, in 1431, that Joan of Arc was burned at the stake. The **Place du Vieux Marche** (old covered marketplace), now a busy modern square, has a stone marker indicating the site of the burning. The principal attraction in this city of many churches is the **Cathedrale Notre-Dame,** a masterful example of the French Gothic style.

Rouen Campground

F–104 ★★ Camping Municipal (Deville-les Rouen). Open year-round. Just off of N15, 4 km (2.4 mi.) northwest of Rouen center. Do not take autoroute to campground. A small, conveniently located, grassy site. Bus to Rouen, 200 yd.

Rouen → Honfleur, 85 km (51 mi.)

From Rouen follow the course of the Seine toward the sea along D982. Cross the river at **Tarcarville** and follow signs to Honfleur.

4. Honfleur

A picturesque seaport on the Seine estuary, Honfleur has been an important art center since the late nineteenth century. The port was an major embarkation point for the early voyages to Canada.

Honfleur Campground

F–105 ★★ Camp du Phare. Open Easter–September 30. Located in town on Boulevard Charles V. Follow signs to the outer harbor and then to campground. The site is at the end of the road just past the tennis courts. A medium, partly shaded campground directly on the Seine estuary. A fifteen-minute walk to Honfleur. No parking in town.

Honfleur → Deauville, 15 km (9 mi.)

Follow the coast road D513 along the cliffs into Deauville.

5. Deauville

Although some of the luster that made Deauville the premiere French seaside resort of the late nineteenth century has faded, the town, with its casino, racetrack and 2-mi.-long boardwalk **(le Promenade des Planches)** still attracts throngs of summertime visitors, some famous, most not so famous.

Deauville Campground

F–106 ★★ Camping de la Vallee (St. Arnoult). Open Easter–October 31. Located 2 km (1.2 mi.) south of Deauville. From Deauville take N177 (Deauville–Pont-l'Eveque) south. After 2.5 km (1.5 mi.) turn off to D27 and follow signs to the campground. A large, level, partly shaded, grassy site. Bus to Deauville, 50 yd. With the exception of July and August, it is possible to park in Deauville. –snacks

Deauville → Caen, 35 km (21 mi.)

Follow the coast road D113 through the fashionable resort towns of **Houlgate** and **Cabourg** into Caen.

Note: To connect with our British Byways itinerary, take the ferry from Cabourg to Portsmouth. For details contact Brittany Ferries, The

Brittany Centre, Wharf Road, Portsmouth PO2 8RU, England; phone (075) 827701.

6. Caen

A large, modern industrial city that was more than 75 percent destroyed following the 1944 Normandy invasion, Caen has great historical significance. Prior to his conquest of England in 1066, this was the headquarters of William of Normandy. The **Abbey aux Hommes** and **Abbey aux Dames,** twin abbeys, are fine examples of the Norman Romanesque style. To orient yourself before touring the Normandy invasion beaches, visit the **Memorial,** a museum in the north end of the city with various exhibits that bring to life the historic events of June 1944.

Caen Campground

F–107 ★ Camping Municipal. Open June 1–September 30. On the Orne River, adjacent to the sports stadium, 2 km (1.2 mi.) southwest of Caen center. From the outer ring road, follow camping signs. A medium-size, partly shaded site. No electrical hookups. Bus to Caen center, 100 yd. –900 yd.

Caen → Bayeux, 23 km (14 mi.)

Follow N13 to Bayeux.

7. Bayeux

The first town in France liberated from German occupation in World War II, Bayeux, unlike its industrial neighbor Caen, was spared major damage. It is a quiet place with a very attractive town center dominated by the imposing eleventh-century **Cathedral of Notre Dame.** The principal attraction is the famed 225-ft. embroidered scroll known as the **Bayeux Tapestry.** This remarkably well-preserved 900-year-old-artwork depicts the 1066 Norman conquest of England.

The Invasion Beaches

Bayeux, with its pleasant municipal campground, makes a good base from which to explore the Normandy invasion beaches. Beginning on

June 6, 1944, the largest invasion force in the history of the world hit the beaches on the Normandy coast. Driving along the coast road D514, you will encounter such historic sites as **Omaha Beach** and **Utah Beach,** where remnants of the German fortifications are still visible. The area is dotted with small museums whose exhibits chronicle the story of the landings.

Bayeux and Invasion Beach Campgrounds

F–108 ★★★★ Camping Municipal (Bayeux). Open March 15–November 15. At the north end of town, adjacent to the N13 bypass. Follow camping signs and turn off at the sign to St. Vigor. Across the street from a large supermarket. A large, well-kept, grassy area with many plants and shrubs. Adjacent municipal swimming pool and sports field. A five-minute walk to Bayeux center and tapestry.

F–109 ★★★ Camping Omaha Beach (Omaha Beach). Open Easter–September 15. In Vierville-sur-Mer, 18 km (11 mi.) northwest of Bayeux. On the cliffs overlooking Omaha Beach. A medium-size terraced site. Remains of a German bunker on the campground. –1,000 yd.

Bayeux → Mont St. Michel, 140 km (84 mi.)

After touring the invasion beaches, take D572 and then D592 through **St. Lo** to **Coutances.** From there follow D971 to **Granville,** and then take the coast road D911 into **Avranches.** From Avranches follow signs to **Pontaubault,** and from there take D75 across the marshy farmlands to intersect with D976. This will take you the last 2 km (1.2 mi.) to the Abbey.

8. Mont St. Michel

One of the most photographed and visited attractions in Europe, the ancient Abbey and Cloister of Mont St. Michel cling to a 250-ft. rocky isle several hundred yards offshore, connected to the mainland by a causeway. One of the best ways to enjoy the spectacular view is to spend the night in your RV in the parking lot at the end of the causeway. The sight of an illuminated Mont St. Michel in the stillness of the evening after all the busloads of tourists have departed and of the monastery looming up out of the early-morning mist is unforgettable.

Free camping at Mont St. Michel

The region is noted for its extreme tides, the highest on the continent. Be careful where you park and where you walk. The returning waters can be treacherous.

Mont St. Michel Campground

F–110 ★★ Camping du Le Mont-St Michel. Open February 1–October 31. Located behind a motel and restaurant at the intersection of D976 and D275, 2 km (1.2 mi.) from the abbey. The approaches are well marked. A large, shaded grassy site that is conveniently located for visits to the abbey. A twenty-minute walk to the abbey; or a bus, 50 yd. Plenty of parking at the abbey.

Mont St. Michel → Dinard/St. Malo, 75 km (45 mi.)

From the abbey take D976 to intersect with D979. Turn right and follow this toward St. Malo. At **Viver** the road changes to D155. Continue to **Les Portes,** where the highway crosses D76. From here you can head directly into St. Malo on D155; or you can follow D76 and then D201, secondary roads that wind and climb along the jagged coastline. This is one of the most scenic stretches of the Brittany coast.

9. Dinard/St. Malo

These old-time twin seaside resorts may have seen better days, but their spectacular setting, facing each other across the broad estuary of the Rance River, is reason enough for a visit. The ancient walled town of St. Malo was once a base for the pirates who ravaged shipping in this region. Badly damaged during World War II, the town has resumed its role as an active fishing port and popular resort. It was from St. Malo in 1535 that Jacques Cartier, the discoverer of Canada, set sail. Dinard, a somewhat tarnished, once very posh Edwardian resort, affords its visitors several lovely sandy beaches and some spectacular vistas of the fjord-like Rance Estuary. **Dinan,** some 20 km (12 mi.) south of Dinard on D766, is one of the best preserved medieval towns in Brittany.

Dinard/St. Malo Campground

F–111 ★★★ Camping la Touesse (St. Lunaire). Open Easter–October 10. In St. Lunaire on the coast road, 3 km (1.8 mi.) west of Dinard. Turn off of D786 at the camping sign. A medium-size, partly shaded, level, grassy site. Quiet location in a residential area. Three hundred yd. to an attractive sandy beach. Bus to Dinard, 50 yd.

Dinard/St. Malo → Quimper, 275 km (165 mi.)

From Dinard follow the coast road D786 through **St. Brieuc** and continue to **Lannion.** This particularly attractive part of Brittany is known as the **Emerald Coast.** At Lannion you can turn off to visit **Perros-Guirec,** a popular seaside resort with lovely beaches and a picturesque fishing harbor. Then continue on D786 to **Morlaix,** a busy yachting center with a colossal viaduct. At Morlaix pick up D785 and take this south into Quimper.

10. Quimper

In a favored location at the head of the **Bay of Kerogan,** Quimper gained recognition in the mid-eighteenth-century as a center for the production of decorative hand-painted ceramics known as *faience.* A fine collection of this type of pottery can be seen in the **Musee Breton,** housed in the former bishop's palace. The twin-towered **Gothic cathedral** is one of Brittany's finest religious structures.

Quimper Campground

F–112 ★★★★ Castel Camping L'Orangerie. Open May 1–September 15. Located 2 km (1.2 mi.) south of town. From Quimper center follow signs toward Quimper Sud and Benodet. Then follow signs to Lanniron. A large, level, grassy area in an idyllic park setting on the grounds of an old chateau that overlooks the Odet River. First-class facilities located in converted outbuildings of the chateau. Music and entertainment in July and August. This is one of the best sites in Brittany. Bus to Quimper, 800 yd.

Quimper → Nantes/Loire Valley, 260 km (156 mi.)

The delightful drive along Brittany's southern coast is highlighted by sandy beaches, rocky cliffs, and quaint fishing villages. Despite its popularity with tourists, for the most part this area has been spared the massive development that has plagued so much of the French Mediterranean coast. There is no single road that follows the entire shoreline. The main highway, N165, generally parallels the coast and runs from Brest, at the western end of the peninsula, to Nantes, at the gateway to the Loire Valley.

To explore the many bays and estuaries that line the coast, follow N165 and take excursions along the secondary roads that intersect with the main highway. The towns of **Auray** and **Locmariaquer** on the **Golfe du Morbihan** and the rugged **Quiberon Peninsula** are particularly attractive. **La Baule,** at the southern base of the Brittany Peninsula, with its palatial mansions and elegant hotels, is one of France's top resorts. The fine sandy beaches that extend for some 10 km (6 mi.) are sheltered from the winds by a 1,000-acre stretch of pines and sandy dunes.

Additional Brittany Campgrounds

F–113 ★★★ Camping Raguenes Plage (Nevez). Open April 17–September 30. On the beach at Raguenes, 9 km (5.4 mi.) south of Pont-Aven. On D783 2.5 km (1.5 mi.) west of Pont-Aven, turn off onto D77 and follow signs to Nevez to campground. A large, pleasant, partly shaded meadow with lots of bushes and flowers. Nice sandy beach, 300 yd.

F–114 ★★★★ Castel Camping La Grande Metairie (Carnac). Open May 29–September 18. Located 2 km (1.2 mi.) north of Carnac. From Auray take N768 toward Quiberon. After 8 km (4.8 mi.) take D119 to Carnac. From there follow campground signs. A large, grassy, partly shaded site that occupies an old Breton farm. Entertainment and music, mini-zoo, small lake, and three swimming pools. Beaches, 3 km (1.8 mi.). No public transportation. Parking is not a problem in this region.

F–115 ★★★ Castel Camping Le Pre du Chateau de Careil (La Baule). Open April 1–October 5. Located 2 km (1.2 mi.) north of La Baule. From La Baule take D92 and turn off at sign to Careil. Then follow campground signs. A medium-size site on the grounds of an old stone chateau. Very pleasant rural setting with many mature trees and shrubs. Adjacent to the Briere National Park and 3 km (1.8 mi.) to the medieval town of Guerande. –600 yd.

11. Nantes and the Loire Valley

This region southwest of Paris that extends west from Gien to Nantes and is traversed by the shallow, meandering Loire River is one of the most enchanting in all of Europe.

The visitor is presented with an architectural potpourri that includes elegant chateaux, medieval fortresses, and the pleasure castles built by the kings of France during the fifteenth and sixteenth centuries. The Loire region contains no fewer than 1,000 historic structures, which range from relatively modest manor houses to the 440-room "hunting lodge" at Chambord. During the summer many of the chateaux stage nighttime sound-and-light shows.

The Loire is an area that rewards those who take the time to linger and explore a bit. Side roads often lead to delightful discoveries—sometimes to an idyllic picnic spot; or, on other occasions, as has happened to us several times, perhaps to the "discovery" of a small, little-known chateau still occupied by the descendants of the original owners.

The Loire region, often referred to as the "Garden of France," produces some of the country's finest foods and wines. It is also said that the purest French is spoken here.

Although there are motorways between Nantes and Angers and between Tours and Orleans and the entire region can be traversed in a few hours, this is a place in which you should linger for at least a few days, driving the secondary roads that run along both river banks and exploring the network of country lanes that link the area's numerous small villages.

Parking in the larger cities such as Tours and Nantes is difficult and the use of public transportation is advised. The chateaux throughout the region, however, provide parking for visitors.

A prosperous Atlantic port on the Loire River, Nantes is the gateway to the Loire Valley. The **Chateau des Ducs (Ducal Castle)** is a fifteenth-century moated fortress where the pirate Bluebeard was once imprisoned.

Nantes Campground

F–116 ★★★ Camping Municipal du Val du Cens. Open April 1–September 30. Located 3 km (1.8 mi.) north of Nantes center, next to the horseracing track on N137, in the direction of Rennes. Entering Nantes from the north, follow campground signs. A large park that is nicely landscaped. Partly shaded site with individual gravel pads. Bus to Nantes, 50 yd. Limited parking at the chateau. –600 yd. –200 yd.

12. Angers

The former capital of Anjou, Angers is located on the Maine River just before it enters the Loire. The town is best known for the production of Anjou wine. The chateau, a thirteenth-century fortress with seventeen large towers, is a classic example of feudal-castle construction. The fortress houses a superb collection of tapestries, including the famous **Apocalypse Tapestry.**

Chateau Montgeoffroy, 25 km (16 mi.) east of Angers on N147, is a delightful, seldom visited eighteenth-century mansion. Still in the possession of the family of the original owners, it remains furnished as it was some 200 years ago.

Angers Campground

F–117 ★★★ Camping Lac de Maine. Open February 10–December 20. At the west end of Angers. All approaches are well marked. Head west from Angers on N23 and turn off at Bouchmaine. A medium-size, partly shaded site that is part of a large vacation complex. This is a good base for touring the region. A five-minute walk to the chateau. –900 yd.

13. Saumur

A pleasant town overlooking the Loire, Saumur is famous for its sparkling wines and mushrooms and as the home of the French National Riding Academy. The chateau, a looming structure with high walls and multiple turrets, is perched on a sheer promontory overlooking the town. It houses the **Musee de Cheval,** which depicts the history of the horse.

Saumur Campground

F–118 ★★★ Camping Ile d'Offard. Open January 15–November 30. Located in Saumur, on an island in the Loire. Next to the sports stadium. A medium-size, partly shaded site. The campus ground is conveniently situated and offers a view of the Saumur Chateau. Summertime music and entertainment. A five-minute walk to town center.

14. Tours

One of the region's major cities, Tours is an active commercial and tourist center. Although it has no major chateaux, the attractive city, with its many parks, gardens, elegant shops, and quaint old town quarter, is nevertheless well worth a visit. A stroll through the streets between the river and the ruins of the ancient **Basilica of St. Martin** will take you past a number of meticulously restored wooden houses that date back to the fifteenth century. The **Cathedral of St. Gatien,** built in the thirteenth to fifteenth centuries, ranks among the country's most attractive churches. The area is full of fine restaurants and inviting outdoor cafes.

Note: To link up with our Bordeaux and the Wine Country itinerary (Itinerary II), follow N10 south from Tours to Poiters (see p. 175 for details).

Tours Area Chateaux

Within a radius of some 50 km (30 mi.) from Tours are some of the Loire Valley's finest chateaux. Although only a small portion of the original Italian Renaissance chateau remains, **Amboise** is well worth a visit. Of interest is the fact that Leonardo da Vinci spent the last years of his life here. He is buried in the **Chapelle St. Hubert.** The **Clos-Luce,** where he lived, is now a museum containing replicas of his numerous inventions.

The imposing **Chateau Azay-le-Rideau,** surrounded by water, is idyllically placed in a forested setting. This is one of the Loire's most graceful structures, whose furnished interior offers a good insight into the Renaissance life of the region.

The chateau at **Blois** commands a hill above the Loire. This huge complex presents visitors with a startling conglomeration of architectural styles that reflect some four centuries of construction. The chateau is richly decorated, full of secret panels, and has a fascinating history of court intrigues and assassinations.

Set in a magnificent 13,600-acre forest, the chateau at **Chambord,** with its 440 rooms and 365 chimneys, is the largest of the Loire chateaux. The building itself is almost devoid of furnishings, but its sheer immensity, impressive Renaissance facade, and assortment of gables, pinnacles, and vast expanse of lawns make a stop here a memorable occasion.

Chenonceaux was a gift from Henri II to his mistress, Diane de Poiters, to celebrate his ascension to the throne in 1547. The most graceful and aesthetically pleasing of all the Loire region chateaux, Chenonceaux is suspended by a series of arches over the Cher River.

The **Chateau Cour-Cheverny** was completed in 1634, in the classical style. Richly decorated and warmly furnished, it is still in the hands of the family of the original owners. This is great hunting country, and in addition to a museum with some 2,000 sets of antlers, the chateau still maintains an active pack of seventy magnificent hunting dogs.

Tours Area Campgrounds

F–119 ★★★ Camping Municipal des Rives du Cher (Tours/St. Avertin). Open March 1–October 30. Located just south of the Cher River in the village of St. Avertin. Located 5 km (3 mi.) southeast of Tours. Adjacent to the municipal swimming pool. A large, grassy

A chateau campground

meadow with some trees. Bus to Tours, 100 yd. A five-minute walk to village with shops and restaurants.

F–120 ★★★ Camping du Moulin (Chenonceaux). Open April 15–September 15. On the river bank at the edge of the village, just east of the bridge over the Cher River. A medium-size, long, narrow, grassy site with little shade. Nearest bus, 1 km (0.6 mi.). –1.2 mi.

F–121 ★★★★ Le Parc de Fierbois (St. Catherine de Fierbois). Open May 24–September 15. In village of St. Catherine de Fierbois, 22 km (13 mi.) south of Tours. From N10 turn off to village and follow campground signs. A large, grassy site on a wooded estate with a lake and swimming pool. A quiet base to use for touring the Loire region. No public transportation.

Tours → Orleans, 114 km (71 miles)

Follow N152 along the north bank of the Loire through **Blois** into Orleans.

15. Orleans

An active commercial center and one of the district's major cities, Orleans was badly damaged during World War II. It is best known as the site where Joan of Arc relieved the city from the siege of the Burgundians. With the exception of the equestrian statue of the Maid of Orleans, the city contains little of interest. The **Benedictine Abbey** at **St.-Benoit-sur-Loire,** 30 km (18 mi.) east on D60, the burial place of the order's founder St. Benedict, is one of the finest Romanesque structures in France.

Orleans Campground

F–122 ★★ Camping Municipal (Olivet). Open April 1–October 15. In Olivet, 2 km (1.2 mi.) south of Orleans. Follow signs from N20. A small, partly shaded, grassy meadow on the banks of the Loire River. Bus to Orleans, 150 yd.

Orleans → Fontainebleau, 77 km (46 mi.)

Take N152 directly into Fontainebleau.

16. Fontainebleau

The palace, gardens, and forest of Fontainebleau are close to the hearts of true Frenchmen—to many even more so than Versailles. The palace was built in the twelfth century, mainly in the Italian Renaissance style. It was at Fontainebleau that Napoleon signed his abdication papers.

Fontainebleau Campground

F–123 ★★ Camping Base de Plein Air (Samois sur Seine). Open year-round. On the Seine River in the Fontainebleau forest, 6 km (3.6 mi.) south of the palace. From Samois sur Seine follow campground signs. A small, shaded, grassy area. International Camping Carnet required. No public transportation. –1.2 mi.

Note: To link up with our Tiptoeing through the Tulips itinerary, take the ring road around Paris and continue north on the A1 Autoroute du Nord to Tournai in Belgium (see p. 139).

Fontainebleau → Paris, 50 km (30 mi.)

To return to Paris take Autoroute A6 or N7 into the city.

Itinerary II: Bordeaux and the Wine Country · The Dordogne

START: Paris

COUNTRY: France

DISTANCE: 2,100 km (1,260 mi.)

MAPS: Michelin #989 *France; #237 Paris Region; #238 Centre; #232 Pays de Loire; #233 Poitou–Charentes;* #234 Aquitaine; #235 *Midi-Pyrenees*

MINIMUM RECOMMENDED TOURING TIME: 14 to 18 days

INTRODUCTION

Appealing to the experienced and the novice European traveler alike, this itinerary combines visits to some of France's less heavily traveled regions—the Poitou–Charentes, the Dordogne and Lot valleys, and the rugged reaches of the Aveyron—with a number of better-known destinations, including Chartres, the medieval walled city of Carcassonne, and the Bordeaux wine country.

WHEN TO GO

The best times for traveling this route are May, June, and September. October, in this part of France, can also be a good time for touring. Many campgrounds close by mid-September, however, and in October the chances of encountering chilly and rainy weather are greatly increased.

HIGHLIGHTS

Paris
Versailles
Chartres
Loire Valley Chateaux
La Rochelle
Bordeaux and the Wine Country
Sarlat-la-Caneda
Rocamadour
Carcassonne
Fontainebleau

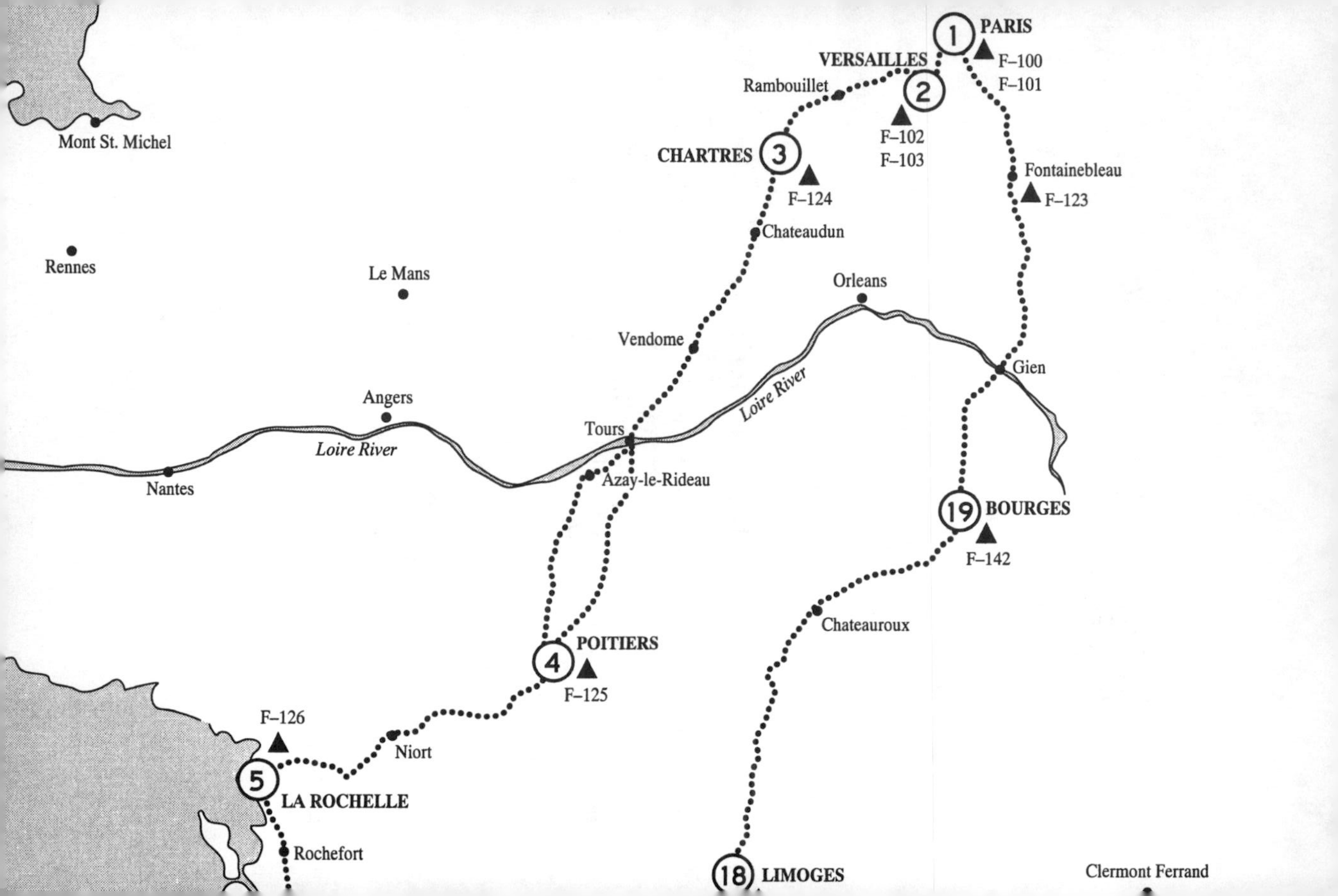

1 PARIS
F–100
F–101
VERSAILLES
2
F–102
F–103
Rambouillet
Mont St. Michel
CHARTRES
3
F–124
Fontainebleau
F–123
Chateaudun
Rennes
Le Mans
Orleans
Vendome
Gien
Angers
Loire River
Tours
Loire River
Nantes
Azay-le-Rideau
19 BOURGES
F–142
Chateauroux
4 POITIERS
F–125
F–126
Niort
5
LA ROCHELLE
Rochefort
18 LIMOGES
Clermont Ferrand

Atlantic Ocean
Medoc
Pauillac
Hourtin
F–129
Blaye
Margaux
Libourne
F–128
BORDEAUX
6
F–127
St. Emilion
7
F–130
Beaumont
BERGERAC
Monpazier
PERIGUEUX
17
F–140
LES EYZIES
16
15
SARLAT-LA-CANEDA
Souillac
F–139
F–138
14
ROCAMADOUR
Brive
F–137
13
FIGEAC
F–136
12
RODEZ
F–135
Fumel
France
F–131
8
MONTAUBAN
Gaillac
ALBI
9
F–132
Requista
Lacaune
St. Gervais
Murat
Herepian
Castres
Toulouse
BEZIERS
11
CARCASSONNE
10
F–133
F–134
Valras Plage
Lourdes
Perpignan
Pyrenees
Andorra
Spain

Expanding Horizons

- **To France Itinerary III:** At Beziers head north to Arles (see p. 199).
- **To Iberian Itinerary:** At Bordeaux follow N10 south toward Madrid (see p. 217).

ON THE ROAD

Numbered sites correspond with circled numbers on the itinerary map.

1. Paris/2. Versailles

See France Itinerary I, pp. 154–58.

Versailles → Chartres, 70 km (42 mi.)

Head south from Versailles on D938 through **Chateaufort** to intersect with N306 at **St. Remy-les-Chevreuse.** Take N306 into **Rambouillet,** a delightful town surrounded by a large forest. The town is known for its fourteenth- to eighteenth-century chateau. From Rambouillet take D906 into Chartres.

3. Chartres

As you approach the town, you can make out the towering twin spires of **Chartres Cathedral** in the distance. One of the best-known cathedrals in Europe, the current thirteenth-century Gothic edifice was built on the site of an earlier Romanesque church that was destroyed by fire in 1194.

Chartres Campground

F–124 ★ Camping Municipal des Bords de L'Eure. Open Easter–September 30. One km (0.6 mi.) southeast of town center. From N154 in the direction of Orleans, turn off and follow camping signs. A medium-size, grassy site on the banks of the Eure River. Very crowded in summer. Pleasant fifteen-minute walk along the river to town. Bus to Chartres, 50 yd. –1.2 mi.

Chartres → Tours (Loire Valley), 140 km (84 mi.)

Take N10 south from Chartres through **Chateaudun** and **Vendome** (attractive gardens and ruined chateau) into **Tours.**

Note: To Tours and the Loire Valley, see Itinerary I, pp. 167.

Tours → Poitiers, 105 km (63 mi.)

From Tours head south on N10 directly into Poitiers. As N10 is often congested with truck traffic, a less direct but more relaxed and scenic route is via D751 west to **Azay-le-Rideau,** then D757 south to Poitiers.

4. Poitiers

During the Middle Ages, thanks to its strategic location midway on the vital Paris–Bordeaux trade route, Poitiers developed into one of France's major commercial, religious, and learning centers. The old-town quarter, little changed over the centuries, enjoys a splendid hilltop position overlooking the Clain River.

Poitiers Campground

F–125 ★★★ Park de Loisers de St. Cyr. Open March 15–October 30. In St. Cyr along the Clain River, 8 km (4.8 mi.) northwest of Poitiers. From Poitiers take N10 north to Beaumont; then follow campground signs. A large, grassy site with young trees. Adjacent lake for water sports. Bus, 500 yd.

Poitiers → La Rochelle, 130 km (78 mi.)

Leave Poitiers southbound on N11 and follow this to **Niort.** Continue on N11 into La Rochelle.

5. La Rochelle

A modern-day yachting center, La Rochelle is centered around **Vieux Port,** the picturesque old port whose entrance is guarded by twin fourteenth-century towers. The **Museum of the New World** chronicles the town's historical links with the Americas.

La Rochelle Campground

F–126 ★★★ Camping Le Trepied du Plumb. Open Whitsunday–September 25. Take N237 toward the bridge. At Lagord turn off onto D104. Then follow signs to L'Houmeau. The campground is just past the airfield. A medium-size, grassy site, slightly inclined and offering little shade. Beach, 800 yd. No public transportation. A thirty-minute walk to old port. Difficult parking in town. –400 yd. –300 yd. –800 yd.

La Rochelle → Bordeaux, 175 km (105 mi.)

Take N137 south along the coast to **Rochefort** and continue on D733 to **Royan** at the mouth of the Gironde Estuary. From Royan take D145 to **Blaye** (ancient fortress) and from there follow D669 to intersect with N10. Take N10 across the bridge into Bordeaux.

6. Bordeaux and the Wine Country

Pleasantly situated on the **Garonne River,** Bordeaux, one of France's most attractive major cities, proudly lays claim to the title of "wine capital of the world."

The expansive **Esplanade des Quinconces,** Europe's largest formal square, was laid out in 1820. Its gardens and impressive monuments overlook the Garonne. The city's rich architectural heritage is reflected in such outstanding buildings as the **Grand Theater,** the **Bourse,** and the **Hotel de Ville.** The **Cathedrale St. Andre,** a stunning edifice with sections dating back to the eleventh century, is Bordeaux's principal church.

Note: To link up with our Iberian Interlude itinerary, follow N10 south from Bordeaux and cross into Spain at Hendaye. Continue to Madrid by way of Burgos (see p. 217).

The Wine Country

The countryside surrounding Bordeaux has been producing fine wines since the days when Bordeaux was a Roman city. The names of the towns and villages in the region read like a who's who in the world of wine. The following wine centers are all within about a half hour's drive of Bordeaux.

With its rambling stone houses, and winding streets, **St. Emilion** is one of the most charming wine villages in the whole of France. Even if you have absolutely no interest in the fermented juice of the grape, be sure to visit this enchanting village.

Libourne is a small, engaging market town on the Dordogne River. Libourne is the shipping point for much of the region's wine.

The tiny village of **Margaux** exists primarily in support of the famous **Chateau Margaux.** The chateau itself, built in the classical style in the beginning of the nineteenth century, is surrounded by fastidiously manicured gardens. The rich-bodied red wine produced here is considered by connoisseurs to be one of the world's finest.

A small town in a pleasant setting on the Gironde River, **Pauillac** is best known as the location of the famous **Chateau Mouton Rothschild** and **Chateau Lafitte Rothschild.**

Soulac-sur-Mer is an attractive seaside resort whose fine sandy beach is backed by dunes and woods that extend for some 7 km (4.2 mi.).

Bordeaux Area Campgrounds

F–127 ★★ Camping les Gravieres (Bordeaux). Open year-round. In Villenave-D'Ornon, 7 km (4.2 mi.) southeast of Bordeaux center. From Bordeaux head south on A630 (ring road) and take exit #20—Begles–Durot—then follow camping signs. A medium-size, well-shaded site in a pleasant setting surrounded by three small lakes. Swimming is not permitted. Bus to Bordeaux, 50 yd. Limited parking available in Bordeaux.

F–128 ★★★ Camping Barbanne (St. Emilion). Open April 1–October 10. From St. Emilion take D122 2.5 km (1.5 mi.) north toward Lussac to the campground. A large, pleasant, grassy site at the edge of a lake surrounded by vineyards. Many large trees. No public transportation. Adequate parking in St. Emilion. A forty-minute walk to town.

F–129 ★★★★ Airotel de la Cote d'Argent (Hourtin Plage). Open May 15–September 15. On the beach at the terminus of D101–E7. Located 60 km (36 mi.) northwest of Bordeaux. From D101 turn off to the beach at Hourtin between Soullac and Lacanau. Approaches are well marked. A large, self-contained camping village located on a broad, sandy beach. Large lake, 4 km (2.4 mi.). Site is sandy with many pines and shade trees. Entertainment and music. An excellent place to relax after city touring.

Bordeaux → Bergerac, 92 km (55 mi.)

Take N89 east to **Libourne** and then D936 along the **Dordogne River** to Bergerac.

7. Bergerac

Spread out on both sides of the Dordogne, Bergerac is the principal town in the southern Dordogne region and the center of an important wine and tobacco industry. Stroll through the flower-bedecked old town with its Renaissance facades and narrow, winding streets. The town is associated with the famed Cyrano de Bergerac, whose statue stands in the **Place de la Myrpe.** Also of interest is the **Tobacco Museum,** housed in a seventeenth-century mansion. Just south of Bergerac are the ornately fortified sixteenth-century **Monbazillac Chateau** and the **Monbazillac Vineyards,** producer of some of the region's finest wines.

Bergerac Campground

F–130 ★★ Camping Municipal la Pelouse. Open year-round. Just south of town on the south bank of the Dordogne. In Bergerac follow CENTRE VILLE signs, then campground signs. A medium-size, partly shaded site. A thirty-minute walk to town. –500 yd. –500 yd.

Bergerac → Montauban, 157 km (94 mi.)

Head west on D660 following the north bank of the Dordogne. At **Port de Couze** cross the river and continue on D660 through the fortified towns *(bastides)* of **Beaumont** and **Monpazier.** From Monpazier stay on D660 to the intersection with D710. Turn here and follow signs to **Fumel,** an industrial town on the **Lot River.** Take D102 south from Fumel and continue over a winding, hilly stretch of road to join D927. Continue into Montauban.

8. Montauban

An important agricultural market center on the **Tarn River,** Montauban is characterized by its pink brick buildings. The town is also the birthplace of the painter Jean Auguste Dominique Ingres. A **museum** displaying his works is located in a former seventeenth-century Episcopal palace.

Montauban Campground

F–131 ★★ Rural Camping de Pech-Boyer. Open year-round. Located 2 km (1.2 mi.) south of town. Take D21 south toward Toulouse. Turn off at Corbarieu and follow signs to campground. A small site with little shade. –1 mi.

Montauban → Albi, 72 km (45 mi.)

Take D999 east to **Gaillac** and from there follow N88 into Albi.

9. Albi

Albi, the birthplace of Toulouse-Lautrec, is a well-preserved town of red brick buildings and winding streets. Of particular interest are the **Musee Toulouse-Lautrec** and the fortresslike **Cathedrale St.-Cecile.**

Albi Campground

F–132 ★★★ Camping de Caussels. Open April 1–October 10. Located 2 km (1.2 mi.) east of town. From Albi head toward Millau on D999 and D100 toward St. Jury. Follow campground signs. Turnoff to the campground is near a large supermarket. A small, well-shaded site. No public transportation. A thirty-minute walk to town. –300 yd.

Albi → Carcassonne, 107 km (64 mi.)

N112 runs south from Albi to **Castres** and then continues to intersect with D118. The road passes through the **Parc Regional du Haut Languedoc** and then crosses the **Noire Mountains** before winding down into Carcassonne.

10. Carcassonne

Carcassonne, which lies at the foot of the **Pyrenees Mountains,** is one of the great fortress cities of Europe. A massive complex of towers and walls, its construction dates back to the fifth century. The medieval town walls, the longest in Europe, enclose an active city filled with artisans, restaurants, and souvenir shops.

Note: To link up with our Iberian Interlude itinerary, head south

The fortress city of Carcassonne (Courtesy French Government Tourist Office)

from Carcassonne across the Pyrenees to Barcelona and continue to Madrid (see p. 217).

Carcassonne Campground

F–133 ★★★ Campeole La Cite. Open March 1–October 30. From Carcassonne town cross the river and head south on D104. Follow signs to campground. A large site with little shade; located on a small river within sight of the walled city. Bus to medieval city, 200 yd. A twenty-minute walk to old town. Plenty of parking.

Carcassonne → Beziers, 70 km (42 mi.)

Head east on N113 and after 5 km (3 mi.), at the interchange, continue northeast on D610 to Beziers. For the first part of the way, the road follows the **Canal du Midi.**

11. Beziers

Located on the **Orb River,** just a few kilometers from the Mediterranean, Beziers is the wine-producing center of the Languedoc–Roussillon region. The **Allees Paul-Riquet** in the old town is a labyrinth of passageways lined with art galleries, craft shops, and museums.

Note: To link up with our French Itinerary III, take either the Autoroute A9 or Hwy. N112 north to Arles (see p. 199).

Bezier Campground

F–134 ★★★★ Camping La Plage et du Bord de Mer (Beziers/Valras Plage). Open June 1–September 10. At the beach in Valras Plage, 12 km (7.2 mi.) west of Beziers on D19. One of the best of many campgrounds at this popular beach resort. A large, self-contained camping complex with private beach. Entertainment, music, and disco. Bus to town, 50 yd.

Beziers → Rodez, 185 km (111 mi.)

This climbing, tortuous route will take you through a little-known and rugged part of France crossing the **Monts de L'Espinouse** and **Monts de Lacaune** in the sparsely populated **Aveyron district.** Head out of Beziers on D909, following signs toward **Bedarieux** and **Herepian.** At Herepian continue on D13 to **St. Gervais,** then on D922 to **Murat.** From Murat take D622 to **Lacaune.** Continue on D607 to **St. Sernin.** From St. Sernin follow D33 to **Requista** and into Rodez D902.

12. Rodez

The capital of the Aveyron district, Rodez is known for its pink sandstone **Cathedral of Notre-Dame.**

Rodez Campground

F–135 ★★ Camping Municipal de Layoule. Open June 1–September 30. In town, next to the river at the bottom of a steep hill. Well marked. A small, terraced site with some shade. Bus to town, 50 yd. A fifteen-minute walk to town center. –1,000 yd. –500 yd.

Rodez → Figeac, 63 km (38 mi.)

Take N140 from Rodez into Figeac.

13. Figeac

Once an important way station on the pilgrimage route to Santiago de Compostela, this delightful little town has many well-preserved medieval houses and an **abbey church** that dates back to the twelfth century.

Figeac Campground

F–136 ★★ Camping les Carmes. Open March 15–October 31. Near the church at the northwest edge of town. From Figeac take N140 toward Brive. Turn off at campground sign. A small meadow, with some shade trees. A fifteen-minute walk to town.

Figeac → Rocamadour, 48 km (29 mi.)

Leave Figeac on N140, following signs toward **Brive.** At km 42 (25 mi.) turn off and take D673 B to Rocamadour.

14. Rocamadour

An important pilgrimage site since the Middle Ages, Rocamadour is one of the most dramatically situated towns in all of France. The medieval town is arranged in tiers and set into the sheer face of a 1,600-ft. cliff. At the top of the cliff, lining the **Place St.-Amadour,** are several impressive churches.

Rocamadour Campground

F–137 ★★ Camping Le Relais du Campeur. Open April 1–October 15. Located behind grocery store at l'Hospitelet, 4 km (2.4 mi.) east of Rocamadour. Approaches are well marked. A medium-size, partly shaded site.

Rocamadour → Sarlat-la-Caneda, 66 km (39 mi.)

Take D673 out of Rocamadour and follow this to **Payrac.** Then take N20 north to **Souillac.** At Souillac turn onto D703, which runs along the Dordogne River into Sarlat-la-Caneda.

15. Sarlat-la-Caneda

One of the most charming medieval towns in the Dordogne region, Sarlat-la-Caneda is a living museum where busy shops and restaurants occupy meticulously restored ancient half-timbered houses.

Sarlat-la-Caneda Campground

F–138 ★★★★ Camping les Perieres. Open Easter–September 30. On D47 1 km (0.6 mi.) east of town. A large, terraced site that is part of a vacation complex, with many trees and shrubs. Good view of Sarlat from the campground. Entertainment and music during July and August. A twenty-minute walk to town. Parking in Sarlat is difficult. No public transportation. –800 yd.

Sarlat-la-Caneda → Les Eyzies, 21 km (13 mi.)

Follow D47 out of Sarlat-la-Caneda to Les Eyzies.

16. Les Eyzies

A tiny village situated in a region of steep cliffs at the confluence of the **Vezere** and **Beune rivers,** Les Eyzies has become a Mecca for students of prehistory. In the mid-nineteenth century a wealth of prehistoric dwellings, skeletons, artifacts, and cave paintings were unearthed in and around Les Eyzies that attracted archaeologists from all over. The **National Museum of Prehistory,** housed in the castle of the former barons of Beynac, contains one of the finest collections of its kind anywhere in the world.

Les Eyzies Campground

F–139 ★★ Camping Le Vezere Perigord. Open Easter–September 30. Located 6 km (3.6 mi.) northeast of Les Eyzies. Turn off of D706 at the campground sign, 800 yd. north of Tursac, in the direction of Montignac. A medium-size, well-shaded site in a wooded area. Individual sites are terraced into a steep hill. No public transportation. Parking available in Les Eyzies.

Les Eyzies → Perigueux, 45 km (27 mi.)

Continue on D47 to D710. Take this to N89 for the last few kilometers into Perigueux.

17. Perigueux

An ancient town with its origins in pre-Roman times, Perigueux, after succumbing to Caesar and his legions, flourished and became one of the most important Roman towns in Aquitaine. Although the city was sacked by the Vandals in the third century, the ruins of a vast **amphitheater,** a **Roman villa,** and the **Tower of Vesunna** are visible remnants of the city's Roman past.

Perigueux Campground

F–140 ★★ Camping Barnabe Plage. Open year-round. On N21–N89 toward **Brive,** 1 km (0.6 mi.) from town center. A medium-size, partly shaded site on the **Isle River.** A fifteen-minute walk to town. No public transportation.

Perigueux → Limoges, 102 km (61 mi.)

Follow N21 north to Limoges.

18. Limoges

The discovery, in 1768, of clay of an unusual degree of purity in nearby Saint-Yrieix, led to the development of Limoges as one of the world's major china-producing centers. Several of the china factories are open to the public.

Limoges Campground

F–141 ★★ Camping Municipal la Vallee de l'Aurence. Open year-round. Located 3 km (1.8 mi.) north of city center on N20 toward Chateauroux. Follow signs toward Limoges Nord Zone Industrielle and then camping signs. A medium-size, level site with little shade. Next to a small, man-made lake and a sports and recreation park. Bus to town, 50 yd. –1,000 yd.

Limoges → Bourges, 192 (115 mi.)

From Limoges take N20 north through the **Forest of Chateauroux** to the cigarette-manufacturing town of **Chateauroux.** From there follow N151 to Bourges.

19. BOURGES

An important cultural center, Bourges is the site of one of the most elaborate Gothic structures in France, the **Palais Jacques-Coeur.**

Bourges Campground

F–142 ★★ Camping Municipal. Open March 15–November 15. On the ring road midway between junction of N144 and N76, 1 km (0.6 mi.) south of town center. A small, partly terraced, gravel site with little shade. No public transportation. Limited parking in Bourges. –800 yd. & –400 yd.

Bourges → Fontainebleau, 165 km (99 mi.)

Head north on N940 to **Gien,** a charming pottery-making center on the Loire River. Continue north to intersect with N7 and follow this into Fontainebleau.

Fontainebleau → Paris

To return to Paris take Autoroute A6 or N7 into the city.

Itinerary III: Paris • Alsace • The Riviera • Provence • Burgundy

START: Paris

COUNTRY: France

DISTANCE: 2,600 km (1,560 mi.)

MAPS: Michelin #989 *France;* #237 *Paris Region;* #241 *Champagne–Ardennes;* #242 *Alsace et Lorraine;* #243 *Bourgogne–Franche–Comte;* #244 *Rhone–Alpes;* #245 *Provence–Cote d'Azur;* #246 *Vallee du Rhone*

MINIMUM RECOMMENDED TOURING TIME: 10 to 14 days

INTRODUCTION

This itinerary offers a wonderful opportunity to combine touring some of France's most appealing but less frequently visited regions with such popular areas as Provence and the Riviera.

In Reims, you can see how champagne is made. In the often disputed region of Alsace–Lorraine, along the German border you will note the interesting melding of German rigor with French *laissez faire.*

For a change of climate and pace, we head south, crossing the Alpes Maritimes to the famed Cote d'Azur, one of the world's most popular adult playgrounds. In Provence, where the architecture of the sun-drenched towns reflects the area's long years under Roman domination, we view some of Europe's most outstanding Roman ruins. Our return route to Paris takes us up the Rhone Valley, through Lyon and into the heart of Burgundy, a region particularly noted for its fine wines and superb food.

WHEN TO GO

Alsace–Lorraine and Burgundy can be explored even in July and August without encountering overwhelming crowds or stifling heat. That is definitely not the case along the Riviera, where travel with an RV or any other mode of travel in July and August is virtually impossible. Campgrounds are hopelessly overflowing, traffic along the coast road doesn't flow at all, and it's difficult even to see the sand on the beaches for all of the basking bodies.

Our recommendations for touring this otherwise charming part of France are May and early June and late September and October. During the winter most campgrounds and other places along the coast are closed and the region takes on a pleasant out-of-season ambience. In late spring and early autumn, Provence offers some of Europe's finest RV touring opportunities.

HIGHLIGHTS

Paris
Versailles
Fontainebleau
Reims
Strasbourg
The Riviera
Arles
Avignon
Beaune

EXPANDING HORIZONS

- **To France Itinerary II:** Connect with this itinerary at Beziers (see p. 181).
- **To France Itinerary I:** Use Paris as a hub to connect with this itinerary (see p. 154).
- **To Italian Impressions Itinerary:** From Monte Carlo head east into Italy and follow the coast to Genoa (see p. 245).
- **To Alpine Heights and Old World Delights Itinerary:** From Strasbourg take the autobahn to Frankfurt (see p. 332). From Annecy head north to Geneva (see p. 349).

ON THE ROAD

Numbered sites correspond with circled numbers on the itinerary map.

1. PARIS/2. VERSAILLES

See France Itinerary I, pp. 154–58.

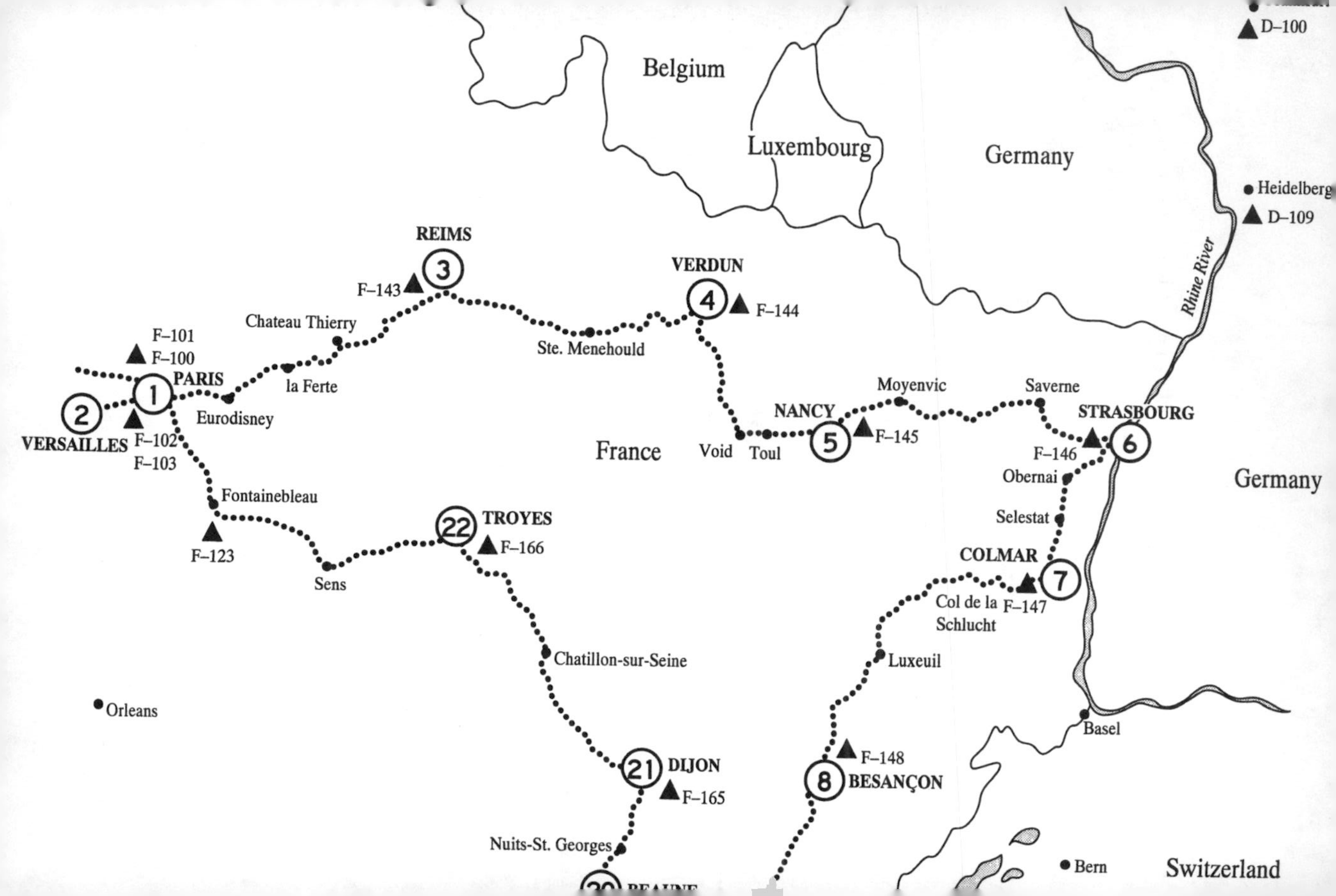
Belgium
Luxembourg
Germany
Heidelberg
D–100
D–109
Rhine River
REIMS
3
F–143
VERDUN
4
F–144
Chateau Thierry
F–101
F–100
PARIS
1
2
VERSAILLES
F–102
F–103
la Ferte
Eurodisney
Ste. Menehould
Moyenvic
Saverne
NANCY
5
F–145
STRASBOURG
6
F–146
France
Void
Toul
Obernai
Germany
Fontainebleau
F–123
22
TROYES
F–166
Sens
Selestat
COLMAR
7
F–147
Col de la
Schlucht
Chatillon-sur-Seine
Luxeuil
Orleans
Basel
F–148
21
DIJON
F–165
8
BESANÇON
Nuits-St. Georges
Bern
Switzerland

Cluny
Nantua
CH–107
Geneva
CH–108
CH–109
Zermatt
Bourg-en-Bresse
Villefranche
9
ANNECY
F–149
Aosta
19
LYON
F–163
France
Aix-les-Bains
Chambery
Vienne
Voiron
Turin
10
GRENOBLE
F–150
Romans
Valence
Rhône River
Gap
Italy
Valreas
DIGNE
18
ORANGE
11
F–162
F–151
NIMES
16
17
F–161
AVIGNON
F–160
Tarascon
Grasse
Nice
Monte Carlo
F–159
ARLES
14
Les Baux
Villefranche
AIGUES-MORTES
15
F–158
Antibes
F–155
CANNES
Ste-Maries-de-la-Mer
Frejus
12
Beziers
F–154
La Couronne
St. Aygulf
Carcassonne
13
MARSEILLES
Saint-Tropez
F–157
Le Lavandou
Toulon
F–153
Mediterranean Sea
F–156
F–152
Mediterranean Se

Versailles → Reims, 175 km (105 mi.)

From Versailles pick up the ring road around Paris and head east on the Autoroute A4 toward Reims. To visit **Eurodisney,** exit the autoroute at **Marne-la-Vallee.** Although you can stay on the high-speed autoroute all the way into Reims, the side roads offer a much more pleasant alternative and afford the opportunity to explore the World War I battlefields around **Chateau-Thierry** and **Belleau Wood.** Exit the autoroute at **la Ferte** and follow D402 and D15 along the **Marne River** into Chateau-Thierry; and from there take RD380 to Reims.

3. Reims

The center of the French champagne industry, Reims is also known for its magnificent thirteenth-century, Gothic **Cathedrale Notre-Dame.** A visit to Reims should also include a tour of one of the several mazelike champagne cellars that have been hewn out of chalk and which lie beneath the city.

Reims Campground

F–143 ★★ Airotel de Champagne. Open Easter–September 30. On N44, 4 km (2.4 mi.) southeast of town. Approaching from A4, take Cathedrale/Reims/Cormontreuil exit and follow campground signs. A large, pleasant, grassy site. Bus to town, 800 yd.

Reims → Verdun, 118 km (71 mi.)

Take N44 southeast from Reims. Then follow RD31 to **Ste. Menehould.** From there continue on N3 traversing the **Meuse–Argonne region** and continuing into Verdun. This region saw some of the fiercest fighting during World War I. Remnants of shell craters and earthen fortifications are still visible.

4. Verdun

During World War I Verdun was the site of a long and bitter siege that stopped the German advance on Paris. Excursions can be made to the battlefields along the route marked **Circuit des Forts.**

Verdun Campground

F–144 ★★ Camping les Breuils. Open April 1–October 15. At the west edge of town, 500 yd. from N3. Approaches are well marked. A large, grassy site with a small lake. Easy walk into town.

Verdun → Nancy, 100 km (60 mi.)

Follow the **Meuse River** south from Verdun on D964. At **Void** take N4 east into the old walled town of **Toul.** Continue on A31 into Nancy.

5. Nancy

The historic capital of the province of Lorraine, Nancy boasts a number of architectural treasures that span from the Middle Ages to the Belle Epoque. Many of the most interesting buildings are clustered around the eighteenth-century **Place Stanislas.**

Nancy Campground

F–145 ★★ Camping Municipal de Brabois. Open April 1–October 31. In the suburb of Villers-les-Nancy, 6 km (3.6 mi.) southwest of Nancy. From A33 take Nancy–Brabois exit and follow camping signs. A large, sloping, grassy area in a pleasant park setting next to a horseracing track. Bus to Nancy, 100 yd.

Nancy → Strasbourg, 145 km (86 mi.)

From Nancy head east across the Alsace. You will pass through a procession of immaculately kept, flower-bedecked villages whose names and architecture reflect the region's strong Germanic heritage. Take N74 to **Moyenvic** and from there continue on D955 to intersect with N4, which will take you to **Saverne.** Stay on N4 into Strasbourg.

6. Strasbourg

The Alsatian capital, separated from Germany by the **Rhine River,** is the seat of a number of important European institutions. Strasbourg, perhaps more than any other city, has come to symbolize the spirit of Franco–German reconciliation and the new Europe that is striving for unity. The **Cathedrale Notre-Dame,** with its pink-colored facade and nearly 500-ft.-high ornate spire dominates the city's center.

Note: To link up with our Alpine Heights and Old World Delights itinerary, cross the Rhine and take the A5 Autobahn north to Frankfurt (see p. 332).

Strasbourg Campground

F–146 ★★ Camping Montagne Verte. Open March 1–October 31. At the southwest edge of the city, off of D392. From Strasbourg follow signs toward St. Die, then follow campground signs. From the autoroute exit at "sortie" #4. Campground is 2 km (1.2 mi.) from city center and train station. A medium-size, grassy site with many trees. Next to the sports stadium. Parking in Strasbourg is very difficult. Bus 3, 13, 23 from campground to downtown.

Strasbourg → Colmar, 75 km (45 mi.)

Head south on N422 to **Obernai,** one of the most attractive towns in the Alsace. Continue on N422 to **Selestat,** site of several impressive churches. Take D10 from **Selestat** to **Ribeauville** and continue to **Riquewhir,** a quaint wine-producing village with an unusual **Postal Museum.** Stay on D10 into Colmar.

7. Colmar

Colmar is an attractive medieval city with many old houses with carved facades and balconies lining the narrow streets. The **Musee Bartholdi** is dedicated to Colmar's native son Frederic Auguste Bartholdi, the creator of the Statue of Liberty. The nearby fortified town of **Turckheim** is a popular resort.

Colmar Campground

F–147 ★★★ Camping Municipal les Cigognes (Turckheim). Open March 15–October 31. From Colmar take N417 to Wintzenheim. Turn off to Turckheim. Do not cross the bridge at Turckheim but continue past the train station and sports stadium to the campground. A medium-size, grassy area with many shade trees, in a pleasant setting alongside a canal. Camping Carnet required. A fifteen-minute walk to town. –800 yd.

Colmar → Besancon, 187 km (112 mi.)

Take D417 west from Colmar. The road winds and climbs over the rugged **Col de la Schlucht** (1,140 m/3,762 ft.) and continues into the village of **Gerardmer.** From there follow signs to **Plombieres** and **Luxeuil.** Take N57 south into Besancon.

8. Besancon

The center of the French watch-making industry, Besancon, in the heart of the **Jura Mountains,** is an attractive fortified town with an impressive citadel. The **Musee des Beaux Arts (Fine Arts Museum),** one of the oldest in France, contains an important collection of ancient timepieces. Besancon also is the birthplace of the nineteenth-century French author Victor Hugo.

Besancon Campground

F–148 ★★ Camping Municipal de la Plage. Open March 1–December 15. Located 5 km (3 mi.) northeast of town off of N83, in the direction of Belfort. Approaches are well posted. A medium-size site with some shade. Bus into Besancon. Limited parking at the Besancon Citadel.

Besancon → Annecy, 250 km (150 mi.)

Follow N83 south from Besancon to **Bourg-en-Bresse,** at the foot of the Jura Mountains. The Juras separate France from Switzerland in this region. From Bourg take D797 east over the mountains to **Nantua.** Continue on D797 to intersect with N84. Stay on N84 and continue over the mountains to N508. Take N508 into Annecy.

9. Annecy

Beautifully situated at the head of the lake of the same name, Annecy is a popular Savoy resort. The old quarter, with its winding canals, flower-covered bridges, and restored medieval houses, is particularly inviting.

Note: To link up with our Alpine Heights and Old World Delights itinerary, head north via N201 to Geneva (see p. 349).

Annecy Campground

F–149 ★★ Camping Au Coeur du Lac d'Annecy. Open Easter–September 30. Located 5 km (3 mi.) south of town. From Annecy take N508 south along the lake toward Albertville. Campground is just south of Sevrier. A medium-size, partly shaded and terraced site. Pleasant lakeside location with scenic views of the mountains. Bus to Annecy. –1,000 yd.

Annecy → Grenoble, 115 km (69 mi.)

Take N201 from Annecy to **Aix-les-Bains,** a pleasant spa on Lake Bourget. Continue on N201 to **Chambery.** From Chambery take N6 and then D520 to **Voiron.** At Voiron pick up N75 and take this into Grenoble.

10. Grenoble

A modern university town, Grenoble is best known for having hosted the 1968 Winter Olympics. Although the center of town has some interesting older buildings, Grenoble attracts attention mostly because of the surrounding Alps.

Grenoble Campground

F–150 ★★ Caravanning Les 3 Purcelles (Seyssins). Open year-round. Located 7 km (4.2 mi.) southwest of Grenoble at the Drac River. From Grenoble take N75 south toward Sisteron; exit at Seyssinet–Pariset and follow campground signs. A small site with lots of shade trees. Bus to Grenoble.

Grenoble → Digne-les-Bains, 195 km (117 mi.)

Take N85 south from Grenoble to **Gap,** then continue on N85 along the Durance River into Digne.

11. Digne

A convenient way station on the **Route du Napoleon,** Digne is a popular spa and resort in the Lavander Alps.

Digne Campground

F–151 ★★★ Camping des Eaux Chaudes. Open April 1–October 30. On D20 in the direction of the spa. Follow signs to Les Thermes. A large, grassy site with some shade trees. In a pleasant setting next to a brook. A fifteen-minute walk to the hot springs. –900 yd.

Digne → Cannes, 80 km (48 mi.)

Exit Digne on N85 and follow the Route du Napoleon (Napoleon traveled in the opposite direction) down to the sea at Cannes. **Grasse,** in the Maritime Alps 17 km (10 mi.) northwest of Cannes, is an important perfume-manufacturing center. You can smell the fragrance as you drive through the town. Tours are available at several of the factories.

12. Cannes and the Cote d'Azur

Although it has suffered much from overcrowding—and "over" just about everything else—the Riviera is still very much a part of the "French experience." In spite of some horrendous pollution and the construction of many tasteless concrete vacation silos, the Riviera still has some lovely stretches of clean sandy beaches, colorful fishing ports, and inspiring scenery. Between June 15 and September 15, when congestion is at a peak, avoid the coastal strip from Menton at the Italian border to Marseilles in the west.

Even in the off season, parking an RV on the Riviera is a difficult proposition. Many of the public parking areas have barriers with vertical height limits.

Nice, the largest city on the Riviera after Marseilles, is the center of many of the region's activities. There is a casino here as well as several golf courses and a horseracing track. The busy harbor is full of yachts, fishing boats, and merchant ships. The **Vieille Ville,** the old-town quarter, with its narrow, teeming streets and colorful hanging laundry, exudes a sort of seedy charm. The shingle beach is not particularly attractive. (The best sandy beaches on the Riviera are in the Saint-Tropez area.) **Musee Chagall,** specially built to house the works of the famous Russian-born artist, is one of the region's finest museums.

Antibes, across the bay some 20 km (12 mi.) from Nice, is a wealthy old town with great charm. The twelfth-century **Chateau**

Downtown Nice (Courtesy French Government Tourist Office)

Grimaldi now houses the extensive collection of the **Picasso Museum.** The villas on the neighboring **Cap d'Antibes** are some of the most elegant on the coast. **Villefranche** has managed, even though most of the fishing boats have been replaced by luxury yachts, to preserve its architectural integrity as a Mediterranean fishing port.

Cannes, with its beautifully manicured flower-lined **Promenade de la Croisette,** is the Riviera's most opulent city. Although many of the fine sandy beaches are private (common practice all along the Riviera), there are some nice public beaches at the west end of town by the port. The **Corniche d'Esterel** is an area southwest of Cannes, between La Napoule and St. Raphael, where rugged cliffs descend into sheltered sandy coves. This is one of the prettiest stretches along the coast.

Saint-Tropez, popularized by Brigitte Bardot in the late '50s, still is for many the ultimate French Riviera experience. The best beaches are out on the cape, a few miles from the village. There are also several good campgrounds out that way. At night the center of action shifts to the old port of Saint-Tropez.

Note: To connect with our Italy itinerary, continue from Nice along the coast to Genoa (see p. 245).

Riviera Campgrounds

As might be expected in this high-rent district, there are few campgrounds that are actually on the beach. Most are located several kilometers inland in the hills overlooking the Riviera. For "sandy beach" camping on the Riviera your best bet is at Saint-Tropez or along the stretch between **le Lavandou** and **Cavalaire.**

F–152 ★★★ Camping du Domaine (La Faviere). Open April 1–October 30. At the beach 1 km (0.6 mi.) west of le Lavandou. A large site with many pine trees. Located in a vacation complex with a fine sandy beach. Bus service.

F–153 ★★★ Camping Kon-Tiki (Saint-Tropez/Ramatuelle). Open April 1–October 7. At the beach 7 km (4.2 mi.) south of Saint-Tropez. From Saint-Tropez follow D93 and turn off at campground sign. A large beachfront vacation complex. Good sandy beach and some shade trees. No public transportation.

F–154 ★★★★ Camping l'Etoile d'Argens (St. Aygulf). Open Easter–September 30. Located 5 km (3 mi.) south of Frejus on the Argens River. Turn off of D8 at the bridge over the river and follow campground signs. A large, fully equipped vacation complex surrounded by vineyards and bamboo trees. Disco, open-air concerts and entertainment mid-June to mid-September. Free boat transportation to the beach, 1.2 mi.

F–155 ★★★★ Caravanning St. Louis (Cannes/Pegomas). Open March 15–October 1. Located in Pegomas in the hills above Cannes, 6 km (3.6 mi.) northwest of the city. Take D9 south from Pegomas and follow campground signs. From Cannes follow signs to Mandelieu and then take D109 to Pegomas. A large, grassy area with many bushes and shrubs. Some individual sites are terraced. Bus stop at entrance.

Cannes → Marseilles, 190 km (114 mi.)

From Cannes follow N98 along the coast through the port city of **Toulon,** an important French naval base and continue into Marseilles. On a sunny day and with no traffic (a rarity) the drive along the stretch of coast from Cannes to Toulon can be one of the most enjoyable and interesting in Europe.

13. Marseilles

Founded by the Greeks in the sixth century B.C., Marseilles is France's largest port and second-largest city. At a major crossroads of world trade for centuries and glorified in countless films and novels, the Port of Marseilles is a bustling blend of many races and influences. The port is ringed with restaurants serving Marseilles's most famous contribution to the world of gastronomy, **bouillabaisse.**

Marseilles Campgrounds

F–156 ★★★ Camping Municipal de Bonneveine. Open year-round. Located in the district of Bonneveine at the southern edge of the city. Adjacent to the Parc Borley. From Marseilles take N559 in the direction of Toulon. A medium-size, level, partly shaded site close to a sandy beach. Convenient for visiting Marseilles. Avoid driving in Marseilles whenever possible. The traffic is horrendous and parking nonexistent. Use the bus from the campground into town.

F–157 ★★★★ Camping Le Mas (La Couronne). Open March 15–October 10. At the beach in La Couronne, 35 km (21 mi.) west of Marseilles. Take N368 west from Marseilles. At the intersection with D49, turn off toward Cape Couronne and follow signs to the campground. A large, terraced site in a quiet location overlooking the sea. Many pine trees. Commuter train to Marseilles.

Marseilles → Arles, 70 km (42 mi.)

From Marseilles take N568 and follow signs into Arles.

14. Arles

Surrounded by the same colorful countryside that served as the inspiration for so many of Van Gogh's paintings, Arles can trace its history back to the Greeks who arrived there in the sixth century B.C. Although not much remains from the Greek period, there are some notable Roman structures in and around the city. The large, well-preserved **amphitheater** is Arles's most important tourist attraction.

Les Baux, an ancient fortified village, is located in an incredible setting atop a bare, rocky pinnacle overlooking the vineyards some 20 km (12 mi.) northeast of Arles.

Arles Campground

F–158 ★★ Camping des Rosiers. Open March 15–October 31. At the southeast edge of the city on the route de Crau. Across from the Europa Hotel. From Arles take N453 toward Pont de Crau and follow campground signs. A medium-size, grassy site with little shade. Well situated for visiting Arles and the Camargue. Bus to Arles.

Arles → Aigues-Mortes and the Camargue, 46 km (28 mi.)

Take D570 south from Arles through the Camargue to Les Saintes-Maries-de-la-Mer. Then return to intersect with D58 and follow this to Aigues-Mortes.

15. Aigues-Mortes and the Camargue

The Camargue is a broad, 800-km² (320-sq.-mi.) swatch of marshes and lagoons in the midst of the Rhone River delta. Once the sole realm of wild horses, steers, and roaming Gypsy bands, the Camargue now shares its haunting beauty with an ever-increasing number of tourists.

Les Saintes-Maries-de-la-Mer at the southern tip of the Camargue is a rather shabby beach town that springs to life each May when thousands of Gypsies from all over Europe converge for a colorful festival in honor of St. Sarah, the patron saint of the Gypsies. Exhibits in the **Baroncelli Museum** document Camargue life in the pre-tourist era.

At the southern gateway to the Camargue, **Aigues-Mortes** is one of the best-preserved walled towns in France. The elaborate ramparts and multiple towers invite exploration.

Note: To link up with France Itinerary II, follow the coast highway N112 or the A9 Autoroute to Beziers (see p. 181).

Camargue Campground

F–159 ★★★★ Camping la Petite Camargue (Aigues-Mortes). Open April 10–September 20. On D62, 3 km (1.8 mi.) southwest of Aigues-Mortes in the direction of La Grande-Motte. Well-marked approach. A large, attractively landscaped site with plenty of shade. Full range of facilities include horseback riding, disco, and entertainment. Good base for exploring the Camargue. Free bus to the beach. Some parking is available in Aigues-Mortes.

Aigues-Mortes → Nimes, 40 km (24 mi.)

From Aigues-Mortes take D979 and N113 to Nimes.

16. Nimes

The gateway to Provence and the Rhone Valley, Nimes is a busy industrial city. Once a major Roman settlement with the name of Nemausus, the town has retained some outstanding Roman structures, including a 20,000-seat **amphitheater,** considered to be the best-preserved Roman amphitheater in the world.

Pont du Gard, spanning a rocky gorge about 20 km (12 mi.) northeast of Nimes on N86, is the remarkably intact remains of a three-tiered, 2,000-year-old Roman aqueduct. Constructed in 18–19 B.C. to supply water to Nimes, this is one of the finest examples of aqueduct construction to be seen anywhere.

Nimes Campground

F–160 ★★★ Camping Domaine de la Bastide. Open year-round.

From Nimes take D13 south toward Generac. After 5 km (3 mi.) turn off to the campground. A large, well-laid-out site with individual hookups. Little shade. No public transportation. Parking in Nimes is difficult.

Nimes → Avignon, 40 km (24 mi.)
Take N86 out of Nimes to Pont du Gard and then N100 to Avignon.

17. Avignon

Avignon was assured its place in history when the seat of the papacy was transferred from Rome in 1309 and, for the next sixty-eight years, seven successive popes reigned from here. When the papacy returned to the Vatican, Avignon remained papal property until the late eighteenth century. The enormous **Palace of the Popes,** built in the fourteenth century as a papal palace and fortress, dominates the city. Avignon is also known for its **Pont St. Benezet,** the bridge made famous by the folksong "Sur le Pont d'Avignon." **Tarascon,** 15 km (9 mi.) south of Avignon, is the site of an imposing twelfth-century castle.

Avignon Campground
F–161 ★★★ Camping Municipal Pont St. Benezet. Open March 1–October 31. Located on the Ile de la Barthelasse in the Rhone. Follow signs from the Pont Daladier. A large, grassy site in a parklike setting. Many trees and bushes. Magnificent views across the river to the Palace of the Popes and the Pont St. Benezet. A good base from which to explore Provence. A ten-minute walk into town.

Avignon → Orange, 30 km (18 mi.)
Follow D980 north along the river to **Roquemaure** and from there D976 into Orange.

18. Orange

A pleasant, quiet town that overlooks the Rhone Valley, Orange is best known for its **Roman Theater,** the best-preserved ancient theater anywhere. Another striking vestige of the town's Roman past is the massive **Triumphal Arch,** the third largest in existence. It was built by Julius Caesar to commemorate his victories over the local Gauls. A few kilometers to the south are the vineyards of **Chateauneuf-du-pape,** where some of Provence's finest wines are produced. There is a small wine museum in the village.

Orange Campground

F–162 ★★ Camping Le Jonquier. Open Easter–October 31. Located just north of the Triumphal Arch off of N7. At the traffic light head west to the site following signs stating CAMPING—INFORMATION. A large, grassy area with little shade. Plots are divided by hedges. Easy walk to town. Bus, 500 yd.

Orange → Lyon, 180 km (108 mi.)

There are several routes to Lyon. The fastest and most direct is via either the A7 Autoroute or Hwy. N7; both follow the course of the Rhone River. There is heavy truck traffic on both routes and little of interest along the way.

If you can spare an extra few hours, we recommend taking D976 from Orange and following this northeast to **Valreas.** From there take D538 to the ancient Roman town of **Vienne.** This route meanders through the pleasant countryside and includes a number of delightful small villages.

19. Lyon

Strategically situated at the junction of the Rhone and Saone rivers and mid-way between Paris and the Mediterranean, Lyon has developed into an important financial center and is also one of the world's leading silk producers. Many gourmets consider the cuisine in Lyon to be the finest in France. The central part of the city has much of interest, including the attractive **old quarter (Vieux Lyon),** on the right bank of the Saone, and several good museums.

Lyon Campground

F–163 ★★ Camping Porte de Lyon. Open year-round. In the suburb of Dardilly, 9 km (5.4 mi.) north of the city. Approaching from the south, follow N7 through Lyon. Then follow PARIS N6 signs. After going through a tunnel, follow campground signs. Turn off by the shopping center. A large, grassy site close to the autoroute. Convenient bus to Lyon. Parking in Lyon is difficult.

Lyon → Beaune, 140 km (84 mi.)

Take N6 out of Lyon and follow signs toward Paris about 20 km (12 mi.). At **Villefranche** turn off onto D504 and follow this west to intersect with D485. Head north to **les Echarmeaux.** Then follow signs to **Cluny,** the site of the medieval **Abbey of Cluny.** Until the construction of St. Peter's in Rome, this was the largest church in Europe. Unfortunately, it now stands in ruins. From Cluny take D981 north to **Chagny,** and then take D974 the remaining few kilometers to Beaune.

20. Beaune

Beaune is a delightful town as well as an important Burgundy wine center. The vineyards at nearby **Nuits-St. Georges** have been producing fine wines since Roman times. While in Beaune, a visit to the **Hospices de Beaune** is a must. Founded in 1443, this was a functioning hospital until 1971. In addition to its fine collection of paintings, the hospice houses a fascinating **medical museum** with some medical implements that date back to the fifteenth century.

Beaune Campground

F–164 ★★★ Camping Municipal les Cent Vignes. Open March 15–October 31. At the north edge of town. Heading toward Dijon on N7, turn off at the St. Nicholas Church and follow D18 and campground signs. A medium-size, pleasantly landscaped site. Individual parcels are separated by hedges. Easy ten-minute walk to the center of Beaune. A convenient base for touring Burgundy.

Beaune → Dijon, 40 km (24 mi.)

Take N74 north through the vineyards at Nuits-St. Georges and continue into Dijon.

Stocking up on French bread

21. Dijon

During the Middle Ages Dijon, the ancient capital of Burgundy, was an independent duchy. The powerful Dukes of Burgundy constructed a magnificent palace, the **Palais des Ducs.** Today the palace houses one of France's most important art museums, the **Musee des Beaux-Arts.**

Dijon Campground

F–165 ★ Camping Municipal du Lac. Open April 1–November 15. At the western edge of the city, on the banks of the Ouche River. Approaches are well marked. A large, partly shaded site. Bus to Dijon center.

Dijon → Troyes, 152 km (91 mi.)

Follow N71 northwest from Dijon to **Chatillon-sur-Seine,** a delightful little town on a hill overlooking the Seine. The local church dates back to the eleventh century. From Chatillon continue on N71, which follows the Seine into Troyes.

22. TROYES

The one-time capital of the province of Champagne, Troyes has a remarkably well-preserved old-town core. There are many attractive half-timbered houses with elaborate turrets and gables.

Troyes Campground

F–166 ★★ Camping Municipal. Open April 1–October 15. From Troyes center take D960 toward Nancy. The campground is on the left after 2 km (1.2 miles). Approaches are well marked. A large, grassy site on the Canal du Labourat. Some shade trees. Bus to Troyes center.

Troyes → Fontainebleau, 120 km (72 mi.)

Take N60 from Troyes to **Sens.** Then take N6 to Fontainebleau.

Fontainebleau → Paris

To return to Paris take Autoroute A6 or N7 into the city.

IBERIAN INTERLUDE

Portugal

CAPITAL: Lisbon

POPULATION: 10,500,000

CURRENCY: escudo ($), divided into 100 centimes

LANGUAGES: Portuguese; English is widely spoken on the Algarve

RELIGION: Roman Catholic

POLICE: 115

FIRE: 115

AMBULANCE: 115

ROAD SERVICE: ACP—Lisbon and south, (01) 942–5092; O'Porto and north, (02) 830–1127 twenty-four hours

BANKS: weekdays 8:30 A.M.–3:00 P.M.

STORES: weekdays 9:00 A.M.–1:00 P.M. and 3:00–7:00 P.M.; Saturday 9:00 A.M.–1:00 P.M.; larger stores or malls remain open until 9:00 or 10:00 P.M.

HOLIDAYS: January 1; Shrove Tuesday (movable); Good Friday; April 25, Liberation Day; May 1, Labor Day; June 10, Portuguese Day; Corpus Christi (movable, Lisbon only); Assumption Day (movable); October 5, Portuguese Republic; All Saints' Day (movable); December 24 and 25

EMBASSIES: *United States,* Avenida das Forcas Armadas, 1600 Lisbon; phone (01) 726–6600, fax (01) 726–9109. *Canada,* Avenida da Liberdade, 4th floor, 1200 Lisbon; phone (01) 347–4892, fax (01) 346–6466. *United Kingdom,* 35/37 Rua de Santo Domingo a Lapa, 1200 Lisbon; phone (01) 396–1191

A small country that occupies less than one-fifth of the Iberian Peninsula, Portugal, often hidden in the shadow of its powerful neighbor

Spain, is one of Europe's last forgotten places. Although Lisbon and the wonderful beaches of the Algarve have long been favorite holiday destinations, particularly for sun-starved British and Northern Europeans, much of the rest of the country remains virtually unknown to European-bound North Americans.

The country's long coastline is blessed with some of Europe's finest sandy beaches. In many of the small fishing villages, hard-working fishermen still ply their ancient trade in small, colorfully painted boats. Away from the sea, in the inland mountains and valleys of the north, where daily life seems far removed from the hectic pace of modern life, tourists are still considered a pleasant curiosity.

In the sprawling Alentejo, Portugal's breadbasket, practically every hill that overlooks the wheat fields and olive groves is crowned by a castle or fortress of some sort. Many are imposing and remarkably well preserved while others have been reduced by the ravages of war and time to ruins. The Portuguese, and especially the rural Portuguese, are a warm and hospitable people who extend a gracious welcome to the foreigners who do venture into their midst.

DRIVING

In spite of the many improvements made in building new roads, in drivers' education, and in traffic law enforcement, Portugal continues to have one of the world's highest accident rates. The ownership of an automobile is still a relatively new thing to many in this country, and Portuguese drivers just do not have the same degree of road savvy found in other parts of Europe. This should not discourage anyone from driving in Portugal—just be a bit more alert when driving there. Enforcement of speeding and traffic regulations is not widespread, although periodic roadblocks are set up to check for drunk drivers.

Recent improvements have brought most of the country's major highways up to the standard of the rest of Europe. A newly completed four-lane motorway connects Lisbon and Porto, and a trans-Algarve motorway is under construction. The motorways are designated with the letter "A" and are subject to tolls. Although many of the country's national highways—which are denoted by the letter "N,"—are in excellent condition, many, particularly in the north, are not. There is an extensive network of secondary roads, a number of which are still cobblestone or dirt. When driving at night in rural areas, be alert for donkey carts without lights.

The wearing of seatbelts is compulsory, and children under age twelve may not ride in the front seats. The speed limit for motorhomes on the motorways is 120 kph (72 mph); in towns and built-up areas, unless otherwise posted, it is 60 kph (36 mph). Outside of built-up areas it is 90 kph (54 mph). Visiting motorists are required to pay fines on the spot for traffic violations.

CAMPING

The majority of Portugal's more than 150 campgrounds are located in the coastal regions; however, a sufficient number of sites are available in the interior to allow extensive exploration of this small country without ever being too far from a campground. Free camping is generally tolerated, although the total number of units at any location may not exceed twenty. Free camping is not allowed in some of the more popular beach resorts.

As Portugal is a favorite wintering spot for many Northern Europeans, most campgrounds, particularly in the Algarve, remain open all year. Facilities and services vary widely and are classified by the tourist authorities with from one to four stars. The International Camping Carnet is required at sites run by the Portuguese Camping Federation.

Electrical hookups are mostly of the two-prong German Schuko type. Foreign gas bottles can be filled in Faro, Porto, and Lisbon. Check at the local campgrounds for details. For additional information regarding camping in Portugal, contact Federacao Portuguesa de Campismo e Caravanismo, Avenida 5 de Outubro 15–3, 1000 Lisboa, Portugal; phone (01) 522–3308.

Spain

CAPITAL: Madrid

POPULATION: 38,600,000

CURRENCY: peseta (Pta), divided into 100 centimos

LANGUAGES: Spanish, Basque, Catalan, and Galician

RELIGION: Roman Catholic

POLICE: 091

FIRE: 080

AMBULANCE: 092

ROAD SERVICE: (091) 593–3333 throughout country

BANKS: weekdays 9:00 A.M.–2:00 P.M.; Saturday 9:00 A.M.–1:00 P.M.

STORES: weekdays and Saturday 10:00 A.M.–8:00 P.M.; some shops close from around 1:00 to 3:00 P.M.; in summer many close on Saturday; department stores in major cities 10:00 A.M.–8:00 P.M.

HOLIDAYS: January 1; January 6, Epiphany; Holy Thursday and Good Friday (movable); May 1, Mayday; Corpus Christi (movable); July 25, St. James Day; Assumption (movable); October 12, National Day; All Saints' Day (movable); December 8, Immaculate Conception; December 25

EMBASSIES: *United States,* Serrano 75, 28006 Madrid; phone (01) 577–4000, fax 577–5735. *Canada,* Edificio Goya, Calle Nunez de Balboa 35, 28080 Madrid; phone (01) 431–4300, fax (01) 431–2367. *United Kingdom,* Calle de Fernando el Santo 16, Madrid 4; phone (01) 319–0200

Occupying most of the Iberian Peninsula, which it shares with Portugal, Spain is Europe's third-largest country and, after Switzerland, its most mountainous. This is a land of enormous contrasts. Madrid and the affluent, sophisticated cities of the north present a sharply different image from the impoverished Andalucian region, which lies in the south of the country and where Gypsy encampments and donkey carts are not unusual sights. It is a country where cheap charter flights and mass tourism have turned once-quaint coastal fishing villages into high-rise tourist ghettos, but it is also the land of Granada and its incomparable Alhambra, glistening hill-top Andalusian villages, the magnificent cathedral of Seville, and the wondrous Moorish architecture of Cordoba. Many areas of great natural beauty, including Europe's largest bird preserve, Parque Nacional Donana, many northern beaches, and the vast mountain ranges, remain unspoiled. In Madrid and Barcelona you will find some of Europe's finest museums. For those visitors who carefully choose when and where they travel, Spain can be one of Europe's most exciting travel destinations.

DRIVING

Driving in Spain is no longer the adventure that it was even a few years ago. Improvements in driver's education and an extensive road-building program have raised driving conditions to the level of most other European countries. Modern four-lane highways (autopistas) extend from the French border south along the Mediterranean coast to Almeria and between the major cities. Many of these highways are toll roads and are designated with the letter "A." Tolls in Spain, particularly for RVs, are steep. The Spanish word for "toll" is *peaje.* Many of the toll roads accept credit cards for payment.

The roads designated with "N" are national highways, which are generally in excellent condition but are often clogged with truck traffic. The letter "C" denotes the extensive network of secondary roads that lace the countryside. These roads are mostly in good condition and provide a wonderful opportunity, for those not in a great hurry, to experience rural Spain.

As Spain was neutral during World War II, the major cities suffered none of the damage inflicted on many other European cities. They have also not benefited from the modern urban planning that has characterized many of the rebuilt cities in other parts of Europe. Extreme traffic congestion is the norm, and parking in the inner cities is very difficult. Most of the larger cities now have bypass highways to avoid the downtown areas.

The wearing of seatbelts is compulsory, and children under age twelve may not ride in the front seats. You are required to carry a spare set of light bulbs for your vehicle. The speed limit for motorhomes on the motorways is 120 kph (72 mph); in towns and built-up areas, unless otherwise posted, it is 50 kph (30 mph). Outside of built-up areas it is 90 kph (56 mph). Visiting motorists are required to pay traffic fines on the spot.

In the event of a serious accident the police may require the posting of a bond. Check with your insurance to see that "Spanish Bail Bond" coverage is included in your policy.

CAMPING

For years a popular pastime with tourists, camping is gaining in popularity among the Spaniards, many of whom set up their trailers at local campgrounds for use as weekend vacation homes. There are approximately 600 official campgrounds, mostly located in the coastal regions and at the principal tourist attractions. In the interior of the country, campsites are sparsely distributed and are confined primarily to the major cities.

Campgrounds are classified by government inspectors as first, second, or third category, on the basis of facilities and services provided; the classification is not based on cleanliness or quality of service. Generally speaking, you will find most Spanish campgrounds to be clean and well maintained. Regular inspections are made by health authorities to ensure drinking-water quality. A free map showing the location of all campgrounds can be obtained from the Spanish National Tourist Office.

Many sites, particularly in the south, limit the amount of electricity available—sometimes to only 2 or 3 A. To avoid blowing fuses, check on the amount provided when registering. Although most of the larger sites have switched over to CEE 17 electrical plugs, a number of the smaller and older campgrounds still use the two-prong German Schuko system. Most of the major cities have stations that fill foreign gas cylinders. For details inquire at local campgrounds.

An International Camping Carnet is not required at most campgrounds. Free camping is generally tolerated unless specifically prohibited by local ordinances. For additional information regarding camping in Spain, contact Federacion Espanola de Campings, General Oraa, 52, 2ºD, 28006 Madrid, Spain; phone (1) 562 99 94.

Itinerary: Madrid • Castile • Andalucia • Southern Portugal • Lisbon • Estremadura

START: Madrid

COUNTRIES: Portugal and Spain

DISTANCE: 1,985 km (1,191 mi.)

MAPS: Michelin #990 *Spain—Portugal;* #440 *Portugal;* #442 *Spain Northern & Central;* #443 *Spain Northern & Eastern;* #444 *Spain Central;* #445 *Spain Central & Eastern;* #446 *Spain Southern*

MINIMUM RECOMMENDED TOURING TIME: 21 to 28 days

INTRODUCTION

The variety of treasures and attractions to be found in Spain and Portugal are practically inexhaustible. In this itinerary we have chosen a representative sample of the best of these two Iberian neighbors. Castles and palaces, great museums and cathedrals, as well as rugged mountains and sprawling sandy beaches are all included.

We begin our itinerary in Madrid, but Lisbon is also a convenient starting point. Rental vehicles are available in both capitals; however, they are in short supply and the selection is limited.

Although Spain and Portugal, which share the Iberian Peninsula, are often considered by tourists as one entity, they are, you will soon notice, two very distinct countries with different traditions, languages, cultures, and even cuisines. Portugal, by far the smaller of the two, has suffered somewhat of an identity crisis in the shadow if its much larger Spanish cousin. As the Moorish occupation lasted nearly four centuries longer in Spain, its influence in all sectors of Spanish life is far more apparent than in Portugal.

WHEN TO GO

This is not an itinerary to be undertaken during July and August, when the broiling Iberian sun is at its most brutal and swarms of Northern European sun-seekers jam the beaches and highways. Early springtime in

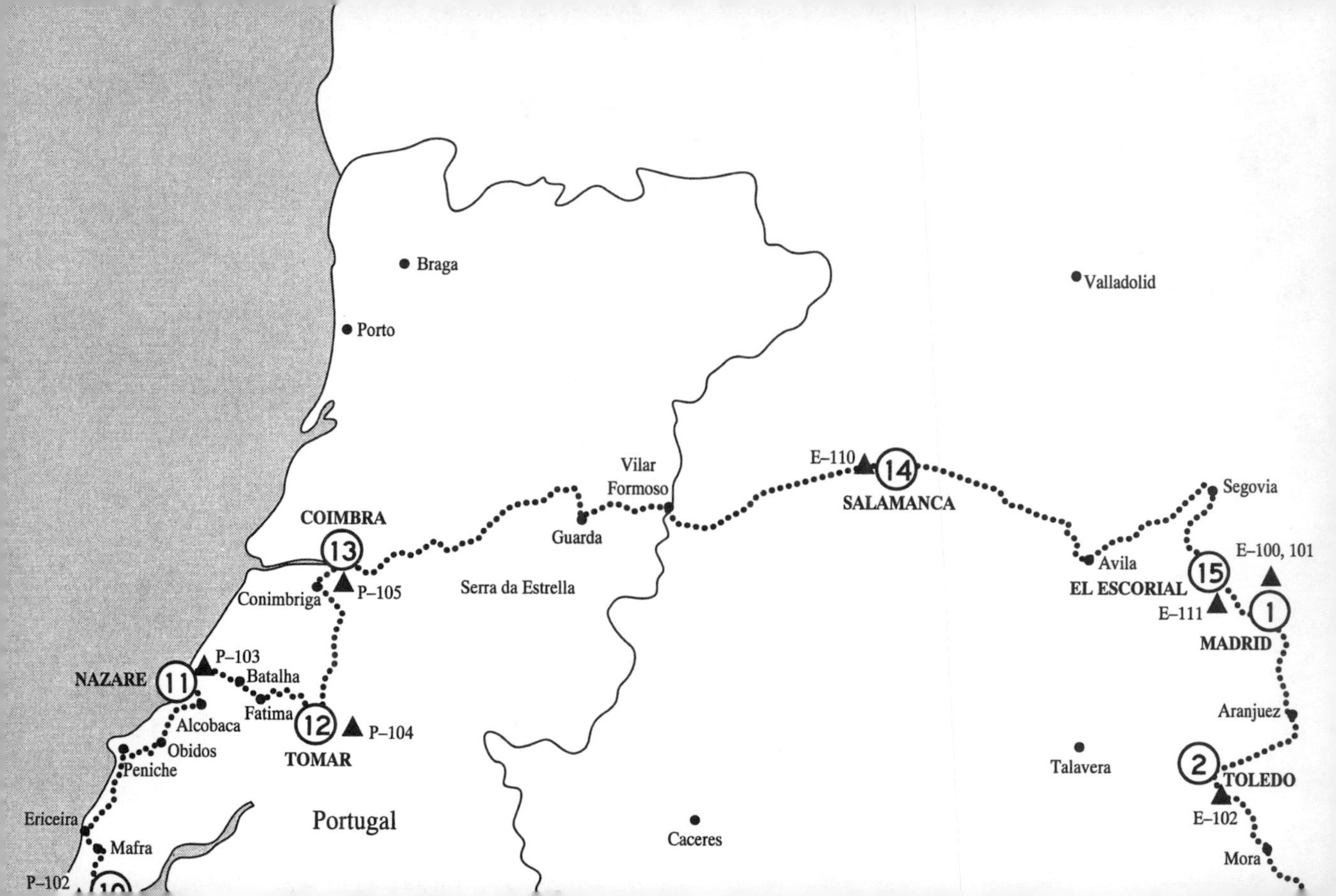
Braga
Porto
Valladolid
Vilar Formoso
E–110
14
SALAMANCA
Segovia
COIMBRA
13
Guarda
Avila
E–100, 101
15
EL ESCORIAL
Conimbriga
P–105
Serra da Estrella
E–111
1
MADRID
P–103
NAZARE
11
Batalha
Fatima
Alcobaca
12
P–104
TOMAR
Obidos
Peniche
Aranjuez
Talavera
2
TOLEDO
Ericeira
Portugal
E–102
Mafra
Caceres
Mora
P–102

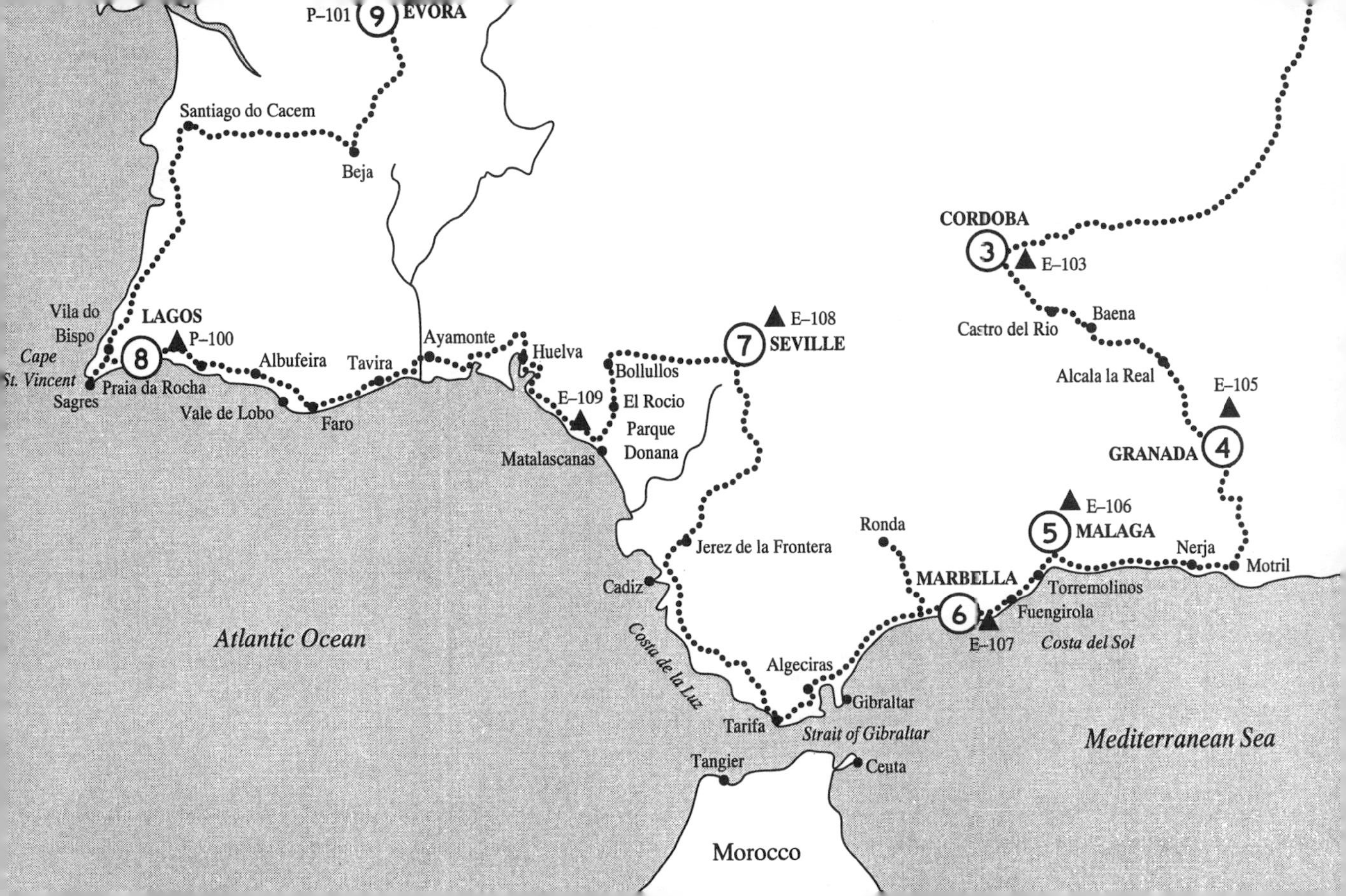
P-101
9
EVORA
Santiago do Cacem
Beja
CORDOBA
3
E-103
Castro del Rio
Baena
Alcala la Real
E-105
4
GRANADA
Vila do Bispo
LAGOS
8
P-100
Cape St. Vincent
Sagres
Praia da Rocha
Albufeira
Tavira
Ayamonte
Vale de Lobo
Faro
Huelva
Bollullos
E-109
El Rocio
Parque Donana
Matalascanas
E-108
7
SEVILLE
E-106
5
MALAGA
Ronda
Jerez de la Frontera
Nerja
Motril
MARBELLA
Torremolinos
Cadiz
6
Fuengirola
E-107
Costa del Sol
Atlantic Ocean
Costa de la Luz
Algeciras
Gibraltar
Tarifa
Strait of Gibraltar
Mediterranean Sea
Tangier
Ceuta
Morocco

Baking bread the traditional way in Portugal

Iberia is lovely. The wildflowers are blossoming, and campgrounds and tourist attractions are pleasantly uncrowded. September and October are also a good time for Iberian touring, but since this season is before the first rains come, much of the landscape is parched from the blistering summer sun.

Winter can also be enjoyable for touring. The climate in the coastal areas is mild, and most campgrounds and attractions stay open all year. In the mountains and the interior, freezing weather and snow are often encountered, and many campgrounds are closed.

Highlights

The Prado, Madrid
The Alhambra, Granada
El Escorial
Roman Aqueduct, Segovia
Lisbon
Obidos

EXPANDING HORIZONS

- **To connect with France Itinerary II:** Head north from Madrid to Bordeaux (see p. 176).

ON THE ROAD

Numbered sites correspond with circled numbers on the itinerary map.

1. MADRID

Madrid, Spain's capital and Iberia's largest city, is a modern, sophisticated metropolis with a population of nearly 4 million. It is a vibrant and exciting place with all of the advantages and drawbacks that one expects in a major urban center. There are world-class museums, including the Prado, expansive parks and broad boulevards lined with some of the continent's finest shops, a marvelous Royal Palace, and hundreds of interesting restaurants and cafes. The Prado and other principal attractions are clustered around the old town in the heart of the city.

Life in Madrid is exciting and goes on at a frenetic pace with the streets, bars, and restaurants filled well into the night. As a visitor you will find the Madrilenos to be urbane, engaging, and remarkably friendly toward foreigners. Madrid's dark side is that shared by most large cities today: stifling air pollution, impossible traffic and parking conditions, and an increasing crime rate.

Madrid is not the place to explore in an RV. Park your rig at one of the city's several campgrounds and avail yourself of the extensive public transportation system. Taxi stands are numerous, and fares are one of the few bargains to be found in Madrid.

Unfortunately, this is one of the few major European cities that do not have a first-rate campground. The sites listed below are conveniently located but leave much to be desired in the way of facilities and maintenance. As an alternative, the campground in El Escorial, 50 km (30 mi.) from Madrid (see p. 229) is excellent, and there is regular bus service into Madrid.

Madrid Campgrounds

E–100 ★ Camping Osuna. Open year-round. At the northeast end of the city near the airport, in the suburb of Barajas. From Hwy. NII (Madrid–Zaragoza) turn off at Barajas, just past airport turnoff, and follow campground signs. A medium-size, dusty site with some shade trees. Facilities in need of renovation. Convenient location. Metro line 5 to Madrid center, 10-minute walk; or bus #101 from campground.

E–101 ★★ Camping Alpha. Open year-round. In the suburb of Getafe, 13 km (7.8 mi.) south of Madrid. Turn off of NIV (Madrid–Cordoba) at Getafe and follow campground signs. A large, partly shaded site with many resident trailers. Convenient public transportation to Madrid center. –900 yd.

Madrid → Toledo, 80 km (48 mi.)

Exit Madrid on NIV and follow signs south to **Aranjuez.** The **Royal Palace** at Aranjuez, a favorite summer residence of the Bourbons, is constructed in the classic Versailles style and features elaborate gardens. After visiting the palace take N400 SE into Toledo.

2. Toledo

Perched on a rocky prominence overlooking the **Tagus River,** Toledo, the long-time spiritual and intellectual capital of Spain, owes much of its fame and wealth to an extended period of fruitful coexistence among Moors, Christians, and Jews. It was in Toledo that El Greco settled in 1577 and produced many of his most famous works. The artist's house is now a museum.

Toledo Campground

E–102 ★★★ Camping El Greco. Open year-round. At the west edge of town on C401/502, in the direction of Puebla de Montalbon. Approaches are well marked. A medium-size, partly shaded site with scenic views of city. Take #7 bus to city. Parking and driving in Toledo are difficult.

Toledo → Cordoba, 350 km (210 mi.)

From Toledo take C400 SE to **Mora** and continue to the intersection with NIV. Follow the divided highway NIV across the **Sierra Morena Mountains** into Cordoba. Part of the route passes through the dry, rugged plateau region known as **La Mancha.** The hilltop windmills along the way are sure to evoke memories of Cervantes's legendary Don Quixote.

3. Cordoba

Located on the banks of the **Guadalquivir River** and surrounded by wheat fields and olive trees, Cordoba has a long and rich history. Founded by the Carthaginians in the second century B.C., the town later became the capital of the Roman province of Baetica, and under Moorish domination it was the capital of Muslim Spain. The city reached its pinnacle as one of Europe's great cultural centers during the tenth century. The **Mezquita** with its graceful lines, curved arches, and intricate ceilings, is one of the finest examples of Islamic architecture outside of the Arab world.

Cordoba Campground

E–103 ★★ Campamento Municipal. Open year-round. Northwest edge of town. Turn off of NIV toward N432 and Badajoz, 5 km (3 mi.) north of Cordoba. Follow signs into Cordoba, then follow signs toward Parador and camping. A small site with little shade, next to municipal swimming pool. Bus to town. Parking in Cordoba is difficult.

Cordoba → Granada, 170 km (102 mi.)

Take N432 southeast into Granada. Along the route there are interesting Moorish castles at **Castro del Rio, Baena,** and **Alcala la Real.**

4. Granada

Situated at the foot of the snowcapped **Sierra Nevadas,** Granada is best known for the **Alhambra,** one of Spain's most magnificent attractions. Over the centuries the beauties of this Moorish masterpiece have been praised by poets and writers the world over. Seeing is believing, however—and no trip to Spain would be complete without a visit to the Alhambra. It was in Granada, in 1492, that nearly eight centuries of Moorish domination in Spain came to an end. Adjacent to the huge cathedral in the center of the city is the ornate **Capilla Real (Royal**

Chapel). The chapel contains the tombs of Isabella of Castile and Ferdinand of Aragon.

Granada Campground

E–105 ★★ Camping Sierra Nevada. Open March 15–October 15. Adjacent to Motel Sierra Nevada, 4 km (2.4 mi.) north of Granada center. Take N323 toward Jaen and follow signs toward Granada Norte, and then follow camping signs. A large site with many mature trees. This is the most convenient of the several Granada campgrounds. Bus from campground to Granada center. Plenty of parking at the Alhambra.

Granada → Malaga, 160 km (96 mi.)

Exit Granada on N323 following signs toward **Motril.** The road climbs over the 3,000-ft.-high **Suspiro del Moro Pass** before dropping down to the **Costa del Sol.** Follow the coast highway to the popular beach resort of **Nerja.** After visiting the **prehistoric caves,** continue along the coast (on N340) the remaining 54 km (32 mi.) into the port of Malaga.

5. Malaga

A busy port and the largest city on the Costa del Sol, Malaga is known for its luxuriant parks and gardens and as the center of a region of mass tourism run rampant, drawing millions of sun-starved Northern Europeans to pack its beaches. The **Museo de Bellas Artes (Fine Arts Museum)** displays a number of works by Malaga-born Pablo Picasso.

Malaga Campground

E–106 ★ Camping Balneario del Carmen. Open year-round. At the beach at the east edge of town, 9 km (5.4 miles) from center. Approaches are well marked. Entry into site possible only when heading east toward Motril on N340. A large site with many mature trees. Small beach. Convenient bus to town. Malaga parking is very difficult.

Malaga → Marbella, 70 km (42 mi.)

Stay on N340 along the coast and through the resorts of **Torremolinos** and **Fuengirola** into Marbella.

6. MARBELLA

One of Spain's poshest resorts, Marbella attracts the wealthy and famous from all over the world. In striking contrast to the overwhelming development along the coast, in the hills just a few kilometers away, you will find much of the beauty and tradition of Old Spain.

Marbella Campground

E–107 ★★★★ Camping Marbella Playa. Open year-round. Located 9 km (5.4 mi.) east of Marbella on N340. Approaches are well marked. A large, sandy site with many young trees. One of the best sites for visiting Costa del Sol. Bus to Marbella.

Marbella → Seville, 320 km (192 mi.)

Head west on the coast road, following signs toward **Algeciras.** To visit one of southern Spain's most beautiful towns, turn off at **San Pedro de Alcantara** and take Hwy. C339 the 50 km (30 mi.) into the mountains to **Ronda.**

Some 35 km (21 mi.) west of Malaga on N340 is the turnoff to the British colony of **Gibraltar.** There are no campgrounds in Gibraltar. The closest site is at **San Roque,** 3 km (1.8 mi.) west of the Gibraltar turnoff.

The coast highway continues into the port city of Algeciras. There is regular ferry service from here to **Tangier, Morocco,** and to the Spanish North African enclave of **Ceuta.**

The highway between the beach at **Tarifa** and the historic port city of **Cadiz** runs along the **Costa de la Luz,** one of Spain's few undeveloped coastal regions. From Cadiz head north to the sherry-producing center of **Jerez de la Frontera.** Many of the sherry bodegas are open to the public for tours and tasting. Take NV or Autopista A4 the 100 km (60 mi.) into Seville.

7. SEVILLE

The romantic setting for numerous plays and operas, including Bizet's opera *Carmen* and Rossini's *Barber of Seville,* Spain's fourth-largest city has retained a charm and ambience unmatched by any other major Spanish city. The principal attractions are clustered around the cathedral, one of the country's grandest. Built in the fifteenth century on the ruins of a Moorish mosque, its cavernous interior and eighty chapels contain numerous art treasures as well as the tomb of Christopher Columbus.

Directly adjacent to the cathedral is the **Giralda Tower.** Built in the twelfth century as a minaret, this is the city's most famous landmark. The observation tower affords a bird's-eye view of Old Seville. **Maria Luisa Park,** with its tall shade trees, tiled murals, and manicured gardens, is one of Spain's loveliest parks.

Seville Campground

E–108 ★★ Camping Sevilla. Open year-round. East of the city near the airport. Turn off of NIV at km 534 in the direction of Carmona/Cordoba. A large, grassy site with some shade. Bus to city center. It is difficult to find parking in Seville, and break-ins are frequent.

Seville → Parque Nacional Donana/Matalascanas, 90 km (54 mi.)

Take A49 heading west from Seville and follow signs toward **Huelva.** Exit the autopista at **Bollullos par del Condado** and follow signs to **El Rocio** and **Parque Nacional Donana.** During Whitsunday weekend the tiny settlement of El Rocio is the gathering place for hundreds of thousands of traditionally dressed pilgrims from all parts of Spain who take part in one of the country's most colorful festivals. A few kilometers farther down the road is the entrance to Parque Nacional Donana, a magnificent wilderness preserve of dunes and salt marshes. Visitors may tour the park on guided half-day Jeep safaris. The closest campground is in the resort town of **Matalascanas.**

Matalascanas Campground

E–109 ★★★ Camping Rocio Playa. Open year-round. At the beach. Turn off of C442 at km 45.2 in the direction of Mazagon. Approaches are well marked. A large, terraced site overlooking the beach. Plenty of parking at El Rocio and at Parque Nacional Donana.

Matalascanas → Lagos, Portugal, 250 km (150 mi.)

Follow the coast road C442 through the pine forests to the industrial port of Huelva, then take N431 west, following signs to **Ayamonte** and Portugal. After crossing the bridge over the **Guadiana River,** which divides Spain and Portugal, continue west on the coast road N125. In this part of Portugal, known as the Algarve, between **Villa Real de Santo Antonio** and Lagos there are a number of popular seaside resorts and interesting towns, including **Tavira, Faro, Vale de Lobo, Albufeira** and **Praia da Rocha.**

8. Lagos

One of the most attractive towns on Portugal's southern coast, Lagos can trace its origin back to the Carthaginians. During Portugal's great era of exploration, this was the starting point for many of the important voyages of discovery. The building that housed Europe's first slave market, now an art gallery, is in the center of the old town, just a few steps from an imposing monument to Prince Henry the Navigator. There are a number of fine beaches in and around Lagos.

Lagos Campground

P–100 ★★★ Camping Imulagos. Open year-round. Overlooking the sea just west of town. From Lagos follow signs toward Porto de Mos. Turnoff to campground is well marked. A large, shaded site with many eucalyptus trees on the cliffs overlooking the sea. Shuttle bus to Lagos. A twenty-minute walk to town center.

Lagos → Evora, 340 km (204 mi.)

Follow N125 west to **Sagres.** The massive **fortress** at the tip of the rocky peninsula is where Prince Henry is said to have had his School of Navigation, where the leading explorers of the era met. Eleven km (6.6 mi.) west of Sagres is the rugged, windswept **Cape St. Vincent,** continental Europe's most southwesterly point. From the cape the road returns to Sagres.

Head east on N125 to **Vila do Bispo.** Pick up N120 and follow this north along the rugged west coast. Some of the finest beaches in Europe are found in this region. Continue along the coast to **Santiago do Cacem.** From there take N121 east to **Beja.** The road runs across the **Alentejo,** the province known as Portugal's breadbasket. From Beja head north on IP2 into Evora.

Camping at a Portuguese beach

9. Evora

Located atop a small hill in the heart of the Alentejo, Evora—with its astonishing variety of inspiring architecture—stands out from any other provincial farm town of its size in the world. The entire inner city is itself a monument. The town is best explored on foot. Wherever you glance, as you stroll the mazes of narrow streets and alleys, you'll come face to face with reminders of the town's rich architectural and cultural heritage. The principal sights include the **Roman Temple of Diana,** the massive fortresslike **Cathedral,** and the **Church of San Francisco,** with its bizarre **bone chapel.**

Parking inside the walls is very difficult. There are, however, several parking lots at the entrances to the old town.

Evora Campground

P–101 ★★ Orbitor Camping. Open year-round. On N380, 2 km (1.2 mi.) southwest of town in the direction of Alcacovas. Approaches are well marked. A pleasant, shaded site with many eucalyptus trees. Bus to town, 100 yd.

Evora → Lisbon (Lisboa), 155 km (93 mi.)

From Evora take N114 to **Montemor-o-Novo.** Continue following signs to **Setubal** and from there take the Via Rapida A2 across the bridge into Lisbon.

10. LISBON (LISBOA)

Spread out over seven hills and overlooking a magnificent harbor, Lisbon is one of Europe's oldest cities and most appealing capitals. The city presents an interesting jumble of architectural styles—an eye-pleasing coexistence of the ancient and ultra-modern.

The bustling **Alfama,** Lisbon's oldest quarter, recalls the labyrinthine medinas of the Arab world. Crowning the hill above the Alfama are the imposing fortifications of the **Castle of St. George.** The view from the walls extends out over the harbor and to the city's sprawling suburbs. At the foot of the Alfama is the fortresslike **Lisbon Cathedral.** The ornate **Jeronimos Monastery** in Belem, built in the uniquely Portuguese Manuline style, contains the tomb of the explorer Vasco da Gama.

Lisbon Campground

P–102 ★★★ Parque Municipal de Campismo de Monsanto. Open year-round. Approaching from the south, just after crossing the bridge, follow campground signs to the site. Approaches are well marked. Located in the heart of Monsanto Park, 5 km (3 mi.) west of city center. A large, sprawling site with many shade trees. Numerous resident campers. Parking in Lisbon is practically impossible and traffic is very heavy. Take the bus to town.

Lisbon → Nazare, 100 km (60 mi.)

Take N9 north from Lisbon to **Mafra.** The **Monastery** and **Royal Palace** comprise one of the most spectacular complexes of its kind in Portugal. From Mafra head west to the seaside resort of **Ericeira.** Then follow the coast road as it winds along the rugged shore to the colorful fishing port and fortress at **Peniche.**

Take N114 inland, following signs to **Obidos.** Crowned by a magnificent **castle,** this well-preserved medieval town brings to life the Portugal of the Middle Ages. Continue north on N8 to **Alcobaca,** site of an impressive church and monastery. From Alcobaca follow N8-4 west to Nazare.

11. Nazare

One of the first quaint Portuguese fishing villages to feel the impact of tourism, Nazare is no longer a village and has long ceased to be quaint. The beach is still lovely, however, and there is a good campground, which makes this a convenient base for exploring this beautiful part of Portugal.

Nazare Campground

P–103 ★★★ Camping Vale Paraiso. Open year-round. On N242, 2 km (1.2 mi.) north of Nazare. A large, inviting, sandy area in a pine forest. Bus to Nazare at entrance.

Nazare → Tomar, 70 km (42 mi.)

Follow N242 north to the intersection with N356 and continue on this to **Batalha.** Built to commemorate a decisive Portuguese victory over the Spanish in 1385, the soaring **Monastery and Church of Batalha** is one of the great masterpieces of Portuguese architecture.

From Batalha follow signs east to the pilgrimage site at **Fatima.** On the thirteenth of each month, pilgrimages are made to the shrine here. The esplanade in front of the basilica can hold as many as 1 million pilgrims. Continue on N113 the remaining 32 km (19 mi.) to Tomar.

12. Tomar

Tomar is a pleasant town laid out on both sides of the Rio Nabo, with the new and old parts linked by a graceful, arched stone bridge. Atop a hill rising from the old town is the **Convent of Christ,** one of Portugal's most remarkable architectural achievements. From 1160 until 1314 this was the headquarters of the Order of the Knights Templar.

Tomar Campground

P–104 ★★ Camping Municipal. Open year-round. In the center of town in a park at the river. Approaches are well marked. Narrow roads make entry difficult for large rigs. A large, grassy site with many shade trees. A twenty-minute walk to Convent of Christ. Plenty of parking at convent.

Tomar → Coimbra, 75 km (45 mi.)

From Tomar take N110 north to **Condeixa-a-Velha.** The ruins of the nearby Roman city of **Conimbriga** are some of the best preserved on the Iberian Peninsula. Continue north the remaining 15 km (9 mi.) into Coimbra.

13. Coimbra

An intriguing city that rises steeply from the banks of the **Mondego River,** Coimbra was once Portugal's capital and is home to one of Europe's oldest universities.

Coimbra Campground

P–105 ★ Parque Municipal de Campismo. Open year-round. At the northeast edge of town, next to the sports stadium. Turn off of N17 in the direction of Guarda. A small site with some shade. Sanitary facilities in need of upgrading. Bus to Coimbra center. Parking in Coimbra is very difficult.

Coimbra → Salamanca, Spain, 320 km (192 mi.)

Leave Coimbra on N17 and take this northeast along the western flank of the **Serra da Estrela,** Portugal's highest mountain range. At the intersection with IP5, follow signs to **Guarda.** At an altitude of 1,000 m (3,300 ft.), Guarda, a strategic fortified bastion guarding the approaches from Spain, is Portugal's highest city. From Guarda take IP5 and cross into Spain at **Vilar Formoso.** The road continues into Salamanca as N620.

14. Salamanca

An early and prominent center of European learning, Salamanca is an attractive city of reddish-golden sandstone buildings whose skyline is dominated by the majestic ancient cathedral. The expansive **Plaza Mayor** is one of the most elegant squares in Spain.

Salamanca Campground

E–110 ★★ Camping Regio. Open year-round. Located 4 km (2.4 mi.) east of Salamanca in suburb of Santa Marta de Tormes. Behind Hotel Regio. Well marked on N501 in the direction of Avila. A large site with plenty of shade. Hourly bus to Salamanca. Limited parking available in city.

Salamanca → El Escorial, 220 km (132 mi.)

Take N501 across the high plateau into **Avila.** Spain's highest provincial capital, Avila is one of Europe's best-preserved walled cities. The massive walls, with a running length of some 2.5 km (1.5 mi.) and containing eighty-eight watchtowers, were constructed in the late eleventh century.

From Avila follow N110 to the old Roman town of **Segovia,** a jewel of a fortified city that crowns a rocky hill. The center of the town is dominated by a huge, remarkably well-preserved **Roman Aqueduct** (still in use), which looms 27 m (89 ft.) above the main street.

La Granja de San Ildefonso, 11 km (6.6 mi.) southeast of Segovia, is a spectacular palace built on the model of Versailles. From Segovia take N630 and follow signs to El Escorial.

15. El Escorial

The traditional burial place of the kings and queens of Spain, El Escorial is a massive, imposing complex of Renaissance-style buildings situated in the foothills of the **Sierra de Guadarrama Mountains,** some 50 km (30 mi.) from Madrid. **Valle de los Caidos (Valley of the Fallen),** just a few kilometers from El Escorial, is a striking memorial to those killed during the Spanish Civil War. General Francisco Franco, ruler of Spain for thirty-six years, is buried here. A towering 150-m (495-ft.) cross looks down over the valley. The underground basilica, carved out of the solid rock, contains a series of sixteenth-century tapestries illustrating the Apocalypse.

El Escorial Campground

E–111 ★★★★ Camping El Escorial. Open year-round. Located 5 km (3 mi.) northeast of town. Turn off of C600 at km marker 14.8. Approaches are well marked. A large site in a pleasant rural setting with plenty of shade. Adequate parking at Valle de los Caidos and El Escorial. This is a good base for touring Avila and Segovia. This is also a good alternative base for visiting Madrid (50 km/30 mi.) and avoiding driving through the city. There is regular bus service into Madrid.

El Escorial → Madrid, 50 km (30 mi.)

To return to the capital take M505 and NVI. The approaches to Madrid are well marked.

ITALIAN IMPRESSIONS

Italy

CAPITAL: Rome

POPULATION: 58,000,000

CURRENCY: Lira, divided into 100 centesimi

LANGUAGE: Italian

RELIGION: Roman Catholic

POLICE: 113

FIRE: 113

AMBULANCE: 113

ROAD SERVICE: Auto Club of Italy (ACI) twenty-four hours, phone 116; includes Vatican City and San Marino

BANKS: weekdays 8:30 A.M.–1:30 P.M. and 2:45–3:45 P.M.

STORES: Monday–Saturday 8:30 or 9:00 A.M.–1:00 P.M. and 3:30 or 4:00–7:30 or 8:00 P.M.; in Rome many shops are closed Monday morning or Saturday afternoon in July and August

HOLIDAYS: January 1; January 6, Epiphany; Easter Monday (movable); April 25, Liberation Day; May 1, Labor Day; June 2, Republic Day; Ferragosto Assumption Day (movable); All Saints' Day (movable); December 8, Immaculate Conception; December 25 and 26

EMBASSIES: *United States,* Via Veneto 119/A, 00187 Rome; phone (06) 467–41, fax (06) 488–2672. *Canada,* Via Zara 30, 00198 Rome; phone (06) 440–3028/31, fax (06) 440–3063. *United Kingdom,* Via XX Settembre 80A, 00187 Rome; phone (06) 482–5441 or 482–5551

Shaped in the form of a jagged boot thrust into the Mediterranean Sea, Italy, its land approaches dominated by a massive alpine wall, has over the centuries developed a character and personality all its own. This is a country that has its own distinctive way of doing things.

Italian designs—in fashion, automobiles, office machines, and even highways and bridges—lead the world. Few who travel in Italy ever get bored, for this is a country that has it all. Visitors can choose from a dazzling array of art and architectural treasures, towering mountains, sandy beaches, medieval hilltop villages, and historic cities—Rome, Florence, Siena, and Venice, to name just a few—that are living Renaissance museums.

Italy is a place where past and present form a viable union; where ancient monuments, such as Verona's Roman amphitheater and Rome's Baths of Caracalla, provide the venue for modern-day opera and concert performances. And, of course, there is Italian cuisine, arguably the best eating in the world.

Although Italy seems constantly to be on the brink of disaster, the country nevertheless manages to survive, often just in time to move on to the next crisis. Many of the disputes revolve around the large disparity in wealth between the industrial north and the poorer agricultural south; as you drive through the countryside, these disparities are readily apparent. Since the end of World War II, there have been more than forty governments in Italy. Italian friends tell us that living in Italy is absolutely chaotic but delightful. For the tourists who don't have to deal with the bureaucracy or face the hassles of everyday life, it is just that much more delightful a place to visit.

DRIVING

Contemporary Italian highway engineers, following the tradition of the early Roman road builders, have created some of Europe's best highways. The old saying, "All roads lead to Rome," still applies, with Rome as the hub of an extensive network of toll roads known as *autostrada.*

Tolls are steep, especially for larger RVs, and these roads will not show you much of the real Italy. They are useful, however, in crossing some of the more tedious mountainous stretches that constitute much of the interior of the country. Payment on the autostrada may be made using a magnetic cash card called a *Viacard,* obtained from the Automobile Club of Italy (ACI) in 50,000- and 90,000-lire denominations. Credit cards are now accepted on some stretches.

The autostrada are marked with white lettering on a green background. State highways are denoted with blue-and-white signs and the letters "SS" followed by a one-, two-, or three-digit number—the more digits the narrower and more tortuous the road. Yellow signs indicate places of touristic interest.

Italian motorists drive much like they talk; rapidly, loudly, with much emotion and a great deal of hand waving and horn honking. This is particularly true in Rome, Naples, and in the south of the country. Drive defensively and you'll do just fine.

Parking is a serious problem in all of the major cities. Should you be lucky enough ever to find a spot, don't leave anything of value in your vehicle, especially around the major tourist areas. Where you encounter signs reading ZONA DISCO, don't reach for your dancing shoes! This has nothing to do with discos and dancing. Rather, it indicates that the use of a parking disk is required and that parking is only for a specified time, usually one and one-half hours.

The previous relaxed attitude toward the combination of alcohol and driving has been replaced by one of strict enforcement, with the imposition of breath tests, heavy fines, and, in some cases, imprisonment for driving under the influence of alcohol or drugs.

The Italian Traffic Police are authorized to collect traffic fines directly and are required to hand over an official receipt for the amount paid. Seatbelts are compulsory, and children between ages four and twelve may not ride in the front seat without a restraining harness. The speed limit for motorhomes on the autostrada is 130 kph (78 mph). The speed limit in towns and built-up areas, unless otherwise posted, is 50 kph (30 mph). Outside of built-up areas it is 90 kph (54 mph).

CAMPING

Camping is a very popular Italian pastime, and with the increasing emergence of a strong middle class, Italian RVs have become a common sight in campgrounds throughout Europe. Within Italy there are some 2,200 officially registered campgrounds. These run the gamut from intimate, secluded mountain sites to camping cities like those found along the beaches near Venice. In summer these latter ones may accommodate 10,000 persons!

Few places of interest in the country are without a campground, with the highest concentration of sites found along the coast, in the lake regions, and in the Dolomite Mountains. If you are traveling in these regions from mid-July through August, try to arrive at your campground early in the day to ensure getting a spot.

In many parts of the country, including the entire Riviera, the water is polluted. Before swimming in the ocean, check locally to be sure that there are no restrictions. The stretches of beach between Rome and Pisa and the beaches in the far south, except those near the larger cities, are suitable for swimming, as are the northern lakes.

In some provinces campgrounds are classified by from one to four stars, depending on the facilities present. The quality of campgrounds is generally best in the northern half of the country. Coin-operated washers and dryers are not as commonly found as in Northern Europe.

The EEC Euro outlets are now widely used throughout the country. In many cases it is necessary to have an adapter for the German Schuko plug. A number of sites, particularly along the Adriatic coast, are miserly about providing sufficient amperage. Check the rating before plugging in any high-wattage items.

German-type propane bottles and tanks can be filled at many campgrounds and filling stations. In some cases an adapter of the type found in the Euro-Set is necessary.

Unless otherwise prohibited, free camping is generally tolerated. There are an increasing number of camper-friendly communities throughout the country where RVs are particularly welcome. These overnight parking areas are usually designated with an RV pictogram.

In many cases you will find water and dumping facilities available. Look for signs that read CAMPER SERVICE or EURO-RELAIS. Usually there is no charge for using these facilities. For additional information about camping in Italy contact Federcampeggio, Via Vittorio Emanuele 11, Casella Postale 23, 50041 Calenzano (FI), Italy; phone (055) 88 23 91, fax (055) 88 25 918.

Itinerary: Rome · Florence and Tuscany · Venice · The Lakes · Naples

START: Rome

COUNTRY: Italy

DISTANCE: 2,075 km (1,245 mi.)

MAPS: Michelin #988 *Italy;* #428 *North West Italy;* #429 *North East Italy;* #430 *Central Italy;* #431 *Southern Italy*

MINIMUM RECOMMENDED TOURING TIME: 18 days

INTRODUCTION

Any tour through Italy is also a tour through the pages of history. No other nation in Europe has as much of cultural and historical interest packed into as small an area. The whole country, in many ways, is one vast museum.

In the three weeks or so that it takes to traverse this route comfortably, you will experience a span of nearly 3,000 years of history—from the founding of Rome in 753 B.C. to the present. Well-preserved medieval fortresses and ancient Roman and Etruscan sites are practically as common a feature of the Italian landscape as are shopping malls in the United States.

This itinerary covers a wide variety of attractions and landscapes that include Siena and the hilltop towns of Tuscany, the canals and regal palaces of Venice, and the relaxing, clear Lombardy lakes at the foot of the Alps. In addition to Rome and Florence, with their incredible art treasures, we also visit Italy's second- and third-largest cities: the northern banking and commercial center of Milan and, in the south, the teeming streets of Naples.

WHEN TO GO

From May through September as well as in early spring and late autumn, when the rest of the places along this itinerary are pleasantly un-

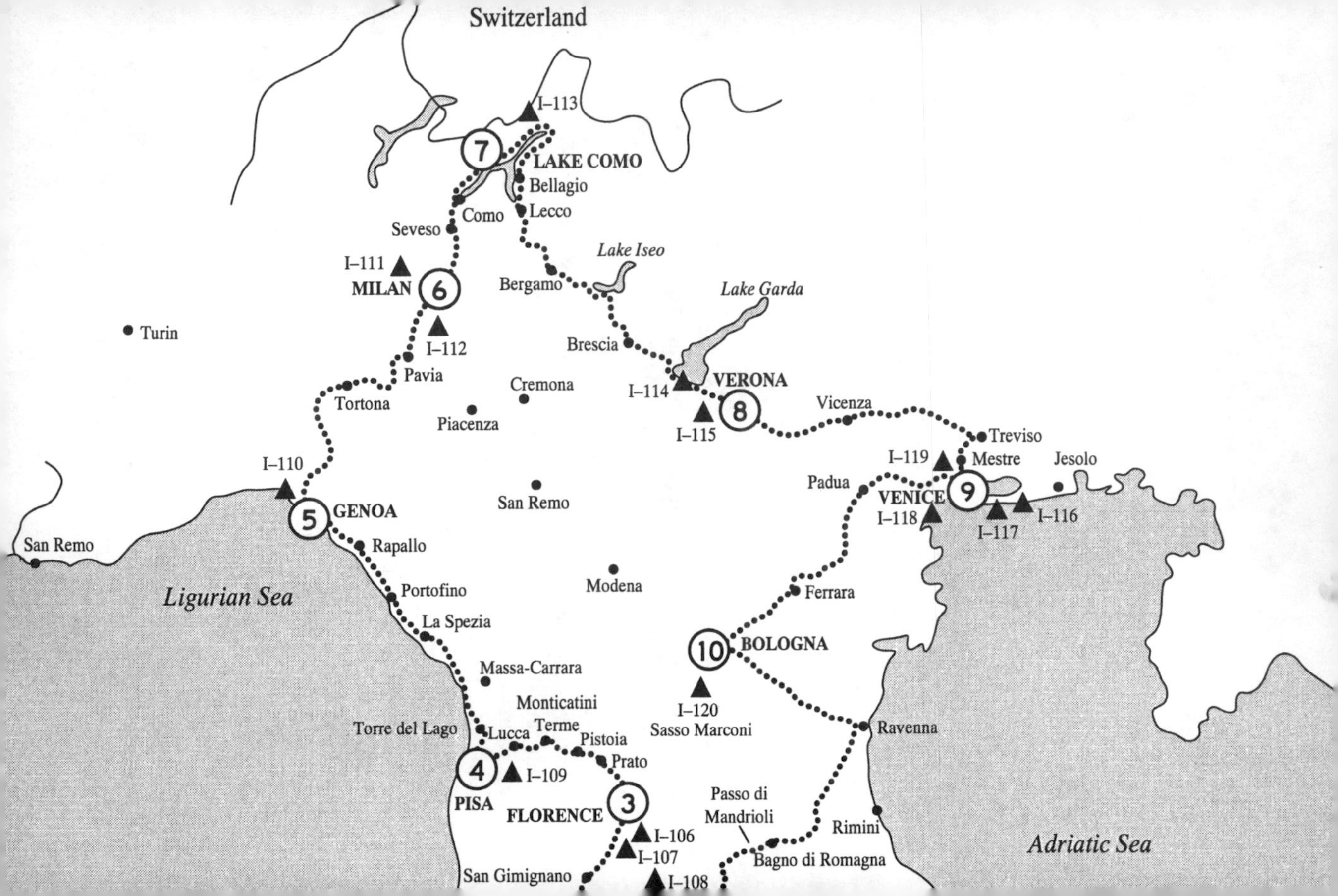
Switzerland
I–113
LAKE COMO
Bellagio
Lecco
Como
Seveso
I–111
MILAN
Bergamo
Lake Iseo
Lake Garda
Turin
I–112
Brescia
Pavia
Cremona
VERONA
I–114
Tortona
Piacenza
I–115
Vicenza
Treviso
I–110
I–119
Mestre
Jesolo
Padua
VENICE
I–118
I–117
I–116
GENOA
San Remo
San Remo
Rapallo
Modena
Portofino
Ligurian Sea
Ferrara
La Spezia
BOLOGNA
Massa-Carrara
I–120
Monticatini
Terme
Sasso Marconi
Torre del Lago
Lucca
Pistoia
Ravenna
Prato
I–109
PISA
FLORENCE
Passo di
Mandrioli
Rimini
I–106
I–107
Adriatic Sea
San Gimignano
Bagno di Romagna
I–108

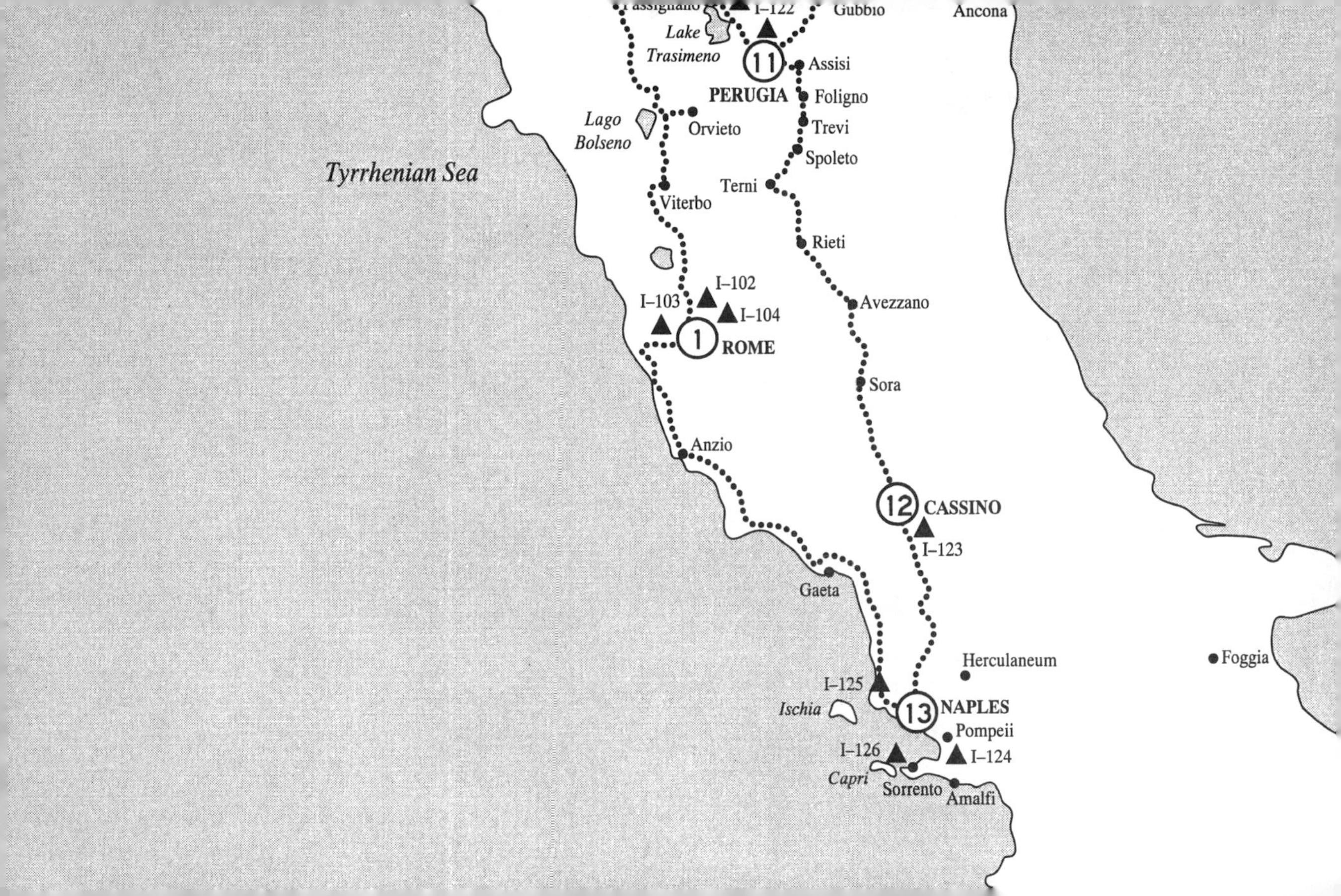

I–122
Gubbio
Ancona
Lake
Trasimeno
11
Assisi
PERUGIA
Foligno
Lago
Bolseno
Orvieto
Trevi
Spoleto
Tyrrhenian Sea
Terni
Viterbo
Rieti
I–102
I–103
I–104
Avezzano
1
ROME
Sora
Anzio
12
CASSINO
I–123
Gaeta
Herculaneum
Foggia
I–125
Ischia
13
NAPLES
Pompeii
I–126
I–124
Capri
Sorrento
Amalfi

crowded, Rome, Florence, and Venice are full of tourists all bent on seeing the same things. Try to schedule your visits to such popular attractions as the Sistine Chapel, Michelangelo's David and the Uffizi Gallery in the early mornings, before the tour buses start rolling in.

July and August in Rome and in the interior of the country are oppressively hot. Although the weather in the Lombardy Lake District in high summer is usually quite pleasant, the hordes of tourists, Italians and foreigners alike, who invade the northern lakes in July and August detract greatly from the enjoyment of this otherwise tranquil region. The best combination of weather and uncrowded conditions for following this itinerary is found in May to mid-June and in September and October.

Highlights

Rome
Florence
Siena
Venice
Pompeii
Amalfi Drive

Expanding Horizons

- **To Alpine Heights and Old World Delights Itinerary:** From Lake Garda take the Brenner Pass into Innsbruck. From Milan follow the road to Aosta (see p. 350).
- **To the Cradle of Western Civilization Itinerary:** From Venice take the ferry to Athens (p. 271) or to Izmir (p. 281). There is also regular ferry service to Greece and Turkey from Bari and Brindisi.

ON THE ROAD

Numbered sites correspond with circled numbers on the itinerary map.

1. Rome (Roma)

Rome is really two cities: Rome, the ancient Eternal City, once the capital of an empire that encompassed most of Europe and North Africa, a realm that stretched from the snows of northern Britain to the desert sands of Syria; and Rome, a sprawling metropolis of 3.5 million, the vibrant capital of a modern industrial state. Today's Rome is an urban colossus, surrounded by relics of its former glory, struggling to cope with the problems and complexities of a united Europe in the approaching twenty-first century.

As the saying goes, Rome was not built in a day, and Rome, as every tourist who has visited it can attest to, cannot be seen in a day. You can easily spend a whole day at the Vatican. The best approach to seeing the city, unless you have a local friend or relative to show you around, is to take an organized sightseeing tour to gain an overall perspective. Then go back and explore the places that interest you on your own. For tour information check with the Rome Provincial Tourist (EPT) office, Via Parigi 5, Rome; phone (06) 43 37 48.

Unlike many European cities, where the major sights are concentrated in a central area easily explored on foot, in Rome the sheer number of interesting things to see and the distance between many attractions makes exploration by foot an undertaking limited to the hardiest of hikers. This does not mean that Rome is not a city for walking.

On the contrary—a good part of the enjoyment of the Eternal City comes from just strolling its busy streets and alleys. For your touring on foot, select several attractions that are within easy walking distance of one another and use public transportation to get to the general areas that you want to explore. Be sure to allow enough time to wander, and, depending on your budget, to shop or at least to look in the inviting shop windows. Stop at a sidewalk cafe in a crowded piazza for a cappuccino and just watch the passing parade. It's all part of the Roman experience.

One part of the Roman experience that's best avoided is driving. The best thing that we can say about driving in Rome is, "Don't!" The traffic defies description, and parking for an RV is nonexistent. Leave your rig at the campground and take the Metro or the city buses or, if your budget allows, a taxi.

Here are just a few of our Roman favorites.

Citta del Vaticano (Vatican City), a sovereign state of 109 acres and 800 inhabitants, lies directly across the Tiber River from the center of Rome. The head of state is the pope, and this mini-state within a state is symbolically protected by a contingent of colorfully costumed Swiss Guards. This tiny enclave is the world headquarters and the seat of the power of the Roman Catholic Church. The Vatican is also one of Europe's principal tourist attractions. It draws believers and nonbelievers alike from all over the world who flock to visit **St. Peter's Square,** the **Vatican museums,** and the recently restored **Sistine Chapel** in **St. Peter's Basilica.**

Piazza Navona is one of the most charming and liveliest of Rome's many baroque squares. At its center is Bernini's masterful **Fountain of the Four Rivers.** Just east of the Piazza is the **Pantheon.** Rebuilt by the Emperor Hadrian in the second century A.D., this architectural masterpiece is dominated by a classically proportioned dome whose height and diameter are perfectly equal.

The **Colosseum,** a massive, 1,900-year-old amphitheater with a seating capacity of 50,000, has been the scene of gladiator contests, chariot races, and simulated naval battles. It has withstood the ravages of time, earthquakes, and modern traffic to remain one of Rome's most popular attractions.

To enjoy a brief respite from the rigors of big-city touring, visit the **Villa Borghese,** the city's biggest public park. The best panoramic view of Rome and the surrounding hill towns is from the **Piazzale Garibaldi** at sunset from the top of the **Gianicolo (Janiculum Hill).**

Rome Campgrounds

Metropolitan Rome is well supplied with campgrounds. The access to and from most of these is relatively painless via the **Grande Raccordo Anulare,** the ring road that circles the city. All of Rome's campgrounds are packed in July and August. To avoid disappointment, schedule your arrival early in the day.

I–102 ★★★ Happy Camping. Open March 15–October 31. Located 9 km (5.4 mi.) north of Rome center. On the Via Prato della Corte. Going in the direction of Viterbo, take exit 5 from the ring road. Then continue on the Via Cassia Veientanna (SS2), following signs to campground. Approach is well marked. Site is about 1 km (0.6 mi.) north of ring road. A medium-size, grassy area with some sites terraced into a hillside. The campground is fenced in and surrounded by fields. A restful place after visiting the crowded city. Shuttle bus to metro station. Ten minutes to Rome center.

I–103 ★★★ Camping Roma. Open year-round. At the west end of town, 8 km (4.8 mi.) from Rome center and 4 km (2.4 mi.) from Vatican. Located on the Via Aurelia at km marker 8.2 on the south side of the dual highway, opposite a large supermarket (Silos). Take exit 1 from the ring road and follow camping signs toward the center of town. A medium-size, grassy site on a hill with many shade trees. Bus to downtown at the entrance.

I–104 ★★ Camping Tiber. Open March 1–November 30. Nine km (5.4 mi.) north of Rome center. Take exit 6 from ring road and head north on Via Fiaminia (SS3), following signs to Prima Porta and campground. A large meadow on the Tevere River with a number of poplar trees. Public transportation at gate. Fifteen minutes to Rome center. Shuttle bus to Metro.

Rome → Siena, 225 km (135 mi.)

Leave Rome via the ring road. Take exit 5 and follow SS2 (Via Cassia) to **Viterbo.** Lying at the foot of the **Cimini Mountains,** Viterbo has a well-preserved medieval city core with an attractive **piazza** and a thirteenth-century **papal palace,** scene of several papal elections.

Continue on SS2 to **Montefiascone.** From there the road follows the shoreline of **Lago Bolsena.** At the town of **Bolsena,** on the lake of the same name, you can turn off and take SS71 the 18 km (10.8 mi.) up to the medieval Umbrian hill town of **Orvieto.** The Gothic **cathedral** in this attractive wine-producing center is one of Italy's most beautiful. Return to the Lakc and follow SS2 the remaining 110 km (66 mi.) to Siena.

2. Siena

Much smaller and more easily manageable for visiting than its archrival Florence, Siena is a wonderful place to just stroll and soak up the atmosphere of medieval Tuscany. The entire old-town center is a living museum. At the center of the old walled city is the **Piazza del Campo,** distinguished by the graceful town hall and site of the famous **Palio** horse race. One of Europe's most colorful spectacles, the race is held every July 2 and August 16. The **Duomo (cathedral)** is a masterpiece of thirteenth- and fourteenth-century Italian Gothic architecture. Siena is also one of Italy's major wine-producing centers. The castle at **Belcaro,** located 7 km (4.2 mi.) southwest of Siena, affords an excellent panoramic view of the town from its open parapets.

Siena Campground

I–105 ★★ Camping Colleverde. Open March 21–November 10. Located 2 km (1.2 mi.) northeast of town. Approach is well marked from the ring road around Siena. A partly sloped, shaded, grassy meadow with some small gravel pads for motorhomes and trailers. Located in a residential neighborhood with view of the old town. Convenient bus to town. Parking in Siena is difficult. –800 yd.

Siena → Florence (Firenze), 65 km (39 mi.)

From Siena take SS2 across the vineyard-clad hills of Chianti to Florence. For an interesting side trip, turn off at **Poggibonsi** and follow signs the 11 km (6.6 mi.) to **San Gimignano,** a delight of a medieval town with three sets of well-preserved city walls. Fourteen of the original fortified towers remain. Continue toward Florence along SS2 and then follow the four-lane highway into the city. Motor vehicles are not allowed in the old town.

3. Florence (Firenze)

The capital of Tuscany lies in the heart of a region of vine-covered hills and fertile valleys. Florence was one of the great centers of the Italian Renaissance, and even though present-day Florence is a bustling city of half a million inhabitants, the old Renaissance core has been meticulously preserved.

Most of the interesting attractions are located within a few minutes walk from the **Duomo (Cathedral of Santa Maria del Fiore),** the magnificent domed structure that rises from the center of the city to dominate the gentle Tuscan landscape.

The list of things to see in Florence reads like the index of an art history text. Here are just a few of the highlights.

Sharing the **Piazza del Duomo** with the Gothic, marble-clad cathedral, whose interior houses numerous priceless artworks, is the **Il Campanile (Bell Tower).** The graceful, freestanding, 265-ft.-tall belfry of the Duomo is one of the most beautiful in Italy.

Ghiberti's fourteenth-century bronze doors on the nearby **Baptistery** rank among the greatest of Europe's art treasures. The **Museo dell Opera di Santa Maria (Cathedral Museum)** includes in its collection of masterpieces Michelangelo's unfinished Pieta. The **Uffizi Museum and Gallery,** with its incredible paintings and sculpture, is yet another world-class museum.

Across the Arno, the **Pitti Palace** contains a wonderful collection of Titians and Raphaels. A visit to the **Palazzo Vecchio** and the **Palazzo Medici** will give you a good insight into the lifestyles of the rulers of Renaissance Florence. The **Ponte Vecchio (Old Bridge),** reconstructed in the fourteenth century, is a Florentine landmark, with craft shops lining its sides. From the **Piazzale Michelangelo,** looking across the Arno, you have a superb panoramic view of the city.

Florence Campground

I–106 ★★ Camping Michelangelo. Open Easter–November 5. Located 1.5 km (0.9 mi.) southeast of town center. South of the Arno near the Piazzale Michelangelo. Approaches are well marked. A large municipal campground that slopes down to the river Arno. Sites are terraced into the hill and afford good views of the city. Many olive trees but little shade. Very crowded in summer. Convenient bus to Florence center, or fifteen-minute walk.

I–107 ★★ Camping International Firenze. Open April 1–October 15. In Bottai, 8 km (4.8 mi.) southwest of Florence. Near the Monastery Certosa. Turn off from SS2 at km 292. Approaches are well marked. A large site terraced into a wooded hill. Steep, narrow approach road. Good base for visiting Siena and Florence. Convenient bus into Florence.

I–108 ★★★★ Camping Norcenni Girasole Club (Figlino–Valdarno). Open year-round. Located 25 km (16 mi.) southeast of Florence center. A nicely landscaped, large, partly terraced meadow in a pleasant rural setting with many shade trees. This is the best of the Tuscany campgrounds, with a full range of facilities, including horseback riding, wine-tasting excursions, disco, and water slides. A good base for touring central Tuscany and Chianti region. Shuttle bus to station for train to Florence.

Florence → Pisa, 80 km (48 mi.)

From Florence follow signs first to **Prato** and then to **Pistoia.** Due to its proximity to Florence, the ancient Roman city of Pistoia is often neglected, but once you get past its heavily industrialized outskirts you will find an old-town core with an authentic and relatively noncommercialized medieval atmosphere. The main attractions are the **Cathedral of San Zemo** and the fourteenth-century octagonal **Baptistery.**

Continue from Pistoia on SS435. This narrow road meanders through the elegant spa town of **Monticatini Terme** and then on to **Lucca,** Puccini's hometown. Behind Lucca's tree-topped sixteenth-century walls lies an important art center with a splendid cathedral. From Lucca take SS12 into Pisa.

4. Pisa

Once a bustling and powerful commercial port near the mouth of the Arno River, Pisa is a city whose glories lie submerged in the past. With the exception of the complex of Romanesque structures that occupy an expansive, open, grassy square in the northwest corner of the city, Pisa has little of interest to hold a visitor's attention.

The main attraction here is the twelfth-century **Campanile,** or **Leaning Tower.** Those who brave the climb up the tower's 294 oddly inclined steps are rewarded with a superb panoramic view of the town. The adjacent cathedral, built between 1068 and 1118, with generous use of marble, is one of Italy's most impressive religious structures.

Pisa Campground

I–109 ★ Camping Torre Pendente. Open April 1–October 15. At the north end of town. From SS1 (Viareggio–Livorno) turn off at km 336/IV and follow signs to campground. A medium-size, level, grassy site with some shade trees. A fifteen-minute walk to the Leaning Tower. Convenient bus to Pisa center. Parking in Pisa is very difficult.

Pisa → Genoa (Genova), 150 km (90 mi.)

From Pisa follow the coastal highway through a series of beach resorts to Genoa. At **Torre del Lago,** just north of Pisa, is the attractive lakeside villa where Puccini composed most of his operas. The road continues through the **Massa-Carrara region.** The beaches here are overshadowed by the towering marble peaks of the Apuan Alps. The fine white marble from Carrara has been the preferred medium for sculptors since Roman times.

La Spezia, a major naval base, has little of interest except for its **Naval Museum. Rapallo** and **Portofino,** along the **Ligurian Coast,** some 20 km (12 mi.) from Genoa, are two of Italy's most popular beach resorts. Beach access here is extremely limited and parking in the summertime with an RV virtually impossible.

5. Genoa (Genova)

Northern Italy's most important port, Genoa is a city that has seen better days. This city of some three-quarters of a million residents fans out like an amphitheater into the hills that rise up from the port. Along with a number of other places in this region, Genoa claims to be the birthplace of Christopher Columbus. An eighteenth-century reconstruction of his reputed childhood home is located in the **Piazza Dante.** The **Via Garabaldi,** in the center of town, contains a number of fine palaces from the sixteenth and seventeenth centuries, a period during which Genoa rivaled Venice in its trade links with the East.

Note: To connect with our France Itinerary III, continue from Genoa following the coast on SS1, or take the autostrada to the French border near Menton, on the French Riviera.

Genoa Campground

I–110 ★★ Camping Villa Doria (Pegli). Open year-round. In Pegli, just west of Genoa. Approach is well marked from SS1 (Genoa–Savona). A small, terraced meadow with many shade trees. Public transportation to Genoa, 300 yd. ▣ ▨–800 yd. ▣ ▢

Genoa → Milan (Milano), 150 km (90 mi.)

Head north from Genoa and follow signs toward Milan. This is one place where we recommend taking the autostrada. (The surface road SS35 climbs and winds considerably and is plagued with heavy truck traffic.)

After exiting the autostrada at **Tortona,** take SS10 and then SS35 to **Pavia.** The well-preserved former capital of Lombardy contains a number of fine old buildings and an ancient university. Several kilometers north of Pavia, located just off of the Milano road, is an impressive Renaissance Carthusian **monastery,** one of northern Italy's grandest. From Pavia continue on SS35 into Milan.

6. Milan (Milano)

With a population of nearly 2 million, Milan is Italy's second-largest city and one of the world's most important banking and business centers. Although much of the cityscape is cluttered with commercial buildings, there is also much of interest here for the tourist.

The white Gothic spires of the enormous **Duomo,** with its 2,200 sculptures, provide the focal point for visitors to Milan. Begun in 1386, the cathedral was not completed until the early nineteenth century. The elegant glass-capped arcade, the **Galleria Vittorio Emanuele,** and the streets radiating out from the Duomo contain some of Europe's most exclusive shops.

The nearby historic **La Scala Opera House** is one of the world's most beautiful. **Sforza Castle,** built in the mid-fifteenth century, houses the **Museum of Antique Art.**

Da Vinci's famous fresco, **The Last Supper,** may be viewed at the **Church of St. Mary of Grace (Santa Maria delle Grazie).** Sketches and scale models of many of Leonardo's inventions are displayed at the **Museo della Scienza e della Tecnica Leonardo da Vinci.** For a glimpse of the Milan of a bygone era, stroll through the **Canal (navigli) District,** one of the city's most colorful quarters.

Note: To connect with our Alpine Heights and Old World Delights Itinerary, head west from Milan to Aosta (see p. 350).

Milan Campgrounds

I–111 ★★★ Campeggio Citta di Milano. Open year-round. At the western edge of the city, 10 km (6 mi.) from center. From Tangante Ovest (Milan ring road) take exit San Siro and follow campground signs. A large, level, grassy site with many young trees. Adjacent to a large water-sports complex. An oasis of green in this sometimes dreary city. Public transport to Milan center, 300 yd.

I–112 ★★ Camping AGIP Metanopole. Open year-round. Located 5 km (3 mi.) southeast of Milan center. Located just off of Autostrada Del Sole (A1) when entering Milan from the direction of Piacenza. Site is visible from the autostrada. This is the closest campground to Milan center. A medium-size, shaded site. Public transportation to Milan, 500 yd.

Milan → Lake Como, 40 km (24 mi.)

Leave Milan and follow signs by way of **Seveso** to the town of **Como.**

7. Lake Como

One of the most beautiful of the sparkling blue Lombardy lakes, Lake Como lies at the foot of the Alps but has a mild climate and subtropical vegetation. After the rigors of sightseeing in Milan, this is a good place to relax. The lake is bordered by a string of enchanting towns, which include **Bellagio, Menaggio,** and Como, with its fine Renaissance **Duomo.**

Como Campground

I–113 ★★ Camping Laguna Beach (Pianello del Lario). Open April 1–October 31. At the northwest shore of the lake in Pianello del Lario. A small, terraced meadow. Approach from town is well marked.

Como → Lake Garda and Verona, 220 km (132 mi.)

From Como follow SS340/SS340D. The narrow winding road hugs the west shore of the lake. This is pleasant but slow going, as the road passes through a number of small lakeside towns. Parking is at a premium all along the lake. Once you reach the north shore, you can either continue to toodle along or you can zip directly into the industrial town of **Lecco** on a four-lane highway that tunnels under a long stretch of steep granite cliffs lining the shore.

As an alternate route there are ferry crossings at **Cadenabbia,** Menaggio, Bellagio, and **Varenna.** You can also skip the ride around the lake and take SS639 east directly to **Lecco.**

From Lecco follow SS639 and then SS342 to **Bergamo.** The modern industrial lower city **(Citta Bassa)** offers little of interest. However, the upper medieval town **(Citta Alta),** some 125 m (412 ft.) above and connected to the lower town by a funicular, is worth a visit. Enclosed within thick walls, old Bergamo is one of the most characteristic of the Lombardy towns.

Continue east from Bergamo to **Sarnico** and then to **Iseo,** on the rocky shores of **Lake Iseo.** From Iseo follow signs to **Brescia,** a major business center and producer of arms since the sixteenth century. There are several Roman monuments and an imposing sixteenth-century castle that affords a fine view of the city. From Brescia take SS11 to Lake Garda.

8. Lake Garda and Verona

With its clean waters, mild climate, and lush Mediterranean vegetation, Lake Garda is one of northern Italy's most popular resort areas. Any one of several campgrounds on the south shore of the lake makes a good base for visiting Verona, 25 km (16 mi.) to the east on SS11.

Verona, immortalized by Shakespeare in *Romeo and Juliet* and *The Two Gentlemen of Verona,* was also an important Roman city. The well-preserved ancient **amphitheater,** which seats 20,000, is used as a venue for opera and concerts. In the old town center stands the thirteenth-century **Casa Capuleti,** with its famous **Juliet's Balcony.** The **Tomba di Giuletta,** reputed to be Juliet's tomb, is located in the Capuchin cloisters overlooking the **Adige River.**

Note: To connect with our Alpine Heights and Old World Delights itinerary, from Lake Garda take SS12 or the Autostrada A22 north over the Brenner Pass to Innsbruck (see p. 341).

Lake Garda and Verona Campgrounds

I–114 ★★★★ Camping del Garda (Peschiera). Open April 1–September 30. On the south shore of the lake, 1 km (0.6 mi.) east of Peschiera. A sprawling, forty-acre, grassy site with many bushes and trees. Swimming pool and private beach. Organized entertainment in summer. Bus from Peschiera to Verona.

I–115 ★★ Camping Romeo e Giulietta. Open March 1–November 30. Located 6 km (3.6 mi.) west of Verona on Hwy. S11 (Verona–Brescia). A medium-size, grassy site in a rural setting surrounded by fields and vineyards. Hourly bus service to Verona. Parking in Verona is difficult.

Verona → Venice (Venezia), 110 km (66 mi.)

Take SS11 east from Verona to **Vicenza.** Filled with the graceful Venetian–Roman-style buildings of Andrea Palladio, Vicenza is virtually an open-air museum dedicated to the works of this famous sixteenth-century Renaissance architect. Leaving Vicenza on SS53, follow signs to **Treviso,** an attractive ancient walled city. Then head south on SS13 to Venice.

9. VENICE (VENEZIA)

Venice, with its 117 islands linked by 400 bridges and 150 canals, is one of those love-hate places. Many visitors are enthralled by the magnificent palaces and inspiring vistas, while others are put off by the polluted canals and crass commercialism. You will have to decide for yourself. In either case, a visit to Venice should be included in any tour of Italy.

Although much of the city can be explored by foot, a ride through the canals in a Venetian gondola is a memorable experience. Be sure to negotiate the price before you depart. For a bird's-eye view of the city's red-tiled roofs, graceful domes, and complex labyrinth of streets and canals, take the elevator or climb the ramp to the top of the 324-ft. bell tower in **Piazza San Marco.** Much of the beauty of Venice can be enjoyed by simply being there and soaking up the atmosphere. Here are some of the places that should be included in any visit.

One of Europe's grande squares, Piazza San Marco is flanked by the **Basilica di San Marco,** originally built in 830 to hold the relics of St. Mark the Evangelist. The basilica was subsequently rebuilt and enlarged during the eleventh to sixteenth centuries. Next to the basilica is the **Palazzo Ducale (Doge's Palace),** an impressive pink-and-white marble structure with an unusual two-tiered loggia. With the ascension of Venice to the role of a major player on the world stage, the palace served as the headquarters for the management of Venice's far-flung interests.

The **Grand Canal,** the most impressive of the canals, winds through the heart of the city and is lined with some 200 Gothic–Renaissance palaces. The **Galleria dell'Accademia** displays of works by Tintoretto, Titian, and other Italian masters form Venice's finest art collection. Quality artistic glass products have been produced for hundreds of years on the island of **Murano** in the **Venice Lagoon.**

Note: To connect with the Cradle of Western Civilization itinerary, take the ferry from Venice to either Athens (Piraeus), Istanbul, or Izmir. The Venice–Izmir crossing takes about sixty hours. There are two

Vegetable market in Italy

crossings weekly. For details contact Turkish Maritime Lines, Central Office, Karakoy, Istanbul, Turkey; phone (1) 24 55 366, fax (1) 25 15 767.

The crossing to Greece takes about thirty hours. There are several crossings weekly, depending on the season. For details contact the Greek National Tourist Office, 645 Fifth Ave, New York, NY (phone 212–421–5777, fax 212–826–6940) or Viamare Travel, Graphic House, 2 Sumatra Road, London NW6 1PU, England (phone 071–431–4560, fax 071–431–5456).

Venice Campgrounds

There is no campground in Venice itself. Within a radius of a few kilometers, however, there are dozens of sites. The long, narrow strip of land that encloses the greater portion of the Venice Lagoon is a popular summer resort and contains one campground after another. Most sites are directly on the beach, and many are large camping "villages" that offer a full range of facilities.

To reach the campgrounds follow signs to **Jesolo,** about 10 miles (6 mi.) northeast of Venice. Access to Venice is by ferry boat from **Punta Sabbioni,** at the tip of the peninsula. There are also several smaller campgrounds on the mainland west of Venice that provide convenient access for a visit. Depending upon the season and the mood of the attendant, it is sometimes possible for self-contained units to camp on the Tronchetto Parking Island. When available, this option provides the closest and most convenient access to the city.

I–116 ★★★★ Camping Union Lido (Lido di Jesolo). Open May 1–September 30. On the road to Punta Sabbioni. Approach is well marked. An expansive, 120-acre camping village, the best and most luxurious of the several large complexes in the area. In addition to a long sandy beach, there are several large swimming pools. The broad range of recreational facilities and organized activities includes excursions to Venice. Seven-day minimum stay in July and August.

I–117 ★★★★ Camping Marina di Venezia (Punta Sabbioni). Open April 1–October 30. On the Cavallino–Punta Sabbioni road. Approaches are well marked. There are 160 acres of parks, grassy sites, dunes, and sandy beaches. Full range of facilities and activities. Three-day minimum in July and August. Shuttle bus to ferry. Twenty minutes to Venice.

I–118 ★★ Camping Fusina (Fusina). Open year-round. On the Venice Lagoon, 10 km (6 mi.) southwest of Venice in the industrial town of Fusina, east of Malcontenta. Approaches are well marked. In spite of its location amid factories and refineries, this site makes a convenient base for visiting Venice. Hourly ferry service to Piazza San Marco. A medium-size, level site with shade trees.

I–119 ★★ Camping Marco Polo (Mestre). Open February 1–November 30. Located 10 km (6 mi.) west of Venice. Turn off from S14 toward the Venice airport. Approach is well marked. A small, level site. Some noise from nearby airport. Bus to Venice, 250 yd.

Venice → Bologna, 155 km (93 mi.)

From Mestre (Venice) take SS11 to **Padua (Padova).** The ancient university in Padua, founded in 1222, is one of Europe's oldest. Padua's major attraction is the **Scovegni Chapel,** which contains magnificent frescos by Giotto. Head south from Padua on SS16 to **Ferrara,** a modern and airy agricultural and industrial center constructed on a filled-in marsh. The imposing moated fortress, **Castello Estense,** was built in the fourteenth to fifteenth centuries. Continue south on SS64 through the vineyard- and tree-covered countryside to Bologna.

10. Bologna

Bologna is often referred to as "Bologna the Fat" because of its reputation as a center of gastronomy and "Bologna the Learned" because of the presence of Europe's oldest university, founded in 1076. The principal attractions are the Gothic structures grouped around the **Piazza Maggiore** and the **Palazzo Comunale,** several palaces that are integrated into a single complex. Many of Bologna's streets are lined with intricate porticos and arcades housing fashionable shops and restaurants.

Bologna Campground

I–120 ★★ Camping Piccolo Paradise (Sasso Marconi). Open year-round. Located 10 km (6 mi.) south of Bologna. On the road to Sirano, 2 km (1.2 mi.) south of Sasso Marconi. A large, shaded, grassy site with many bamboo trees. Part of a large vacation complex. Bus from Sasso to Bologna. Parking in Bologna is difficult.

Bologna → Perugia, 295 km (177 mi.)

From Bologna follow SS253 east to **Ravenna** on the Adriatic coast. The city is known for its many **Byzantine monuments** and for its fine mosaics. Take SS71 southwest from Ravenna into the Tuscan Mountains. At the spa of **Bagno di Romagna,** the road forks. Continue over the serpentine 3,800-ft. **Passo di Mandrioli** and follow signs to the ancient Etruscan town of **Arezzo.** One of the most attractive of the Tuscan hill towns, Arezzo is known for its fine ceramics and goldwork. The major attractions are the frescos of Piero della Francesca in the fourteenth-century **Basilica di San Francesco.** From Arezzo continue south on SS71 to **Lake Trasimeno.** It was here in 217 B.C. that Hannibal's Carthaginians defeated Rome's legions. Take SS75 east the rest of the way into Perugia.

11. PERUGIA

The battlement-encircled Umbrian capital, Perugia, is perched on a hill that overlooks the **Tiber Valley.** The principal attractions in the old-town center are the thirteenth-century **San Lorenzo Cathedral,** the Gothic **Prior's Palace,** and the **National Gallery of Umbria. Gubbio,** 40 km (24 mi.) northeast of Perugia on SS298, is one of Italy's most attractive and best-preserved medieval towns.

Perugia Campgrounds

I–121 ★★★ Camping Kursaal (Passignano). Open April 1–October 10. On Lake Trasimeno at Passignano, 25 km (16 mi.) west of Perugia. Approach is well marked. A six-acre, grassy site with many trees. Small beach on the lake. Bus to town. Parking in Perugia difficult.

I–122 ★★ Camping Paradise d'Ete (Colle della Trinita). Open year-round. Located 6 km (3.6 mi.) northwest of Perugia. Turn off of S75 at km 13/VIII. Steep approach to campground. A grassy site that is terraced into a wooded hill.

Perugia → Cassino, 300 km (180 mi.)

Take SS147 east from Perugia to **Assisi.** The **Basilica of St. Francis of Assisi** is one of Christendom's most honored sites. The interior of the church is decorated with superb frescos by Giotto. From Assisi continue to **Foligno,** and from there follow SS3 through **Trevi** and the festival town of **Spoleto** to **Terni.** Then take SS79 to **Rieti** and SS578 along the winding course of the **Salto River** to **Avezzano.** From there follow signs to **Sora,** and then take SS627 and SS509 to Cassino.

12. CASSINO

This small town is best known as the location of the hilltop **Abbey of Montecassino.** Founded by St. Benedict in 529, the abbey, the cradle of the Benedictine Order, was used for military purposes by the Germans during World War II. The structure, badly damaged in an assault by Allied troops and planes, has been restored and is open to the public.

Cassino Campground

I–123 ★ Camping Terme Varroniane. Open year-round. Located

1 km (0.6 mi.) south of town. A medium-size, shady site. Simple but adequate facilities. Convenient base for visiting the monastery.

Cassino → Naples (Napoli), 85 km (51 mi.)

From Cassino take SS6, the **Via Casilina,** into Naples.

13. Campania: Naples, Pompeii, and the Gulf of Naples

Italy's third-largest city and one of the Mediterranean's major seaports, Naples attracts visitors more for what the city once was and for the surrounding areas of Pompeii and the bay region than for any current charms that it might have. Beset today by overpopulation, rampant decay, urban blight, gridlock traffic, pollution, unemployment, and widespread crime, Naples is not a city in which to linger. See the fine antiquities collection at the **Museo Archelogico Nazionale** and move on to the surrounding countryside. Driving or parking an RV in Naples is not recommended.

Pompeii, buried under a deep layer of lava and ash in A.D. 79, lies at the foot of the still-active **Mt. Vesuvius,** 15 km (9 mi.) southeast of Naples on SS18. The excavations cover some 160 acres and present a fascinating record of life in this region 1,900 years ago.

Herculaneum, 7 km (4.2 mi.) southeast of Naples, was buried under the same eruption as Pompeii. Although it has not been as extensively excavated as Pompeii, its villas are more elegant. One of the most spectacular drives in all of Italy is the twisting stretch of highway that skirts the peninsula separating the gulfs of Naples and Salerno. This includes the **Amalfi Coast Drive** and passes through the delightful resorts of **Sorrento** and **Positano.**

Note that sections of this drive are quite narrow and winding and are not recommended for large rigs.

Campania Campgrounds

I–124 ★★ Camping Zeus (Pompeii). Open year-round. In Pompeii. Approaches are well marked. A five-acre, level site with some shade. Conveniently located, 150 yd. from ruins. Train to Naples.

I–125 ★★ Camping Vulcano Solfatara (Solfatara). Open April 1–October 15. Located 5 km (3 mi.) southwest of Naples. On Via Domiziana at km 60. Coming from the north on SS7, go through Pozzuoli and follow signs to Solfatara. A level, shaded, sixteen-acre site in the crater of the extinct volcano Solfatara. Adjacent sulfur baths. Train to Naples from Pozzuoli, 900 yd. Bus, 50 yd. Excursions to Capri, Ischia.

I–126 ★★★ Camping Nube d'Argento (Sorrento). Open year-round. At the west end of Sorrento on the Sorrento–Massa Lubrense road. Difficult approach for large rigs. A small, terraced site. Shade trees. Good view of the bay. Bus to Sorrento, 50 yd.

Naples → Rome, 200 km (120 mi.)

From Naples follow SS7 along the coast to **Gaeta** and continue following the coast past the World War II invasion site at **Anzio** to Rome.

THE CRADLE OF WESTERN CIVILIZATION

Bulgaria

CAPITAL: Sofia

POPULATION: 9,000,000

CURRENCY: lev (Lv), divided into 100 stotinki; import and export prohibited

LANGUAGES: Bulgarian with some Turkish, Russian, and Greek; in Sofia and Black Sea resorts, some English and German are spoken

RELIGION: Bulgarian Orthodox

POLICE: 166 (Sofia)

FIRE: 160 (Sofia)

AMBULANCE: 150 (Sofia)

ROAD SERVICE: SBA—#146; in Sofia, 6:00 A.M.–10:00 P.M., call (02) 883978

BANKS: Foreign Trade Bank open Monday–Friday 8:00 A.M.–noon

STORES: weekdays 8:00 A.M.–5:00 P.M., Saturday 8:00 A.M.–2:00 P.M.; some shops remain open all day

HOLIDAYS: January 1; March 3, Liberation Day; Easter Monday (movable); May 1 and 2, Labor Day; May 24, Education Day; September 9 and 10, National Holiday; December 25 and 26

EMBASSIES: *United States,* 1 Sabornia Street, unit 25402, 1000 Sofia; phone (02) 884–801, fax (02) 801–977. *Canada,* no embassy. *United Kingdom,* Boulevard Marshalo, Marshal Tolbukhin 65/67, 1000 Sofia; phone (02) 885–361/2

Occupying the eastern half of the Balkan Peninsula, Bulgaria is the smallest of the Eastern European countries. Before the overthrow of the Communist regime in 1989, this fascinating land of some 9 million people, closely aligned with the Soviet Union and somewhat shrouded in mystery and intrigue, was seldom visited by Westerners.

Bulgaria is a country of great natural beauty that offers its visitors a wide range of scenic attractions ranging from fine sandy beaches along the Black Sea to the 8,000-ft. peaks of the rugged Balkan Mountains. In this essentially peasant and agricultural society, old traditions are maintained and folk arts and crafts are encouraged.

In its architecture, art, and cuisine, the country projects a decidedly Eastern feeling, a by-product of its early association with the Byzantine Empire and Bulgaria's nearly 500 years under Turkish occupation. Throughout the country there are a number of fine icon-filled monasteries and churches decorated with lovely frescoes. Bulgaria is also know as the "rose capital of the world." The Valley of the Roses, in the center of the country, produces more than 70 percent of the world's supply of rose oil, an essential ingredient in the manufacture of perfume.

Away from Sofia and the Black Sea resorts, language can be a problem. While some English is spoken, the principal foreign language is Russian. At campgrounds and restaurants, however, you can usually find someone who speaks a bit of English. Be sure to bring along an English–Bulgarian phrase book that includes a translation of the widely used Cyrillic alphabet. Time spent studying this alphabet will greatly enhance your trip, as the appearance of even such common words as "restaurant" *(pectophat)* can be baffling. Another confusing aspect of Bulgarian travel is the custom of giving an affirmative answer by shaking the head from side to side and saying no by a nod of the head. But it's like driving on the "wrong" side of the road in Britain: One soon gets used to it.

DRIVING

A good network of paved main roads connects the major tourist destinations. Since relatively few Bulgarians own automobiles, traffic is light, with the exception of along the heavily traveled Black Sea coast. There are no toll roads, and a major motorway-construction program is under way to link the principal cities and the Black Sea coast. Highway maintenance, while adequate, is not up to Western European standards; in your trip planning allow some extra time for rough potholed stretches of road.

Gasoline stations are adequately spaced on the main highways, but are few and far between in the outlying districts. The free road map available from Balkantourist shows the location of gas stations. Prepaid vouchers for the purchase of fuel are no longer required. If you intend to do a lot of back-country exploring, take along a jerry can of fuel and keep an eye on your gas gauge. Repair facilities and spare parts for most Western-made and Japanese vehicles are very limited. It is a good idea to carry a spare-parts kit.

Front seatbelts are compulsory, and it is against the law to drive after consuming any alcohol at all. Road signs are in both Cyrillic and Roman letters; however, in some of the more remote regions, only Cyrillic signs may be found.

The speed limit for motorhomes on the expressways is 120 kph (72 mph); outside of built-up areas it is 80 kph (51 mph). The speed limit in towns, unless otherwise posted, is 60 kph (36 mph).

Be sure that your international proof of insurance (Green Card) is valid for driving in Bulgaria. If it is not, you will be required to purchase more expensive insurance at the border.

CAMPING

Of the some 110 campgrounds in Bulgaria, nearly half are located along the Black Sea coast. Group camping vacations are a favorite pastime among Eastern Europeans, and it is not unusual to find many sites, particularly those near the beaches, swarming with busloads of tent and bungalow campers. Most campgrounds devote a large part of their space to so-called camping bungalows or huts. Motorhome travel is virtually nonexistent among Bulgarians, and the few motorhomes and trailers that you may see will most likely belong to German tourists.

The casualness and friendly atmosphere prevailing at these campgrounds, coupled with the fact that you and your RV will be objects of great curiosity, provide an unusually good opportunity for making contact with a diverse assortment of Eastern Europeans. You will find that the curiosity about lifestyles, politics, and material things is mutual and in most cases is enough to break down language barriers. To help further bridge the communications gap, always carry a bottle of *slivova,* the local firewater, with you. It will be indispensable.

Although sanitary facilities are often inadequate and facilities in general not up to Western campground standards, an effort is made to maintain an acceptable level of cleanliness. Most sites have some sort of campstore and snack bar; while the larger campgrounds, particularly those along the Black Sea coast, often are a part of a hotel–vacation complex that includes restaurants, discos, folklore programs, and concerts. During July and August the Black Sea resorts are packed, so plan to arrive at a campground as early in the day as possible to ensure obtaining a site.

Campgrounds are classified with from one to three stars, according to the facilities provided. An International Camping Carnet is not required, and no discounts are given. With the increase in the number of privately operated campgrounds, this is likely to change. Free camping is officially prohibited, but if you are discreet, you will generally have no problem.

Electrical connections are generally of the German Schuko type. Do not plan on filling your gas bottles or tanks in Bulgaria.

A map showing the location of campgrounds is available from the Bulgarian National Tourist Office (see p. 357). Most campgrounds are open only from May through September.

Greece

CAPITAL: Athens

POPULATION: 10,300,000

CURRENCY: drachma (Dr), divided into 100 lepta

LANGUAGE: Greek

RELIGION: Greek Orthodox

POLICE: 100

FIRE: 100

AMBULANCE: 100

ROAD SERVICE: OVELPA—104 (most areas), twenty-four hours

BANKS: weekdays 8:00 A.M.–2:00 or 2:30 P.M.

STORES: Tuesday–Friday 9:00 A.M.–6:30 P.M., Monday 9:30 A.M.–2:30 P.M.; there is much variance in the regions

HOLIDAYS: January 1; January 6, Epiphany; Monday before Ash Wednesday (movable); March 25, Independence Day; Good Friday and Easter Monday (movable); May 1, Labor Day; Ascension Day (movable); Pentacost (movable); October 28, National Day; December 25 and 26

EMBASSIES: *United States,* 91 Vasilissis Sophia Boulevard, 10160 Athens; phone (01) 721–2951, fax (01) 721–8660. *Canada,* 4 10 Annou Gennadiou Street, Athens; phone (01) 723–9511/9, fax (01) 724–7123. *United Kingdom,* 1 Odos Ploutarchou, 10675 Athens, phone (01) 723–6211

The cradle of Western civilization, ancient Greece was responsible for numerous contributions to our literature, music, poetry, architecture, politics, medicine, and law. The visitor to modern-day Greece is confronted throughout the country with reminders of its glorious past. When you have tired of temples and ancient artifacts, Greece's many attractive islands and more than 15,000 km (9,000 mi.) of coastline offer a wonderful variety of beaches and swimming opportunities.

DRIVING

Driving in Greece is a hair-raising experience. Greek drivers and roads are among the worst in Europe. Extreme caution is advised. When driving at night, be alert for animals and unlit horse or donkey carts on the road.

Two stretches of toll roads run from Athens north to the border with former Yugoslavia and south from Athens to the Peloponnese. Road signs and place names are in both the Greek and Roman alphabets.

The use of seat belts is mandatory. The permissible blood-alcohol level is 0.05 percent.

The speed limit for motorhomes on the tollways is 100 kph (60 mph). The speed limit in towns and built-up areas, unless otherwise posted, is 50 kph (30 mph). Outside of built-up areas it is 80 kph (48 mph).

A bewildering number of ferries can transport you and your RV to the various islands. For details check with the Greek National Tourist Office.

CAMPING

With its fine beaches and sunny weather, Greece is one of Europe's favorite camping destinations. The country's 250 campgrounds are located primarily in the coastal regions, at the popular tourist destinations, and on many of the more popular islands. Although much progress has been made in improving facilities, Greek campgrounds, with few exceptions, are not on a par with those of Northern Europe. The best facilities and service are found at the sites that are privately owned.

Free camping is officially prohibited; however, enforcement varies from place to place and is often arbitrary. For additional information about camping in Greece, contact Greek Camping Association, 102 Solonos Street, 106 80 Athens, Greece; phone (01) 36 21 560, fax (01) 86 41 693.

Turkey

CAPITAL: Istanbul

POPULATION: 59,200,000

CURRENCY: Turkish lira (TL), divided into 100 kurus

LANGUAGES: Turkish, Kurdish, and Arabic

RELIGION: Islamic (mostly Sunni)

POLICE: check local directories

FIRE: check local directories

AMBULANCE: check local directories

ROAD SERVICE: TTOK Istanbul, twenty-four hours, 177–8339

BANKS: weekdays 8:30 A.M.–noon and 1:00–3:00 P.M.

STORES: weekdays 8:30 A.M.–1:00 P.M. and 2:00–7:00 P.M.; Saturday 8:30 A.M.–noon and 1:00–7:30 P.M.; in resort areas shops often remain open until 9:00 P.M.

HOLIDAYS: January 1; April 23, National Independence and Children's Day; Seker Bayrami (sugar feast), three-day feast marking the end of Ramadan, a month-long daytime fasting period (movable); May 19, Sports Day; Kurban Bayrami (movable); August 30, Victory Day; October 28 (half) and 29,

EMBASSIES: *United States,* 110 Ataturk Boulevard, Ankara; phone (04) 426–5470, fax 426–5470. *Canada,* Nenehatun Caddesi 75, Gaziosmanpasa, 06700 Ankàra; phone (04) 436–1275/9, fax 446–4437. *United Kingdom,* Sehit Ersan, Caddesi 46/a, Ankara; phone (04) 127–4310/15

A fascinating country that forms the traditional bridge between the Orient and the Occident, Turkey offers the RV traveler a taste of the exotic right on Western Europe's doorstep. From Thessaloniki in northern Greece, it's just a half day's drive to Istanbul and then across the Bosporus bridge, and you are in Asia.

For the student of history, Turkey offers a wealth of fascinating material. In 1964, for example, a settlement dating back to 6000 B.C. was uncovered near Konya, the home of the famous "whirling dervishes."

Mt. Ararat, in the northeastern part of the country, near the Armenian border, is where Noah's ark is said to have come to rest; and on the west coast, at the historic Dardanelles, are the ruins of the legendary city of Troy, which Homer described in the *Iliad.* In more recent times both Byzantine and Ottoman Turkey have had profound influences on the development of Western Europe. The entire country is a virtual open-air museum of art and architectural treasures. Turkey is also a land of many contrasts where, in some regions, in the shadow of modern industrial plants, peasants till the soil with wooden plows in scenes reminiscent of biblical times.

Note: At present the southeastern part of Turkey is off limits to tourists due to problems with Kurdish insurgency. Before heading east from Istanbul, we would advise checking with your consular representative in Istanbul.

DRIVING

A recent program of highway construction has greatly improved driving conditions in Turkey. All of the major cities are now linked by a system of good all-weather roads. Driving in the cities, especially in Istanbul, is chaotic, and extreme caution is advised. Turkish drivers are not known for their expertise, and the accident rate is one of the highest in Europe.

Although parking is provided at most historical sites, it is extremely difficult to park in the cities and larger towns.

Traffic outside of the cities, with the exception of the main Istanbul–Ankara highway, is sparse and driving is easy; however, highways are often poorly marked. The letter "E" indicates an international European route, while "M" stands for Middle East International Highway and "A" for Asian International. Construction sites are often unmarked. Historical and archeological sites are indicated by yellow markers. Try to avoid driving at night, as sheep and cattle often wander across the roads and unlit farm vehicles and carts are quite common.

Keep an eye on your gas gauge and fill up whenever possible, as service stations are far apart. Unleaded fuel is readily available in the cities but scarce in the outlying regions. Diesel fuel is also known as "Mersin." It is a good idea to carry spare parts, as parts for vehicles not sold in Turkey are difficult to obtain.

View from a campground in central Turkey

The combination of drinking and driving is strictly prohibited, with severe penalties for offenders. Penalties for drug offenses are often draconian.

The speed limit for motorhomes on the short stretch of motorway is 80 kph (48 mph). The speed limit in towns and built-up areas, unless otherwise posted, is 50 kph (30 mph). Outside of built-up areas it is 80 kph (48 mph).

CAMPING

Although camping in Turkey is still somewhat in its infancy, there are a sufficient number of campgrounds at the major tourist destinations. Standards vary considerably, ranging from abominable to quite good. The best facilities are found at the chain of Kervansaray Mocamps run by the British Petroleum Company.

Free camping is permitted throughout the country. In risky areas it is often possible to park your vehicle at the local police or militia station.

Electrical outlets are the German two-prong Schuko type. Gas cylinders can be filled at the AYGAS depot at Ambarli, located approximately 10 km (6 mi.) west of Istanbul on the road to Edirne. For additional information about camping in Turkey, contact Turkize Kamp Ve Karavan Dernegi, Nenehatun cad. 96 Gayiosmanpasa, Ankara, Turkey; phone 136 31 51.

Itinerary: Athens · The Peloponnese · Central Greece · Thrace · Istanbul · Cappadocia · The Turkish Riviera · Sofia and Central Bulgaria

START: Athens

COUNTRIES: Bulgaria, Greece, Turkey

DISTANCE: 5,480 km (3,288 mi.)

MAPS: Michelin #980 *Greece;* Bartholomew RV *Eastern Turkey/ Cyprus;* Bartholomew RV *Romania–Bulgaria*

MINIMUM RECOMMENDED TOURING TIME: 35 to 42 days; without eastern Turkey, 21 days

INTRODUCTION

This itinerary offers the opportunity to explore three fascinating and exotic countries in the southeastern corner of Europe. There are several options for doing this tour. To cover the entire itinerary, involving more than 3,000 miles of sometimes difficult driving, requires a minimum of five to six weeks. Anything less than five weeks would leave little time for anything but driving.

By eliminating the eastern portion of Turkey and going from Istanbul directly to Edirne, the distance traveled is reduced to just over 2,300 km (1,380 mi.). This makes for a very pleasant three-week journey.

You can fly into Athens or Istanbul and pick up a rental motorhome (see pp. 11–16 for details). If you already have a vehicle, you can take the long ferry trip from Venice to Athens (Piraeus) or the shorter crossing from Bari, Italy, to the Greek west-coast port of Igoumenitsa. Until the situation in the former Yugoslavia is resolved, the most direct surface route from Austria through Belgrade is not open.

Within the circle traced by this itinerary you will encounter well-preserved vestiges of many ancient civilizations that include, among others, the Hittites, Greeks, Romans, and Byzantines. Athens, Istanbul, and Sofia are three of Europe's most fascinating major cities, each

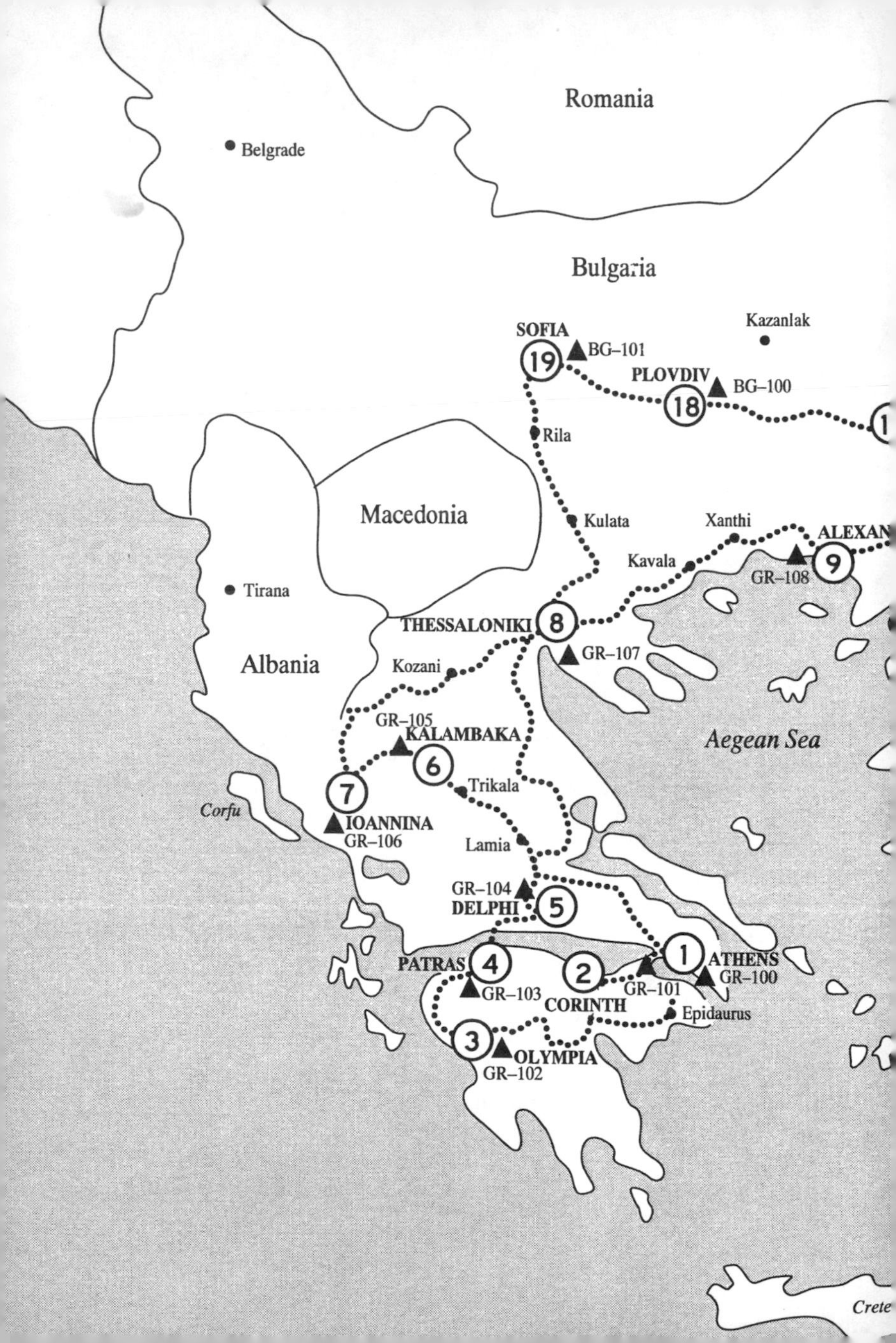
Romania
Belgrade
Bulgaria
Kazanlak
SOFIA
19
BG-101
PLOVDIV
18
BG-100
Rila
Macedonia
Kulata
Xanthi
ALEXAN
Kavala
GR-108
9
Tirana
THESSALONIKI
8
GR-107
Albania
Kozani
GR-105
KALAMBAKA
6
Aegean Sea
Trikala
7
Corfu
IOANNINA
GR-106
Lamia
GR-104
DELPHI
5
PATRAS
4
2
1
ATHENS
GR-100
GR-103
GR-101
CORINTH
Epidaurus
3
OLYMPIA
GR-102
Crete

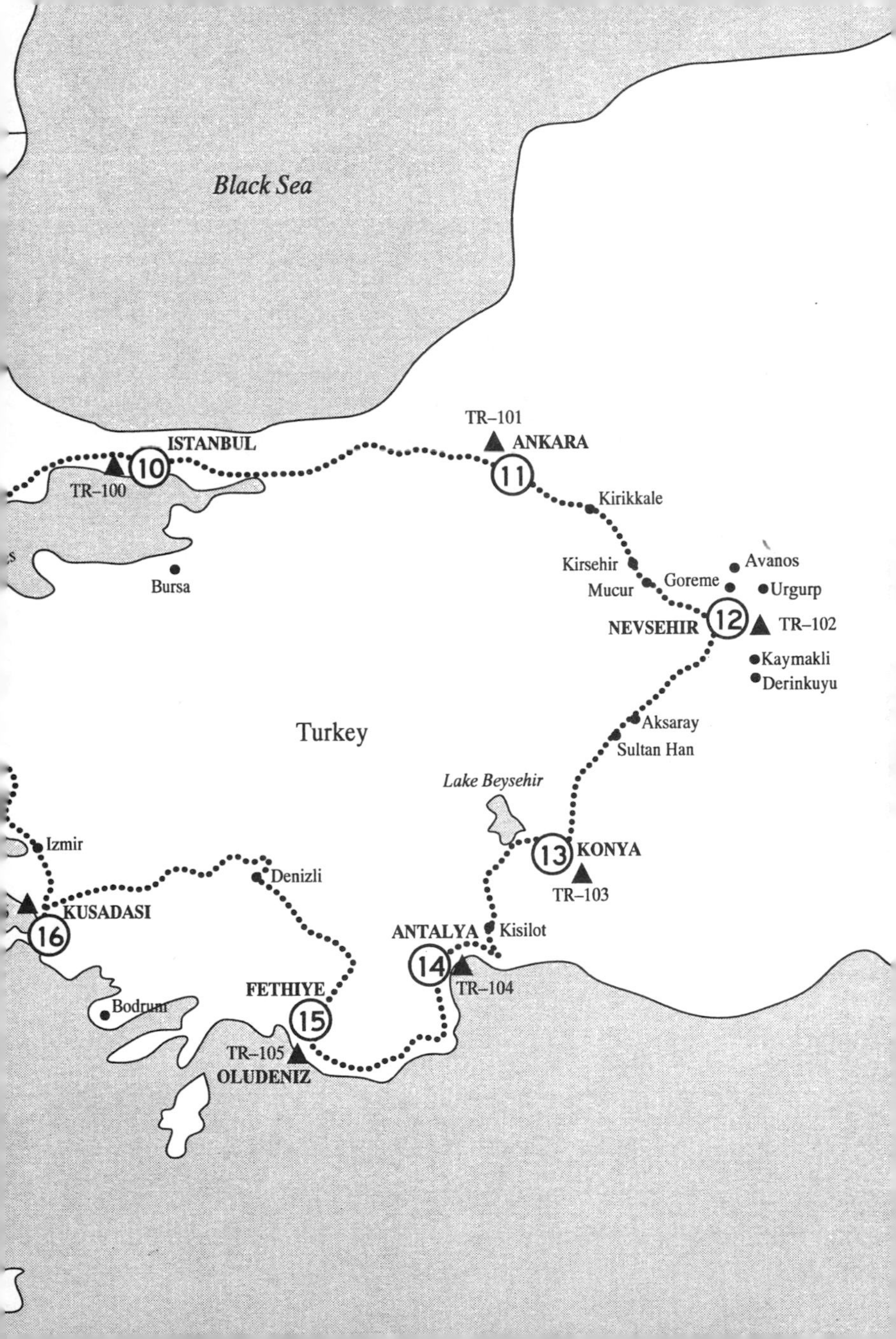
Black Sea
ISTANBUL
10
TR-100
TR-101
ANKARA
11
Kirikkale
Bursa
Kirsehir
Mucur
Goreme
Avanos
Urgurp
NEVSEHIR
12
TR-102
Kaymakli
Derinkuyu
Aksaray
Sultan Han
Turkey
Lake Beysehir
13
KONYA
TR-103
Izmir
Denizli
KUSADASI
16
ANTALYA
Kisilot
14
TR-104
FETHIYE
15
Bodrum
TR-105
OLUDENIZ

unique in its own right and all of them totally different from anything that you will experience in the western part of Europe.

Along the way, traveling through one of Europe's poorest and least developed regions, you will encounter simple villages and agricultural practices little changed over the centuries. Away from the major cities, you will meet some of the most genuinely hospitable people that you will find anywhere in your travels.

This itinerary can easily be expanded to include any number of the many Greek islands. There is regular car ferry service to most of the important islands. Crete, with its Minoan site at Knossos, rugged interior, and charming coastal villages, is well worth the twelve-hour ferry trip from Pireaus.

When to Go

With the exception of the coastal and mountain portions, this route is best avoided in July and August. Athens, Istanbul, and much of the interior of Greece and Turkey are unbearably hot. Early spring and late September and October are the best times for touring this region.

Highlights

Athens
Delphi temple
Meteora monasteries
Mycenae excavations
Istanbul
Cappadocia
Ephesus
Oludeniz
Museum of Anatolian Civilizations, Ankara
Old town, Plovdiv
Sofia
Monastery, Rila

Expanding Horizons

- **To Italian Impressions Itinerary:** Take the ferry from Igoumenitsa to Brindisi or from Piraeus to Venice (see p. 249).

ON THE ROAD

Numbered sites correspond with circled numbers on the itinerary map.

1. Athens (Athina)

Hopelessly overcrowded and ravaged by pollution, Athens nevertheless deserves to be seen for its incredible antiquities, which include the **Acropolis** and the **Agora.** The **National Archaeological Museum** contains many of the treasures uncovered throughout Greece.

Do not attempt to drive an RV in Athens. Leave your rig at the campground and take the bus or a taxi.

Athens's busy port, **Piraeus (Pireefs),** is the jumping-off point for ferries to many of the Greek islands. **Cape Sounion (Sounio),** 70 km (42 mi.) southeast of Athens, is an inspiring spot with the ruins of a once magnificent **Temple of Poseidon.**

Note: To connect with our Italian Impressions itinerary, take the ferry from Piraeus or from Patra to Venice or to Brindisi. For details contact The Greek National Tourist Office, 645 Fifth Avenue, New York, NY (phone 212–421–5777, fax 212–826–6940) or Viamare Travel, Graphic House, 2 Sumatra Road, London NW6 1PU, England (phone 071–431–4560, fax 071–431–5456).

Athens Campground

GR–100 ★★ Camping Athens. Open year-round. On the main Corinth–Athens road, 7 km (4.2 mi.) west of Athens center. Located east of the sixth-century Dafni monastery, this is the closest of the several Athens campgrounds. A small site, in a residential area. There is little shade. Convenient bus to city.

Athens → Corinth (Korinthos), 90 km (54 mi.)

Head west from Athens, following the coastline through **Elefsina** and **Ag Theodori.** Cross the bridge over the narrow **Corinth Canal** to Corinth.

2. Corinth (Korinthos)

The largest city in ancient Greece, Corinth was destroyed twice by earthquakes. The modern city is of little interest. All that remains of ancient Corinth is the ruins of the **Temple of Apollo.** At **Acrocorinth,** on a hill overlooking the ancient city, is an imposing **Byzantine-Crusader fortress.**

Fifty km (30 mi.) south of Corinth lies the ancient city of Mycenae (Mikinai). The fabled city of Agamemnon, **Mycenae** was once the most powerful city in Greece. This incredible archeological site, mentioned in the writings of Homer, was excavated by the German archeologist Heinrich Schliemann at the end of the nineteenth century.

Epidaurus (Epidavros), 30 km (18 mi.) east of the port of **Nafplio,** was the sanctuary of Aesculapios, son of Apollo and the god of medicine. There is an excellent **amphitheater** on the site.

Corinth Campground

GR–101 ★★★ Camping Isthmia Beach. Open April 1–October 31. At the beach on the road from Corinth to Epidaurus. Approaches are well marked. A medium-size, nicely landscaped site. In a scenic location on a bay with a gravel beach. Well situated for visiting Corinth, Epidaurus, and Mycenae.

Corinth → Olympia, 225 km (135 mi.)

From Mycenae follow the road south to **Argos,** one of the principal cities of classical Greece. From there head east to the Arcadian capital of **Tripoli,** and then continue over the winding mountain road down to Olympia.

3. Olympia

It was here, in this fertile, cypress-covered valley, that the first Olympic Games were held in 776 B.C. Of interest are the ruins of a 20,000-seat **stadium** and the **Temple of Zeus.**

Olympia Campground

GR–102 ★★★ Camping Alphios. Open April 1–October 31. Located 2 km (1.2 mi.) southwest of town. From Olympia follow signs toward Flokas/Drouva. A medium-size, level, hilltop site. Archeological site, 900 yd.

Olympia → Patras (Patrai), 115 km (69 mi.)

Follow E55 along the western Peloponnese to Patras.

4. Patras (Patrai)

An important port city and former Roman military outpost, Patras is the present-day capital of the **Peloponnese,** a rugged, mountainous region that is separated from mainland Greece by the man-made Corinth Canal. This region contains many of Greece's finest archeological sites. The interior of the Peloponnese is relatively unspoiled and has a number of attractive mountain villages.

Patras Campground

GR–103 ★★★ EOT Beach Camping. Open May 1–October 31. From the ferry port follow the coast road north to the campground. A lovely, parklike site on the bay with access to a nice beach. Individual pads for motorhomes, separated by bushes.

Patras → Delphi (Delfi), 115 km (69 mi.)

From Patras follow the coast road north to **Rio.** From there take the ferry across the straits to the mainland at **Andirio.** Then follow E65 along the gulf to **Itea.** Head inland toward Mount Parnassos and Delphi.

5. Delphi (Delfi)

In a beautiful hillside setting at the foot of Mount Parnassos, Delphi is one of the most inspiring of the ancient Greek sites. In addition to the famed fourth-century B.C. **Temple of Apollo,** there is also a well-preserved **amphitheater** and an interesting **museum.**

Delphi Campground

GR–104 ★★★ Delfi Camping. Open year-round. Located 3 km (1.8 mi.) west of Delphi, on the road to Itea. A five-acre site in a lovely rustic setting among the olive and pine trees. Fine view of the Bay of Itea. Three km (1.8 mi.) from the Apollo temple.

Delphi → Kalambaka/Meteora, 235 km (141 mi.)

From Delphi head west to **Amfissa.** From there take E65 north with Mount Parnassos on your right. Continue to **Lamia** and then to **Trikala.** From Trikala take E92 to Kalambaka.

6. Kalambaka/Meteora

Here, in the rugged mountains of central Greece, is one of the most fascinating assemblages of monasteries anywhere in the world. Atop a series of rocky pinnacles that have been etched over the centuries by nature to form a unique set of solitary pillars are several unique monasteries. Built in the fourteenth century by Byzantine monks, these represent an amazing feat of construction. Until recently, the only access to the monasteries was to be hauled up in a cargo net.

Kalambaka/Meteora Campground

GR–105 ★★ Camping Meteora Garden. Open year-round. Located 1 km (0.6 mi.) northwest of Kalambaka on the road to Ioannina. A small, level field with plants and trees. View from the site toward Meteora.

Kalambaka → Ioannina, 125 km (75 mi.)

Continue west from Kalambaka on E92, a twisting mountain road with spectacular scenery, to Ioannina.

7. Ioannina

In a pleasant location on Lake Ioannina, Ioannina is a major trading center that shows a strong Turkish influence in its architecture and people. The bazaar is known for its fine-quality hand-woven goods. There are several interesting monasteries in the region. North of Ioannina the road leads to **Vikos Gorge,** a region with a number of picturesque mountain villages.

Note: To connect with our Italian Impressions itinerary, continue west down to the ferry port of Igoumenitsa. There is regular service to Brindisi and Bari, with a stop possible along the way at Corfu. The crossing takes ten to eleven hours. For details contact Viamare Travel, Graphic House, 2 Sumatra Road, London NW6 1PU, England; phone (071) 431–4560, fax (071) 431–5456.

Ioannina Campground

GR–106 ★★ Camping Limnopoula. Open year-round. On the lake next to the local boating club. Approaches are well marked. A pleasant, level, lakeside site.

Ioannina → Thessaloniki, 365 km (219 mi.)

From Ioannina take E92, a winding scenic road that skirts the rugged mountains of central Greece and then continues into Thessaloniki.

8. Thessaloniki

Founded in the third century B.C., Thessaloniki, Greece's second-largest city, is a bustling metropolis with few reminders of its historic past. The **Archaeological Museum** displays a number of finds from the nearby tomb of Philip II, father of Alexander the Great.

Thessaloniki Campground

GR–107 ★★ EOT Camping Akti Termaikou (Agia Trias). Open May 1–October 31. At the beach, 12 km (7.2 mi.) southwest of Thessaloniki Airport. Approach is well marked. A twenty-five-acre park with many pine trees. Individual sites partitioned by bushes and hedges.

Thessaloniki → Alexandroupolis, 365 km (219 mi.)

From Thessaloniki take E90 east to **Kavala,** an ancient Roman city with a picturesque fishing harbor. From Kavala continue east to **Xanthi** and then on to Alexandroupolis.

9. Alexandroupolis

An attractive small town with a good beach, Alexandroupolis is a convenient stopping place on the main route to Istanbul.

Alexandroupolis Campground

GR–108 ★★ Camping Alexandroupolis. Open year-round. On E90, 1.5 km (0.9 mi.) west of town. A pleasant, fifteen-acre, level, grassy site directly at the beach. Plots are divided by shrubs. Some hard pads for trailers and motorhomes.

Alexandroupolis → Istanbul, 300 km (180 mi.)

From Alexandroupolis continue east across the plains of Thrace and the heavily fortified no man's land that divides Greece and Turkey. The border crossing is at the **Evros River.** Once in Turkey, follow Hwy. 18/E84 the rest of the way into Istanbul.

10. ISTANBUL

With its fine Byzantine and Islamic architecture, exotic markets, teeming streets, and colorful harbor, Istanbul is one of the world's most fascinating cities. Straddling both sides of the Bosporus, it serves as an important link between the European and Asian continents.

Of the city's numerous mosques, the most famous is the **Sultanahmet Camii** or **Blue Mosque,** so named for its blue-tiled interior. The imposing **Aya Sofya (St. Sophia),** consecrated in 537 by Emperor Justinian, is one of the world's finest examples of Byzantine architecture. Looking out over the Bosporus are two extraordinary palaces, the fifteenth-century **Topkapi Palace** and the ornate **Dolmabahce Palace,** official residence of the last Ottoman sultans.

Istanbul's **Kapali Carsisi (Covered Bazaar)** is a shopper's paradise, an incredible labyrinth of some 4,000 shops, stalls, and restaurants that is the Turkish precursor of a modern shopping mall.

Istanbul Campground

TR–100 ★★ Londra Camping (Bakirkoz). Open year-round. On Hwy. 1/E80, 10 km (6 mi.) west of Istanbul center, near the airport. Campground is next to a large truck stop and hotel. A small, walled-in, grassy site with little shade. Very crowded in summer. Convenient bus or co-op taxi to Istanbul.

Istanbul → Ankara, 370 km (222 mi.)

From Istanbul take the city bypass E80 and cross the Bosporus bridge to the Asian side of the city. Continue east on E80, following signs to Ankara.

11. Ankara

Turkey's capital since 1923, Ankara is not a particularly attractive place. The climate is severe, with broiling hot summers and bitter cold winters. The main attraction is the **Museum of Anatolian Civilizations,** which features an excellent collection of artifacts from the region's early civilizations, with many fascinating Hittite pieces.

Ankara Campground

TR–101 ★★ Altinok–Susuzkoy Mocamp (Susuzkoy). Open May 1–October 15. On E89, 23 km (14 mi.) north of the city. Entrance at the BP service station. A four-acre field with little shade. Bus to Ankara at entrance.

Ankara → Nevsehir, 240 km (144 mi.)

Take E88 east from Ankara to **Kirikkale,** then head southeast on Hwy. 765 to **Kirsehir.** *(Note:* Due to road construction in this area, road numbers might be different.) Continue to **Mucur** and from there follow signs to Nevsehir and Goreme, in the heart of Cappadocia.

12. Nevsehir

This region of central Turkey presents a fascinating, stark moonscape that contains some of the most incredible and bizarre natural rock formations found anywhere. **Urgurp, Goreme,** and **Avanos** are the principal bases for exploring this area. The underground cities at **Derinkuyu** and **Kaymakli,** built by the early Christians, extend some ten to fifteen stories below the ground and once housed as many as 20,000 people.

Nevsehir Campground

TR–102 ★★ Kaya Camping (Ortahisar). Open year-round. Turn off of Hwy. 300 (Nevsehir–Urgup) and follow signs to campground. A large dirt-and-gravel area with few trees. Beautiful views of the valley and rock formations. Convenient base for exploring Cappadocia. Ample parking at sightseeing attractions. Interesting underground restaurant.

Nevsehir → Konya, 225 km (135 mi.)

From Nevsehir follow signs to **Aksaray,** and continue southeast on Hwy. 300 to Konya. Thirty km (18 mi.) from Aksaray is **Sultan Han,** Anatolia's largest and best-preserved **caravansary.** This served as a refuge for the travelers and their camels who plied these ancient caravan routes.

13. Konya

One of the world's most ancient cities, Konya lies in the heart of the Anatolian Plateau. The region is believed to have been inhabited as early as 7000 B.C. It is best known in modern times as the home of the "whirling dervishes."

Konya Campground

TR–103 ★ Camping Konya. Open year-round. Next to sports stadium in southwest corner of town. A very small area on the grounds of the sports stadium. No shade. Convenient bus to town center.

Konya → Antalya, 295 km (177 mi.)

From Konya take Hwy. 330 west to **Beysehir,** on the lake of the same name. From Beysehir head south over the rugged mountains that separate the interior from the coast. The road (Hwy. 695) crosses two 4,000-ft. passes before winding down to the sea at the village of **Kisilot.** Continue along the coast road the remaining 75 km (45 mi.) to Antalya.

14. Antalya

A popular beach resort that has experienced an explosive tourist boom over the past few years, Antalya, the center of the **Turkish Riviera,** is ideally situated on a calm bay surrounded by high mountains. The nearby archeological excavations at **Perge** and **Aspendos** are worth a visit.

Antalya Campground

TR–104 ★★ Bambus Camping. Open April 1–October 31. Located 2 km (1.2 mi.) from town center on the road to Lara Plaji. A small, terraced site overlooking the sea. No sandy beach. Access to water over the rocks. –900 yd.

Antalya → Fethiye/Oludeniz, 265 km (159 mi.)

Continue south from Antalya. The highway climbs along the mountains that hug the coast. There are fantastic sea views and several fine beaches along this stretch of coast. From Fethiye there is a good road down to the beach at Oludeniz.

15. FETHIYE/OLUDENIZ

Fethiye is a small, modern port city with a number of interesting Lycian tombs. Oludeniz, with its white sandy beach and blue-water lagoon, is one of Turkey's most beautiful seaside resorts.

Oludeniz Campground

TR–105 ★★ Han Camp. Open year-round. Across from the beach. Approach is well marked. A small, pleasant site with some shade trees. One of several campgrounds along the beach road. Excellent restaurant.

Fethiye → Kusadasi, 375 km (225 mi.)

Head north from Fethiye across the mountains, following the signs to **Denizli.** From there continue on to visit the amazing terraced hot springs and pools at **Pamukkale.** Take E87 east to Kusadasi.

16. KUSADASI

Situated on a beautiful bay and surrounded by fine sandy beaches, Kusadasi makes an excellent base for visiting **Ephesus (Efes), Priene,** and **Didyma,** which rank among Turkey's most important archeological sites.

Kusadasi Campground

TR–106 ★★ Yat Camping. Open year-round. At the north edge of town, opposite the harbor. Access to the beach across the coast road. A ten-minute walk to town center.

Kusadasi → Edirne, 650 km (390 mi.)

From Kusadasi pick up Hwy. 6/E87, the main highway that runs

The monastery at Rila, in southwest Bulgaria (Courtesy Balkan Holidays USA Ltd.)

through **Izmir,** Turkey's third-largest city, and then follows the coast to the port city of **Canakkale.** There are many campgrounds along the coastal section of this route.

Eighteen km (11 mi.) south of Canakkale are the excavations of the famous city of **Troy (Truva).** From Canakkale take the ferry across the **Dardanelles Strait** and continue following Hwy. 6/E87 to the intersection with Hwy. 1/E80 the main Edirne–Istanbul road. Continue the remaining 27 km (16 mi.) into Edirne.

Note: To connect with our Italian Impressions itinerary, take the ferry from Izmir to Venice. The crossing takes about sixty hours. There are two crossings weekly. For details contact Turkish Maritime Lines, Central Office, Karakoy, Istanbul, Turkey; phone (1) 24 55 366, fax (1) 25 15 767.

17. Edirne

One of Turkey's most attractive cities, Edirne was the capital of the Ottoman Empire for some one hundred years. With its splendid mosques, bazaars, palaces, and old wooden houses, Edirne is a living museum.

Edirne Campground

TR–107 ★★ Fifi Touristik Camping. Open April 1–October 31. Located 6 km (3.6 mi.) southeast of town, near the turnoff to Kirklareli. A small, grassy site with few trees. Bus to town at entrance. Adequate parking in Edirne.

Edirne → Sofia, Bulgaria, 160 km (96 mi.)

Leave Edirne on E 80. It is 18 km (11 mi.) to the border crossing into Bulgaria at **Kapitan Andreevo.** Continue on Hwy. 5/E80 into Plovdiv.

18. Plovdiv

Bulgaria's second-largest city is a major industrial center that can trace its origins back to the fourth century B.C. The **old town** is a living open-air museum whose narrow, tree-lined streets are filled with colorfully decorated wood and stucco houses from the Ottoman period. A well-preserved **Roman amphitheater** has recently been excavated.

Plovdiv Campground

BG–100 ★ Camping Trakia. Open May 1–September 30. On Hwy. 5/E80, 5 km (3 mi.) west of town. A large site in a pleasant, wooded setting.

Plovdiv → Sofia, 145 km (87 mi.)

Continue west on E80 following signs to Sofia.

19. Sofia

Situated at an elevation of 550 m (1,815 ft.) and surrounded by a ring of high mountains, Sofia is one of Eastern Europe's most attractive cities. The main attractions are concentrated in a small central area easily explored on foot.

Sofia's most prominent landmark is the golden-domed, Byzantine-style **Alexander Nevsky Memorial Church.** Also of interest, just across from the Nevesky Church, is the sixth-century **Sveta Sophia Church,** named for the city's patron saint. The **Boyana Church,** 10 km (6 mi.) south of Sofia, contains some excellent thirteenth-century frescos.

Sofia Campground

BG–101 ★★ Camping Vranja. Open year-round. Located 10 km (6 mi.) west of downtown Sofia, off of the Plovdiv road. Coming from Plovdiv, the turnoff is just before the bridge over the Iskar River. A large, wooded site that spans the river. Convenient bus to Sofia center.

Sofia → Thessaloniki, Greece, 320 km (192 mi.)

Leave Sofia on E770/E79. After 25 km (16 mi.), the road splits. Follow E79 south to **Stanke Dimitrov.** Continue south to **Kocerinovo.** From there take the turnoff to visit the **monastery** at **Rila.** The more than 1,000-year-old fortresslike structure is a showcase of Orthodox religious art. With its intricately carved balconies and numerous fine paintings and icons, it is one of Eastern Europe's most impressive sites. From Rila return to the main highway and continue south to the Greek border at **Kulata.** Stay on E79 the rest of the way into Thessaloniki.

20. Thessaloniki (see p. 275).

Thessaloniki → Athens (Athini), 500 km (300 mi.)

From Thessaloniki follow E75 into Athens.

THE HEART OF EASTERN EUROPE

Austria

CAPITAL: Vienna

POPULATION: 7,900,000

CURRENCY: Austrian shilling (S), divided into 100 groschen

LANGUAGES: German; English is widely spoken in tourist regions

RELIGION: Roman Catholic

POLICE: 133

FIRE: 122

AMBULANCE: 144

ROAD SERVICE: Austrian Auto Club—120; ARBO—123

BANKS: Monday–Friday 8:00 A.M.–noon and 1:30–3:00 or 4:00 P.M.; varies from city to city; main offices in large cities do not close at noon

STORES: weekdays: 8:00–6:30 P.M. with one to two hours for lunch; Saturday 8:00 A.M.–1:00 P.M., first Saturday of the month open until 5:00 P.M.

HOLIDAYS: January 1; January 6, Epiphany; Easter Monday (movable); May 1, Labor Day; Ascension Day (movable); Pentacost (movable); Corpus Christi (movable); Assumption (movable); All Saints' Day (movable); December 8, Immaculate Conception; December 25 and 26

EMBASSIES: *United States,* Boltzmanngasse 16, 1011 Vienna; phone (01) 313–39, fax (01) 310–0682. *Canada,* Dr. Karl Lueger Ring 10, 1010 Vienna; phone (01) 533–3691, fax (01) 533–4473. *United Kingdom,* Jauresgasse 12, 1030 Vienna; phone (01) 713–1575

When the victorious Allied powers carved up Austria–Hungary at the end of World War I, they didn't leave much of the Hapsburg empire that once dominated so much of Europe. With Austria what they did leave was a country that must have been created with the vacationer in mind.

Austria offers its visitors an incredible variety of year-round attractions and activities, ranging from the spectacular alpine scenery of the Tirol and Vorarlberg to the sophistication and elegance of Vienna and Salzburg. All of this and much more is packed into an area slightly smaller than the state of Maine.

If your taste is for the outdoors, you can enjoy hiking, climbing, tennis, horseback riding, sailing on pristine mountain lakes, and some of the world's finest skiing. Should you wish to accent your vacation with a bit of culture, how about a world-class concert or opera in Vienna or Salzburg, or a visit to one of the many museums and palaces laden with treasures accumulated during the nearly seven centuries of Hapsburg rule? Just about the only thing in Austria that you can't do is swim in the ocean—and you can do that in neighboring Italy or Slovenia, just a few hours' drive away.

Following its joint post–World War II occupation by the United States, Great Britain, France, and the Soviet Union, Austria was granted its independence in 1955 and, with occasional setbacks, has prospered since then.

The Austrian tourist authorities are well organized and can provide a wealth of useful information. Each province and just about every town of interest has a tourist office. Look for signs that read FREMDENVERKEHRSVEREIN.

DRIVING

The once fearsome Austrian alpine roads have been largely tamed by a series of tunnels and modern highways that have provided access to the Alps and the rest of the country for larger recreational vehicles. In general roads throughout the country are excellent. The high-speed autobahns and tunnels that cut through the Alps are wonderful for covering great distances in a short time, but the real charm and beauty of Austria are best experienced along the many country roads that wind through picturesque villages and towns. Take note that on such roads, where livestock have the right-of-way, you will occasionally find yourself behind a herd of cows coming or going to pasture. In September the back roads are often clogged with colorfully decorated cows being brought down from the high alpine pastures to spend the winter in the villages.

While most Austrian roads are free, there are a number of exceptions. These include the Grossglockner High Alpine Highway, Brenner Autobahn, and most of the major tunnels. Toll charges are steep by U.S. standards but, considering the awesome engineering and construction feats involved in building these roads and tunnels, the costs are not unreasonable. For example it costs approximately $15 to zip through the 13.7-km (8.2-mi.) -long Arlberg Tunnel in the western Alps.

Keep in mind when driving in the mountains that weather conditions can change rapidly. Sudden snowstorms are not unusual in spring and autumn. We have even encountered snow in mid-August in the higher elevations, although this is rare. During the winter months it is essential to carry snow chains. Rental chains are available at the approaches to most of the main Alpine pass roads; but if you plan on doing any substantial amount of winter driving in the mountains, it's best to buy your own. Many rental points do not carry chains to fit the larger RVs.

Many mountain roads and passes are kept open all year, and there are tunnels to bypass the most difficult pass stretches. On narrow mountain roads the "common-sense rule" applies. The vehicle that can most easily reverse to a passing place is obliged to do so. For information on current road conditions and a listing of roads closed to trailers, contact the Austrian Automobile Club (OAMTC) Main Office, Schubertring 1–3, 1010 Vienna, Austria; phone (01) 711 990. Branch offices are located throughout the country.

Traffic regulations are similar to those in other European countries. Children under age twelve are not allowed to ride in the front seat, and the wearing of seatbelts is obligatory. The permissible blood-alcohol level is 0.8. Drunk drivers are subject to loss of license and heavy fines.

Speed limits for motorhomes on the autobahn are 130 kph (78 mph) and on surface roads 100 kph (60 mph). Be careful when driving through towns; unless otherwise posted, the speed limit is 50 kph (30 mph). All accidents involving injuries must be reported to the police.

CAMPING

There are approximately 500 campgrounds scattered throughout this small alpine paradise. Just about every place of interest has a conveniently located campground. Vienna, Austria's exciting capital, has five modern campgrounds, all with convenient access by public transportation to the city's center.

Campgrounds in the alpine regions may vary from a small farmyard with modest, but clean, facilities to luxurious camping villages with every imaginable convenience. Many sites in the Alps afford spectacular mountain vistas and are well suited to use as a base for hiking and exploring the local area.

The overall standard of service and facilities throughout the country is high. Hot showers and electrical hookups with sufficient amperage are universal. Electrical connections are mostly of the German Schuko type; however a number of sites are converting to the new EEC standard three-prong blue plugs and outlets. To play it safe while camping in Austria, carry a Schuko/EEC adapter. Most vehicles rented in Austria and Germany are furnished with these. They can also be obtained at camping-supply stores.

An increasing number of Austrian campgrounds are installing U.S.-style dump stations to service RVs with built-in holding tanks. Individual gray-water hookups are found at some of the three- and four-star sites, while individual black-water connections are not generally available.

German and Austrian gas bottles are interchangeable, and you can exchange an empty for a full bottle at most campgrounds. If you have a built-in propane tank, look for filling stations that display an AUTO GAS sign.

The southern province of Karnten (Corinthia), with its multitude of clear lakes and the towering peaks of the Hohe Tauren Mountains, attracts the greatest number of camping visitors.

Although the International Camping Carnet is not required, many sites grant a discount to holders of this card. At a number of resort areas, a supplemental *Kurtax*, or tourist tax, is added to the campground price. This money is used to maintain and improve public recreation facilities in the area.

Free camping on public lands is prohibited; however, camping in state forests is permitted with permission from the local authorities. Camping on farms and other private lands is possible as long as the owner's permission is obtained. The Austrians are generally friendly toward visitors, so this option provides a wonderful, inexpensive alternative to official campgrounds. Overnight stops are permitted at highway parking and rest areas as well as on most city streets. Such overnight stops are prohibited in Vienna, however, and wherever specifically posted. Camping equipment may not be set up alongside the vehicle.

In a country where winter sports are so popular, it is no surprise to find that many campgrounds are open year-round. A number of these are located close to ski lifts and cross-country loops. Detailed lists of campgrounds along with a map can be obtained free of charge from the Austrian National Tourist Offices (see p. 357), the Provincial Tourist Boards, or the Austrian Automobile Club. Additional information about camping in Austria may be obtained from Camping Club Austria, Schubertring 1–3, A–1010 Vienna, Austria; phone (01) 711 991 272, fax (01) 711 991 498.

Czech Republic and Slovakia

CAPITALS: Prague (The Czech Republic)
Bratislava (Slovakia)

POPULATION: 15,700,000

CURRENCY: koruna or crown (Kc), divided into 100 haleru

LANGUAGES: Czech, Slovak

RELIGIONS: Roman Catholic, Protestant, others

POLICE: 158

FIRE: 150

AMBULANCE: 155

ROAD SERVICE: Prague, twenty-four hours—(02) 123 or 747–400

BANKS: weekdays 8:00 A.M.–2:00 P.M.

STORES: weekdays 9:00 A.M.–6:00 P.M.; Thursday until 8:00 P.M.; some close between noon and 2:00 P.M.; Saturday 9:00 A.M.–noon for many shops

HOLIDAYS: January 1; Easter Monday (movable); May 1, Labor Day; May 9 and October 28, Independence days; December 25 and 26

EMBASSIES: *United States,* Triziste 15, 12548 Prague 1; phone (02) 536–641/6, fax (02) 532–457. *Canada,* Mickiewiczova 6, Prague 6; phone (02) 312–0251, fax (02) 311–2791. *United Kingdom,* Thunovska 14, 11800 Prague; phone (02) 533–347/8 or 9

Emerging in 1918 from World War I as the newly formed republic of Czechoslovakia, this tiny nation's experience with democracy was short-lived, as the country fell prey to German invaders during World War II. After a brief period of independence, Czechoslovakia came under a Communist regime, which lasted until December 1989. In 1993 the country, in a peaceful process that came to be known as the "velvet divorce," split into two independent republics: the Czech Republic and Slovakia. Of the two, the Czech Republic, with its great capital of Prague, is the more highly developed.

DRIVING

The overall road network is adequate in both republics, with the roads in the western Czech Republic better than those in Slovakia. There are only a few short sections of motorways, and there are no toll roads. The principal motorway links the two capitals of Prague and Bratislava.

Rural roads, especially in the east, are sometimes unsurfaced and are often used by horse-drawn vehicles. Extreme caution is advised when driving these roads at night. Be on the lookout for slow-moving vehicles without lights.

The speed limit (in both countries) for motorhomes on the motorways is 110 kph (66 mph). Outside built-up areas it is 90 kph (54 mph). The speed limit in towns, unless otherwise posted, is 60 kph (36 mph). A right turn on a red light is permitted only when indicated by a green arrow. Police are empowered to collect fines from foreign motorists on the spot!

Seatbelts are compulsory, and children under age twelve are not allowed in the front seat. The penalties for driving under the influence of alcohol are severe. The permissible blood-alcohol level is 0.00 percent. An International Driver's License is currently not required for visitors from the United States, Canada, and the United Kingdom.

There is an adequate network of service stations in the western regions, with fewer in Slovakia. Not all stations sell unleaded gasoline, known locally as "Natural." Diesel fuel is sold at stations displaying the sign TT DIESEL.

CAMPING

As is the case in other Eastern European countries, camping is very popular with the local residents. The fall of communism and the introduction of a more tourist-friendly government policy has encouraged many Western Europeans to explore these newly emerged republics in their RVs.

The countries combined have approximately one hundred official campgrounds, which are designated as *Autocamps* and rated in four categories. Most of these, even the four-star sites, are not up to Western European standards. In Slovakia many of the campgrounds are quite primitive, with few amenities or facilities. With the expansion of free enterprise into the camping sector, this situation is rapidly improving.

Except for city campgrounds, many sites are located in idyllic mountain or wooded settings. Most campgrounds have some sort of snack bar and campstore. Washers and dryers are rare.

The International Camping Carnet is not required, but most campgrounds will give a small discount to card holders. Foreigners often wind up paying considerably more than local residents. Most campgrounds are open from June 15 to September 15. Those sites that also have cabins for rent are often open all year. During July and August sites in the Prague area and in the Tatra Mountains are very crowded.

Free camping is officially prohibited in forested areas and is generally tolerated in most other places. In areas where there are no campgrounds, it is best to ask permission.

The German-style Schuko electrical plugs and outlets are the most commonly used. Additional information may be obtained from the Ministry of Tourism, Staromestke nam. 6, 1100 00 Praha 1, The Czech Republic (phone 231 28 39, fax 232 57 20) and the Ministry of Tourism, Spitalska, 800 00 Bratislava, Slovakia.

Germany

CAPITAL: Berlin; seat of government: Bonn.

POPULATION: 80,600,000

CURRENCY: deutsche mark (DM), divided into 10 groschen or 100 pfennige

LANGUAGE: German

RELIGIONS: Protestant and Roman Catholic

POLICE: 110

FIRE: 112

AMBULANCE: 110 and 115 in eastern Germany

ROAD SERVICE: Auto Club of Germany (ADAC), twenty-four hours: 19211 or (01) 308 19211 in eastern Germany

BANKS: weekdays 8:30 A.M.–12:30 P.M. and 2:00–4:00 P.M. (until 3:30 P.M. on Thursday)

STORES: weekdays 8:30 or 9:00 A.M.–6:30 P.M.; Thursday until 9:00 or 10:00 P.M. in large shops; Saturday 7:30 or 8:00 A.M. until 2:00 P.M.

HOLIDAYS: January 1; January 6, Three Kings Day; Good Friday, Easter Monday (movable); May 1, Labor Day; Ascension Day (movable); Pentacost (movable); Corpus Christi (movable); Assumption Day (movable); October 3, Unification; November 1, All Saints' Day; December 25 and 26

EMBASSIES: *United States,* Deichmanns Ave, 53179 Bonn; phone (0228) 3391, fax (0228) 339–2663. *Canada,* Godesberger Allee 119, 53179 Bonn; phone (0228) 810–0630, fax (0228) 375–739. *United Kingdom,* 77 Friedrich Ebert Allee, 53113 Bonn; phone (0228) 234–061

West Germany, once part of the Germany that was virtually destroyed during World War II, experienced a phoenixlike rise to become Europe's dominant economic power in the mid-1980s. After more than forty years of bitter division, a recently reunited Germany is now in the throes of coming to grips with the serious economic and social consequences of this unification. Germany has much to offer the visitor, including exciting cities, such as Berlin, Munich, and Hamburg, and charming towns and villages—Rothenburg, on the quiet Tauber River, and the wood-carving center of Oberammergau are just two of many that come to mind. For lovers of mountains the Bavarian Alps, which form a portion of Germany's southern border with Austria, are hard to beat. The landscape in the north, while less dramatic, is nevertheless attractive, as shown by the thatched-roof cottages and white sandy beaches of Schleswig Holstein. Germany's rich cultural heritage is reflected in the country's many fine museums and concert halls.

DRIVING

For most people the first time driving in Germany is quite an experience. Where else can you be overtaken by a Porsche legally whizzing by at 200 kph (120 mph)? The region that was formerly West Germany enjoys a highway network that is second to none. An extensive system of high-speed autobahns, in some areas eight lanes wide, connects all of the country's major towns and cities.

At present, except in posted areas, there is no speed limit on the autobahns. A proposal is currently being considered to impose a toll for use of these speedways. Under the burden of rush-hour and vacation traffic, the term speedway is less appropriate than perhaps "crawlway" or "parking lot," as near-gridlock conditions prevail. The autobahns are also subject to heavy truck traffic, although trucks are not allowed on weekends and holidays.

The autobahns are designated with the white letter "A" on a blue background. The major trunk roads, known as "Bundesstrassen," are indicated by the letter "B" and a number on a yellow background.

Unless you are in a great hurry to get from one point to another, we would advise staying off of the autobahns and concentrating on the more scenic and interesting local roads. It is on these roads, many of which carry such charming names as the Romantic Road, The Castle Road, or the Fairy Tale Road, that you encounter much of the enchantment of Germany.

Germans, while usually in a great hurry on the road, are mostly courteous and excellent drivers. This not so much the case in the former East Germany, where until recently automobile ownership was limited to a privileged few and the level of road savvy is far lower. The state of the highway system in the eastern part of the country is also considerably inferior to that of the west. A massive infusion of funds has been allocated to remedy this situation.

Unless otherwise posted, there is no speed limit on the autobahns for motorhomes under 2,800 kg (6,160 lb). On highways outside built-up areas, the speed limit is 100 kph (60 mph). In towns the speed limit is 50 kph (30 mph) unless otherwise posted. Police are empowered to collect fines from foreign motorists on the spot.

The penalties for driving under the influence of alcohol are severe. The permissible blood-alcohol level in the western part of the country is 0.08 percent; at this writing the permissible level in the former East Germany is 0.00 percent.

There is an excellent network of service stations in the west, and many new stations are being built in the east. Unleaded gasoline, known as "Bleifrei," is readily available, as is diesel fuel.

An International Driver's License is currently not required for visitors from the United States, Canada, and the United Kingdom.

The wearing of seatbelts is compulsory, and children under age twelve may not ride in the front seat unless a suitable child-restraint system is employed.

CAMPING

The former West Germany has an extensive network of more than 2,000 campgrounds that serves just about every place of interest to the visitor. Standards, particularly with respect to cleanliness, are among the highest in Europe. Restaurants, camp stores, and coin-operated laundry facilities are standard at practically every campground, and a high percentage of sites are wheelchair-accessible. At many campgrounds the restaurants, also open to the public, are among the best in the area.

In the former East Germany, the situation is quite different. The network of campgrounds is not nearly as dense, and many sites have antiquated and inferior facilities. This condition is changing rapidly with the influx of funds from the west, but it will take at least several years before the gap between east and west can be appreciably closed.

Most German campgrounds close their gates at night and observe a midday quiet period, known as *Mittagsruhe,* usually between noon and 2:00 P.M. During this time the reception and gates are closed. To avoid being locked out after a busy morning or evening on the town, inquire about the hours before leaving.

Many campgrounds, particularly the newer ones, use the CEE 17 Euro plugs. Others use the two-pin Schuko system. Trash disposal in Germany is taken seriously, and containers are provided at campgrounds and other points for various categories of refuse.

Free camping for one night is allowed at highway and autobahn rest stops. An increasing number of local communities are making facilities, including dump and filling stations, available for RVs at little or no charge. These are usually posted with signs showing a motorhome pictogram.

For additional information about camping in Germany, contact the German Camping Club (DCC), Mandlstrasse 28, Postfach 400428, 8000 Munchen 40, Germany (phone 089 38 01 42 0, fax 089 33 47 37) or the German Automobile Club (ADAC), Am Westpark 8, 81373 Munchen 70, Germany (phone 089 76 76 0, fax 089 76 76 2500. A booklet listing RV-friendly communities may be obtained from VDWH, in der Schildwacht 13, 65933 Frankfurt am Main 80, Germany; phone (069) 39 34 00, fax (069) 38 08 574.

Hungary

CAPITAL: Budapest

POPULATION: 10,300,000

CURRENCY: forint (Ft), divided into 100 filler

LANGUAGE: Hungarian

RELIGION: Roman Catholic and Protestant

POLICE: 07

FIRE: 05

AMBULANCE: 04

ROAD SERVICE: MAK, open twenty-four hours throughout the country; (061) 1151220; Budapest 1151220

BANKS: Monday 8:15 A.M.–6:00 P.M.; Tuesday, Wednesday, and Thursday 8:15 A.M.–3:30 P.M.; Friday 8:15 A.M.–1:00 P.M.

STORES: weekdays 10:00 A.M.–6:00 P.M.; Saturday 9:00 A.M.–1:00 P.M.

HOLIDAYS: January 1; March 15, National Day; Easter Monday (movable); May 1, Labor Day; Pentacost (movable); August 20, Constitution Day; October 23, Proclamation of the Republic; December 25 and 26

EMBASSIES: *United States,* v. Szabadsag Ter 12, Budapest; phone (01) 112–6450, fax (01) 132–8934. *Canada,* Budakeszi ut. 32, 1121 Budapest; phone (01) 176–7312, fax (01) 176–7689. *United Kingdom,* Hamincad UTCA 6, Budapest V; phone (01) 118–2888

This small, landlocked country, long an important crossroads between West and East, offers its visitors a wonderful blend of the old Hapsburg Empire and the exotic East. The present-day Hungarians are the proud descendants of the hordes of Magyar tribesmen who ravaged Western Europe more than 1,000 years ago from bases in the Ural Mountains.

DRIVING

Hungary has one of the best road networks of the Eastern European countries and is, with the exception of the Budapest area, a pleasure to drive through. Many secondary roads in the countryside are unpaved; in these regions be alert, particularly after dark, for unlit horse-drawn wagons and carts.

A high-speed motorway links Budapest with Lake Balaton, and there are short stretches of motorway that radiate out in several directions from Budapest. There are no tolls for using these roads. Motorways are designated by the letter "M" and a single digit. Other roads are numbered with one, two, or three digits, with the major highways having a single digit.

Although the network of service stations throughout the country is adequate, it is often difficult to find stations that are open at night. Visa and MasterCard may be used in payment for gasoline in many places.

The speed limit for motorhomes on the few motorways is 120 kph (72 mph); outside built-up areas it is 80 kph (48 mph). The speed limit in towns, unless otherwise posted, is 60 kph (36 mph). Throughout the country the police are empowered to collect fines from foreign motorists on the spot. The penalties for driving under the influence of alcohol are severe. The permissible blood-alcohol level is 0.00 percent.

Seatbelts are compulsory, and children under age twelve are not allowed in the front seat. An International Driver's License is currently required for visitors from the United States and Canada. U.K. drivers can use their local licenses. To avoid difficulties when leaving the country, if your vehicle has any visible damage, point this out to border authorities upon entry into the country.

CAMPING

As in many Eastern European countries, camping is very popular with the locals, who take full advantage of this inexpensive way of seeing their own country. The great influx of camping tourists from Western Europe results in very crowded conditions during the peak season, in July and August, and during holiday periods. Crowded campgrounds are a particularly acute problem in the Budapest and Lake Balaton regions.

Following the fall of the Communist regime, many government-owned sites are now in private hands. Standards throughout the country are rapidly improving but have generally not yet reached Western European standards. Hungary's some one hundred campgrounds are rated with from one to three stars, based on facilities and space allotted to each visitor. Many sites offer discounts for the International Camping Carnet.

Opening times vary, with most campgrounds staying open from May 1 to September 30. There are also a few year-round sites, usually associated with a health spa.

The majority of campgrounds have either a small campstore or are close to a grocery store. When traveling in Hungary, however, it is best not to plan on doing your grocery shopping at campgrounds. Coin-operated washers and dryers, while not universal, are found at an ever increasing number of campgrounds.

Although Budapest and Lake Balaton are well supplied with campgrounds, the more remote regions, such as the eastern plains, have few campgrounds. A large number of Hungarian campgrounds are either associated with motels or have cabins for rent. Free camping is officially prohibited but is generally tolerated. In areas where there are no campgrounds, it is best to ask permission locally.

The German-style Schuko electrical plugs and outlets are the most commonly used. There are gas bottle filling stations in Budapest, Eger, and Estergom. For details inquire at local campgrounds. Additional information about camping in Hungary may be obtained from Hungarian Camping and Caravanning Club, ulloi ut 6, Budapest, Hungary; phone (01) 33 65 36.

Poland

CAPITAL: Warsaw

POPULATION: 38,400,000

CURRENCY: Zloty (zl), divided into 100 groszy

LANGUAGE: Polish

RELIGION: Roman Catholic

POLICE: 997

FIRE: 998

AMBULANCE: 999

ROAD SERVICE: most towns 981; or PZM (022) 293–541 or 290–467, twenty-four hours in the entire country

BANKS: weekdays 8:00 A.M.–6:00 P.M.; some banks open Saturday 8:00 A.M.–1:00 or 3:00 P.M.

STORES: food shops, weekdays 7:00 A.M.–7:00 P.M.; Saturday 7:00 A.M.–1:00 P.M.; other stores, weekdays 11:00 A.M.–7:00 P.M., Saturday 9:00 A.M.–1:00 P.M.

HOLIDAYS: January 1; Easter Monday (movable); May 1, Labor Day; May 3, Constitution Day; Corpus Christi (movable); Assumption Day (movable); All Saints' Day (movable); November 11, Independence Day; December 25 and 26

EMBASSIES: *United States,* Aleje Ujazdowskie 29/31, Warsaw; phone (02) 628–3041, fax (02) 628–8298. *Canada,* Ulica Matejki 1/5, Warsaw 00-481; phone (022) 298–051, night line 298–050, fax (022) 296–457. *United Kingdom,* aleja Roz No. 1, 0, 00–556 Warsaw; phone (072) 281–001/5

It was the birth of the Polish Solidarity movement in the mid-1980s that set much of the tone for the dramatic changes that have swept across Eastern Europe, and it is in Poland that many of these changes are most evident. A country of great natural beauty, Poland offers its visitors a broad spectrum of historical and cultural attractions.

DRIVING

Great improvements have been made in recent years in the condition of its roads; however, Poland still has a lot of catching up to do before Western European standards are obtained. Driving a car is a new experience for many Poles, and this lack of road savvy is reflected on the highways. With the exception of short stretches near Warsaw and Wroclow, there are no modern freeways, and divided highways are still the exception rather than the rule. Secondary roads are often poorly maintained, and many unpaved and cobblestone roads remain. Horse-drawn carts and wagons are common on country roads and are occasionally encountered even on major highways. These vehicles are often poorly lit or carry no lights at all and constitute a serious hazard when driving at night.

Over the past few years, many highway numbers have been changed. To avoid confusion, try to obtain the most recent road maps available. Since much of Poland has, at one time or another, been under German control, you will encounter many German place names, particularly on maps and in guidebooks published in Germany.

The network of service stations on the major roads is adequate; however, it is often difficult to find stations on the secondary roads. Few stations are open at night. As spare parts for most vehicles are not readily available, it is a good idea to carry the items that are most likely to cause problems for you.

When driving in cities, look out for tiny green arrows under the traffic lights; these allow a right turn on a red light. Seatbelts are compulsory. Children under age ten are allowed in the front seat only with a children's seat.

The speed limit for motorhomes on the few existing motor ways is 110 kph (66 mph); outside built-up areas it is 90 kph (54 mph). The speed limit in towns, unless otherwise posted, is 60 kph (36 mph). Throughout the country the police are empowered to collect fines from foreign motorists on the spot.

The penalties for driving under the influence of alcohol are severe. The permissible blood alcohol level is only 0.2 percent.

CAMPING

The wave of change that is sweeping the country has also been felt in the camping sector. Many previously state-owned campgrounds are reverting to private ownership. Names, opening times, and conditions described in guidebooks are often changed by the time the guide is published. Many of these new privately operated campgrounds approach Western European standards.

There are some 200 official sites, designated by number and rated as category 1, 2, or 3. These generally are inferior to Western European sites in facilities and cleanliness.

You will have no difficulty finding campgrounds in the main tourist regions. Campgrounds in the more remote regions are rare. Although free camping is officially prohibited, it is generally tolerated. Farmers are often happy to receive a few Zlotys to allow you to park on their land.

Most campgrounds are open from mid-June through mid-September. There are only a few year-round campgrounds. At many sites restaurants and camp stores are opened only in July and August. Washing machines and dryers are rarely found at Polish campgrounds.

Electrical outlets are mostly of the German Schuko type, although the French-type socket is also found. Additional information about camping in Poland may be obtained from Camptur, Polish Federacja Camping Caravanning, 00-060 U1 Krolewska 27-A, Warsaw, Poland.

Itinerary: Berlin • Gdansk and the Baltic Coast • Warsaw • Krakow • The Tatra Mountains • Budapest and the Danube • Vienna • Prague and the Czech Republic

---

START: Berlin
COUNTRIES: Austria, The Czech Republic, Germany, Hungary, Poland, Slovakia
DISTANCE: 2,740 km (1,644 mi.)
MAPS: Hallwag *Czech Republic; Slovakia; Hungary; Poland*
MINIMUM RECOMMENDED TOURING TIME: 18 to 21 days

INTRODUCTION

This tour explores a region that has, in the space of just a few years, experienced revolutionary upheaval. Not so long ago our entry into Poland from Berlin, across what was then Communist East Germany, entailed a major bureaucratic hassle to obtain the necessary visas, and the inspection of our vehicle and belongings took place under the watchful eyes of machine gun-toting border guards.

On our most recent visit, the scowling, heavily armed guards and the barbed wire were gone, and the new border officials were barely interested in looking at our passports. In Poland and what was then Czechoslovakia (today the Czech Republic and Slovakia) shops where we had witnessed long lines of people waiting for the chance to buy a few inferior items or a scraggly piece of meat have been supplanted by modern stores full of goods that approach Western European standards of quality.

This is not to say that all is rosy. On the contrary; the cataclysmic changes that have taken place in Eastern Europe have left many people dazed and in dire financial straits. For the traveler from the West, however, there are now wonderful opportunities to experience the new, emerging Eastern Europe first-hand and in relative comfort.

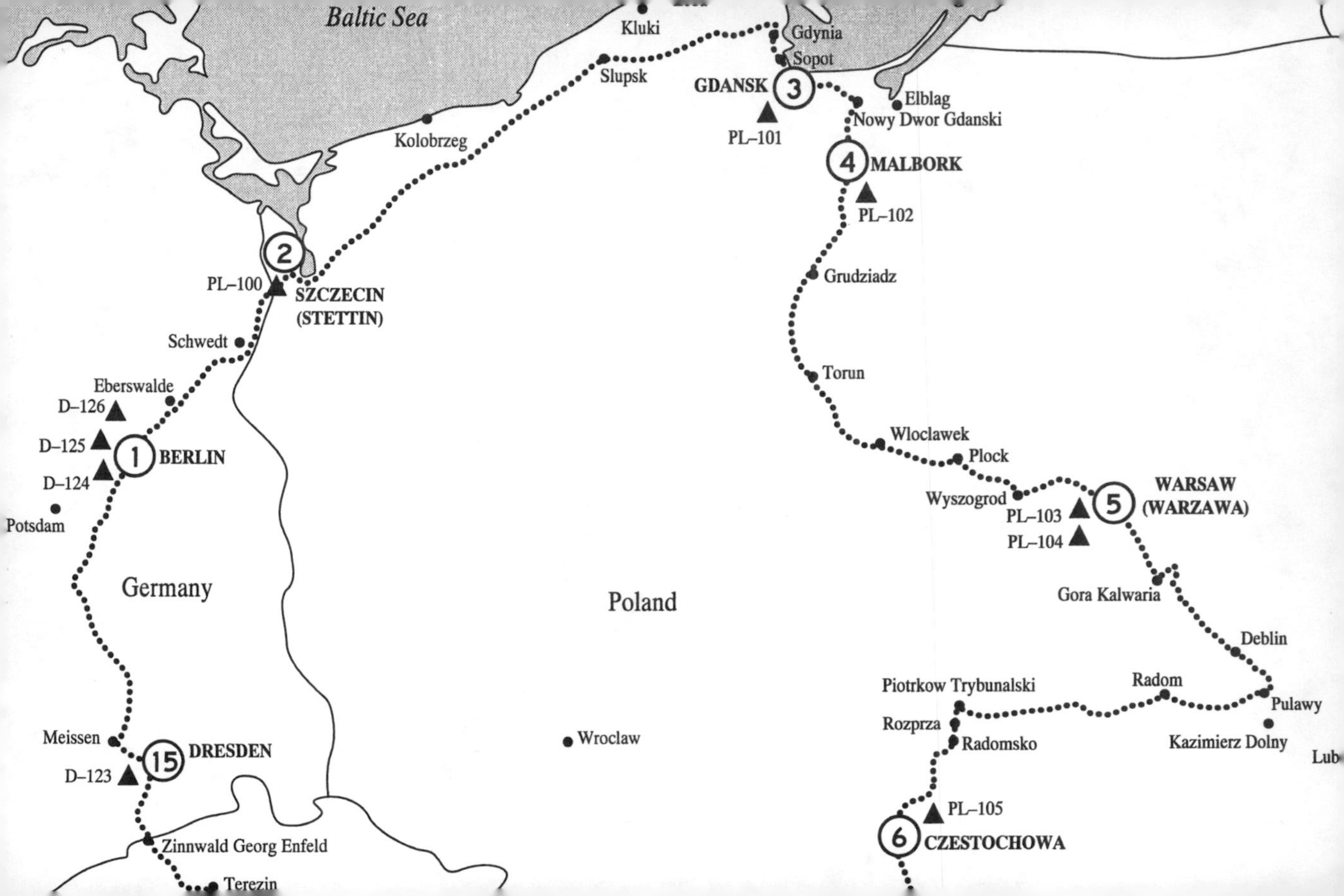
Baltic Sea
Kluki
Gdynia
Sopot
Slupsk
GDANSK
3
PL–101
Elblag
Nowy Dwor Gdanski
Kolobrzeg
4
MALBORK
PL–102
2
PL–100
SZCZECIN
(STETTIN)
Grudziadz
Schwedt
Torun
Eberswalde
D–126
D–125
1
BERLIN
D–124
Wloclawek
Plock
Potsdam
Wyszogrod
5
WARSAW
(WARZAWA)
PL–103
PL–104
Germany
Poland
Gora Kalwaria
Deblin
Piotrkow Trybunalski
Radom
Pulawy
Rozprza
Radomsko
Kazimierz Dolny
Meissen
15
DRESDEN
Wroclaw
Lub
D–123
PL–105
6
CZESTOCHOWA
Zinnwald Georg Enfeld
Terezin

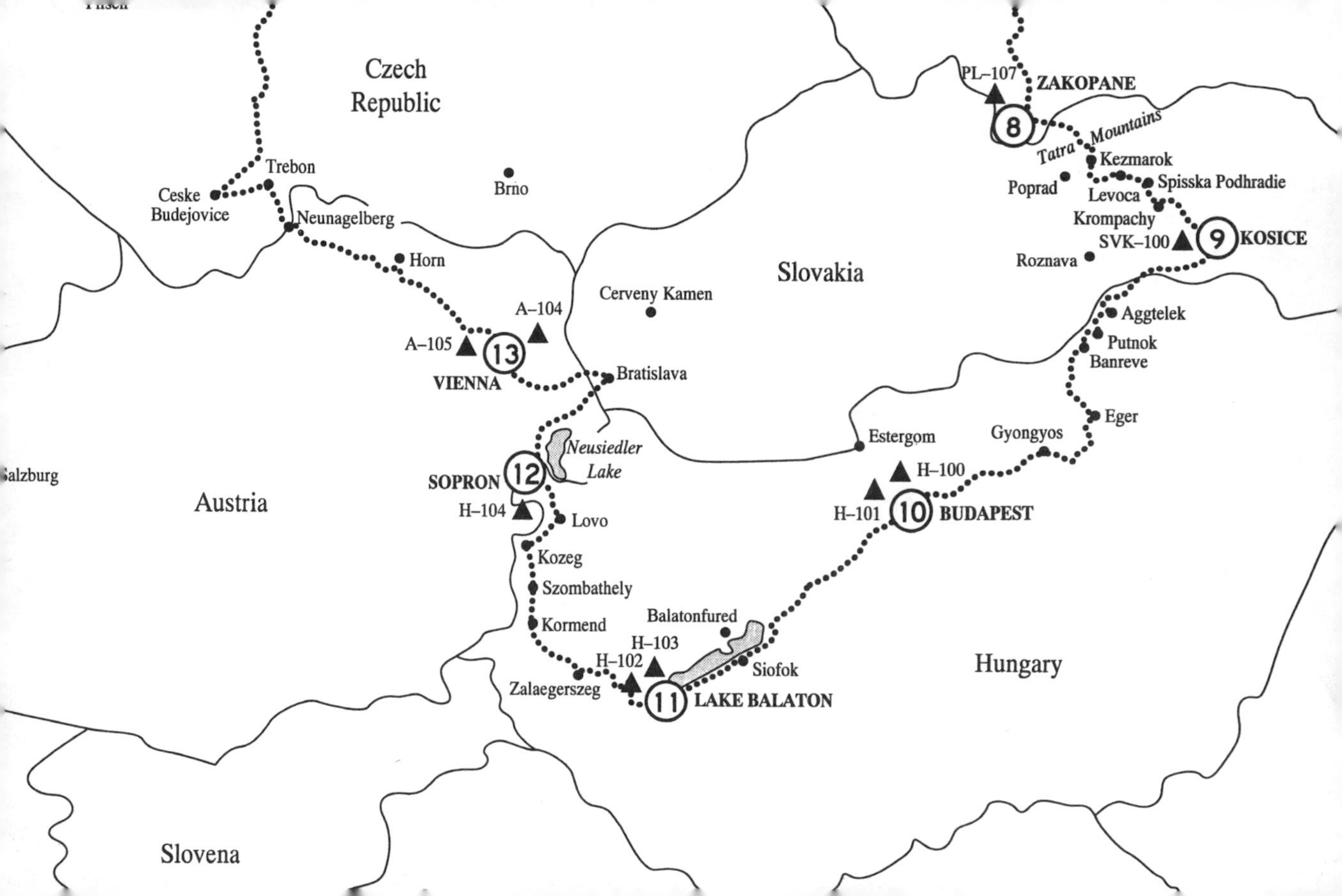
Czech
Republic
Trebon
Ceske
Budejovice
Brno
Neunagelberg
Horn
A–104
A–105
13
VIENNA
Cerveny Kamen
Bratislava
Slovakia
Neusiedler
Lake
12
SOPRON
H–104
Lovo
Kozeg
Szombathely
Kormend
Zalaegerszeg
H–102
H–103
11
LAKE BALATON
Balatonfured
Siofok
Austria
Slovena
Estergom
H–101
H–100
10
BUDAPEST
Gyongyos
Eger
Banreve
Putnok
Aggtelek
Hungary
PL–107
8
ZAKOPANE
Tatra Mountains
Kezmarok
Poprad
Levoca
Spisska Podhradie
Krompachy
SVK–100
9
KOSICE
Roznava

Starting in Berlin, the newly designated capital of a unified Germany, we trace a circular route that takes us along Poland's Amber Coast to the historic Baltic seaport of Gdansk, birthplace of the Solidarity movement. En route to the Polish capital of Warsaw, we visit the thirteenth-century castle at Malbork, one-time headquarters of the legendary Teutonic Knights. The historic capitals of Prague, Budapest, and Vienna are also a part of our tour. In southern Poland we visit Krakow, one of the most beautiful cities in all of Europe. In addition to these bustling cities, we pass through areas of great natural beauty, including the High Tatra Mountains, whose scenic vistas rival those of the Alps.

Our visits to the former Nazi concentration camps at Auschwitz and Teriesenstadt are sober reminders that this is also a region in which much suffering took place during World War II.

When to Go

One disadvantage of the "opening up" of Eastern Europe is the flood of tourists who all want to visit Prague, Budapest, and Warsaw in July and August. Spring and fall are the best times for finding that elusive combination of good weather and a tolerable level of tourism. The Hungarian plains and the mountains of Poland and Slovakia are relatively uncrowded even in August, while the Baltic coast of Poland and Hungary's Lake Balaton are best visited in the spring and fall.

Keep in mind when traveling in this region that many campgrounds are only open from June through September. See individual listings for dates.

Highlights

Auschwitz, Poland
Berlin
Budapest
Kazimierz Dolny, Poland
Krakow
Lake Balaton, Hungary
Malbork Castle, Poland
Charles Bridge, the old town, Prague
Vienna
The Old Town, Warsaw

Expanding Horizons

- **To Alpine Heights and Old World Delights Itinerary:** From Vienna take the autobahn west to Salzburg (see p. 339).

- **To Viking Trails Itinerary:** From Gdansk take the ferry to Helsinki. The crossing takes thirty to forty hours (see p. 99).

ON THE ROAD

Numbered sites correspond with circled numbers on the itinerary map.

1. Berlin

With the collapse of the Communist East German regime and the subsequent reunification of Germany in 1990, the infamous Berlin Wall, which symbolized Berlin's existence as a divided city for nearly forty years, came crashing down. Only a few token fragments are left standing as a reminder. Checkpoint Charlie, the best-known crossing point between the two Berlins (East and West) during the cold war, is now just another tourist attraction, with a museum that documents the history of the wall.

The combined city of Berlin, the continent's largest, is a vast metropolis that encompasses individual villages and towns along with numerous parks and lakes. Unlike most European cities, Berlin's attractions are spread out over a large area, which makes exploration on foot difficult. Fortunately, the city has an excellent public-transportation system. Although things are changing rapidly, given impetus by the decision to move the seat of the German government from Bonn to Berlin, there is still much in the eastern sector that has not been brought up to Western European standards.

The bustling **Kurfurstendamm** or **Ku'damm,** one of Europe's busiest boulevards, is Berlin's best-known shopping street and the focal point for the city's active nightlife. At the eastern end of the Ku'damm you will see the bombed-out ruins of the **Kaiser Wilhelm Gedachtniskirche (Memorial Church),** left standing as a reminder of the senseless destruction of war. The 630-acre **Zoologischer Garten** (Berlin's zoo) is one of Europe's most modern animal parks. The **Brandenburger Tor (Gate),** built in 1788 as a triumphal arch for victorious Prussian armies, was the scene of the celebrations that marked Germany's reunification.

Berlin has several world-class museums, which include the **Egyptian Museum,** the **Gemaldegalerie (art museum),** and, on the **Museum Island** in the former eastern sector, the **Pergamon Museum,** with its impressive collection of Greek and Babylonian antiquities. The **Sans Souci Palace,** built by Frederick the Great in the southern suburb of Potsdam, is one of the finest rococo structures in Europe.

Berlin Campgrounds

There are a number of year-round campgrounds spread around the greater Berlin area. Most of these have a high percentage of resident campers, with limited space set aside for travelers. At present there is no really first-class campground for the new German capital. We expect that this will change in the near future.

Berlin is not currently an RV-friendly city. Leave your rig at the campground and use the extensive public-transportation system.

D–124 ★★ DCC Campingplatz Kladow. Open year-round. At the southwest edge of city, 20 km (12 mi.) from city center. From Autobahn ring A10 take exit Potsdam Nord. Go through Potsdam and follow signs to Kladow, then to campground. A fifteen-acre, level, partly shaded site on the south shore of Glienicker Lake. Bus to town, #135, #138, 250 yd. –250 yd.

D–125 ★★ Campingplatz Kohlhasenbruck. Open year-round. In the southwest corner of the city near Griebnitzsee, 13 km (7.8 mi.) from city center. Take Autobahn ring A115 to Zelendorf–Kleeblatt. Take Wannsee exit and follow Konigstrasse to Wannsee city hall, then signs to campground. A large, mostly level site with some terracing. In a rural setting on a small lake (no swimming). Commuter train from Griebnitzee station, or bus to downtown. –500 yd.

D–126 ★★ Campingplatz Dreilinden. Open year-round. Located 14 km (8.4 mi.) southwest of city center. Same approach as D–124, then Albrechtstrasse to campground. A small, level, partly shaded site. Commuter train to downtown, 2 km (1.2 mi.). Bus #118 (a fifteen-minute walk).

Berlin → Szczecin (Stettin), Poland, 130 km (78 mi.)

Leave Berlin heading northeast and pick up Hwy. 2 in the direction of **Bernau.** Continue on Hwy. 2 through **Eberswalde** and **Schwedt,** following the **Odra River** into Szczecin.

2. Szczecin (Stettin)

An industrial town located on the Odra River, Szczecin was once the capital of the Prussian state of West Pomerania. The thirteenth-century **Zamek Ksiazat Pomorskich (Castle of the Pomeranian Dukes),** leveled by bombing during World War II, has been reconstructed and serves as a cultural center and art gallery.

Szczecin Campground

PL–100 ★ Camping No. 25 Dabie. Open June 1–September 30. In the suburb of Dabie, 8 km (4.8 mi.) east of Szczecin center. From the center of Szczecin, take E14 east toward **Swinoujzcie** and follow signs to campground. A shaded, level, grassy site on Lake Dabie. Next to local airport.

Szczecin → Gdansk (Danzig), 300 km (180 mi.)

Leave Szczezecin and follow Hwy. E28/6 to Gdansk via **Slupsk,** site of a restored, fourteenth-century castle with a working mill. Continue via **Gdynia** and **Sopot** into Gdansk. The highway parallels the Baltic coastline. This is a region of broad, white, sandy beaches backed by gentle dunes and dense pine forests. **Kolobrzeg** is one of the most popular of the coastal resorts. There is an interesting **open-air museum** at **Kluki,** just west of the fishing village of **Leba.** The eastern part of the coast is known for its rich Amber deposits.

3. Gdansk (Danzig)

A seaport of some 500,000 that was once an important member of the medieval Hanseatic Trading League, Gdansk was the scene of some of the earliest fighting during World War II. The Lenin shipyards here were the birthplace of the Polish Solidarity movement. There is a touching monument at the entrance that commemorates the workers who died in a bloody 1970 uprising. Although the city was virtually destroyed during World War II, the **Glowne Miasto (main town)** has been meticulously restored to its former splendor. The 250-ft. steeple of the Gothic **Kosciol Mariacki (Church of Our Lady)** affords a bird's-eye view of the city. One of Europe's largest churches, this towering brick structure holds 25,000 people. **Sopot,** at the northern edge of Gdansk, is one of

A roadside stop in Poland

the oldest and most popular of the Baltic Sea resorts.

Note: To connect with our Viking Trails itinerary, take the ferry from Gdansk to Helsinki. For details contact Pol Ferries, Matkakeskus, P.O. Box 1002, Helsinki, Finland, phone (9)0 680 901, fax 680 9633.

Gdansk Campground

PL–101 ★★ Camping Wita No. 18. Open May 1–September 30. In Sopot, 5 km (3 mi.) north of Gdansk center. Follow coast road north from Gdansk to Sopot. Site is located 300 yd. past the Marina Hotel, across the road from a sandy beach. A large, level site with some shade. Tram to Gdansk, 300 yd. –900 yd.

Gdansk → Malbork, 50 km (30 mi.)

From Gdansk take E77 east toward **Elblag.** At **Nowy Dwor Gdanski** head south, following signs to Malbork.

4. Malbork (Marienburg)

Constructed in the late thirteenth century as the headquarters of the Teutonic Knights, this spectacular red-brick castle has one of the largest medieval defense systems in Europe. At various times the castle has served as a residence for Polish kings, a barracks for Prussian soldiers, and, during World War II, a German prison camp. The castle has been fully restored, and guided tours are available.

Malbork Campground

PL–102 ★★ Camping Osrodek No. 197. Open May 15–September 30. In the city, at the Nogat River. Approaches are well marked. A medium-size site in a pleasant riverside location with some shade trees. Plenty of parking at the nearby castle.

Malbork → Warsaw (Warzawa), 320 km (192 mi.)

Head south from Malbork to **Grudziadz;** from there follow signs to **Torun.** One of the country's best-preserved Gothic medieval towns, Torun is the birthplace of the astronomer Nicolaus Copernicus. You may visit the house in which he was born.

From Torun follow E75/1, which parallels the **Vistula (Wista) River** to **Wloclawek,** a city known for its hand-decorated faience. Continue along the large artificial lake formed by a dam in the Vistula to **Plock,** a former Polish capital. The road follows the river into Warsaw. The bridge at **Wyszogrod** is Europe's largest wooden span.

5. Warsaw (Warzawa)

Modern Poland's cultural and intellectual center, Warsaw has been the country's capital since 1596. Although it is a sprawling metropolis of 2 million people, most of the interesting places to visit are clustered together within an hour's walking radius of the old town. The **Stare Miastro (old town)** and most of the rest of the city were nearly totally destroyed during World War II. The city's faithful restoration from original plans and drawings was a masterpiece of historical reconstruction. This impressive undertaking is documented with pictures and models in the **Historical Museum,** in the center of the old town. The best vantage point for an overall view of Warsaw is from the thirtieth floor of the Stalinesque **Palace of Culture and Science.**

The **Lazienki Palace,** a favorite summer residence of Polish royalty, is set in a beautiful park on an artificial lake. The ornate eighteenth-century **Wilanow Palace,** with gardens modeled after Versailles, was built by King Jan Sobieski. It was Sobieski who, at the head of the Polish Army, rescued Vienna from the Turks in 1683. The palace contains much of the original furniture and an extensive portrait gallery.

The gripping **Monument to the Ghetto Heroes,** erected on what was a part of the Warsaw ghetto, is the only thing in the area to remind visitors of what was once a section of the city in which some 400,000 Jews lived. By the end of World War II, they were gone, most sent to their deaths in the Nazi gas chambers.

Warsaw Campgrounds

Most Warsaw-area campgrounds have ready access to public transportation. There is limited parking available on the river embankment below the old town and at the Palace of Culture.

PL–103 ★★ Camping Gromada No. 34. Open June 1–September 30 (considering extending opening times). Located 5 km (3 mi.) southwest of Warsaw center. One km (0.6 mi.) south of main train station (Warzawa Centralina). From station take Aleje Jerozolimskie toward Kielce; after a few hundred meters, turn left onto Raszynskka and follow signs to campground. Site is next to sports stadium (SKRA) and Pilsudski Park. A medium-size, uneven, grassy field. This is the most pleasant and conveniently located of Warsaw's several campgrounds. Take bus #175 from entrance to Warsaw center. Very crowded in July and August.

PL–104 ★★ Camping Astur No. 123. Open May 1–September 30. Located 8 km (4.8 mi.) west of Warsaw center. From Warsaw center take Hwy. 7/8 toward Katowice. Follow signs to campground. Site is located opposite Hotel Vera. A small, level site with some shade. Bus to Warsaw center.

Warsaw → Czestochowa, 350 km (210 mi.)

Leave Warsaw at the south end of the city, near the Wilanow Palace, and follow the road that runs along the Vistula River. At **Gora Kalwaria** cross the Vistula and continue with the river, now on your right, to **Deblin** and then into **Pulawy.** The white-and-yellow, eighteenth-century neo-classical **Pulawy Palace** is surrounded by lovely parks and formal gardens.

Continue south to **Kazimierz Dolny.** This charming town on the Vistula, described as a "pearl of the Polish Renaissance," has been a favorite retreat of Polish artists and intellectuals for the past century. From Kazimierz return to Pulawy and pick up the main Lublin–Radom highway. Follow signs to Radom, a rather dull industrial center, and continue east on Hwy. 44 to **Piotrkow Trybunalski.** From there head south to Czestochowa. To avoid the heavy truck traffic on Hwy. 1, the main artery between Warsaw and the heavily industrialized **Katowice** region, take the alternate route that passes through **Rozprza** and **Radomsko** into Czestochowa.

6. CZESTOCHOWA

This primarily industrial town draws religious pilgrims from all over the world who come to view a mysterious fifteenth-century painting of a dark-skinned Madonna and Child. Designated as the savior of Poland, the painting, known as **The Black Madonna,** is located in the thirteenth-century Paulite Monastery of **Jasna Gora.**

Czestochowa Campground

PL–105 ★★ Camping Mosir. Open June 1–September 30. At the north edge of town. Approaches are well marked from all directions. A large, level, partly shaded site. Easy walk to visit town and Black Madonna.

Czestochowa → Krakow, 145 km (87 mi.)

Leave Czestochowa on E75/1 and head south, skirting Katowice to **Tychy.** From there follow Hwy. 92 east toward Krakow.

Twenty-two kilometers (13 mi.) southeast of Tychy is the drab industrial town of **Oswiecim,** better known by its German name of **Auschwitz.** The ivy-covered brick buildings, well-kept lawns, and tranquil atmosphere belie the fact that some 4 million victims of Nazi terror met their deaths here. The Auschwitz and Birkenau camps are now Polish state museums. Continue east from Auschwitz the remaining 55 km (33 mi.) to Krakow.

7. Krakow

Among the few major European cities to have escaped serious damage during World War II, Krakow is listed by UNESCO as one of the twelve great historic cities of the world. The **Rynek Glowny,** often referred to as "Krakow's drawing room," is Europe's largest medieval marketplace and a bustling center of activity. The area is alive with food vendors, flower sellers, street performers, and gypsy musicians.

From the steeple of the adjacent **Kosciol Mariacki (Church of Our Lady),** a plaintive trumpet is played at the beginning of each hour. This haunting melody, never played to completion, is suddenly interrupted to honor the Trumpeter of Krakow who was shot in the throat by a Tartar's arrow as he was warning the city of an ensuing attack.

One of Krakow's principal attractions is the well-preserved complex of sixteenth-century fortified buildings occupying a rise overlooking the Vistula. The old Jewish synagogue, now a museum of Jewish history, is practically all that is left of a once vibrant, thriving Jewish community. A visit to the Jewish cemetery on Miodowa at Podbrezie, where toppled headstones lie beneath a decades-old overgrowth of brush and ivy, is a moving experience.

The **Salt Mines at Wieliczka,** 13 km (7.8 mi.) southeast of Krakow, are the oldest in Europe, with an inspiring underground chapel and many figures carved from salt.

Krakow Campground

PL–106 ★★★ Motel Camping Krak No. 45. Open May 1–October 15. Located 5 km (3 mi.) northwest of Krakow center. From city center take E40/4 toward Katowice. At traffic circle take Hwy. 914 toward Katowice, then follow signs to Campground/Motel Krak. A large, grassy, partly sloping site with some shade. Sites are divided by hedges. Bus #173 to Krakow center, 500 yd.

Krakow → Zakopane, 85 km (51 mi.)

Take E77/7 south from Krakow into the foothills of the **Tatra Mountains** to the resort town of Zakopane.

8. Zakopane

Lying at an elevation of approximately 3,281 ft., Zakopane is Poland's highest town and most popular year-round mountain resort. The town has many fine examples of the intricate carved-wood architecture that is distinctive to this mountainous region.

Zakopane Campground

PL–107 ★★ Comfort Auto Camping. Open May 1–September 30. At the western edge of town. Follow signs from town. A recently opened private campground that is conveniently located, ten minutes' walking distance from Zakopane center.

Zakopane → Kosice, Slovakia, 150 km (90 mi.)

From Zakopane take the road east across the Tatra Mountains to **Lysa Polana** and the border crossing into Slovakia. The Tatras are a rugged, compact, alpinelike range whose highest peak, **Gerlachovsky Stit,** reaches 8,710 ft. Continue through this mountainous region on Hwy. 67 to **Kezmarok,** a former German settlement dating back to the twelfth century. The main attraction here is the massive Gothic Renaissance palace in the town center.

From Kezmarok take the road through **L'ubica** and **Vrbov,** and bypass the drab industrial town of **Poprad** to intersect with Hwy. E50/18, the main Presov–Poprad road. Head east on E50/18 to **Levoca,** an attractive medieval town with a large Renaissance square. The huge Gothic **St. Jacob's Church** contains an incredible carved-wood altar from the early sixteenth century.

From Levoca continue along E50/18 to **Spisska Podhradie.** From there take Hwy. 547, a beautiful, curving mountain drive that passes through the mountain villages of **Spis Vlachy** and **Krompachy,** in the heart of the **Spis kingdom,** to Kosice.

9. Kosice

Kosice, a sprawling, modern city, the second largest in Slovakia, straddles the main route between Hungary and Poland and has a centuries-old tradition as an important trading center. The **Katova Basta** is a medieval fortress complete with a torture chamber that has been converted into a regional museum. The town's expansive medieval square is flanked by Slovakia's largest cathedral.

Kosice Campground

SVK–100 ★ Autocamping Salas Barca. Open June 1–September 30. At the south edge of town on Hwy. 50, in the direction of Roznava. A small, level site with no shade. Bus to center of town, 300 yd. –900 yd.

Kosice → Budapest, Hungary, 280 km (168 mi.)

Take Hwy. 50 south from Kosice and follow this along the Hungarian border in the direction of **Roznava,** as far as the border town of **Turna n. Bodya.** Cross into Hungary and follow the **Bodya River** west to **Aggtelek.** This is the jumping-off point for exploring one of Europe's most extensive subterranean cave systems.

From Aggtelek continue on the winding mountain road to **Putnok.** Then head north for 5 km (3 mi.) on Hwy. 26 to the border town of **Banreve.** Leave Banreve heading south on Hwy. 25 to **Eger,** an attractive town in the heart of the **Bukk Mountains** that is known for its fine wines.

From Eger continue south on Hwy. 25 to intersect with E71/3 that runs by way of **Gyongyos** into Budapest. Located in the beautiful **Matra Mountains,** Gyongyos is at the center of one of Hungary's principal wine-producing regions.

10. Budapest

Affectionately dubbed by its residents the "Pearl of the Danube," Hungary's cosmopolitan capital is to a great extent defined by this great river, which flows through Budapest's center and divides it into its component towns of Buda and Pest. United in 1873, Buda and Pest present visitors with two entirely different faces. Pest, on the east bank of the Danube, is the administrative and business side of the city; on the west bank the sprawling hills of Buda, the older of the two sections, are covered by a maze of narrow cobblestone streets lined with ancient buildings. Unlike many major European cities, Budapest doesn't easily lend itself to exploration by foot. There is, however, a good public transportation network, and taxis are reasonably priced.

The city's main attractions include the graceful **Danube bridges;** the **Royal Palace,** which houses the **Hungarian National Gallery;** and the **Matthias Church,** the traditional coronation church of the Hungarian monarchs. The **Cathedral** above the Danube at **Esztergom,** 30 km (18 mi.) northwest of Budapest, is Hungary's largest.

Budapest Campgrounds

There are at least twenty campgrounds, of varying quality, within a 25-km (16-mi.) radius of the center of Budapest. The following are recommended for their facilities and convenient access to the city. Parking in Budapest is difficult, except on weekends and holidays. Your best bet is to use public transportation.

H–100 ★★ Hars Hegy Camping. Open Easter–October 20. In the Buda hills, 5 km (3 mi.) northwest of Budapest center. From Budapest center follow signs to Budakesi and then to Europa Camping/Hotel. A seven-acre, wooded site terraced into a hill between two hotels. Convenient bus to Budapest center. Sightseeing excursions leave from campground.

H–101 ★★ Romai Camping. Open year-round. Located 10 km (6 mi.) north of Budapest center on Hwy. 11, the road to Esztergom. A fifteen-acre, wooded area next to large outdoor swimming pool. Metro and bus to Budapest center. Organized excursions.

Budapest → Lake Balaton, 110 km (66 mi.)

Take Hwy. 70 southwest from Budapest to Lake Balaton.

11. Lake Balaton

With some 200 km (120 mi.) of shoreline, Balaton is Europe's largest inland body of water. The lake is surprisingly shallow and rarely exceeds a depth of 10 ft. An area of great natural beauty, the Balaton region has experienced tremendous tourist development in recent years; there is hardly a place along the lake that doesn't have some sort of tourist complex.

Siofok, on the south shore, is the center for the region's tourist industry. There is a car ferry from **Szantodrev** on the south shore across the lake to the **Tihany Peninsula.** The crossing takes just eight minutes. **Balatonfured,** on the north shore, has been drawing an international clientele to its eleven medicinal springs for the past two centuries. The **Festetics Palace,** in **Keszthely,** the largest town on the north shore, is one of the finest examples of Baroque architecture in Hungary.

Lake Balaton Campgrounds

The lake is ringed with dozens of campgrounds. During July and August they are all very crowded, so arrive early to ensure a spot. Most campgrounds are open from mid-May through mid-September.

H–102 ★★★ Kurcamping Castrum Heviz. Open year-round. From Keszthely follow lake west toward Zalaegerszeg. Approaches are well marked. A five-acre, grassy area with many mature trees. Site is not on Lake Balaton but borders a small "inland" lake fed by hot springs. One of the few year-round sites in the region. Thanks to the hot springs, bathing is possible all year. –900 yd.

H–103 ★★ Camping Castrum Keszthely. Open April 1–October 31. At the east edge of Keszthely. At km 103.2, next to AFOR station, turn off to lake. A large, level, pleasantly laid out site with little shade. Easy walk (ten minutes) to resort town of Keszthely.

Lake Balaton → Sopron, 125 km (75 mi.)

From Keszthely follow signs to **Zalaegerszeg** and continue north on Hwy. 76 to **Kormend.** Take E65/86 farther north to **Szombathely.** Founded by the Romans in A.D. 43, Szombathely was an important settlement on the route that transported amber from the Baltic Sea to Rome. **Kozeg,** on Hwy. 87 at the Austrian border 20 km (12 mi.) north of Szombathely, is one of Hungary's most delightful towns. From Kozeg take the road to **Lovo,** and from there follow Hwy. 84 to Sopron.

12. Sopron

Another important way station on the Roman amber route, Sopron is an attractive border town with a number of well-preserved medieval and baroque buildings. The 200-ft.-high **Fire Tower,** at the entrance to the old town, has foundations dating back to Roman times.

H–104 ★★ Camping Ozon. Open April 1–October 31. At the southwest corner of town on the road to Brennbergbanya. A small, terraced site in an orchard. Bus to town.

Sopron→ Vienna (Wien), Austria, 110 km (66 mi.)

From Sopron cross into Austria at **Morbisch** and follow the road around the **Neusiedlersee.** Cross over the Danube (Donau, Duna) into Bratislava, the capital of the recently formed independent republic of Slovakia.

At first glance the city presents a drab industrial face; however, the ancient inner city has some interesting structures and a fine hilltop castle. One of the region's most intriguing castles is the pink-tinted, thirteenth-century Renaissance fortress at **Cerveny Kamen,** 50 km (30 mi.) to the northeast. From Bratislava cross back over the Danube and follow signs into Vienna.

13. VIENNA (WIEN)

A bustling modern city of 1.6 million inhabitants, Vienna retains much of the charm and allure of its imperial past. Although this is a huge, sprawling metropolis that fans out to encompass the famed **Vienna Woods,** most of the main attractions are within the relatively compact inner core.

Stephansdom (St. Stephen's Cathedral), whose towering 450-ft.-high spire is a Vienna landmark and Austria's finest Gothic structure. The **Hofburg (Imperial Palace),** an extensive complex of buildings whose architecture spans the thirteenth to the twentieth centuries, is the former winter residence of the Hapsburgs.

Vienna is home to a number of fine museums, including the **Kunsthistorisches Museum (Fine Arts)** and the **Albertina,** with an impressive collection of graphics and etchings. **Schonbrunn Palace,** the opulent Hapsburg summer residence, is located in a huge park at the west end of the city. Although parking in the inner city is difficult, there is plenty of parking at Schonbrunn.

Note: To link up with our Alpine Heights and Old World Delights itinerary take the A1 Autobahn west to Salzburg (see p. 339).

Vienna Campgrounds

A–104 ★★★★ Aktiv-Camping Neue Donau. Open May 15–September 15. Located 4 km (2.4 mi.) east of city center, just east of A22–A23 interchange. Located near the Prater amusement park and Neue Donau recreation area, this is the closest to the city center of the Vienna campgrounds. Approaches are well marked. A large, level, grassy area with little shade. Good access to city via bus 91A and Metro.

A–105 ★★★★ Donaupark Camping Klosterneuburg. Open year-round. In Klosterneuburg, on the Danube. From Vienna take Hwy. 14 along the river to Klosterneuburg. Approaches are well marked. A beautifully laid out campground in a park setting. Adjacent to full-facility recreational complex. Ten minutes to Vienna center via commuter train or campground shuttle bus.

Vienna → Prague (Praha), the Czech Republic, 290 km (234 mi.)

Leave Vienna on E49/4 and head northwest to **Horn.** Continue on Hwy. 303 to the Czech Republic border at **Neunagelberg.** E49/34 continues into the village of **Trebon.** The intact sixteenth-century walls ringing the town are some of the best in the country. Just off of the main square is **Trebon Castle,** with a faithfully re-created sixteenth-century interior.

Continue on Hwy. 34 into **Ceske Budejovice,** a well-preserved medieval town with an enormous eighteenth-century main square. The town is also well known for its excellent original Budweiser beer. From Ceske, head north to Prague on Hwy. E55/3.

14. Prague (Praha)

One of Europe's most beautiful cities, the ancient Czech capital on the banks of the **Vltava River** is a treasure chest of historical buildings and romantic vistas. Prague escaped World War II with little physical damage, so many of these sites can be enjoyed in their original form.

The city's more than ten centuries of history are reflected in its architecture, a pleasing combination of Romanesque, Gothic, Baroque, neoclassical, and modern. The skyline shows some five hundred towers and steeples.

Although Prague's attractions are somewhat scattered, it is nevertheless a delightful city to explore on foot. Parking in the city is very difficult, and much of the city center is closed to motor vehicles.

The heart of Prague lies in the center of the **Stare Mesto (old town).** The **Staromestske Namesti (Old Town Square)** is dominated by the Town Hall with its elaborate **astronomical clock.**

The **Jewish quarter** was once one of the most important centers of Jewish culture in Europe. The **Staronova Synagoga,** a fine Gothic structure built in 1270, is the oldest synagogue in Europe.

Lined on both sides with baroque statues, the graceful **Charles Bridge** is a Prague landmark that links the old town with the **Mala Strana (lesser town),** a pleasant, cobblestone-lined quarter full of old palaces, churches, and cozy wine bars. **Hradcany,** the section of Prague that contains the **Prague Castle,** is an intriguing complex of ancient fortifications, courtyards, and structures that include the **St. Vitus Cathedral,** one of Europe's most beautiful Gothic structures.

Prague Campground

CZ–100 ★★ Camping Sokol Troja. Open April 1–October 31. At the northwest edge of the city. From Prague follow signs toward Teplice and then follow campground signs. A small, partly shaded site with convenient access to city via bus #112, tram, or train.

Prague → Dresden, Germany, 130 km (78 mi.)

From Prague head north on Hwy. 8 toward **Teplice.** At **Veltrusy,** 15 km (9 mi.) north of Prague, stop and visit the **Castle and Gardens. Nelahozeves,** 2.5 km (1.5 mi.) from Veltrusy on a marked footpath, is the birthplace of Anton Dvorak, Czechoslovakia's foremost composer.

Farther along Hwy. 8 you will come to **Terezin,** site of a former Nazi concentration camp, better known by its German name, **Theresienstadt.** There is a museum, and films are shown. At **Zinnwald-Georgenfeld** cross into Germany and continue on the same road, now called E55/170, into Dresden.

15. Dresden

The capital of **Saxony** since the fifteenth century, Dresden, before its destruction in a massive bombing raid in 1945, was one of the great European centers of culture and architecture. Many of the buildings along the **Elbe River** have been rebuilt in the old style. Dresden is well known for its fine art museums, in particular the **Zwinger,** an intriguing Baroque complex whose galleries contain several outstanding collections. The other pride of Dresden is the sixteenth-century, glass-domed **Albertinum Museum.**

Dresden Campground

D–123 ★★ Camping Altfranken. Open March 1–October 30. At the west edge of the city, 6 km (3.6 mi.) from city center. From Dresden center take B173 in the direction of Freiberg. Approaches are well marked. A sixteen-acre, grassy site pleasantly located on the grounds of an old castle. Sites are terraced and many are graveled. Bus to Dresden center, 500 yd.

Dresden → Berlin, 165 km (99 mi.)

Take B6 northwest from Dresden to **Meissen,** known worldwide for its fine china. The porcelain works are open to the public. From Meissen follow B101 to Berlin.

ALPINE HEIGHTS AND OLD WORLD DELIGHTS

Austria, France, Germany, and Italy

For profiles of these countries, see the pages listed below.

Austria, 283
France, 145
Germany, 291
Italy, 231

Principality of Liechtenstein

CAPITAL: Vaduz

POPULATION: 30,000

CURRENCY: Swiss franc (SwF), divided into 100 centimes

LANGUAGES: German; English is widely spoken in Vaduz

RELIGIONS: Roman Catholic and Protestant

POLICE: 118

FIRE: 117

AMBULANCE: 114

ROAD SERVICE: 140

BANKS: weekdays 8:30 A.M.–4:30 P.M.; Thursday until 5:30 P.M.

STORES: weekdays 8:00 A.M.–noon and 1:30–6:30 P.M.; Saturday 8:00 A.M.–4:00 P.M.

HOLIDAYS: January 1 and 2; January 6, Epiphany; Shrove Tuesday;

March 19, Feast of St. Joseph; Good Friday; Ascension Day; Whitmonday; Corpus Christi; August 15, Assumption; December 8, Immaculate Conception; December 25 and 26

EMBASSIES: *United States,* Jubilaeum Str. 93, 3005 Bern, Switzerland; phone (031) 437–011, fax (031) 437–344. *Canada,* Kirchenfeld Str. 88, 3005 Bern, Switzerland; phone (031) 446–381, fax (031) 447–315. *United Kingdom,* Thun Str. 50, 3005 Bern, Switzerland; phone (031) 445–021/6

Sandwiched between Austria and Switzerland, the sovereign Principality of Liechtenstein occupies a mere 155 m^2 (62 sq. mi.) and has a population of 30,000 with one of the highest per capita incomes in the world. A constitutional monarchy ruled by Hans Adam, a Hapsburg prince, Liechtenstein is the smallest member of the United Nations, which it joined in 1990. The royal family occupies the imposing thirteenth-century castle that is perched on a mountain overlooking the capital city of Vaduz.

Although Liechtenstein is an independent nation, it has, for practical purposes, integrated its money, postal, and customs services as well as international relations and defense with those of neighboring Switzerland. Because of its liberal tax laws, tiny Liechtenstein is the nominal headquarters for more than 20,000 foreign firms.

DRIVING

Driving conditions are the same as in Switzerland.

CAMPING

There are two campgrounds in Liechtenstein. Both are in the vicinity of Vaduz and maintain high standards.

Switzerland

CAPITAL: Bern

POPULATION: 6,900,000

CURRENCY: Swiss franc (SF), divided into 100 centimes

LANGUAGES: German, French, Italian, and Romansch

RELIGIONS: Roman Catholic and Protestant

POLICE: 118

FIRE: 117

AMBULANCE: 114

ROAD SERVICE: Touring Secours, 140 (including Liechtenstein)

BANKS: weekdays 8:30 A.M.–4:30 P.M.; Thursday until 5:30 P.M.

STORES: Tuesday–Friday 8:00 or 8:30 A.M.–6:30 or 7:00 P.M.; Monday 1:00 or 2:00 P.M.–6:30 P.M.; Saturday 8:30 A.M.–4:00 or 6:00 P.M., depending on region

HOLIDAYS: January 1; Good Friday and Easter Monday (movable); Ascension Day (movable); Pentacost (movable); August 1, National Day; December 25 and 26

EMBASSIES: *United States,* Jubilaeum Str. 93, 3005 Bern; phone (031) 437–011, fax (031) 437–344. *Canada,* Kirchenfeld Str. 88, 3005 Bern; phone (031) 446–381, fax (031) 447–315. *United Kingdom,* Thun Str. 50, 3005 Bern; phone (031) 445–021/6

A tiny nation with a population that is less than that of greater Los Angeles, Switzerland encompasses three distinct ethnic groups within its borders, each group with its own culture and language. In Zurich and the north of the country, the language and the culture are German; in the central and western cantons, French predominates. When you visit the southern canton of Tessin, you might easily believe that you are in Italy (albeit with a degree of neatness and organization that is rarely found in that country).

Although Switzerland boasts some fine museums and interesting churches, it is the great beauty and variety of its scenic attractions—

idyllic alpine villages, pristine mountain lakes, and towering peaks such as the Matterhorn, that make this such a special place to visit. In the south of the country, along the palm-lined shores of Lake Maggiore, the landscape and architecture take on a Mediterranean air. Wherever you travel in Switzerland, you will find a level of quality, service, and cleanliness that is seldom matched anywhere in Europe.

DRIVING

Like everything else in this country, driving is controlled and disciplined. Traffic, except during holiday periods, is seldom a problem. A network of well-maintained autobahns links all of the important cities and towns. The autobahns are designated with white numbers on a green background. Main highways are marked with white numbers on a blue background. This—the opposite of the system used by Switzerland's neighbors—at first is a bit confusing. Throughout the country place names and roads are clearly indicated.

The massive chain of Alps that traverses Switzerland's heartland has been conquered and penetrated by a series of superbly engineered all-weather roads and tunnels. When you drive in the Alps, always check the status of the pass roads, as the weather and driving conditions can change rapidly. We have, on several occasions, encountered snow on the higher pass roads even in August. Signs on the access roads to the mountain passes indicate whether a pass is open or closed. Red denotes closed and green indicates open. You can also obtain current highway condition information by call the Touring Club Suisse (TCS) in Geneva (022) 73 71 212 or via a recording by dialing 163.

On mountain postal roads, designated by a blue rectangle with a yellow horn, postal vehicles always have the right-of-way. On other mountain roads slow-moving vehicles are required to pull over where possible to let backed-up traffic pass. On narrow mountain roads the descending vehicle must stop to allow an ascending vehicle to pass. When driving on these roads you should be aware of the height and width of your vehicle in meters and centimeters; warnings of narrow stretches and low overhangs are posted in metric dimensions.

To use the autobahns, it is necessary to purchase a "Vignette." These windshield stickers, on sale at the border crossings for 30 Swiss francs, are valid for the balance of the year in which they are purchased. Several of the major trans-alpine tunnels are subject to tolls.

Gasoline stations are well distributed throughout the country, although many are closed at night. There are, however, many automated self-service stations, open twenty-four hours a day, that operate with 10 and 20 Swiss frank notes. While most, but not all, service stations have diesel fuel, Switzerland is the only country in Europe in which diesel is higher priced than gasoline.

The use of seat belts is obligatory, and children under age twelve may not sit in the front seat. Low-beam headlights are required in tunnels. The speed limit for motorhomes on the autobahns is 120 kph (72 mph). The speed limit in towns and built-up areas, unless otherwise posted, is 50 kph (30 mph). Outside of built-up areas it is 80 kph (48 mph).

CAMPING

There are some 500 official campgrounds distributed throughout the country. Most cities and areas of interest have at least one conveniently located campground. Although there are a number of privately owned sites, the majority of Swiss campgrounds are run by municipalities, camping clubs, or the Swiss Touring Club. The standard of cleanliness and range of facilities throughout the country are excellent. A high percentage of Swiss campgrounds are wheelchair-accessible. Most sites are relatively small and there are none of the huge camping villages found in parts of Spain and Italy.

The normal season is from mid-April to early October. There are, however, enough year-round sites to accommodate off-season travelers.

Most campgrounds have a snack bar or restaurant and a campstore. Coin-operated laundry facilities are the norm. Trash disposal is regulated throughout the country, and campgrounds provide separate containers for various categories of refuse.

In Tessin and some other popular resort areas, free camping is prohibited, and this regulation is strictly enforced. Discreet free camping is generally tolerated in other cantons. Overnight parking at autobahn and highway rest stops is allowed.

The ECC electrical plugs and outlets are not used in Switzerland. Swiss campgrounds use a unique three-prong plug; most campgrounds will supply an adapter for a small deposit. German-type propane bottles can be exchanged at most campgrounds.

The International Camping Carnet is accepted but not required. For additional information about camping in Switzerland contact the Swiss Touring Club, Division Camping, chemin de Riantbosson 11/13, case postale 176, 1217 Meyrin 1, Switzerland (phone 022–78 51 333, fax 022–78 51 262) or the Swiss Camping and Caravanning Federation, Habsburgerstrasse 35, 6004 Luzern, Switzerland (phone 041–23 48 22).

Itinerary: Frankfurt · The Rhine · Heidelberg · Rothenburg and the Romantic Road · Munich and Bavaria · The Alps · Salzburg · Innsbruck and Tyrol · Liechtenstein · The Swiss Heartlands and Lake Geneva · Chamonix and Mont Blanc · The Aosta Valley · Zermatt and the Matterhorn · The Black Forest

---

START: Frankfurt, Germany

COUNTRIES: Austria, France, Germany, Italy, Liechtenstein, Switzerland

DISTANCE: 3,226 kilometers (1,936 mi.)

MAPS: Falk *Sud-Deutschland (Frankfurt bis Venedig);* Michelin #984 *Deutschland/Germany;* Michelin #988 *Italy/Switzerland*

MINIMUM RECOMMENDED TOURING TIME: 21 days

INTRODUCTION

To many of us Europe evokes romantic visions of turreted castles, towering snow-clad Alps, and fairy-tale medieval villages. This tour, although it covers a relatively short distance, passes through six countries and affords a wonderful opportunity to turn those visions into reality. Of all our itineraries, this one offers the greatest variety and is the most representative of traditional Old Europe.

For your first European venture, we recommend that you start with this tour. Frankfurt, our starting point, is a convenient and inexpensive place to rent motorhomes.

Along the route we cross several spectacular mountain passes and experience the grandest of the Alps, Mont Blanc, in France, as well as Switzerland's famed Matterhorn. As we follow the Romantic Road, Germany's best-known theme highway, we encounter a delightful assortment of enchanting medieval towns and castles. Rudisheim, a charming old town on the banks of the Rhine River, is a wonderful

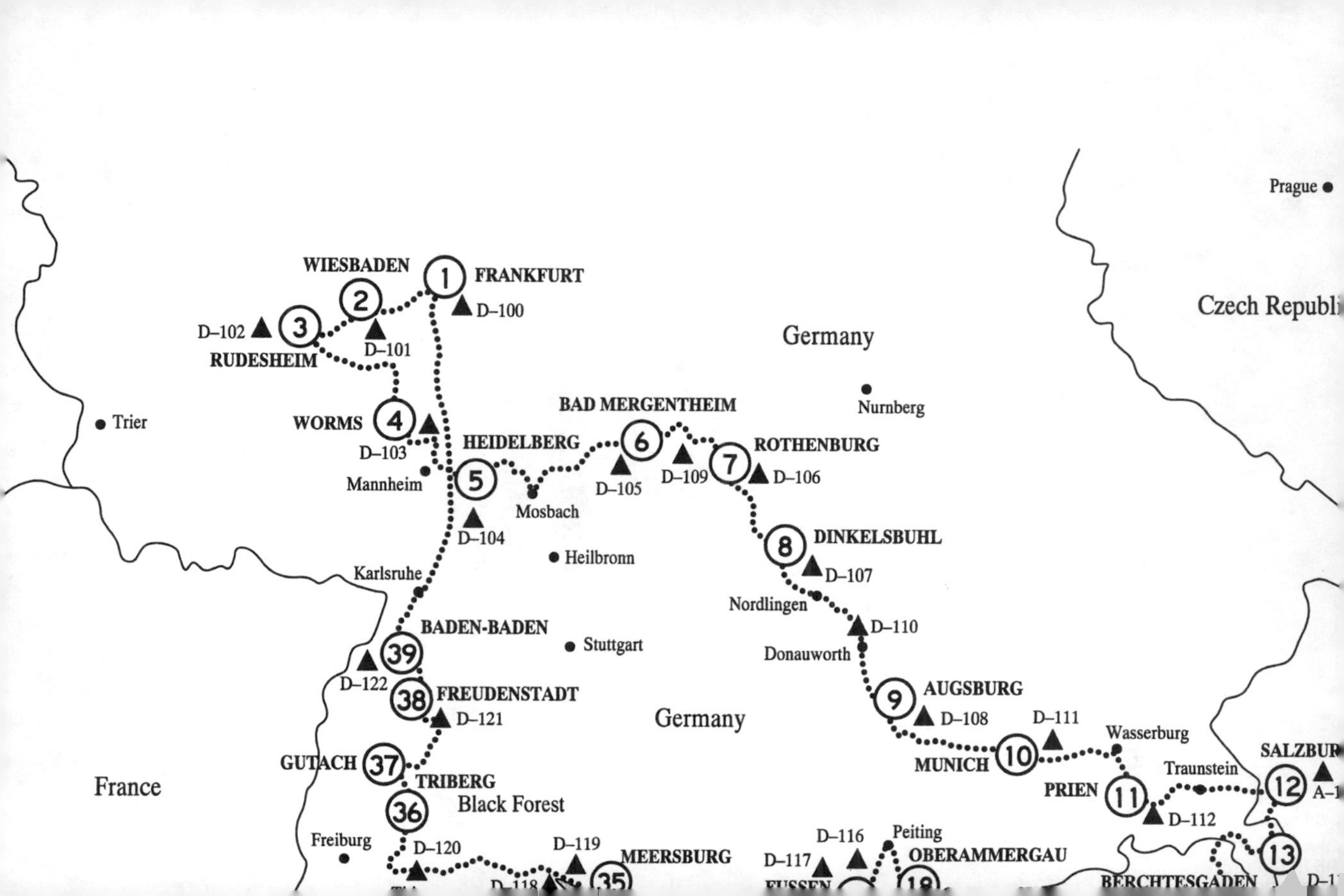
Prague
Czech Republi
Germany
Nurnberg
WIESBADEN
FRANKFURT
D–100
D–102
D–101
RUDESHEIM
Trier
WORMS
D–103
Mannheim
HEIDELBERG
BAD MERGENTHEIM
ROTHENBURG
D–105
D–109
D–106
Mosbach
D–104
DINKELSBUHL
D–107
Heilbronn
Karlsruhe
Nordlingen
D–110
BADEN-BADEN
Stuttgart
Donauworth
D–122
FREUDENSTADT
D–121
Germany
AUGSBURG
D–108
D–111
Wasserburg
GUTACH
TRIBERG
MUNICH
France
Black Forest
PRIEN
Traunstein
D–112
Freiburg
D–120
D–119
MEERSBURG
D–116
Peiting
D–117
OBERAMMERGAU
BERCHTESGADEN

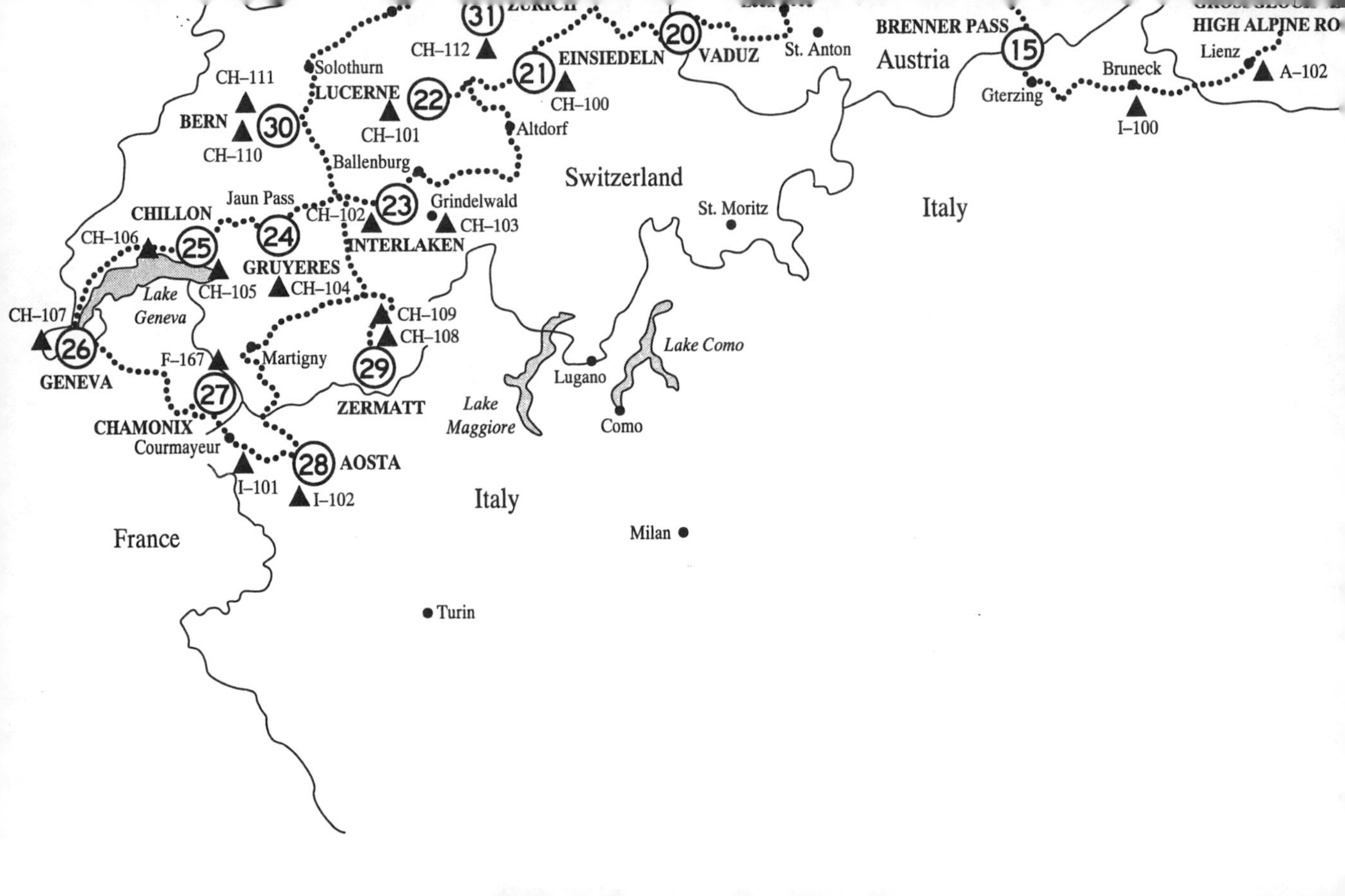

31
CH–112
20
VADUZ
St. Anton
BRENNER PASS
15
Austria
Lienz
A–102
Bruneck
Gterzing
I–100
Solothurn
LUCERNE
22
CH–101
21
EINSIEDELN
CH–100
Altdorf
CH–111
BERN
30
CH–110
Ballenburg
Switzerland
Italy
Jaun Pass
23
Grindelwald
CH–102
CH–103
INTERLAKEN
St. Moritz
CHILLON
24
CH–106
25
GRUYERES
CH–105
CH–104
Lake
Geneva
CH–107
26
GENEVA
CH–109
CH–108
Martigny
29
ZERMATT
F–167
27
CHAMONIX
Courmayeur
Lake Como
Lugano
Lake
Maggiore
Como
28
AOSTA
I–101
I–102
Italy
France
Milan
Turin

place to sample the fine wines for which the Rhine Valley is so well known. Quaint villages nestled in the heart of Germany's Black Forest feature, along with such irresistible local specialties as Black Forest cakes and tasty smoked meats, an incredible assortment of cuckoo clocks and traditional wood carvings. To enjoy European city life at its liveliest, we have included the Bavarian capital of Munich.

While in Austria our city visits include Salzburg, the city of Mozart, and the centuries-old Hapsburg stronghold, Innsbruck. Between these two cities we cross several breathtaking alpine-pass roads.

Our excursions into France and Italy, although brief, are nevertheless dramatic, with visits to Chamonix and Mont Blanc in the French Alps and to Italy's magnificent Aosta Valley.

When to Go

The best time to cover this route is in late spring or early autumn. Although the weather is best in July and August, the onslaught of tourists to many of the places on this itinerary and the grossly overcrowded conditions of so many otherwise tranquil campgrounds are enough to dampen the brightest holiday spirits. Our preference for touring this region is mid-September to mid-October. The weather is marginally better, or at least statistically that is the case, and the likelihood of encountering closed passes and snow in the high mountains is also a bit less in the autumn. Our most compelling reason for doing this route at that time is the chance it gives us to take part in Munich's rollicking Oktoberfest. This annual mega–beer bust takes place during the two weeks preceding the first weekend in October.

Highlights

Castle and old town, Heidelberg
Munich
Neuschwanstein Castle, Germany
Fortress and old town, Salzburg
Zermatt and the Matterhorn, Switzerland
Chamonix and Mont Blanc, France
Grindelwald, Switzerland
Rothenburg and the Romantic Road, Germany
Black Forest, Germany
Fortress of Chillon, Switzerland

On the road in the Alps

EXPANDING HORIZONS

- **To Heart of Eastern Europe Itinerary:** From Salzburg take the A1 Autobahn east to Vienna (see p. 317).
- **To France Itinerary III:** From Geneva head south to Annecy, or from Baden-Baden cross the Rhine to Strasbourg (see p. 191).
- **To Italian Impressions Itinerary:** From Aosta continue east to Milan (see p. 246).
- **To Tiptoeing through the Tulips Itinerary:** From Rudesheim cross the Rhine and continue to Luxembourg (see p. 137).

ON THE ROAD

Numbered sites correspond with circled numbers on the itinerary map.

1. Frankfurt

Germany's principal banking center, despite its numerous Manhattan-like high-rise towers (locals wryly refer to it as "Manhattan on the Main") has a rich history. Enough of this past has been preserved to recommend a visit. As is the case with major cities throughout Europe, however, we cannot recommend it as a place to drive. Swarms of trucks and monumental traffic jams are commonplace, and parking for RVs is nonexistent. Take the commuter train into town. Start your sightseeing in the old-town center with a visit to the birthplace of Johann Wolfgang von Goethe, Germany's most famous poet. The **Goethe House** and adjacent **Museum** are about a ten-minute walk from the **Hauptbahnhof** (main train station). The three gabled patrician houses referred to collectively as the **Romer,** on the square of the same name, have served as Frankfurt's city hall since 1405. Across the **Main River** from the Romer are seven notable museums, including Germany's first **Film Museum** and the recently opened **Jewish Museum.**

Frankfurt Campground

D–100 ★ Stadt-Campingplatz Heddernheim. Open year-round. In northwest suburb of Heddernheim. From junction A5/E451 with A66, take A66 east toward Frankfurt to exit Nordweststadt (by TV tower) and follow Rosa Luxemburg Str. to Heddernheim–Industriegebiet. Then follow signs to campground. A level, partly shaded site along River Nidda. This is the most convenient campground for visiting Frankfurt. Frankfurt subway, 180 yd.

Frankfurt → Wiesbaden, 40 km (24 mi.)

Leaving Frankfurt from the Heddernheim campground, follow signs to the A66 Autobahn. This will take you to Wiesbaden.

2. Wiesbaden

An ancient spa, founded by the Romans in the first century A.D., the old-town part of Wiesbaden projects the image of a classic mid-nineteenth-century European resort.

Wiesbaden Campground

D–101 ★★ Camping Maarau. Open April 1–September 30. There is no campground in Wiesbaden. This is the best in the area. Located on an island near the junction of Main and Rhine rivers, 3 km (1.8 mi.) southeast of Mainz center. From A66 take exit for Mainz/Kastel/Kostheim. Continue to Kostheim. Cross the Main River and then follow signs to campground. A flat, partly shaded, grassy area surrounded by hedges. Good view of Mainz Cathedral. Public transportation, 900 yd.

Wiesbaden → Rudesheim, 20 km (12 mi.)

From Wiesbaden continue on B42 along the banks of the Rhine into Rudesheim.

3. Rudesheim

The vine-clad hills in the vicinity of Rudesheim that rise steeply from the river produce some of Germany's best wines. As you explore the narrow cobblestone alleys lined with well-preserved half-timbered houses, inviting wine cellars, and cozy restaurants, you will have ample opportunity to sample these fine local wines. Don't pass up the chance to stroll along the **Drosselgasse,** Rudesheim's famed restaurant row.

The best way to view the romantic old castles that line the historic stretch of the Rhine between Rudesheim and **Koblenz** is from the deck of a comfortable **Rhine cruise** excursion boat. You can leave your rig at the campground and walk along the river to the Rudesheim boat dock in about fifteen minutes. Parking in Rudesheim during the summer months is very difficult.

Note: To connect with our Tiptoeing through the Tulips itinerary, from Rudesheim cross the Rhine to Bingen. Then take Autobahn A61 northwest to Hwy. 50. Follow this to Bernkastel am Mosel. Continue along the river to Trier and then to Luxembourg (see p. 137).

Rudesheim Campground

D–102 ★★★ Campingplatz am Rhein. Open April 30–October 1. At Rudesheim turn off of B42. Head toward the river and follow campground signs. A large, grassy area with some trees in a pleasant, parklike setting on the banks of the Rhine. Delightful fifteen-minute walk along the river to town center.

Rudesheim → Heidelberg, 125 km (75 mi.)

From Rudesheim the most direct route to Heidelberg is via the Rhine ferry to Bingen and then on the autobahn, following signs first to **Mannheim** and then to Heidelberg. If you are not in a hurry, it is far more interesting to leave the usually congested and monotonous autobahn and explore the countryside.

Rudesheim → Worms, 80 km (48 mi.)

Another choice is to go to Heidelberg via Worms and the scenic route. From Rudesheim cross the Rhine to **Bingen** and follow B50 south. Then take B420 to intersect with B9 at **Nierstein.** Head south on B9 to Worms. The Rhine is on your left.

4. Worms

It was in Worms in 1521 that Martin Luther made his historic plea for the reformation of the church. The **Worms Cathedral,** whose lofty spires dominate the town center, is one of Germany's most inspiring churches. This region is the center for the production of the popular Liebfraumilch wines.

Worms Campground

D–103 ★★ Camping Nibelungenbrucke. Open April 1–September 30. After entering Worms on B9, turn left and cross over the Rhine bridge. The campground is along the river next to the bridge and occupies a large meadow with trees and shrubs. Convenient bus to town or easy walk, 900 yd.

Worms → Heidelberg, 45 km (27 mi.)

From Worms continue south on B9. Just north of **Mannheim** take Autobahn A6 and follow signs to Heidelberg.

5. Heidelberg

Although student dueling societies have long been banned, much of the romantic Old Heidelberg immortalized in Sigmund Romberg's operetta *The Student Prince* remains. Germany's oldest **university,** still going strong, attracts students from all parts of the world, lending a youthful, international flavor to this venerable old town. Heidelberg's most popular attraction is the **ruins of the hillside castle** destroyed by the troops of France's Sun King, Louis XIV, in 1689.

Heidelberg Campground

D–104 ★★ Camping Neckartal. Open May 1–October 15. On the Neckar River in the suburb of Schlierbach, 5 km (3 mi.) east of Heidelberg center. From Heidelberg follow B37 toward Eberbach. Turn off toward the river at camping sign. The campground consists of a long, narrow, grassy area at the riverbank. Facilities are adequate. This a great place to watch the barges glide by. Bus #35 to Heidelberg center.

Heidelberg → Bad Mergentheim, 120 km (72 mi.)

From Heidelberg take B37 and follow the Neckar River to **Eberbach.** Note the castles perched in strategic positions along the river. This stretch of highway is part of the **Burgenstrasse (Castle Road),** which extends from Mannheim in the west to Nuremburg (Nurnberg) in the east. At **Mosbach** turn off onto B292 and follow signs to Bad Mergentheim on the Romantic Road.

6. Bad Mergentheim

A popular health spa on the Romantic Road, Bad Mergentheim was once the headquarters of the Order of Teutonic Knights. The town's imposing **Renaissance palace** now houses a **museum** that chronicles the exploits of this historic order during the Crusades.

Bad Mergentheim Campground

D–105 ★★ Camping Willinger Tal. Open year-round. Just south of the town on B19, in the direction of Kunzelsau. Turn off at sign for Wachbach and follow camping signs. A long, narrow, grassy area. Occasional noise from nearby shooting range. Bus to town, 100 yd.

Bad Mergentheim → Rothenburg ob der Tauber, 45 km (27 mi.)

Stay on the Romantic Road as it follows the winding Tauber River.

7. Rothenburg ob der Tauber

Take away the TV antennas and a few other modern trappings and it is easy to imagine yourself in a typical sixteenth-century fortified German town. Rothenburg, perhaps more than any other town in the region, has retained its essential medieval character. For a spectacular bird's-eye view of the town, climb to the top of the **Town Hall Tower. St. Jacobs,** Rothenburg's principal church, houses the intricately carved Holy Blood Altar, a fine example of the woodcarver's art by Renaissance sculptor Tilman Riemenschneider.

Rothenburg Campground

D–106 ★★★ Camping Tauber-Idyll. Open April 1–October 31. In Detwang, 2 km (1.2 mi.) northwest of Rothenburg on the road from Creglingen. Follow camping signs into village and past church to site. (Detwang church houses a fine Riemenschneider altar.) A small, well-run site. Grassy area with plenty of trees. A twenty-minute walk to Rothenburg. Convenient bus to town.

Note: There is free overnight camping with an RV service area in Plarkplatz 1, just outside the Rothenburg town walls.

Rothenburg → Dinkelsbuhl, 45 km (27 mi.)

Continue south on B25.

8. Dinkelsbuhl

Dinkelsbuhl, 50 km (30 mi.) south of Rothenburg along the Romantic Road (B25), is a smaller but equally delightful medieval town.

Dinkelsbuhl Campground

D–107 ★★★ DCC Campingpark Romantische Strasse. Open year-round. Follow signs to turnoff from B25 at Dinkelsbuhl. Located 1.5 km (0.9 mi.) northeast of Dinkelsbuhl. A large, scenic, grassy site adjacent to a small lake. View across the lake to walled city. A twenty-minute walk, or take a bus to town.

Dinkelsbuhl → Augsburg, 102 km (61 mi.)

Head south on B25 past the walled city of **Nordlingen,** the stately castle at **Harburg,** and the medieval town of **Donauworth.** Just past

Donauworth the highway number changes to B2 and continues into Augsburg.

9. AUGSBURG

In medieval times Augsburg was an important trading and banking center and the home of the powerful Fugger family, bankers to the Hapsburgs. These sixteenth-century merchant princes established the **Fuggerei,** the world's first social housing project. Located just east of the town center, the project is still in operation.

Augsburg Campground

D–108 ★★ Camping Augusta. Open year-round. Just north of Autobahn A8 Munchen–Stuttgart, in the Augsburg suburb of Gersthofen. From Augsburg-Ost exit follow signs toward Neuburg. After 400 yd. turn to the right and follow signs to campground. A pleasant, parklike setting on a small lake. Two km (1.2 mi.) to Augsburg center. No convenient bus to town.

Additional Romantic Road Campgrounds

D–109 ★★★ AZUR Camping Romantische Strasse (Creglingen-Munster). Open year-round. On the Romantic Road midway between Rothenburg and Bad Mergentheim. At Creglingen turn off towards Munster then 3 km (1.8 mi.) to campground. An attractive partly terraced, grassy site with many mature shade trees. Adjacent to a lake. Bus to town, 200 yd.

D–110 ★★★ Donau-Lech Camping (Donauworth). Open April 1–October 31. In Eggelstetten, 6 km (3.6 mi.) southeast of Donauworth. Turn off of B2 toward Oberndorf and follow signs to campground. A large, lakeside, grassy meadow in a quiet rural setting. Bus stop, 500 yd.

Augsburg → Munich (Munchen), 75 km (45 mi.)

From Augsburg take either Autobahn A8 or Hwy. B2 into Munich.

10. MUNICH (MUNCHEN)

Of all the cities you will visit on this itinerary, Munich, more than any other, personifies the Europe on the verge of the twenty-first century. Vibrant and exciting, it is a place where tradition and folklore are as highly regarded as are high-tech research and industry. The people in *lederhosen* and *dirndls* that you see in the beer gardens and cafes dress that way not for the tourists' sake but out of an authentic respect for tradition, a trait that runs deeper in Bavaria than in any other part of Germany.

Munich offers its visitors a broad palate of attractions that range from world-class museums to centuries-old beer halls. The **Marienplatz** is the busy hub of Munich's bustling outdoor street scene. The pedestrian zone that radiates in all directions from the Marienplatz is lined with outdoor cafes, souvenir shops, and elegant boutiques and is an impromptu stage for street performers of all kind. The **Oktoberfest,** the granddaddy of all European folk festivals, is held during the two weeks that precede the first Sunday in October.

Munich Campground

D–111 ★★★ Camping Thalkirchen. Open March 15–October 13. Approaching Munich from Augsburg on Autobahn A8 or Hwy. B2, follow signs to Mittlerer Ring. From the ring street follow camping and zoo signs. Centrally located on the Isar River in a parklike setting. A large, grassy area with little shade. Very crowded in summer and during Oktoberfest. City bus, 300 yd.

Munich → Prien (Lake Chiemsee), 90 km (54 mi.)

From Munich the most interesting route to Salzburg is by way of the twelfth-century fortress town of **Wasserburg,** located on the banks of the Inn River. After a stop to explore Wasserburg's delightful old town, continue on to Chiemsee, Germany's largest lake. Exiting Munich from Thalkirchen Campground, head out of town on the Mittlerer Ring (an expressway that rings the old town). Continue east to B304 and stay on this to Wasserburg. Then follow signs to Prien.

11. Prien

From this pleasant lakeside resort you can catch an excursion boat for the twenty-minute trip to the **Herreninsel,** a small, wooded island that is the site of **Schloss Herrenchiemsee,** King Ludwig of Bavaria's most opulent castle.

Prien Campground

D–112 ★★ Panorama-Camping Harras. Open May 1–September 30. Exit Autobahn Munchen–Salzburg at Bernau. Follow signs toward Prien. Three km (1.8 mi.) from autobahn exit, turn toward Harras and follow campground signs. Part grass, part gravel site directly on the lake. Very popular with locals. A ten-minute walk along lake to Prien and boat for Ludwig's castle.

Prien → Salzburg, 65 km (39 mi.)

From Prien you can either pick up Autobahn A8 directly into Salzburg or you can follow the more pleasant lakeshore drive to **Seebruck** and then head for Salzburg by way of **Traunstein** and B304.

12. Salzburg

In an idyllic setting that spans both sides of the **Salzach River,** Salzburg is one of Europe's most attractive cities. This in spite of the monumental number of visitors who make the annual pilgrimage to pay homage to Wolfgang Amadeus Mozart, the city's most famous native son. They flood the famed **Getreidegasse** and other narrow old-town shopping streets, causing the pedestrian equivalent of gridlock.

The old town, a small area nestled between the river and the massive hilltop **Hohensalzburg Fortress,** the one-time stronghold of the archbishops and princes of Salzburg, has managed to preserve a surprising degree of Old World charm and ambiance. To visit the fortress climb the hill or take the funicular to the top for a wonderful bird's-eye view of the domes and rooftops of Salzburg.

The surrounding countryside, known as the **Salzkammergut,** is a delightful melange of quaint villages, crystal-clear lakes, and alpine meadows. It was here that Julie Andrews romped through the hills during the filming of *The Sound of Music.* Great fun for adults and children of all ages are the "trick fountains" that spray unsuspecting visitors in the gardens of **Hellbrunn Palace.**

Note: To connect with our Heart of Eastern Europe itinerary, take A1 Autobahn east to Vienna (see p. 317).

Salzburg Campground

A–100 ★★★ Camping Nord-Sam. Open April 1–October 31.

Located 3 km (1.8 mi.) north of Salzburg old town. From Autobahn A1 Salzburg–Wien take exit Salzburg–Nord. Follow signs toward Zentrum for 300 yd., then campground signs. Individual sites divided by thick bushes and many trees. Convenient access to city bus. Forget about parking an RV in Salzburg!

Salzburg → Berchtesgaden, 30 km (18 mi.)

Follow signs south from Salzburg for 30 km (18 mi.) to the German alpine resort of Berchtesgaden.

13. Berchtesgaden/14. Grossglockner Hochalpine Strasse/15. Brenner Pass

An ancient market town in a spectacular mountain setting, Berchtesgaden is one of Germany's most popular year-round resorts. Be sure to visit the **Salzbergwerk (Salt Mine),** where guests don miner's garb and take a miniature open train into the depths of the ancient mine. A short distance from Berchtesgaden, in **Obersalzberg,** is the **Eagle's Nest,** Hitler's World War II mountaintop redoubt.

Berchtesgaden Campground

D–113 ★★★ Camping Allweglehen. Open year-round. In direction of Salzburg turn off of B305. Located 3 km (1.8 mi.) from Berchtesgaden center. Steep access road behind Rossfeldstrasse. A large, terraced, alpine meadow with spectacular panoramic views. Bus to town, 600 yd. Limited parked available in Berchtesgaden.

Berchtesgaden → Innsbruck, 335 km (201 mi.)

From Berchtesgaden take B305, the German Alpine Highway, to B312. Crossing into Austria, follow signs to **Zell am See,** a popular lakeside resort. For a breathtaking driving experience, continue on to the **Grossglockner Hochalpine Strasse,** the Grossglockner High Alpine Road (a toll road). Opened in 1935, this serpentine alpine highway was one of the first modern roads to cross the Alps.

From **Lienz** head west to **Bruneck (Brunico),** crossing through a mountainous region of Italy that is known as **Sud Tirol (South Tyrol).** Formerly part of Austria, this region was ceded to Italy following World War I. A few kilometers west of Bruneck is the historic **Brenner**

Pass, for centuries Northern Europe's principal gateway to the Mediterranean. Along this route the towns of **Brixen (Bressanone)** and **Sterzing (Vipiteno),** with their many flower-bedecked stone houses, are particularly attractive. From the pass summit it's an easy downhill drive into the Tyrolean provincial capital of Innsbruck.

Berchtesgaden → Innsbruck Campgrounds

A–101 ★★★ Seecamp Zell am See (Zell am See). Open year-round. At the north shore of the lake, 2 km (1.6 mi.) north of town. Turn off of Hwy. 311 toward Thumersbach. A large, part grass, part gravel site with many trees and lovely panoramic views of lake and surrounding mountains. Bus to town, 200 yd. Parking available at ski lifts in Zell am See.

A–102 ★★ Camping Falken (Lienz). Open January 1–November 1. From Lienz train station follow signs past swimming pool and tennis courts to Tristach, then follow campground signs. A small, pleasantly situated site with mountain panorama.

I–100 ★★★★ Camping Corones (Bruneck). Open January 1–April 15, May 15–October 15. Turn off from S49 about 10 km (6 mi.) east of Bruneck toward Rasen, then follow campground signs. A large, part grass, part gravel site in an idyllic wooded mountain setting with first-rate facilities. No public transportation.

16. Innsbruck

In a favored location nestled at the foot of an imposing wall of sheer Alpine peaks, Innsbruck, a popular winter-sports center, hosted the Winter Olympics in 1964 and 1976. From the fourteenth century until the collapse of the Austrian monarchy after World War I, the town was a stronghold of the Hapsburgs. Innsbruck's most popular sights include the **Goldenes Dach (Golden Roof),** which adorns the exterior of the **Olympic Museum,** the rococo-style **Hofburg (Imperial Palace),** and the twenty-eight larger-than-life **statues** of Emperor Maximilian and his ancestors that grace the Imperial Church. **Schloss Ambras,** 3 km (1.8 mi.) southeast of the town center, is one of Austria's best-preserved castles.

Innsbruck Campground

A–103 ★★★★ Terrassen-Camping Natters. Open year-round.

Located 4 km (2.4 mi.) south of Innsbruck. Take Natters turnoff from Hwy. 182 or, from Brenner Autobahn, exit Innsbruck–Sud and follow signs through the village of Natters to campground. A large, grassy, wooded, lakeside area in the hills overlooking Innsbruck. Superb alpine panoramas. Difficult entrance for large campers. Good restaurant. No convenient bus to Innsbruck. Parking in Innsbruck itself is difficult. The best bet is to park at the ski jump or ice stadium and take public transportation.

Innsbruck → Garmisch–Partenkirchen, 100 km (60 mi.)

From Innsbruck follow Hwy. 189 along the **Inn River** to the **Fern Pass,** once a strategic link in the principal trading route between Augsburg and Venice. A few kilometers past the summit, turn off the main road and follow signs to **Biberwier** and **Ehrwald.** Then pick up B24 and stay along the **Loisach River** as it runs back into Germany. The road continues to follow the river into Garmisch–Partenkirchen.

17. Garmisch–Partenkirchen

The neighboring villages of Garmisch and Partenkirchen were united in 1936 to host the Winter Olympic Games. Situated in a beautiful, narrow valley ringed by the Bavarian Alps that include Germany's tallest mountain, the Zugspitze, Garmisch–Partenkirchen provides a wonderful base for hiking and other Alpine sports.

Garmisch–Partenkirchen Campgrounds

D–114 ★★ Camping Zugspitze. Open year-round. In Grainau, 2 km (1.2 mi.) south of Garmisch, on B24 in the direction of Fern Pass. A flat, grassy area on the banks of the Loisach River. Views of the Zugspitze. Bus to town, 200 yd.

D–115 ★★★★ Alpen Caravanpark Tennsee. Open January 1–October 25. In Klais, 16 km (10 mi.) east of Garmisch. Turn off of B2 at Klais and follow camping sign. Rustic, wooded setting with alpine vistas. Excellent restaurant. Private bathrooms available. One of Germany's finest campgrounds. Bus, 400 yd.

Garmisch–Partenkirchen → Oberammergau, 20 km (12 mi.)

Head north out of Garmisch on B23/2 to **Farchant** and then to

Oberau. Turn off to the left as the road splits and follow B23 up the hill, past the monastery at Ettal, and into Oberammergau.

18. Oberammergau

Noted for its ornately painted house facades and talented woodcarvers, this normally quiet village receives worldwide attention during the first year of each decade as the site of the famous **Passion Play. Schloss Linderhof,** 12 km (7.2 mi.) southwest of Oberammergau, with its bizarre underground grotto and elegant furnishings, is one of the most intriguing of King Ludwig's castles.

Oberammergau Campground

There is no campground in Oberammergau, but Camping Zugspitze, 20 km (12 mi.) down the hill in Garmisch–Partenkirchen, provides a good base for visiting Oberammergau.

Oberammergau → Fussen, 48 km (29 mi.)

Continue from Oberammergau on B23 toward **Peiting.** Just before Peiting turn off and follow signs to **Wildsteig** and **Wies.** Here, in an idyllic alpine setting, is the **Wies Kirche (the Church in the Meadow),** one of Germany's finest rococo churches. Join up with B17 (the Romantic Road) and follow this south the 23 km (14 mi.) to Fussen.

19. Fussen

Fussen is the site of the most famous of King Ludwig's castles, **Neuschwanstein.** This multiturreted manifestation of the king's vivid imagination was the inspiration for the Fantasy Castle at Disneyland.

Fussen Campgrounds

D–116 ★★★★ Camping Hopfen am See. Open January 1–November 10. On the shores of Hopfensee. Turn off of B16 Marktoberdorf–Fussen to Hopfen am See and follow camping signs. Located 5 km (3 mi.) northwest of Fussen. A pleasant, lakeshore meadow with views of surrounding mountains. Health spa, private bathrooms available. Well situated for visiting King Ludwig's castles. Bus to Fussen, 300 yd. There is adequate parking at all of Ludwig's castles.

The village of Lech, Austria

D–117 ★★★ Camping Bannwaldsee. Open year-round. In Schwangau, on the shores of Bannwaldsee. Approaching Schwangau from the north on B17, turn off to the right at the camping sign 3 km (1.8 mi.) north of Schwangau. A large, grassy site on the shores of a small lake. Good restaurant. This is the most convenient site for visiting Neuschwanstein castle. Bus stop at campground.

Fussen → Vaduz, 175 km (105 mi.)

From Fussen head south and cross back into Austria. Follow Hwy. 314 and signs toward **Reutte.** Turn onto Hwy. 198. The signs read **Lechtal.** The road winds and climbs through a narrow valley formed by the **Lech River** and traverses some of Europe's choicest ski country, the legendary **Arlberg region.** After a stop in the delightful ski village of **Lech,** cross the **Flexen Pass** and then it's an easy downhill run all the way to Liechtenstein.

20. Vaduz/21. Einsiedeln

The capital of the tiny principality of Liechtenstein, Vaduz is well known for its **Postage Stamp Museum,** which attracts philatelists from all over the world. The massive sixteenth-century fortress that looms over the town is the royal residence (currently closed to the public).

Vaduz Campground

FL–100 ★★ Camping Mittagsspitze. Open year-round. Located 4 km (2.4 mi.) south of Vaduz on road to Balzers. Turn off at Lawena bus stop and follow camping sign. An attractive, terraced, grassy area at the foot of the mountains. Bus to Vaduz, 300 yd.

Vaduz → Lucerne (Luzern), 140 km (84 mi.)

Cross the Rhine at Buchs and you are in a little-known but charming region of the Swiss Alps known as **Toggenburg.** The signs to follow are **Wildhaus** and **Wattwil.** From Wattwil stay on Hwy. 8 to **Rapperswil.** Note the wonderful twelfth-century castle on the shores of the **Zurichersee (Lake of Zurich).**

Cross the lake and follow signs to Lucerne. The most interesting route is via Hwy. 8 with a stop in Einsiedeln, to visit Switzerland's largest pilgrimage church. Continue on Hwy. 2 into Lucerne. En route, stop in **Schwyz** at the **Schwyzerland Model Cheese Making Works** (next to the train station).

Einsiedeln Campground

CH–100 ★★ Camping Gruene Aff. Open year-round. From Einsiedeln follow signs to Willerzell, 4 km (2.4 mi.). A pleasant, grassy meadow on the shores of the Shilsee. Bus to town, 400 yd.

22. LUCERNE (LUZERN)

Located on a sparkling lake and surrounded by snow-capped Alps, Lucerne is one of Central Europe's most delightful cities. Be sure to stroll through the well-preserved old town and across the elaborately decorated fourteenth-century **Kappelenbrucke (Chapel Bridge).** The **Swiss Transport Museum,** adjacent to the campground, has the best collection of old planes, trains, cars, and boats in Europe. For an unforgettable alpine experience, take the cog railway to the top of nearby **Mt. Pilatus.** A fleet of excursion boats is available to take you to all corners of the **Vierwaldstattersee,** Lucerne's lovely lake.

Lucerne Campground

CH–101 ★★★ Camping Lido. Open March 15–October 31. At the west end of Lucerne, off of Hwy. 2 (Kussnacht–Luzern). Turn at sign for Lido Camping or Verkehrshaus. Situated in a park complex next to the lake. Just a few steps from Transport Museum. Convenient access to Lucerne via bus or boat. Parking in Lucerne is difficult.

Lucerne → Interlaken, 160 km (96 mi.)

From Lucerne follow the lakeshore road first to **Kussnacht** and then to **Vitznau** and **Brunnen.** Before continuing on to the **Susten Pass,** check with the tourist office in Brunnen to ensure that the pass road is open. The **Susten Pass Road** and the nearby **Furka Pass Road** afford some of the most spectacular driving in the Alps. In **Altdorf,** on the approach road to the Susten Pass, you will find a monument to Swiss hero **William Tell.** If the pass road is closed or the weather is poor, take the autobahn via **Sarnen** to Interlaken. Stop at **Ballenburg** near the terminus of the Susten Road to see the **Open-Air Museum** where traditional farm houses from all parts of Switzerland have been reconstructed.

23. Interlaken

Interlaken is a delightful, small but sophisticated town nestled between two pristine lakes. It and the nearby village of **Grindelwald** are excellent bases from which to explore the surrounding Alps. This region, known as the **Berner Oberland,** is a hiker's paradise that offers an extensive network of well-marked trails for all levels, from casual walkers to experienced climbers. A "not to miss" experience is the cog railway trip to the massive sea of snow and ice at the 11,550-ft.-high **Jungfraujoch,** Europe's highest train station.

Interlaken Campgrounds

CH–102 ★★★★ Camping Manor Farm. Open year-round. From Autobahn N8 take exit Guten/Beatenberg and follow signs to "Camping 1." A large, parklike site directly on the lake. Good base for exploring Berner Oberland. First-class restaurant. Bus to town at site. Parking by the casino.

CH–103 ★★★ Camping Eigernordwand (Grindelwald). Open year-round. At entrance to village. From Interlaken turn off at Grund and continue past the train station. Then turn right at camping sign. Entrance at Restaurant Bodenwald. A grassy meadow with spectacular alpine vistas. Excellent base for hiking and Jungfraujoch excursion. Good restaurant. Bus/train, 500 yd.

Interlaken → Gruyeres, 85 km (55 mi.)

After leaving Interlaken take Hwy. 1 along the **Thuner See** to **Spiez,** then follow Hwy. 11 to the **Jaun Pass** and continue over the pass to Gruyeres. Check with the tourist office in Interlaken, as the pass is often snowed in between November and May. If that is the case, stay on Hwy. 11 and follow signs to **Saanen, Chateau d'Oex,** and Gruyeres.

24. Gruyeres

At the cheese factory you can watch the famous Gruyere cheese being made and then sample the tasty product in the adjacent shop or at one of the attractive restaurants that line the approach to Gruyeres's impressive fifteenth-century hilltop fortress.

Gruyeres Campground

CH–104 ★★ Camping du Lac. Open May 15–September 15. At the Lake of Gruyeres. Turn off of Hwy. 12 Bulle–Freibourg at Gumefens, 6 km (3.6 mi.) north of Bulle. A small, grassy site on the lakeshore. Campers longer than 6 m (20 ft.) not allowed. Bus, 300 yd. Large parking lot at Gruyeres.

Gruyeres → Montreux, 40 km (24 mi.)

From Gruyeres follow the road to **Bulle** and then take the autobahn, which winds down a steep grade, to **Lake Geneva.** At the bottom of the hill follow the lake road to the chic resort of **Montreux.** From there continue along the lake to Chillon.

25. CHILLON

As you leave Montreux you will see a remarkably well-preserved turreted fortress that rises up out of the lake. This is the famed **Fortress of Chillon,** the inspiration for Lord Byron's epic poem, *The Prisoner of Chillon.* Parking is available at the fortress.

Chillon Campgrounds

CH–105 ★★ Camping les Horizons Bleus. Open April 1–September 30. Located in Villeneuve on the lakeshore road 2.5 km (1.5 mi.) southeast of Chillon. A small, grassy site at the lakeshore. Bus to Chillon or a twenty-five-minute walk along the lake.

CH–106 ★★★ Camping de Vidy. Open year-round. In Lausanne, directly on the lake. In Lausanne Sud at La Maladiere, turn onto Chemin du Camping and follow signs to campground. A large, grassy area in the center of a lakeside park and sports complex. Bus to Lausanne center, 500 yd.

Chillon → Geneva, 86 km (52 mi.)

After touring the fortress take Hwy. 1 along the lake into Geneva.

26. Geneva (Geneve)

The capital of French-speaking Switzerland, Geneva (Geneve) is an attractive, cosmopolitan city beautifully situated on **Lake Geneva.** The seat of several important international organizations, Geneva has hosted numerous historic conferences. Guided tours of the United Nations and the former League of Nations complex are available.

Note: To connect with our France Itinerary III, follow signs south from Geneva on Hwy. N201 to Annecy, 40 km (24 mi.). (See p. 193.)

Geneva Campground

CH–107 ★★ Camping Pointe a la Bise. Open April 3–October 10. In the suburb of Vesenaz, 4 km (2.4 mi.) northeast of Geneva, turn off to the lake and follow camping signs. A pleasant, grassy meadow on the shores of Lake Geneva. Bus to Geneva, 300 yd.

Geneva → Chamonix, 90 km (54 mi.)

Exit Geneva and cross into France. Your best bet for this stretch is to take Autoroute A40 as far as it goes and then continue into Chamonix on N205. The surface streets are uninteresting and congested.

27. Chamonix

An attractive winter-sports resort, at the foot of Mont Blanc, Chamonix was chosen in 1924 to host the first Winter Olympic Games. Don't miss the thrilling ride on the world's highest cable car up the 12,600-ft.-high **Aiguille du Midi.**

Chamonix Campground

F–167 ★★ Camping de la Mer de Glace. Open May 1–September 30. Located 3 km (1.8 mi.) from Chamonix on N506. In Les Praz follow signs from church toward Le Bois and then to campground. Large meadow enclosed by tall evergreens. Bus to Chamonix, 700 yd.
–600 yd.

Chamonix → Aosta, 60 km (36 mi.)

From Chamonix take the **Mont-Blanc Tunnel,** an engineering masterpiece that runs for 11.7 km (7 mi.) under the Alps and exits at the Italian ski resort of **Courmayeur.** Continue on S26 to Aosta.

28. Aosta

Aosta lies in the center of a broad valley in the heart of the Italian Alps. The surrounding mountains are one of Italy's most popular winter vacation areas. Twelve km (7.2 mi.) outside of Aosta, on the road to **St. Vincent,** is the imposing fourteenth-century **Castle of Fenis.**

Note: To connect with our Italian Impressions itinerary, continue east from Aosta, following signs to Milan (see p. 246).

Aosta Campgrounds

I–101 ★★★ Camping Green Park (Courmayeur/La Salle). Open year-round. Turn off from Hwy. SS26 (Aosta–Morgex) at km 128. Cross railroad tracks and follow campground signs. A large, terraced, wooded, area with panoramic views. Bus to town, 500 yd.

I–102 ★★ Camping Monte Bianco (Sarre/Aosta). Open April 1–October 31. In Sarre, on main road SS26, 6 km (3.6 mi.) west of Aosta. A small, wooded site near the river. Bus to Aosta, 100 yd.

Aosta → Zermatt, 180 km (108 mi.)

From Aosta return to Switzerland over the famed **Great St. Bernard Pass.** This important link across the Alps dates back to Roman times. It was here that the famed St. Bernard dogs were first used by the monks to aid in rescuing stranded travelers. As an alternate route, in bad weather, you can zip under the mountains in a few minutes through the 5.8-km (3.5-mi.) -long **St. Bernard Tunnel.**

Continue through the **Vallee d'Entremont** to **Martigny** and then along the **Rhone Valley** to **Sion.** At **Visp** turn off and follow the road up the narrow valley to **Tasch.** As Zermatt is an auto-free village, you must leave your rig at the campground or in the large parking lot by the train station and take the cog train into Zermatt.

29. Zermatt

It spite of its enormous popularity, Zermatt has retained much of its original alpine-village ambiance. The focus of this popularity is one of the world's most photographed and visited mountains, the **Matterhorn.**

For an inspiring climber's-eye view of this unique pyramid-shaped peak, take the **Gornergrat** train to the 10,266-ft.-high summit station.

Zermatt Campgrounds

CH–108 ★★ Camping Alpenhubel. Open May 1–October 15. Located 100 yd. south of train station in Tasch at the terminus of the Zermatt road. A small, grassy site. This is the most convenient campground for visiting Zermatt and the Matterhorn. Zermatt cog train station, 100 yd.

CH–109 ★★ Camping Atermenzen. Open Easter–October 15. Midway between Randa and Tasch, on the Zermatt road. A large alpine meadow with outstanding mountain vistas. Train to Zermatt and Matterhorn in Tasch, 1.2 mi.

Zermatt → Bern, 115 km (69 mi.)

Head back down the valley to Visp and take Hwy. 9 toward Sion. Eleven km (6.6 mi.) past Visp turn off to **Goppenstein.** There you can load your vehicle on a train that runs under the mountains to emerge a few minutes later on the other side of the Alps, in **Kandersteg.** Proceed down the valley to **Frutigen** and then, at **Spiez,** join up with Hwy. 6, which will take you into Bern.

30. Bern

One of the smallest of the European capitals, Bern, which lies on the border between the French- and German-speaking parts of Switzerland, presents a pleasing blend of these two diverse cultures in its architecture and cuisine. The several kilometers of graceful medieval arcades lined with elegant shops and the many tempting cafes and restaurants make exploring Bern on foot a delight in any weather.

Bern Campgrounds

CH–110 ★★ Camping Eichholz. Open May 1–September 30. In the suburb of Wabern. Exit Hwy. 70 at Bern–Belp and follow signs to Wabern. Campground approaches are well marked. A pleasant, wooded site directly on the Aare River. A fifteen-minute walk along river to Bern center.

CH–111 ★★★ TCS Camping Kappelenbrucke. Open year-round.

Exit N1 Bern–Murten and follow signs toward Wohlen. Campground approach is well marked. A large, pleasant, grassy area surrounded by a forest. Bus to Bern center, 300 yd. –snacks

Bern → Zurich, 115 km (69 mi.)

From Bern you can take Autobahn N1 directly to Zurich or you can choose a more interesting route that will take you via Hwy. 12 through **Solothurn, Olten,** and **Baden.** From Baden follow signs into Zurich.

31. Zurich

Switzerland's largest city and one of the world's major financial centers occupies both banks of the **Limmat River.** With its many broad plazas and parks, Zurich is a city that invites exploration on foot. The nearby campground occupies a pleasant lakeside site and has frequent bus service to the city's center. Even if you do not have an account at one of the many international banks that have made Zurich their headquarters, be sure to stroll along the world-famous **Bahnhofstrasse.** Lined with banks, chic cafes, and exclusive shops, this is one of the world's most exclusive thoroughfares. The thirteenth-century **Fraumunster (church)** with its remarkable stained-glass windows by Marc Chagall is one of Zurich's principal tourist attractions.

Zurich Campground

CH–112 ★★★ Camping Seebucht. Open May 1–September 30. In Zurich–Wollishofen, directly on the left bank of Lake Zurich, 4 km (2.4 mi.) southwest of Zurich center. Approaching from Autobahn Bern, take Wollishofen exit. From Zurich center follow signs to Chur and turn off in Wollishofen. Approaches are well marked. A small, pleasant lakeside park with excellent access to city. Take bus #61 or #63 from campground entrance. There is no place to park an RV in Zurich.

Zurich → Rhine Falls, 38 km (23 mi.)

From Zurich center follow signs to FLUGHAFEN (airport), then continue on Hwy. 4 toward **Schaffhausen** and the Rhine Falls.

32. Rhine Falls/33. Stein am Rhein

Rhine Falls, in Schaffhausen, is Europe's most powerful waterfall. From Schaffhausen take Hwy. 13 to Stein am Rhein, where you can admire the colorful painted house facades that line the town's cobbled streets. There is a large parking lot just outside the town walls.

Rhine Falls/Stein am Rhein Campground

CH–113 ★★ Camping Rheinwiesen. Open May 1–October 3. In Langwiesen, directly on the Rhine. Adjacent to municipal swimming pool 3 km (1.8 mi.) from Schaffhausen on the Schaffhausen–Frauenfeld highway. A small, grassy site with many mature trees. Public transportation, 500 yd.

Stein am Rhein → Constance, 20 km (12 mi.)

Continue along the Rhine to Constance.

34. Lake Constance/35. Meersburg

Constance is a busy university town and commercial center on Lake Constance (Bodensee). **Mainau,** an island in Lake Constance bursting with delightful gardens and flower exhibits, is accessible from a pedestrian causeway on the outskirts of the town of Constance. Overnight parking is not permitted at Mainau. After visiting the gardens take the ferry from Constance across the lake to Meersburg, site of a magnificent seventh-century castle.

Lake Constance Campgrounds

D–118 ★★★ Camping Klausenhorn (Constance/Dingelsdorf). Open Easter–October 31. On Lake Constance, in the suburb of Dingelsdorf. Follow signs from Constance to Mainau and then Dingelsdorf. The site is 300 yd. north of the town and next to the municipal swimming area. Pleasant, grassy area directly at lake. Little shade. Bus, 500 yd.

D–119 ★★★ Campingpark Uberlingen (Uberlingen/Lake Constance). Open April 1–October 15. At the west end of town, directly on the lake. From B31 turn off at Uberlingen Stadt Mitte. From town follow signs to Uferstrasse and then to campground. A large, grassy site with access to lake. No public transportation.

Lake Constance → Freudenstadt, 204 km (127 mi.)

Continue along the lake on B31 to **Stockach** and then to the fashionable lakeside resort of Titisee. Just outside of Titisee pick up B500 and head north for a drive through the enchanting Black Forest.

36. TRIBERG/37. GUTACH/38. FREUDENSTADT

At Triberg visit the **Black Forest Museum;** if a cuckoo clock is on your wish list, this is the place for some serious shopping. Here you will find a vast selection of locally made clocks in the many shops that line the main street.

The expansive **Open-Air Museum** at Gutach, 15 km (19 mi.) north of Triberg on B33, features an exhibition of traditional Black Forest farmhouses. Stay on B33 to Freudenstadt, an attractive regional market center with an enormous town square that is lined with inviting cafes and restaurants. This is a wonderful place for sampling a piece of tasty Black Forest cake.

Black Forest Campgrounds

D–120 ★★★ Campingplatz Bankenhof (Titisee). Open year-round. Turn off of B31 at Titisee. Then follow camping signs. A grassy meadow between a pine forest and the lake. At the southern gateway to the Black Forest. Bus to village, 300 yd.

D–121 ★★★ Camping Langenwald (Freudenstadt). Open Easter–October 31. Located 3 km (1.8 mi.) west of Freudenstadt. From town take B28 toward Strasbourg. Turn off to the left into campground. An attractive, large, rustic site with many trees and a creek. Bus #12 to town at entrance.

Freudenstadt → Baden-Baden, 45 km (27 mi.)

From Freudenstadt pick up the tortuous, winding **Schwarzwald Hochstrasse** and continue to Baden-Baden.

39. BADEN-BADEN

The healing waters at Baden-Baden have been drawing people to this region since the Roman emperor Caracalla discovered the bubbling **hot**

springs in the first century. The casino here is one of Europe's most exclusive.

Note: To connect with our France Itinerary III from Baden-Baden, cross the Rhine and follow signs to Strasbourg (see p. 191).

Baden-Baden Campground

D–122 ★★★ Camping Adam (Baden-Baden/Buhl). Open year-round. There is no campground in Baden-Baden. Camping Adam is located approximately 20 km (12 mi.) southwest of Baden-Baden. This is the best and closest of several in the area. From Baden-Baden head west for 10 km (6 mi.) to B3, then south 10 km (6 mi.) to Buhl. From Buhl follow signs to Lichtenau and then to campground. A large camping "village" bordering a lake. Bus, 500 yd.

Baden-Baden → Frankfurt, 162 km (97 mi.)

The last stretch of our itinerary, from Baden-Baden to Frankfurt, is best done on Autobahn A5.

Appendix

NATIONAL TOURIST OFFICES

Austria

Austrian National Tourist Office

United States: 500 Fifth Avenue 20th Floor, New York, NY 10110; phone (212) 944–6880

Canada: 2 Bloor Street E., Suite 3330, Toronto, Ontario M4W 1A8, Canada; phone (416) 967–3381

United Kingdom: 30 St. George Street, London W1R OAL, England; phone (071) 629–0461

Belgium

Belgian Tourist Office

United States: 745 Fifth Avenue, New York, NY 10151; phone (212) 758–8130, fax (212) 355–7675

United Kingdom: Premier House, 2 Gayton Road, Harrow, Middlesex HA1 2XU, England; phone (081) 861–3300

Bulgaria

Bulgarian National Tourist Office

United States and Canada: Balkan Holidays, 161 E. 86th Street, New York, NY 10028; phone (212) 573–5530

United Kingdom: 18 Princess Street, London W1R 7RE, England; phone (071) 499–6988

The Czech Republic

Cedok

United States: 1109 Madison Avenue, New York, NY 10028; phone (212) 535–8814

United Kingdom: 17–18 Old Bond Street, London W1X 4RB, England; phone (071) 629–6058

Denmark

Danish Tourist Board

United States: 655 Third Avenue, New York, NY 10017; phone (212) 949–2333

Canada: Box 115, Station N, Toronto, Ontario M8V 3S4, Canada; phone (416) 823–9620

United Kingdom: P.O. Box 2LT, London W1A 2LT, England; phone (071) 734–2637, fax (071) 494–2170

Finland

Finnish Tourist Board

United States: 655 Third Avenue, New York, NY 10017; phone (212) 949–2333

Canada: 1200 Bay Street, Suite 604, Toronto, Ontario M5R 2A5, Canada; phone (416) 964–9159

United Kingdom: 66–68 Haymarket, London SW1Y 4RF, England; phone (071) 839–4048

France

French Government Tourist Office

United States: 610 Fifth Avenue, New York, NY 10020; phone (212) 757–1125; France by Telephone (900) 990–0040 (50 cents/minute)

Canada: 1981 McGill College Avenue, Suite 490, Montreal, Quebec H3A 2W9, Canada; phone (514) 288–4264, fax (514) 845–4868

United Kingdom: 178 Piccadilly, London W1V OAL, England; phone (071) 491–7622

Germany

German National Tourist Office

United States: 122 East 42nd Street, New York, NY 10168–0072; phone (212) 661–7200, fax (212) 661–7174

Canada: 175 Bloor Street, North Tower, Suite 604, Toronto, Ontario M4W 3R8, Canada; phone (416) 968–1570, fax (213) 688–7574

United Kingdom: 65 Curzon Street, London W1Y 7PE, England; phone (071) 495–3990

Great Britain

British Tourist Authority

United States: 551 Fifth Avenue, New York, NY 10176; phone (212) 986–2200, fax (212) 986–1188

Canada: 94 Cumberland Street, Suite 600, Toronto, Ontario M5R 3N3, Canada; phone (416) 925–6326, fax (416) 961–2175

United Kingdom: Thames Tower, Black's Road, Hammersmith, London W6 9EL, England; phone (081) 846–9000

Greece

Greek National Tourist Organization

United States: 645 Fifth Avenue, New York, NY 10022; phone (212) 421–5777, fax (212) 826–6940

Canada: 1233 rue de la Montagne, Montreal, Quebec H3G 1Z2, Canada; phone (514) 871–1535, fax (514) 871–1498

United Kingdom: 4 Conduit Street, London W1R ODJ, England; phone (071) 734–5997

Hungary

IBUSZ Hungarian Travel Bureau

United States and Canada: One Parker Plaza, Suite 1104, Fort Lee, NJ 07024; phone (201) 592–8585, fax (201) 592–8736

United Kingdom: Danube Travel Ltd., 6 Conduit Street, London W1R 9TG, England; phone (071) 734–5997

Italy

Italian Government Tourist Office

United States: 630 Fifth Avenue, Suite 1565, New York, NY 10111; phone (212) 245–4822, fax (212) 586–9249

Canada: 3 Place Ville Marie, Montreal, Quebec, Canada (514) 866–7667

United Kingdom: 1 Princess Street, London W1R 8AY, England; phone (071) 408–1254

Liechtenstein

See Switzerland.

Luxembourg

Luxembourg National Tourist Office

United States: 801 Second Avenue, New York, NY 10017; phone (212) 370–9850, fax (212) 922–1685

The Netherlands

Netherlands Board of Tourism

United States: Lexington Avenue, 21st Floor, New York, NY 10017; phone (212) 370–7367, fax (212) 370–9507

Canada: 25 Adelaide Street East, Suite 710, Toronto, Ontario M5C 1Y2, Canada; phone (416) 363–1577, fax (416) 363–1470

Norway

Norwegian Tourist Board

United States and Canada: 655 Third Avenue, New York, NY 10017; phone (212) 949–2333, fax (212) 983–5260

United Kingdom: Charles House, 5/11 Regent Street, London SW1Y 4LR, England; phone (071) 839–6255

Poland

Polish National Tourist Office

United States and Canada: 275 Madison Avenue, Suite 1711, New York, NY 10016; phone (212) 338–9412, fax (212) 338–9283

United Kingdom: 82 Mortimer Street, London W1N 7DE, England; phone (071) 580–8028

Portugal

Portuguese National Tourist Office

United States: 590 Fifth Avenue, 4th Floor, New York, NY 10036; phone (212) 354–4403, fax (212) 764–6137

Canada: 4120 Yonge Street, Yonge Corporate Center, Suite 414, Willowdale, Toronto, Ontario M2P 2B8, Canada; phone (416) 250–7577, fax (416) 250–7579

Spain

Spanish National Tourist Office

United States: 665 Fifth Avenue, New York, NY 10022; phone (212) 759–8822

Canada: 60 Bloor Street W, Suite 201, Toronto, Ontario M4W 3B8, Canada; phone (416) 961–3131
United Kingdom: 57–58 St. James Street, London SW1A 1LD, England; phone (071) 499–1169

Sweden
Swedish Tourist Board
United States and Canada: 655 Third Avenue, New York, NY 10017; phone (212) 949–2333, fax (212) 983–5260
United Kingdom: 29–31 Oxford Street, 5th Floor, London W1R 1RE, England; phone (071) 487–5007, fax (071) 935–5853

Switzerland and Liechtenstein
Swiss Tourist Board
United States: 608 Fifth Avenue, New York, NY 10020; phone (212) 757–5944, fax (212) 262–6116
Canada: 154 University Avenue, Suite 610, Toronto, Ontario M5H 3Y9, Canada; phone (416) 971–9734, fax (416) 971–6425
United Kingdom: Swiss Center, 1 New Coventry Street, London W1V 8EE, England; phone (071) 734–1921

Turkey
Turkish Government Information Office
United States and Canada: 821 United Nations Plaza, New York, NY 10017; phone (212) 687–2194, fax (212) 599–7568
United Kingdom: 170–173 Piccadilly, London W1V 9DD, England; phone (071) 734–8681

INTERNATIONAL ROAD SIGNS

REGULATORY SIGNS

PRIORITY ROAD SIGNS

Priority for oncoming traffic

Priority over oncoming traffic

Give way

Stop

Priority road

End of priority road

MANDATORY SIGNS

Pass this side

Direction to be followed

Compulsory roundabout

Compulsory footpath

Compulsory cycle track

Compulsory track for horseback riders

End of compulsory minimum speed

Compulsory minimum speed

Snow chains compulsory

PROHIBITORY OR RESTRICTIVE SIGNS

Closed to all vehicles in both directions

No entry

No entry for any power-driven vehicle except two-wheeled motorcycles without side cars

No entry for any power-driven vehicle drawing a trailer other than a semi-trailer or a single-axle trailer

No entry for goods vehicles

No entry for mopeds

No entry for cycles

No entry for motorcycles

No entry for vehicles carrying more than a certain amount of explosives or readily inflammable substances

No entry for vehicles carrying more than a certain quantity of substances liable to cause water pollution

No entry for power-driven agricultural vehicles

No entry for hand carts

No entry for animal-drawn vehicles

No entry for pedestrians

No entry for vehicles having an overall height exceeding __ meters (__ feet)

No entry for vehicles having an overall width exceeding __ meters (__ feet)

No entry for vehicles or combination of vehicles exceeding __ meters (__ feet) in length

No entry for vehicles having a weight exceeding ___ tons on one axle

No entry for vehicles exceeding ___ tons laden weight

Driving of vehicles less than___ meters (___ feet) apart prohibited

PROHIBITORY OR RESTRICTIVE SIGNS

No entry for power-driven vehicles

No entry for power-driven vehicles or animal-drawn vehicles

No left turn

No right turn

No U-turns

Maximum speed limited to the figure indicated

Overtaking prohibited by goods vehicles

Overtaking prohibited

End of all local prohibitions imposed on moving vehicles

End of speed limit

End of prohibition overtaking

Passing without stopping prohibited

Use of audible warning devices prohibited

Parking prohibited

Standing and parking prohibited

Alternate parking: prohibited on odd number dates

Alternate parking: prohibited on even number dates

Limited duration parking zone

Exit from the limited duration parking zone

INFORMATIVE SIGNS

USEFUL INFORMATION SIGNS

Tourist information

Filling station

Telephone

Restaurant

Hotel or motel

Refreshments or cafeteria

Picnic site

Camping site

Starting point for walk

Trailer site

Camping and trailer site

Youth hostel

Hospital

Hospital

USEFUL INFORMATION SIGNS

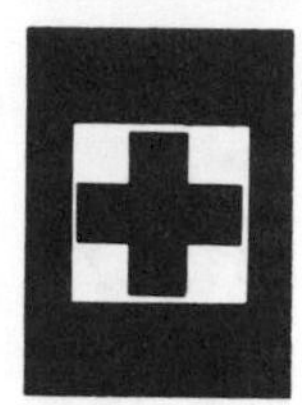
First aid station

Breakdown service

Parking

One way

One way

Road for motor vehicles

End of road for motor vehicles

Motorway

End of motorway

No through road

Tramway stop

Bus stop

Road open or closed

Car-sleeper train

Car-carrier train

Ferry

ADVANCE DIRECTION SIGNS

Advance diversion sign

No through road

General case

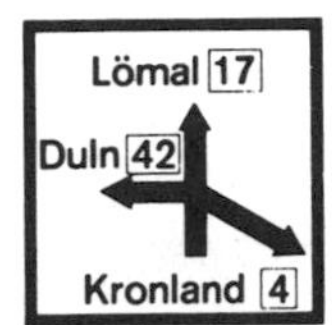

General case

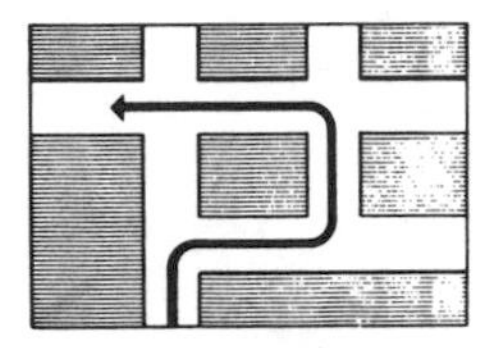
Route to be followed for left turn

Layout of priority road

Lane preselection at intersection

Direction to airfield

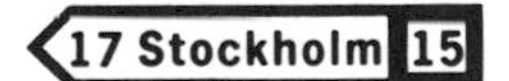

Direction to a place

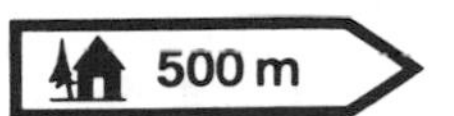

Direction to a youth hostel

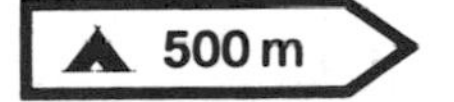

Direction to a camping site

Beginning of a built-up area

End of a built-up area

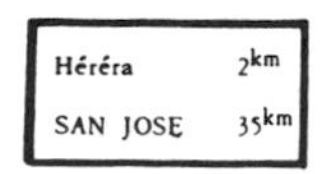

Confirmatory sign

Pedestrian crossing

WARNING SIGNS

Dangerous bend

Carriageway narrows

Carriageway narrows

Steep ascent or descent: dangerous descent ___ %

Dangerous bend: double bend

Dangerous bend: left bend

Uneven road: dip

Uneven road: hump bridge or ridge

Uneven road: bad condition

Road leads on to quay or river bank

Swing bridge

Children

Pedestrian crossing

Falling rocks

Loose gravel

Slippery road

Airfield

Light signals

Road works

Animal crossing

WARNING SIGNS

Cattle crossing

Cyclists

Level crossing: without gates

Level crossing: with gates or staggered half gates

Other dangers

Two-way traffic

Cross wind

Approach to intersection

Approach to intersection: general priority rule

Approach to intersection: roundabout

Approach to intersection: merging traffic

Approach to intersection: side road

Location of level crossing without gate or barrier: one track

Location of level crossing without gate or barrier: at least two tracks

Intersection with tramway line

Count-down posts

COUNTRY ABBREVIATIONS

AL	Albania
AND	Andorra
A	Austria
B	Belgium
BG	Bulgaria
CR	Croatia
CS	The Czech Republic
DK	Denmark
SF	Finland
F	France
D	Germany
GB	Great Britain
GR	Greece
H	Hungary
I	Italy
FL	Liechtenstein
L	Luxembourg
NL	The Netherlands
N	Norway
PL	Poland
P	Portugal
RO	Romania
SVK	Slovakia
SLO	Slovenia
E	Spain
S	Sweden
CH	Switzerland
TR	Turkey

CONVERSION TABLE

The following are some of the most commonly used measures and examples to make the necessary conversions from the metric system (in use throughout Europe, except for Great Britain and Ireland) to the familiar North American values. The formulas and values given are rough approximations, accurate enough for travel purposes.

From	**To**	**Formula**	**Example**
Miles	Kilometers (km)	Multiply by 1.6	100 mi. x 1.6 = 160 km
Kilometers	Miles (mi.)	Multiply by 0.6	100 km x 0.6 = 60 mi.
Feet	Meters (m)	Divide by 3.3	10 ft./3.3 = 3 m
Meters	Feet (ft.)	Multiply by 3.3	10 m x 3.3 = 33 ft.
Inches	Centimeters (cm)	Multiply by 2.5	10 in. x 2.5 = 25 cm
Centimeters	Inches (in.)	Divide by 2.5	10 cm/2.5 = 4 in.
Pounds	Kilos (kg)	Divide by 2.2	10 lb/2.2 = 4.5 kg
Kilos	Pounds (lb)	Multiply by 2.2	10 kg x 2.2 = 22 lb
Gallons	Liters (l)	Multiply by 3.8	10 gal x 3.8 = 38 l
Liters	Gallons (gal)	Divide by 3.8	10 l/3.8 = 2.6 gal
Liters	Quarts (qt)	Multiply by 0.91	10 l x 1.06 = 10.6 qt
Quarts	Liters (l)	Divide by 1.06	10 qt/1.06 = 9.4 l
°Fahrenheit	°Centigrade (°C)	(°F - 32) x 5/9 = °C	68°F - 32 = 36 x 5/9 = 20°C
°Centigrade	°Fahrenheit (°F)	(°C x 1.8) + 32 =°F	20°C x 1.8 = 36 + 32 = 68°F

Index